T0178285

Lecture Notes of the Institute for Computer Sciences, Social Informatics and Telecommunications Engineering 450

More information about this series at https://link.springer.com/bookseries/8197

Tanya Zlateva · Rossitza Goleva (Eds.)

Computer Science and Education in Computer Science

18th EAI International Conference, CSECS 2022
On-Site and Virtual Event, June 24–27, 2022
Proceedings

 Springer

Editors
Tanya Zlateva
Boston University
Boston, MA, USA

Rossitza Goleva 🆔
New Bulgarian University
Sofia, Bulgaria

ISSN 1867-8211   ISSN 1867-822X (electronic)
Lecture Notes of the Institute for Computer Sciences, Social Informatics
and Telecommunications Engineering
ISBN 978-3-031-17291-5   ISBN 978-3-031-17292-2 (eBook)
https://doi.org/10.1007/978-3-031-17292-2

This Springer imprint is published by the registered company Springer Nature Switzerland AG
The registered company address is: Gewerbestrasse 11, 6330 Cham, Switzerland

Preface

We are delighted to introduce the proceedings of the eighteenth edition of the International Conference on Computer Science and Education in Computer Science (CSECS 2022). The event is endorsed by the European Alliance for Innovation (EAI), an international professional community-based organization devoted to the advancement of innovation in the field of information and communication technologies. The conference took in Sofia, Bulgaria, during June 24–27, 2022, and was also transmitted online for all remote participants from the USA, Germany, India, Portugal, China, and North Macedonia.

CSECS 2022 was dedicated to a wide range of computer science research areas starting from software engineering and information systems design and ending with cryptography, the theoretical foundation of the algorithms, and implementation of machine learning and big data technologies. Another important topic of the conference was education in computer science which covered the introduction and evaluation of computing programs, curricula, and online courses, including syllabus, laboratories, teaching, and pedagogy aspects. The technical and education topics spanned multiple existing and emerging technologies, solutions, and services for design and training, providing a heterogeneous approach towards the delivery of Software 4.0 and Education 4.0 to a broad range of citizens and societies. CSECS 2022 brought together technology experts, researchers, and industry representatives contributing to the design, development, and deployment of modern solutions based on recent technologies, standards, and procedures.

The papers were selected from 55 submissions following a double-blind review process, with each submission being reviewed by at least 3 members of the Program Committee. The reviewers have been selected among Program Committee members that are not directly related to the author to avoid potential conflict of interest. The acceptance rate is 50%. The selection process was made in consensus with the Program Committee before opening authors' names and strictly based on the review results.

The technical program of CSECS 2022 consisted of 24 papers in oral presentation sessions on-site or online at the main conference tracks. The papers cover many systems technologies, applications, and services as well as solutions. Multiple topics have been addressed including the theory of computation, models of computation, computational complexity and cryptography, logic, design, and analysis of algorithms, network architectures, performance evaluation, network services, software engineering, software creation, and management, applied computing, machine learning, and education.

Coordination with the steering chair, Imrich Chlamtac, and the valuable support of Ivan Landjev, Vladimir Zlatev, Lou Chitkushev, Dimitar Atanasov, Constandinos Mavromoustakis, Eugene Pinsky, Metodi Traikov, Irena Vodenska, and Vijay Kanabar were essential for the success of the conference. We sincerely appreciate their continuous work and assistance.

We strongly believe that CSECS 2022 provided a good forum for all researchers, developers, and practitioners to discuss all science and technology aspects that are relevant to computer science and computer science education. We also expect that the CSECS 2023 conference will be as successful and stimulating as this year's, as indicated by the contributions presented in this volume.

October 2022

Tanya Zlateva
Rossitza Goleva

Organization

Steering Committee

Imrich Chlamtac   University of Trento, Italy

Organizing Committee

General Chair

Ivan Landjev   New Bulgarian University, Bulgaria

General Co-chair

Tanya Zlateva   Boston University, USA

Technical Program Committee Chairs

Tanya Zlateva   Boston University, USA
Rossitza Goleva   New Bulgarian University, Bulgaria

Technical Program Committee Co-chair

Lou Chitkushev   Boston University, USA

Sponsorship and Exhibit Chair

Vijay Kanabar   Boston University, USA

Local Chair

Rossitza Goleva   New Bulgarian University, Bulgaria

Workshops Chair

Eugene Pinsky   Boston University, USA

Publicity and Social Media Chair

Rossitza Goleva   New Bulgarian University, Bulgaria

Publications Chair

Rossitza Goleva   New Bulgarian University, Bulgaria

Web Chair

Metodi Traikov   New Bulgarian University, Bulgaria

Posters and PhD Track Chair

Irena Vodenska   Boston University, USA

Panels Chair

Dimitar Atanasov   New Bulgarian University, Bulgaria

Demos Chair

Gregory Page   Boston University, USA

Tutorials Chair

Vladimir Zlatev   Boston University, USA

Community and Industry Outreach Chair

Vijay Kanabar   Boston University, USA

Technical Program Committee

Petya Asenova	New Bulgarian University, Bulgaria
Dimitar Atanasov	New Bulgarian University, Bulgaria
Olena Chebanyuk	National Aviation University, Ukraine
Hao Chen	China University of Mining and Technology, China
Radu-Ioan Ciobanu	University Politehnica of Bucharest, Romania
António Cunha	Universidade de Trás-os-Montes e Alto Douro, Portugal
Andreas Deuter	OWL University of Applied Sciences and Arts, Lemgo, Germany

Contents

Education in Computer Science

Computer Science Implementations

A Clustering Approach to Analyzing NHL Goaltenders' Performance

Ruksana Khan[2], Patrick Schena[1], Kathleen Park[1], and Eugene Pinsky[2(✉)]

[1] Administrative Sciences Department, Metropolitan College, Boston University,
Boston, MA 02215, USA
{pschena,epinsky}@bu.edu
[2] Computer Science Department, Metropolitan College,
Boston University, Boston, MA 02215, USA
{ruksanak,epinsky}@bu.edu

Abstract. Ice hockey is among the top 10 sports in the world by global popularity, and the National Hockey League (NHL) is one of the major professional sports leagues in United States and Canada. In the NHL there are 32 teams, 25 in the U.S. and 7 in Canada. In ice hockey, the goaltender, also known as the goalie, is one of the most important players in the game. The result of the game greatly depends on the performance of the goaltender. One of the most important statistics of the goaltender is save percentage SV% (calculated as the number of saves divided by the total number of shots attempted on the goal). In spite of the goaltender being a key player in the game, there are shortcomings in existing methods of ranking goaltenders, as these methods do not comprehensively capture the performance of the goaltender. This paper proposes the use of clustering methods from machine learning to compare performance of NHL goaltenders by using SV% and to look for patterns in their performance.

Keywords: Clustering · NHL performance comparison · Goaltender statistics

1 Introduction

One of the most important statistics of a goaltender in ice hockey is save percentage (SV%). It is a statistic that represents the percentage of attempted shots on the goal that the goaltender stops. The higher the SV% is, the better the performance of the goaltender. In this paper, we have analyzed the NHL goaltenders' SV% patterns over 5 years by applying the k-means clustering method with Manhattan distance. Inputs to the k-means model are the annual SV% for each goaltender.

We use the quantile statistics to split the SV% into clusters [3]. In this way, for each year and for each goaltender, we can describe his performance in terms

---

Supported by Metropolitan College, Boston University.

T. Zlateva and R. Goleva (Eds.): CSECS 2022, LNICST 450, pp. 3–10, 2022.
https://doi.org/10.1007/978-3-031-17292-2_1

of a cluster (defined by a quantile range). The performance of each goaltender over 5 years will be described by a 5-value tuple of these clusters.

We will then use k-means clustering [1,2,5–7] and divide our goaltenders into $k = 5$ groups. The outputs of the k-means are the 5 clusters defined as: World Class, Elite, Competitive, Serviceable, and Inadequate.

2 Data Analysis and Visualization

2.1 Data

We collected goaltenders performance data from two sources:

1. Worldwide ice hockey statistics (https://www.eliteprospects.com). From this source, we collected the data for each player, individually searched each player, and used a filter to view the data for the NHL goaltenders only. We obtained SV% from this dataset.
2. Instat sports performance database (https://hockey.instatscout.com). We used this dataset to obtain information about time on ice, for analyzing goaltenders who have played more than 7,000 min total in 5 years.

Apart from the minutes on ice, we have considered only goaltenders who have more than five years of playing history in the NHL. We are left with 37 goalies after applying all the above filters.

2.2 Visualization and Statistics

SV% ranges from a min of 0.750 to a max of 0.934. Inter-quartile range is defined as $Q_3 - Q_1$ and for our dataset, it is $Q_3 - Q_1 = 0.013$. Quantile skewness A is defined in Eq. (1) as the difference between the range of the lower quartile and median M (i.e. $M - Q_1$) and range of the upper quartile and median M (i.e. $Q_3 - M$) divided by inter-quartile range. For our dataset, this skewness $A = -0.61$, and the median $M = 0.915$ (Table 1).

$$A = \frac{(Q_3 - M) - (M - Q_1)}{Q_3 - Q_1} \tag{1}$$

Table 1. Save percentage (SV%) quartile statistics

Statistics	Value
Min	0.750
First quartile Q_1	0.907
Median M	0.915
Third quartile Q_3	0.920
Max	0.934
Deviation σ	0.007
Quantile skewness A	−0.61
Mean μ	0.912

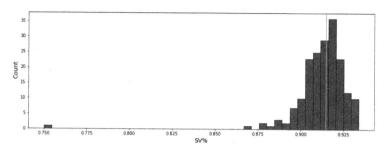

Fig. 1. Save percentage (SV%) distribution

The histogram of SV% (Fig. 1) shows that SV% is skewed to the left with a mean $\mu = 0.912$ and a standard deviation $\sigma = 0.007$.

We will use non-parametric analysis using simple quantile statistics to analyze SV% [4]. Using the Q_1, Q_2 (median M), and Q_3 we defined the patterns of SV% for every goaltender over the five years. We assign SV% values to clusters according to Table 2.

Table 2. Save percentage (SV%) pattern

Range	SV% Pattern (cluster)
$<Q_1$	1
$Q_1 \longleftrightarrow M$	2
$M \longleftrightarrow Q_3$	3
$>Q_3$	4

In Fig. 2, we plotted 5-year SV% trajectories for 37 goaltenders. Table 4 (Appendix A) contains the details of these trajectories.

As an example, consider the trajectory for the goaltender Tristan Jarry (Pittsburgh Penguins). His 5-year pattern is $[1, 2, 1, 4, 2]$. In the first year, Tristan Jarry's SV% is in cluster 1 (SV% below $Q_1 = 0.907$). In the second year, he was in cluster 2 (SV% was between Q_1 and - median M, namely in range $(0.907–0.915)$). In the third year, his performance was in cluster 1 again. In the fourth year he was in the top cluster 4 (SV% was above 0.920), and, finally, in the fifth year it was again between Q_1 and the median M. His trajectory shows that his performance improved over the 5 years.

By contrast, let us consider Brandon Holtby (Dallas Stars). His 5-year cluster trajectory is $[4, 4, 1, 2, 1]$. His trajectory shows that he had top performance in the first 2 years but his performance declined drastically over the next 3 years.

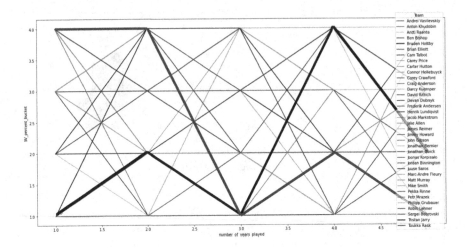

Fig. 2. Save percentage (SV%) pattern trajectories

3 *k*-Means Clustering of 5-Year SV% Trajectories

We extracted data for 37 goaltenders and their SV% pattern over 5 years. We divided these goaltenders into clusters using their 5-year performance patterns. We rank these goaltenders according to cluster trajectories and cluster signatures as explained below.

3.1 Cluster Trajectories

Clustering divides the data into groups based on certain similarities in the data. We use a standard *k*-means clustering to group goaltenders into *k* groups. Each cluster is represented by its centroid, an arithmetic mean of all the data points assigned to a cluster. In other words, a centroid represents a typical member of its cluster. In our case, a centroid is a "average" 5-year trajectory of its members. We rounded the centroid values to the nearest SV% cluster values.

The *k*-means algorithm works iteratively until each point has less inter-cluster distance than intra-cluster distance. Both the number of clusters *k* and the distance metric are the hyperparameter inputs to the model and need to be specified. Since we are working with a SV% pattern for distance, we used Manhattan distance as an input distance metric. We also decided to use $k = 5$ clusters as we believe that this number would be adequate to analyze similarities in historical goaltender performance. With this choice of hyperparameters, we divided the historical performance of 37 goaltenders into 5 clusters: *World Class, Elite, Competitive, Serviceable,* and *Inadequate*.

Table 3 shows the statistics for each of the 5 clusters. We note that there are no outlier clusters (i.e. clusters with just one member).

Table 3. k-means clusters

Cluster	Cluster name	Count	5-year SV% trajectory
0	Inadequate	10	3,2,2,1,1
1	Serviceable	4	1,4,2,2,1
2	Competitive	4	4,4,1,2,1
3	Elite	8	3,4,4,2,1
4	World class	11	3,2,3,3,3
–	Average goaltender	–	3,3,3,2,2

As can be seen from Table 3, the distribution across the 5 clusters is not equal. Instead, the *"Inadequate"* and *"World Class"* clusters each have dispro-portionately high representation of 10 and 11 each. In general, once past the large representation in *"Inadequate"*, the trend is toward increasing represen-tation as the cluster rankings climb from *"Serviceable"*, to *"Competitive"* to *"Elite"* to *"World Class"*. For instance, the *"Elite"* and *"World Class"* clusters combined contain over half the players in the sample. There are implications for the longevity of play within a 5-year period being skewed toward the higher performers, with, interestingly a relatively deep bunch of backup reserve players classified as *"Inadequate"* for consistent first-rung starting play, but who have nevertheless at occasional key moments made significant enough contributions to have exceeded our baseline of 7,000 min aggregate NHL play in 5 years.

The performance of each cluster is represented by the cluster path of its centroids, as shown in Fig. 3.

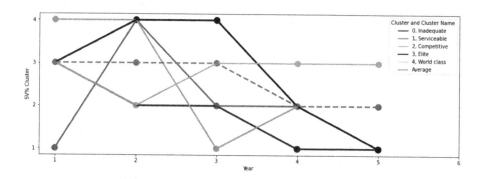

Fig. 3. Centroid trajectories

Let us examine the 5-year cluster trajectories for the centroids in more detail. We start with "world class". The goaltenders in this group have consistent and good performance over 5 years (level 3). By contrast, consider the "elite" group. Goaltenders in this group the highest performance (3–4) for at least 3 years but then much lower performance (1–2) in the last 2 years. If we examine "com-petitive", we see that goaltenders in this group start out very strong (highest level 4) but decline drastically in the next 3 years (1–2). Goaltenders in the "serviceable" cluster had a period of early glory (level 4 in the second year) and otherwise, show substandard performance (level 1 and 2). Finally, goaltenders in "inadequate" group never achieve a very high level (highest level is 3) and they mostly perform at the lower level (1–2).

We note that all clusters show declining performance over time. These results suggest that, with rare exceptions (e.g. Darcy Kuemper), unless goaltenders show early promise, they tend not to improve over time.

In Appendix A we show 5-year cluster trajectories for each goaltender in our dataset.

3.2 Cluster Signatures

Centroid-Signatures. From the previous discussion we have shown that the performance of every goaltender can be represented by 5 year trajectory. We now consider simplified representation which we will call signature. To compute the signature we compute two values the average cluster that best represent the first two year, and the cluster that represent the last two year. In other words, the signature is computed by taking a simple average of the first 2 years and last 2 years from 5-year cluster trajectory.

As a result we reduce 5-tuple representation to 2 values. The first value reflects the performance in the first two year whereas the last value in the signature represent the performance in the last two year.

For example, consider the performance of Tristan Jarry's in the previous section. His 5-year cluster path was $[1, 2, 1, 4, 2]$ corresponding to cluster *"World Class"*. His corresponding signature is $[2, 4]$ showing that his performance improved over the 5 years. By contrast, consider Braden Holtby. His 5-year cluster path was $[4, 4, 1, 2, 1]$ corresponding to cluster *"Competitive"*. His corresponding signature is $[2, 4]$ showing that his performance decreased over the 5 years.

Using signatures gives us a very simple summary of 5-year goaltender performance.

4 Conclusion

In this paper, we applied machine learning methods to analyze the performance of NHL goaltenders. We used the standard metric of SV% and, for every year, divided NHL goaltenders into five clusters using the k-means clustering method. We examined the 5-year performance pattern for each goaltender. We applied clustering again to these 5-year patterns using Manhattan distance and identified groups of goaltenders with similar performance over time. We use 5-year cluster trajectory and a simplified performance measure, "signature", to describe goaltenders' performance over time. This approach provides a simple and visually intuitive method to analyze and classify goaltenders. It could also be used for NHL teams to evaluate the performance of their goaltenders compared to others in the league on a game-by-game basis by entering SV% for each game played, rather than a cumulative season SV%. This method can be generalized to other sports as well. We hope to address this in our subsequent work.

Acknowledgement. The authors would like to thank Brian Daccord, the goaltending coach at Boston University, for his helpful suggestions [8]. We would also like to thank the Office of the Dean at Boston University Metropolitan College for their support.

Appendix A

Table 4. SV% trajectory patterns and signatures

Last name	First name	SV% pattern	SV% signature	Cluster
Allen	Jake	[3, 2, 1, 1, 4]	[2, 2]	Inadequate
Andersen	Frederik	[3, 3, 3, 3, 2]	[3, 2]	World class
Anderson	Craig	[3, 4, 1, 1, 1]	[4, 1]	Competitive
Bernier	Jonathan	[2, 2, 2, 1, 1]	[2, 1]	Inadequate
Binnington	Jordan	[1, 4, 2, 2, 1]	[2, 2]	Serviceable
Bishop	Ben	[4, 2, 3, 4, 3]	[3, 4]	World class
Bobrovski	Sergei	[2, 4, 4, 2, 1]	[3, 2]	Elite
Crawford	Corey	[4, 3, 4, 2, 3]	[4, 2]	World class
Dubnyk	Devan	[3, 4, 3, 2, 1]	[4, 2]	Elite
Elliott	Brian	[4, 2, 2, 1, 1]	[3, 1]	Inadequate
Fleury	Marc-Andre	[4, 2, 4, 2, 1]	[3, 2]	Elite
Gibson	John	[3, 4, 4, 3, 1]	[4, 2]	Elite
Grubauer	Philipp	[3, 4, 4, 3, 3]	[4, 3]	World class
Hellebuyck	Connor	[3, 1, 4, 2, 4]	[2, 3]	World class
Holtby	Braden	[4, 4, 1, 2, 1]	[4, 2]	Competitive
Howard	Jimmy	[1, 4, 2, 2, 1]	[2, 2]	Serviceable
Hutton	Carter	[2, 4, 2, 1, 1]	[3, 1]	Serviceable
Jarry	Tristan	[1, 2, 1, 4, 2]	[2, 3]	World class
Khudobin	Anton	[2, 4, 4, 1, 1]	[3, 1]	Elite
Korpisalo	Joonas	[3, 1, 1, 1, 2]	[2, 2]	Inadequate
Kuemper	Darcy	[2, 1, 4, 4, 4]	[2, 4]	World class
Lehner	Robin	[4, 3, 2, 4, 3]	[4, 4]	World class
Lundqvist	Henrik	[3, 2, 2, 1, 1]	[2, 1]	Inadequate
Markstrom	Jacob	[2, 2, 2, 2, 3]	[2, 2]	World class
Mrazek	Petr	[4, 1, 2, 2, 1]	[2, 2]	Inadequate
Murray	Matt	[4, 4, 1, 3, 1]	[4, 2]	Competitive
Price	Carey	[4, 4, 1, 3, 2]	[4, 2]	Competitive
Quick	Jonathan	[3, 3, 4, 1, 1]	[3, 1]	Elite
Raanta	Antti	[3, 4, 4, 4, 1]	[4, 2]	Elite
Rask	Tuukka	[2, 2, 3, 2, 4]	[2, 3]	World class
Reimer	James	[3, 3, 2, 1, 2]	[3, 2]	Inadequate
Rinne	Pekka	[2, 3, 4, 3, 1]	[2, 2]	Elite
Rittich	David	[1, 1, 2, 1, 1]	[1, 1]	Inadequate
Saros	Juuse	[1, 4, 4, 2, 2]	[2, 2]	Serviceable
Smith	Mike	[3, 2, 3, 1, 1]	[2, 1]	Inadequate
Talbot	Cam	[3, 3, 2, 1, 3]	[3, 2]	Inadequate
Vasilevskiy	Andrei	[2, 3, 3, 4, 3]	[2, 4]	World class

References

1. Bishop, C.M.: Pattern Recognition and Machine Learning. Information Science and Statistics. Springer, Heidelberg (2006)
2. Deisenroth, M.P.: Mathematics for Machine Learning. Cambridge University Press, Cambridge (2020)
3. Everitt, B.S., Landau, S., Leese, M., Stahl, D.: Cluster Analysis. Wiley, Hoboken (2011)
4. DeGroot, M.H., Schervish, M.J.: Probability and Statistics, 4th edn. Pearson, London (2018)
5. Hastle, T.: Elements of Statistical Learning. Springer, Heidelberg (2016)
6. Kroese, D.P., Botev, Z., Taimre, T., Vaisman, R.: Data Science and Machine Learning. Chapman and Hall CRC Publishing (2019)
7. Wilmott, P.: Machine Learning: An Applied Mathematics Introduction. Panda Ohana Publishing (2019)
8. Doomany, C.: Cluster names (personal communication). Bentley University, April 2022

Synopsis of Video Files Using Neural Networks: Component Analysis

Georgi Kostadinov[(⊠)] [iD]

New Bulgarian University, 21 Montevideo str, 1618 Sofia, Bulgaria
grgkostadinov@gmail.com

Abstract. The following paper provides a detailed analysis of the components of a novel framework for generating synopsis of CCTV videos. A synopsis is a video file obtained by overlaying the main objects from a source video on a single scene. This allows for a file length reduction and optimization of the storage of such files. This paper extends the presented work based on convolutional neural networks by discussing the effect that such algorithms may have on the final synopsis result which in turn helps in understanding how they can be further improved for this task. For the purposes of the component analysis presented in this paper, specialized datasets and metrics were selected to quantify the quality of the algorithms of the video synopsis framework.

Keywords: Video synopsis · Convolutional neural networks · Machine learning · Object localization · Multiple object tracking · Feature extraction · Background segmentation · Person re-identification

1 Introduction

1.1 Current Challenges and Opportunities

Recent years have witnessed an explosive growth of video surveillance technologies. Constant video monitoring is required in order for governments and owners of private properties to ensure the security and safety of their people and assets. However, the effectiveness of analysis and storage of raw videos remain a challenge. In most of the cases in video surveillance, the static repetitive frames can have a length of hours whilSe the segments that contain useful information are no more than several seconds. An emerging solution called video synopsis is developed to cope with these challenges. It enables the reduction of hours of video footage in minutes showing the most important events while at the same time retains the quality of the source video.

In [1], an end-to-end framework is proposed, that can generate a synopsis of CCTV video footage of pedestrians using convolutional neural networks (CNN). A "synopsis" of a video file is an output file containing only the main moving objects from the source video file, placed together on the extracted background. The output file generated during the process is much smaller in size compared to the source file, making its storage cost-effective, and at the same time shorter in length, making the manual analysis and review of such CCTV footage a much easier process.

T. Zlateva and R. Goleva (Eds.): CSECS 2022, LNICST 450, pp. 11–23, 2022.
https://doi.org/10.1007/978-3-031-17292-2_2

1.2 Classification of Video Synopsis Methods

Over the years numerous methods for video condensation have been developed. They can be classified broadly in two categories: frame-based and object-based approaches.

Frame-based approaches are extracting the key frames from the source video either by skipping several frames or analysing each of them individually using certain criteria and extracting only those with the highest importance. The extracted frames are then blended to create the output video summarization. Earlier methods are based on video skimming approach [2], which skip several low interest frames. More advanced methods [3] analyse the structured motion of the frames to extract the key ones. Although frame-based approaches are simple and fast condensation methods, they result in unrealistic artifacts due to the frame skipping and are ineffective with highly dynamic scenes with little to no repetitive frames.

Modern video condensation methods are object-based. Such methods extract sequences of the main moving objects in the source video called *tubes* that are shifted along temporarily and placed together on the extracted background. This allows for the simultaneous visualization of all moving objects from the source video allowing for higher condensation ratio than the frame-based approaches. For example, both [4] and [5] are using estimation algorithms where object's positions are chronologically rearranged with no trajectory analysis. Whereas [6] is clustering the objects trajectories via event-based trajectory kinematics descriptors extracted from each object.

The rest of the paper is structured as follows. Section 2 discusses the details of the synopsis framework for videos with pedestrians presented in [1] as well as the importance of understanding the effect each component has on the final output. Section 3 analyses the background extraction method, whereas Sect. 4 measures the quality of the pedestrian localization, tracking, and pedestrian re-identification algorithms. Finally, in Sect. 5 conclusions are drawn, and future work is presented.

2 Video Synopsis Framework Overview

In [1] a novel framework for creating a synopsis of CCTV footage of pedestrians is presented. The framework can be divided into five main components: (1) extracting the background using mixture of Gaussian models (GMM) [7]; (2) localization of pedestrians using the convolutional neural network *You Only Look Once v3* (YOLOv3) [8]; (3) extraction of their visual features for accurate re-identification via the CNN for person re-identification *Omni-Scale Feature Learning for Person Re-Identification* (OSNet) [9]; (4) tracking them in the source video scenes using *Deep Simple Online and Realtime Tracking* (DeepSORT) [10] and the visual features from (3); and (5) generating the synopsis file for the joint visualization of the tracked identities from (4) on the extracted background from (1). The structure of the framework is visualized on Fig. 1.

The synopsis is generated via two main processes – *analysis* and *generation*. During the *analysis*, each frame is fed into the object localization algorithm YOLOv3 and the pedestrians are localized and segmented. For each pedestrian a structure determining its spatial-temporal data is created that includes the position and the time of occurrence in the original video. Moreover, using OSNet the visual features for each pedestrian localized on the scene are extracted. These visual features are later used as part of the

DeepSORT algorithm to re-identify the pedestrians in subsequent frames based on the accumulated state of the previous frames. This way the object tubes or in the context of pedestrians – their *identities*, are created. Each identity is a sequence of the occurrences of a given pedestrian from the source video. In parallel, the background is extracted using the algorithm from [7]. The output from the analysis step is both the extracted background and tracked identities. The *generation* process takes the tracked identities, filters any whose occurrence is low, and uses two control parameters to render the identities on the extracted background – m for the maximum number of identities to render at once and k for the number of frames to wait before rendering a new identity on the scene. The final output of the process is the rendered synopsis file where each identity is temporarily shifted along for their joint visualization.

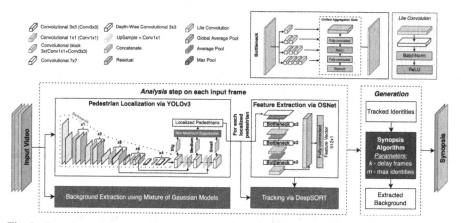

Fig. 1. Overview of the presented video synopsis framework in [1]. Two convolutional neural networks are used – YOLOv3 [8] for localization of the pedestrians and OSNet [9] for the extraction of their visual features. The localized pedestrians are then tracked via DeepSORT [10] and put on the extracted using mixture of Gaussian models [7] background to create the synopsis.

Comparing the presented framework in [1] with prior art [4–6] shows that the frame reduction is much higher while maintaining the same visual quality as in the source video. The comparison results achieved in [1] on a CCTV video of a hall room from [5] are presented in Table 1 (the video synopsis framework in [1] is marked as **VSF**) and the synopsis output is visualized on Fig. 2.

Table 1. Comparison with prior art on the hall video dataset [5]. *SynopsisO* is the frame reduction rate or the ratio between the number of synopsis frames F_o and number of source frames.

Metric	Huang et al. [4]	Huang et al. [5]	Wang et al. [6]	**VSF** [1]
F_o	14379	11271	8814	**1566**
SynopsisO	0.785	0.831	0.868	**0.977**

Fig. 2. Visualization of the hall dataset [5] synopsis.

As seen from the results in Table 1, the framework presented in [1] achieves state-of-the-art frame reduction rate. However, being a multi-component solution, no further analysis has been presented in [1] to understand the effect that each component may have on the final synopsis file, and which are the situations where they work sub-optimally. To do so, each component must be examined individually using specialized datasets and metrics for each task to get a quantitative measure of its accuracy and the effect on the final output. Moreover, the achieved results can be used as a base to determine how these algorithms could be further improved.

This paper presents a methodology of such analysis for each task and to the extent of the conducted research, no prior works, that discuss the effect each component used in a multi-component object-based video synopsis algorithm may have, exist.

3 Analysis of the Background Extraction

The algorithm for the adaptive Gaussian mixture model presented in [7] and shown on Fig. 1, is an important component of the video synopsis framework. A mixture of Gaussian models is used to model the multimodal background image of the source video. The algorithm is adaptive, which means that it iteratively updates the background mixture model to cope with illumination changes and scene noise. The extracted background is then used as a base where the tracked identities will be later rendered. This means that the algorithm must work as precisely as possible in segmenting the background from the foreground. Failing to do so will result in a lesser quality of the final synopsis output. A quantitative assessment of the quality of the algorithm must be generated to understand the effect that such algorithms have on the final output.

3.1 Control Dataset

For the overall assessment of the algorithm, a specialized dataset for motion detection called CDnet 2014 is used [11]. The goal of CDnet is to provide a balanced dataset with multiple scenarios that are common in motion recognition algorithms. The dataset includes 53 video files with a total of ~158,000 frame annotations. In addition, the video files are divided into 11 categories, each of which represents a different type of challenge – from easy to segment videos, to more challenging scenes with bad weather or night vision. CDnet's annotations are hand-made images for each frame of a video, which on a pixel level annotate the moving objects on the stage.

The official metrics presented in [11] were used to generate the results and rank them with other methods: *Recall* (Re), *Specificity* (Sp), *False Positive Rate* (FPR), *False Negative Rate* (FNR), *Percentage of Wrong Classifications* (PWC), *Precision* (Pr) and *F1-Score* (F1). For their specific descriptions, refer to [11].

3.2 Results

Measurements for the algorithm used in the synopsis framework [1] were obtained by calculating the metrics presented by CDnet for each category from the dataset. Then an average of these per-category metrics was calculated to obtain the overall results. The final results are presented in Table 2 and marked as **VSF**. They are also compared with the results of six other background segmentation methods, calculated in the same way. The data of the other methods is taken from the public results page of CDnet.

Table 2. Comparison of the background extraction algorithm used in [1] with other methods. Ordered in descending order of *F1*. Arrows are an indicator of low or high optimal values.

Methodology	$Re\uparrow$	$Sp\uparrow$	$FPR\downarrow$	$FNR\downarrow$	$PWC\downarrow$	$Pr\uparrow$	$F1\uparrow$
FTSG [12]	0.77	**0.99**	**0.01**	0.23	**1.38**	**0.80**	**0.73**
SuBSENSE [13]	**0.81**	**0.99**	**0.01**	**0.19**	1.84	0.75	**0.73**
CwisarDH [14]	0.66	**0.99**	**0.01**	0.34	1.53	0.77	0.68
VSF [1]	0.64	0.98	0.02	0.36	3.32	0.68	0.58
CP3-online [15]	0.72	0.97	0.03	0.28	3.43	0.56	0.58
GMM [7]	0.68	0.98	0.03	0.32	3.77	0.60	0.57
Euclidean [16]	0.68	0.94	0.06	0.32	6.54	0.55	0.52

The presented methods in Table 2 show both more classical algorithms for background segmentation such as Euclidean distance [16] and GMM [7], and recent developments such as FTSG [12] and SuBSENSE [13]. [16] is a simplified method for background segmentation, which makes a direct comparison of pixels in two consecutive frames. This is followed by many errors, thus higher percentage of PWC (classification errors). GMM Stauffer-Grimson [7] is the adaptive Gaussian mixtures model of Stauffer and Grimson, that the algorithm in [1] is based on. In CP3-online [15], instead of modelling each pixel individually, the colour distribution of the pixels is modelled with strong spatial correlation. According to the authors, this type of spatial model copes with abrupt changes in scene's lighting.

The algorithm in the video synopsis framework (VSF) [1], which is based on [7] shows an improvement in accuracy and a lower error rate than the original work. This is due to the additional steps to post-process the resulting segmentation by blurring and morphological transformations to remove smaller regions of pixels that have been misclassified as foreground by the algorithm. Figure 3 shows an example segmentation of a video frame from CDnet, as well as the result of the additional processing that is performed by VSF.

Newer methodologies significantly improve F1-Score, precision (Pr) and reduce error rate (PWC). CwisarDH [14] uses a neural network that, for any set of previous pixel values in the image, approximates corresponding values of background or foreground components. The main disadvantage of this approach is the need for the neural network to be trained with pre-segmented frames. In [13], colour and local binary signs of similarity

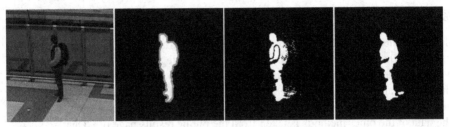

Fig. 3. Sample segmented frame via VSF [1]. Left to right: video frame snippet from CDnet [11]; CDnet frame annotations; GMM [7] output before processing; final result after blur processing, threshold filtering and morphological transformation.

are used to give approximations at the pixel level. In addition, it automatically adjusts the parameters and adapts locally according to the dynamics of the scene. FTSG [12] is a three-step algorithm: (1) recognizing moving objects using a pixel energy flux tensor, and a GMM [7] algorithm; (2) combining the recognized scene movements; and (3) removing artifacts obtained from stagnation of moving objects in one place. The results show that, despite the improvement in F1-Score compared to the baseline GMM model, the algorithm in [1] is far behind state-of-the-art methods that are either using neural networks or based on more complex frame analysis. However, to better understand where the algorithm in [1] lacks the necessary accuracy, Table 3 presents a more thorough analysis for each dataset category showing the F1-Score of the algorithm.

Table 3. Results of the background extraction from [1] for the CDnet dataset categories [11].

Video	Description	$F1$
badWeath	Different weather conditions, 4 videos	0.79
baseline	Easy to segment foreground, 4 videos	0.79
shadow	Dynamic scene shadow, 6 videos	0.75
dynamic	Dynamic movement on the background, 6 videos	0.68
cameraJ	Unstable CCTV footage, 4 videos	0.64
thermal	Infrared thermal sensor videos, 5 videos	0.62
turbule	Infrared videos with turbulence due to hot air, 4 videos	0.60
lowFram	Low FPS videos, 4 videos	0.50
intermi	With objects that are static for long periods of time, 6 videos	0.42
nightVi	Videos captured in low-light conditions, 6 videos	0.40
PTZ	From cameras with pan, tilt, and zoom control, 4 videos	0.22

The results in Table 3 indicate that the hardest category is the one from PTZ cameras due to the pan, tilt, and zoom movements of the camera. This result is expected as the algorithm used in the framework which is based on GMM [7] relies on the fact that the scene composition will be mostly static. The lack of lighting in the *nightVi* category leads to much higher number of pixels being recognized as a background, whereas the result for the *intermi* category shows the inability of the algorithm to adapt if an object has stayed static for a longer period of time. Moreover, the lower frame rate in the *lowFram* category creates situations where the algorithm does not adapt fast enough. Sample background visualizations of the worst performing categories are shown on Fig. 4. The PTZ video background visualized is corrupted due to the pan and tilt movements of the camera. Meanwhile, the background for both *nightVi* and *lowFram* videos show artefacts due to either the low light conditions or the lower frame updates.

Fig. 4. Sample extracted backgrounds by [1] for the worst performing CDnet [11] categories.

The results on the CDnet dataset show that a more robust methodology needs to be developed in [1] to be able to cope with low-light conditions and adapt quickly to sudden scene changes. This will increase both the quality of the backgrounds extracted in such conditions and the overall quality of the final synopsis output.

4 Analysis of the Pedestrian Localization, Extraction, and Tracking Components

As visualized in Fig. 1, the algorithms for pedestrian localization, re-identification, and tracking are core to the video synopsis framework. If the localization algorithm does not recognize a pedestrian in a sequence of frames, it will be also missing in the synopsis video. On the other hand, if the feature extraction algorithm for re-identification does not extract robust-enough features, the tracking algorithm won't be able to correctly identify the identities on the scene. To understand the impact of these algorithms to the final output, a control dataset of CCTV videos of pedestrians is required that contains both annotations of their positions within each frame as well as their identities.

4.1 Control Dataset

Based on the defined requirements, the datasets from the MOTChallenge [17] competition were selected. Being a specialized dataset for multi-object tracking algorithms, MOTChallenge consists of several video files that capture pedestrians in busy public places with frequent, partial, or complete occlusions from other objects. Videos differ in shooting angle, scene brightness, subject size, camera sensor quality. The competition consists of several different tracking tests. For testing the localization, tracking, and re-identification algorithms, the test dataset MOT17 [18] has been selected.

The MOT17 dataset consists of a total of 7 videos that have public results from three different localization algorithms – DPM [19], Faster R-CNN [20] and SDP [21]. Moreover, it has additional detailed annotations for each frame that can be used to measure the quality of the tracking algorithm. One such annotation contains an identifier of the object, a region with its exact position in the frame, a value between 0 and 1, indicating how occluded the object is, as well as the type of object. Sample video frames for each of the 7 videos from MOT17 are visualized on Fig. 5.

Fig. 5. Sample frames from the MOT17 dataset [18].

MOTChallenge also includes official metrics for calculating the performance of an algorithm on their test sets. For measuring the accuracy of the tracking and re-identification algorithms, the following metrics from MOTChallenge were used: *Multiple Object Tracking Accuracy* (MOTA), *Multiple Object Tracking Precision* (MOTP). And for measuring the precision of the object localization algorithm *Recall* (Re), *Precision* (Pr), *F1-Score* (F1) were selected. For their specific descriptions, refer to [17].

4.2 Results for Pedestrian Localization with YOLOv3

YOLOv3 [8] consists of a single feed-forward 53-layer convolutional neural network Darknet-53 [8] as well as three scaled detection layers for detecting small, medium, and large objects. The algorithm considers the object localization task as a regression problem and in a single feed-forward pass can make predictions both for the regions of the objects within the image as well as their class affiliation. A visualization of its architecture is presented on Fig. 1. At the final stage, the three scaled detection layers are fused together and post-processed with a Non-maximum Suppression [22] algorithm to produce the localization output. Being a one-stage object detector, YOLOv3 is a very efficient and fast algorithm, making it an extremely good choice for real-time video processing applications.

The YOLOv3 algorithm in the video synopsis framework (VSF) is trained on the *person* category from two datasets – *Common Objects in Context (COCO)* [23] and *Pascal Visual Objects Classes (VOC)* [24]. The final dataset consists of 66,109 images for training and *4,786* for validation. Training on *15,000* iterations with learning rate of *0.001* achieved a validation accuracy of *93%*. However, measurement of the real-world performance is required in order to understand how the algorithm behaves in different occlusion situations or scene changes, all of which are present in the MOT17 dataset.

To test the localization algorithm, the metrics *Re*, *Pr*, and *F1* were calculated on each video of the MOT17 dataset and then averaged to get the overall results for the whole dataset. Moreover, public results for the algorithms DPM [19], Faster R-CNN [20], and SDP [21] were used to compare the results of the YOLOv3 algorithm used in the framework. DPM is a model that combines different parts of pedestrian recognition objects, but due to the hand-built descriptors it is inaccurate in abrupt changes in scene lighting or in recognizing pedestrians from a distance. The other two algorithms – Faster R-CNN and SDP, are using two neural networks to localize objects – one for region proposals and the other for classification of these regions. The difference between the two algorithms is that SDP is using an additional algorithm to clean the regions so that the bounding boxes approximations are more accurate.

Table 4 presents the results for each method. The YOLOv3 model used in the video synopsis framework is labelled as **VSF**. The frames per second (FPS) values have been measured on the same hardware – NVIDIA GTX 1080Ti, for SDP, VSF, and Faster R-CNN. The DPM algorithm was tested on a 3.4 GHz Intel CPU.

Table 4. Results of the YOLOv3 [8] localization algorithm compared with the results of the methods used in MOT17 [18]. Ordered by F1-Score. Arrows indicate low or high optimal values.

Methodology	*Re* ↑	*Pr* ↑	*F1* ↑	*FPS* ↑
SDP [21]	**0.682**	0.954	**0.795**	4
VSF [1]	0.624	0.916	0.742	**78**
Faster R-CNN [20]	0.520	**0.958**	0.674	5.6
DPM [19]	0.314	0.935	0.470	30

Based on the results presented on the table and in terms of F1-Score, YOLOv3 proves to be the most optimal method for the video synopsis framework out of these four, as it achieves 19.5 times faster frame rate compared to SDP for 5.3% lower *F1*. However, further training of the algorithm is required to surpass the localization accuracy of SDP.

4.3   Results for Pedestrian Tracking with DeepSORT

DeepSORT [10] is tracking-by-detection algorithm that uses Kalman filtering for tracking multiple objects localized in new frames based on how their state changed in past frames and a convolutional neural network for object re-identification. The DeepSORT algorithm in the video synopsis framework is also responsible for creating the identities within a single video, making it an important component that has a direct impact on the final synopsis. The inability to correctly identify the pedestrians, can lead to less identities created, thus missing important frames from the source video.

For testing the tracking algorithm, the *MOTP* and *MOTA* metrics were calculated. Outputs from DPM, SDP, and Faster R-CNN were also used as tracked object regions to compare how the tracking algorithm's performance changes with methods other than the YOLOv3 used in VSF. As seen from the results in Table 5 the YOLOv3 algorithm, when paired with DeepSORT, is both less precise and accurate than SDP and Faster R-CNN. This is since YOLOv3 approximates the regions in a single feed-forward pass instead in a dedicated neural network as in Faster R-CNN and SDP. This leads to less precise and varying regions, therefore lower tracking precision.

Table 5. Results of the DeepSORT [10] algorithm. Arrows indicate low or high optimal values.

Methodology	$MOTP \uparrow$	$MOTA \uparrow$
SDP [21]	0.832	**0.643**
VSF [1]	0.798	0.558
Faster R-CNN [20]	**0.883**	0.493
DPM [19]	0.776	0.290

4.4 Results for Pedestrian Re-identification with OSNet

An essential component of a tracking algorithm is the ability to re-identify the same object in a new video frame. The most common way is by creating an associative matrix, whose elements determine a score whether a tracked object correlates to a newly localized object. In SORT [25] such score is calculated using the Mahalanobis distance between the object states from the Kalman filter and the objects from the localization algorithm. SORT does not use any additional data such as object's visual similarity. However, this leads to an issue where the identities of two objects can be misidentified or switched by the tracking algorithm when their paths cross on the same scene. DeepSORT improves SORT and mitigates this issue by adding a second distance metric to the final score in the associative matrix – an Euclidean distance between the visual features of a given localized object and those of the last 100 tracked objects. These visual features are encoded using a convolutional neural network.

The convolutional neural network used to extract the visual features of the pedestrians in the video synopsis framework from [1] as shown in Fig. 1 is OSNet [9]. OSNet is a specialized CNN for pedestrian re-identification that uses residual blocks composed of convolutional streams for detecting features in different spatial scales – from small, local features (shoes, glasses) to more global, bigger features (size, age, clothing). It also uses a novel unified aggregation gate [9] that fuses the different-scaled features together with the input-dependent weights to learn spatial correlations. The final output is a 512-D feature vector that is used for re-identification as part of DeepSORT. The OSNet model used as part of the framework is trained on three datasets for person re-identification: *Market1501* [26], *DukeMTMC* [27], and *CUHK03* [28].

To test the accuracy of the OSNet model, the *MOTA* metric is calculated for SORT and compared with the same for the video synopsis framework (VSF) using DeepSORT and OSNet from Table 5. Table 6 presents these results with an additional column IDSW which is the number of times there was an identity switch. The results indicate that the accuracy improvement of using OSNet is 3.7% and, at the same time, this leads to

39.4% less identity switches. Figure 6 visualizes these results. Although they show a major improvement in decreasing the identity switches, the total number for [1] is still too high. Improvements to the algorithm will be required to decrease them even further.

Table 6. Comparison of the results on the MOT17 [18] dataset for the VSF [1] (that uses DeepSORT [10] and OSNet [9]) and SORT [25]. Arrows indicate low or high optimal values.

Methodology	MOTA ↑	IDSW ↓
VSF [1]	**0.558**	**941**
SORT [25]	0.521	1554

Fig. 6. Frames from MOT17 [18]. Top row are results using SORT [25], bottom row – using VSF [1] (DeepSORT [10] and OSNet [9]). VSF correctly identifies the pedestrian in red rectangle with an identity 3, whereas SORT incorrectly assigns him three different identities – 48, 65, 75.

5 Conclusions

This paper reviewed and analysed the components of the video synopsis framework presented in [1]. Results were generated on specialized datasets, namely CDNet [11] for evaluation of the background extraction algorithm and MOTChallenge [17] for the pedestrian localization, tracking, and re-identification algorithms. Moreover, the algorithms in [1] were compared with other methodologies. Results show that, despite being optimal for the framework, cases exist where the algorithms are not precise enough – there are still high number of identity switches from the tracking algorithm and the background subtraction algorithm could be further improved to handle more challenging scene situations. Future work will include incremental improvements to the algorithms increasing their accuracy in order to have higher quality synopsis videos.

References

1. Kostadinov, G.: Synopsis of video files using neural networks. In: Proceedings of the 23rd EANN 2022. https://doi.org/10.1007/978-3-031-08223-8_16

2. Smith, M.A., Kanade, T.: Video skimming and characterization through the combination of image and language understanding. In: Proceedings CAIVD, pp. 61–70 (1998)
3. Fu, W., Wang, J., Gui, L., Lu, H., Ma, S.: Online video synopsis of structured motion. Neurocomputing **135**, 155–162 (2014)
4. Huang, C.R., Chen, H.C., Chung, P.C.: Online surveillance video synopsis. In: IEEE International Symposium on Circuits and Systems (ISCAS), pp. 1843–1846. IEEE (2012)
5. Huang, C.R., Chung, P.C.J., Yang, D.K., Chen, H.C., Huang, G.J.: Maximum a posteriori probability estimation for online surveillance video synopsis. IEEE Trans. Circuits Syst. Video Technol. **24**(8), 1417–1429 (2014)
6. Wang, W.C., Chung, P.C., Huang, C.R., Huang, W.Y.: Event based surveillance video synopsis using trajectory kinematics descriptors. In: Fifteenth IAPR International Conference on Machine Vision Applications, pp. 250–253 (2017)
7. Stauffer, C., Grimson, W.E.L.: Adaptive background mixture models for real-time tracking. In CVPR (1999)
8. Redmon, J., Farhadi, A.: Yolov3: an incremental improvement. arXiv preprint arXiv: arXiv: 1804.02767 (2018)
9. Zhou, K., Yang, Y., Cavallaro, A., Xiang, T.: Omni-scale feature learning for person re-identification. In: ICCV, pp. 3702–3712 (2019)
10. Wojke, N., Bewley, A., Paulus, D.: Simple online and realtime tracking with a deep association metric. In: ICIP, pp. 3645–3649 (2017)
11. Wang, Y., Jodoin, P.-M., Porikli, F., Konrad, J., Benezeth, Y., Ishwar, P.: Cdnet 2014: an expanded change detection benchmark dataset. In: CVPR, pp. 387–394 (2014)
12. Wang, R., Bunyak, F., Seetharaman, G., Palaniappan, K.: Static and moving object detection using flux tensor with split Gaussian models. In: CVPR, pp. 414–418 (2014)
13. St-Charles, P.-L., Bilodeau, G.-A., Bergevin, R.: Flexible background subtraction with self-balanced local sensitivity. In: CVPR, pp. 408–413 (2014)
14. De Gregorio, M., Giordano, M.: Change detection with weightless neural networks. In: CVPR, pp. 403–407 (2014)
15. Liang, D., Kaneko, S.: Improvements and experiments of a compact statistical background model. arXiv preprint arXiv:1405.6275 (2014)
16. Benezeth, Y., Jodoin, P.-M., Emile, B., Laurent, H., Rosenberger, C.: Comparative study of background subtraction algorithms. J. Electron Imaging **19** (2010)
17. Leal-Taixé, L., Milan, A., Reid, I., Roth, S., Schindler, K.: Motchallenge 2015: towards a benchmark for multi-target tracking. arXiv preprint arXiv:1504.01942 (2015)
18. Milan, A., Leal-Taixé, L., Reid, I., Roth, S., Schindler, K.: Mot16: a benchmark for multi-object tracking. arXiv preprint arXiv:1603.00831 (2016)
19. Felzenszwalb, P.F., Girshick, R.B., McAllester, D., Ramanan, D.: Object detection with discriminatively trained part-based models. TPAMI **32**(9), 1627–1645 (2009)
20. Ren, S., He, K., Girshick, R., Sun, J.: Faster r-cnn: towards real-time object detection with region proposal networks. In: ANIPS, pp. 91–99 (2015)
21. Yang, F., Choi, W., Lin, Y.: Exploit all the layers: fast and accurate CNN object detector with scale dependent pooling and cascaded rejection classifiers. In: CVPR (2016)
22. Neubeck, A., Van Gool, L.: Efficient non-maximum suppression. In: ICPR (2006)
23. Lin, T.Y., et al.: Microsoft coco: common objects in context. In: ECCV, pp. 740–755 (2014)
24. Hoiem, D., Divvala, S.K., Hays, J.H.: Pascal VOC 2008 challenge. World Literature Today, p. 24 (2009)
25. Bewley, A., Ge, Z., Ott, L., Ramos, F., Upcroft, B.: Simple online and realtime tracking. In: ICIP, pp. 3464–3468 (2016)
26. Zheng, L., Shen, L., Tian, L., Wang, S., Wang, J., Tian, Q.: Scalable person re-identification: a benchmark. In: ICCV, pp. 1116–1124 (2015)

27. Ristani, E., Solera, F., Zou, R., Cucchiara, R., & Tomasi, C.: Performance measures and a data set for multi-target, multi-camera tracking. In ECCV, pp. 17–35. (2016)
28. Li, W., Zhao, R., Xiao, T., Wang, X:. Deepreid: deep filter pairing neural network for person re-identification. In: CVPR, pp. 152–159 (2014)

Image Decluttering Techniques and Its Impact on YOLOv4 Performance

Maryam Asghari and Farshid Alizadeh-Shabdiz$^{(\boxtimes)}$

Boston University, Boston, MA 02215, USA
{masghari,alizadeh}@bu.edu

Abstract. Object detection and specifically face detection are challenging computer vision problems. The purpose of this study is to explore the effect of data augmentation and image decluttering technique on performance of YoloV4 model. In this work, we proposed the idea of image decluttering technique and evaluated its effect on the face detection. We have also investigated Mosaic augmentation technique and identified some drawbacks of using that and suggested an enhancement to the existing Mosaic augmentation to address the drawbacks and showed the impact of the new proposed mosaic augmentation technique on performance of face detection using YoloV4 model. This study is structured to find the effect of the proposed techniques on various images with diverse backgrounds, illumination, occlusions, and viewpoints. We achieved promising results that prove the effectiveness of the proposed techniques on detection probability, specifically in the challenging conditions.

Keywords: Image decluttering · Data augmentation · Face detection · Image processing · Image enhancement · Object detection · YOLO

1 Introduction

Object detection is one of the most important aspects of computer vision that has been widely studied in the past. Since 2012, many studies have been done on object detection techniques using deep learning, which resulted in many algorithms with high accuracy. The goal of object detection is to find and recognize objects that are in each image and give it a label from predefined classes. The second goal is to predict the location of the object in the image by drawing a bounding box around the detected object.

Deep learning-based object detection solutions can be divided into two main categories: (i) Two-step architectures, like region-based Convolutional Neural Networks (R-CNN) [1] and its improved versions like Fast R-CNN [2] and Faster R-CNN [3] and (ii) one stage architectures, like You Only Look Once (YOLO) [4], YOLO9000 [5] and Single Shot multi-box Detector (SSD) [6]. Two-step architectures select a number or region proposals and use CNN to extract features from these proposals and feed the extracted features into a classifier like Support vector machines (SVM) to predict the class of the proposed region. One-step architectures techniques combine detection and

© ICST Institute for Computer Sciences, Social Informatics and Telecommunications Engineering 2022
Published by Springer Nature Switzerland AG 2022. All Rights Reserved
T. Zlateva and R. Goleva (Eds.): CSECS 2022, LNICST 450, pp. 24–44, 2022.
https://doi.org/10.1007/978-3-031-17292-2_3

classification steps together. Two stage architecture techniques usually have better performance in comparison with one stage architectures, but they are significantly slower. Furthermore, unlike one-step architecture, they have lower applicability in real-time object detection applications.

Applications of object detection are on the rise in many different fields including face detection. Face detection is a technique that detects the location and size of faces in images. Face detection is the first step in many tasks like face recognition and face verification. Face recognition has several applications in smartphones, social media, and security systems for authentications. Face detection is still a challenging problem in the field of computer vision because of the varieties of illumination, occlusions, and viewpoints.

In this research we used YOLOv4 [7] model in both Darknet and TensorFlow frameworks and trained both models using different combination of datasets by applying various data augmentation and image pre-processing techniques and then applying the proposed image decluttering technique. Image decluttering is the step which is applied to an image before feeding it to the face detection module.

In this paper, Sect. 2 presents related work of face detection algorithms. Datasets, data augmentation, data enhancement and proposed decluttering methods are discussed in Sect. 3. Results are analyzed in Sect. 4. Conclusion remarks and future work are described in Sect. 5.

2   Related Work

In this section, we provide a literature review of image augmentation, test time augmentation, and image processing methods.

2.1   Image Augmentation

Image augmentation is a key step and most common method to reduce overfitting in computer vision tasks. It is almost impossible to include images for all scenarios in real life. However, with image augmentation, we can provide wider variety of images by modifying existing images and enlarging the training dataset. There are wide variety of augmentation methods that researchers have employed when training a convolutional neural network.

Bochkovskiy et al. called these methods "Bag of freebies" [7]. They defined bag of freebies as a series of techniques that only increased the training cost and improved the performance of models without affecting the inference time. They divided the image augmentation techniques into distortions and occlusion. Distortions can further be divided into photometric (which includes adjusting the contrast, brightness, saturation, hue, and noise), and geometric distortions (which includes shifting, cropping, flipping, rotating, and scaling). Both distortion methods are pixel-wise adjustments to the original image and the original image can be easily recovered. Geometric distortion also affects the bounding boxes, so the labels must be updated after these augmentation methods.

LeCun et al. in [8] applied randomly distorting patterns with random distortion parameters. These distortions include horizontal and vertical translation, scaling, squeezing, and horizontal shearing. They increased the training set ten times by adding instances of distorted images to improve the accuracy and robustness of their model. Bengio et al. in [9] applied a large variation of transformations including thickness, slant, affine transformation, local elastic deformation, pinch, motion blur, occlusion, gaussian smoothing, pixels permutation, gaussian noise, background image addition, salt & pepper, scratches, and grey level & contrast. Krizhevsky et al. in [10] applied image translations, horizontal reflections and random changes in the intensity and color of the illumination. They reduced the error rate and prevented their model to suffer from overfitting by applying these augmentation methods. Wu et al. in [11] applied red, green, and blue color casting, vignette, left and right rotation, pincushion distortion, barrel distortion, and vertical and horizontal stretch to improve the result of training.

In the second group of augmentation, researchers focus on occlusion issues in object detection. There are several methods introduced by researchers that result in better performance in object detection and image classification. Zhong et al. in [12] introduced random erasing data augmentation technique. In this technique random rectangle regions from images are chosen and masked either with a random value or the average of the ImageNet's images' pixel values [13]. In [12], they applied random erasing in three methods: 1) Image-aware Random Erasing (IRE) 2) Object-aware Random Erasing (ORE), and 3) Image and object-aware Random Erasing (I + ORE). In IRE, a random region is chosen from the entire image. In ORE, a random region is applied to each object bounding box. In I + ORE, a random image is chosen from both entire image and each bounding box. They also combined random erasing with random cropping to generate more images. By applying random erasing, they achieved improvements in image classification, object detection and person re-identification. Like random erasing, DeVries et al. [14] introduced Cutout data augmentation. In this method, they used zero-masking to obstruct a random square region. In [14], they proposed that Cutout can be also used in combination with other augmentation methods. They achieved better results on popular image recognition datasets. Singh et al. [15] introduced a data augmentation technique called Hide-and-Seek to improve the performance of object localization. In Hide-and-Seek method, each training image will be divided into SxS grids. Then in each epoch different random patches will be masked by all zeros. This can cause that the most discriminative section of the object will not be visible to the model. Therefore, the model must focus on the other parts of the object and learn them. Chen et al. [16] proposed similar idea called Grid mask. The goal of this method was to find a balance between deleting and reserving to avoid excessive deletion that could cause complete removal of an object and reservation of continuous regions which could, consequently, lead to leaving some objects untouched. Grid mask could control the size and density of deleted squares. They used a set of spatially uniformly distributed squares to delete these regions. In [16], they claimed that they can achieve better results in comparison with other information dropping augmentation methods like [12, 14] and [15].

In addition to these augmentation methods, there are other methods that will use multiple images and combine them together. Zhang et al. [17] proposed a method called Mix-up, which overlays a pair of images with different coefficient ratios and adjusts their labels based on the changes. Yun et al. [18] proposed a new augmentation method called CutMix, which is a combination of Cutout [14] and Mix-up [17]. It could cut a patch from an image and paste it to another image, following by adjusting the labels. In [18], they claimed that Mix-up data augmentation will improve the results of classification, localization, and detection on popular datasets. Bochkovskiy et al. in [7] introduced a new data augmentation method called Mosaic. Mosaic is a new method for image augmentation that mix four random images together with different ratios. This will help the model to detect objects in smaller scales, also in context outside their usual context. Hao et al. [19] improved mosaic augmentation of YOLOv4. The applied improvements are considering the number of target objects in composite image, using three fixed grid layouts with 6 and 9 grids instead of 4, considering the change in image size, and considering the ground truth of the objects that are hardly visible after combining all the images. Wei et al. [20] introduced adaptive cropping, which considers the scale of the objects and the number of objects in the cropped section. They applied partitioning or padding to solve the problem of scale variation. They also used YOLOv4 mosaic augmentation in a way that cropped out the region of interests from sparse samples. To prevent scale variation, they first applied zooming in or out to have objects with reasonable scales and then combined multiple regions in one image. Jiankang, et al. [21] for training RetinaFace, used Wider Face training set, they crop random square patches from original images and resized them to generate larger faces during training. This is because 20% of faces in Wider face data set are very tiny. If the center of the bounding box is within the patch, they would consider the faces that ended up on the boundary of cropped patches and they would keep the label. Besides cropping, they also applied random horizontal flip and photo-metric color distortion.

2.2 Test-Time Augmentation

Test-Time Augmentation (TTA) is applying data augmentation to test dataset. The idea of TTA is to perform random augmentation and modification to test images, create multiple versions of each image in the test set, run the prediction on each, and process the results to return the final prediction. In general, we can expect to improve the prediction by using multiple augmented images instead of one original image. We need to keep inference time low but adding each augmented image would increase it. Therefore, we prefer to use few augmented images along with original image during testing. Simonyan et al. [22] applied horizontal flipping to a test set, used the average of soft-max class posteriors of both original and flipped images to get the image final score. Szegedy et al. [23] used cropping during test time, which they referred to as multi-crop evaluation. Multi-crop technique will use multiple cropped variation of the image to predict and use the average of the scores for final prediction.

TTA can also be utilized for object detection. However, in object detection, we cannot use averaging to get the result as in classification and we need to aggregate the outputs of the model and perform non-maxima-suppression (NMS) for final prediction. In [21], for testing Retinanet on Wider Face, they followed [24] and [25] and applied flip and multi-scale strategies. They followed [26] and used box voting with IoU threshold at 0.4 to choose the final prediction.

2.3 Image Processing

Image processing is the process of adjusting digital image and providing a better and more suitable input for other image analysis purposes. Many images suffer from poor contrast and noise. The goal of image processing is to improve the quality and clarity of the image, emphasize and sharpen the image features and details such as boundaries and edges, so they can be detected easily. This will be done by feature enhancement, suppressing unwanted distortions and noise, and increasing contrast. There are many image processing methods to improve a digital image. These methods can broadly be divided into two categories: Spatial Domain and Frequency Domain methods. Spatial domain techniques are based on direct manipulation of image pixels. In Frequency Domain techniques, images will be converted to Frequency Domain using Fourier transform followed by the required processing. These enhancement methods are applied to refine the quality of images by improving the brightness or contrast of the images or working on the edges and features of images. [27, 28], and [29] provided a comprehensive analysis on various image enhancement methods. In [27] they discussed Point Processing Operation methods like: Create Negative of an Image, Thresholding Transformations, Intensity Transformation, Logarithmic Transformations, Powers-Law Transformations, Piecewise Linear Transformation Functions, Grey Level Slicing and Histogram Processing such as Histogram Equalization, Histogram Matching, Local Enhancement, and Use of Histogram Statistics for Image Enhancement.

In [29] they provided an overview of image enhancement methods such as Filtering with morphological operators, Histogram equalization, Noise removal using a Wiener filter, Linear contrast Enhancement, Median Filtering, unsharp mask filtering, Contrast-limited adaptive histogram equalization (CLAHE), and Decorrelation Stretch. [28] presented comparative study of various Image enhancement techniques using Retinex theory and Fuzzy Logic. Retinex theory states that an image is the product of illuminance and reflectance. There are many Retinex-based approaches that have been proposed and implemented such as SSR (Single Scale Retinex), MSR (Multi Scale Retinex), MSRCR (Multi Scale Retinex Color Restoration) and MSRCP (Multi Scale Retinex Color Preservation). In [28], they provided a review for latest development in Retinex theory such as: Luminance adaptation, Genetic algorithm, Guided filter, and Wavelet transform. They also provided a summary of latest development using fuzzy theory such as Intuitionistic fuzzy set theory, Interpolation method based on fuzzy logic, Fuzzy conceptual contrast enhancement (FCCE), Optimization on membership function, Illuminate normalization and Fuzzy contrast mapping.

One common image enhancement technique is removing unwanted noise. This is usually done by Gaussian smoothing that is the result of blurring the image by a Gaussian function to reduce image noise. Applying Gaussian smoothing can destroy the edges of an image. On the other hand, edge enhancement, which is another image enhancement method, might create unnecessary noise while sharpening the edges. Farbiz et al. in [29] presented a method to overcome these problems by removing impulsive noise and smooth Gaussian noise while preserving edges and image details on gray level images. Shen et al. [30] proposed a novel method to improve the quality of images called (QoE) based MAP-HMGCRF fusion. They proposed the two perceptual quality measures of perceived local contrast and color saturation which are embedded in their hierarchical multivariate Gaussian conditional random field (HMGCRF) model to illustrate improved performance for multi-exposure fusion. In their research they also considered human perceptual parameters to evaluate pixel contributions. Given a source image sequence, the contributions from individual pixels to the fused image were perceptually tuned by perceived local contrast and color saturation. After this process, the perceived contrasts (luminance and color) were used in the MAP-HMGCRF model for pixel-level contribution evaluation. HMGCRF is a hierarchical architecture of MGCRF. It was used to efficiently estimate the pixel contributions/fusion weights (MAP) configuration on a lattice graph.

Kuldeep Singh et al. [31] developed a robust contrast enhancement algorithm based on histogram equalization methods named Median-Mean Based Sub-Image-Clipped Histogram Equalization (MMSICHE). The proposed algorithm has three steps: (i) The Median and Mean brightness values of the image are calculated; (ii) The histogram is clipped using a plateau limit set as the median of the occupied intensity; (iii) The clipped histogram is first bisected based on median intensity then further divided into four sub-images based on individual mean intensity, subsequently performing histogram equalization for each sub-image. This method achieves multi objective of preserving brightness as well as image information content (entropy) along with control over enhancement rate, which suits for consumer electronics applications.Suthaharan et al. [32] proposed two techniques to restore images that are degraded by blur and noise. Their first method was based on fuzzy logic which was used to perform detail sharpening. In their second method, they used improved Wiener filter method to restore blurred-noisy images. In fuzzy image filtering, intensity of the central pixel will be determined by reasoning the intensity value of its surrounding pixels. Two characteristics of proposed method in [32] are that they used a hierarchical order for reasoning rules and the reasoning can be terminated at any stage that the condition is satisfied. They used an averaging process in their approach to find the estimate for the intensity value of the diagonal pixels. Then, they used average defuzzification, that is to get the defuzzificated difference (i.e., the average of four values for differences of intensities between the center pixel and its vertical, horizontal, and diagonal pixels from NW to SE, and from SW to NE). Then, the filtered intensity value of the center pixel is determined by its own value and the defuzzificated difference. In the second proposed method in [32], they used generic algorithm to improve Wiener filter approach. The results of both proposed methods show that the proposed techniques reduce the MSE values of the images significantly.

Hemalatha et al. in [33] proposed a three-step pre-processing technique for facial images. First, they applied median filter for RGB images with salt and pepper noise removal. Then, they used Gabor filter for edge enhancement for the noise-free median filtered image. At the end, they applied histogram for contrast equalization. The median filter uses a sliding window and go pixel by pixel over the entire image. It will replace the value of each pixel by the median intensity in the window. The benefit of the median filter is that the unrepresentative pixel in the window does not have any effect on the median value. Gabor filter is a linear filter used to enhance the feature at every pixel. The parameters of the Gabor filter were fine-tuned with different orientation and wavelength in their method.

Singh et al. in [34] proposed an image enhancement technique that uses both local and global enhancement methods on the same image. Their method has 4 steps: first step is converting the RGB image to saturation and value (HSV) color space and take the luminance of that image. Second step is enhancing local details of image by applying the local enhancement method on the V component or the luminance component. They used unsharp masking method [35] to employ local enhancement. Unsharp masking method has three steps; First blurring of the image, second creating a mask by subtracting the blurred image from the original image and adding the weighted portion of the mask to the original image to get the sharpened image. Third step is applying one of the global contrasts stretching methods to apply global image enhancement to sharpened image. In this method, they used histogram equalization. The last step is combining the enhanced luminance with hue and saturation or the chrominance and convert back to color image.

3   Model Description

In this study, we use YOLOv4 [7] object detection algorithm. YOLOv4 is a real time object detection from YOLO [4] object detection family that was published in April 2020 and achieved state-of-the-art performance on the COCO dataset [43]. YOLOv4 is a result of contribution of many researchers with many new features. Bochkovskiy et al. [7] introduced bag of specials and bag of freebies in their paper. They made some modifications to existing methods like SAM, PAN, CmBN and added innovative designs like Mosaic augmentation, Self-Adversarial Training (SAT) to make the model more suitable for training on a single GPU. YOLOv4 [7] is originally implemented in darknet framework and it consists of CSPDarknet53 [37], SPP [38] and PAN [39] neck, with YOLOv3 [40] head. For this study we trained YOLOv4 model in both darknet and TensorFlow frameworks. We Trained and tested YOLOv4 using NVIDIA Tesla V100 SXM2 16 GB 300W GPU 54.8 GB RAM in Google Colab and NVIDIA GeForce 8 GB 151W in Ubuntu 20.04 using a local server.

3.1   Dataset Description

There are several datasets available for face detection. In this study, our goal is to choose different datasets with various levels of difficulties to test the effect of data augmentation, image enhancement, and image decluttering. For this purpose, we chose three public datasets Labeled Faces in the Wild (LFW), Wider Face, Common Objects in Context (COCO) and Unconstrained Face Detection Dataset (UFDD) datasets.

LFW is a public benchmark for face verification. The dataset contains 13,233 images from 5,749 people. 1,680 of these peoples have two or more images. This dataset is not labeled for face detection. The images are all the same size, and the faces are mostly in the center of the images. There are four different sets of LFW images including the original ones and three distinct types of "aligned" images [41].

Wider face dataset is an exceptionally large dataset for face detection. The images are organized in 61 distinct categories. This dataset consists of 393,703 labeled faces in 32,203 images. Images vary in occlusion, scale, pose, lighting conditions, race, gender, and age. The dataset is randomly divided in training (40%), validation (10%) and testing (50%) [42].

COCO is a large dataset for object detection and segmentation. COCO contains 330k images with more than 200k labeled images. COCO contains 80 object classes with 1.5 million object instances. The first category of COCO objects is "person" object which contains images with various parts of the human body [43].

UFDD is a challenging dataset for face detection that includes issues like weather-based degradations, motion blur, focus blur and several other issues. The images are provided in seven categories of rain, snow, haze, blur, illumination, lens impediments and distractions [44].

3.2 Data Preprocessing

For this study, we used three different datasets for training and four datasets for testing. The LFW dataset is not annotated for face detection. We used MTCNN [15] to label the LFW dataset followed by manual checking to label small faces in the background, blurry faces and missed detections by MTCNN.

Wider face dataset has labels for face detection, although there is a need for preprocessing the format of the labels to match each framework.

We also used random images from COCO dataset. We chose a few thousands COCO images that did not contain any person. This was done to improve the false detection. The COCO and UFDD images have been used for testing.

3.3 Data Augmentation

In this study, we tested the effect of different data augmentation methods on the detection results. The LFW dataset is a simple dataset for face detection without any augmentation. Training a model based on LFW dataset gets overfitted, since in all the LFW images the main face is in the middle of the image. Therefore, the trained model with LFW dataset without any data augmentation, learns that there should be a face in the middle of the image. When the model gets tested with the COCO images, all the false positives are a box in the middle of the image. To improve the model, we applied two random shifts while keeping the entire bounding box in the image and trained the model with three versions of each image to see how a minor change can affect the results.

In the next step, we added mosaic augmentation. Mosaic augmentation combines four random images into one. Images were selected and randomly cropped with random ratios. Standard mosaic augmentation was not a good option for face detection. It resulted in detecting parts of the face alongside of detecting the face. For example, detecting the forehead or ear as it is shown in Fig. 1. To apply mosaic augmentation for face detection we need to keep the entire bounding boxes when cropping each image to prevent the negative effect.

3.4 Image Processing and Enhancement

There are several image enhancement methods that can be applied to the images during the testing and detection. In this study, we work with changing the brightness of images

Fig. 1. False detection

and applying Contrast Limited Adaptive Histogram Equalization (CLAHE). CLAHE could be used to equalize images. CLAHE operates on a small portion of the image instead of the entire image. To remove the created boundaries between neighbor parts, CLAHE use bilinear interpolation to smooth the image. There are several ways to apply CLAHE to an image. We can apply CLAHE to all the channels of the RGB image or only apply on the luminance channel of an HSV image (see Fig. 2). Applying CLAHE to the luminance channel would have better results than applying that on all the channels. We can also change the clip limit and tile grid size when applying CLAHE on images (see Fig. 3).

Fig. 2. Left to right: Original Image, LAB, L_channel, Applying CLAHE to L_channel, merging CLAHE output with a and b channel, Converting LAB to RGB: Final image

Fig. 3. Left: clipLimit = 3, tileGridSize = (5,5) and (17,17) Right: clipLimit = 5, tileGridSize = (5,5) and (17,17)

3.5 Image Decluttering

In most images, there are areas with similar pixels and same or close tone. In this study, we proposed a method called image decluttering which removes those areas from images before running the detection. For applying this procedure there are several approaches that are tested. At a high level, we used clustering algorithms and histogram-based approaches to detect and remove these areas from the images.

Density-Based Spatial Clustering of Applications with Noise (DBSCAN). DBSCAN is the most common density-based clustering algorithm. The density-based algorithms are highly efficient with arbitrary shaped clusters and clusters with noise. The idea behind DBSCAN is that a point belongs to a cluster if it is close to many points from that cluster. It has two key parameters of eps and minPts. Eps is the maximum distance between the neighbors and minPts is the minimum number of points to consider the points as a cluster. The problem with DBSCAN is that choosing these hyperparameters is often a challenging task. In Fig. 4, we showed a few samples of applying DBSCAN to one image from the LFW dataset.

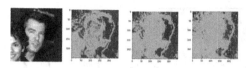

Fig. 4. Different eps and minPts applied to the image. Left to Right: Original image, DBSCAN eps = 0.5, min_samples = 20 - eps = 0.5, min_samples = 40, eps = 0.4, min_samples = 80

Ordering Points to Identify the Clustering Structure (OPTICS). OPTICS is similar to DBSCAN. However, the main problem of DBSCAN is fixing the desired density. OPTICS introduces two more parameters of core distance and reachability distance. Core distance is the minimum value of the radius of a possible cluster that contains the minimum number of points. Reachability distance is the distance between each point and a core point which cannot be lower than the core distance. OPTICS creates a reachability plot for all the data points and then uses the plot to cluster the data. There is also a hyperparameter maximum epsilon that can help to speed up the clustering (See Fig. 5).

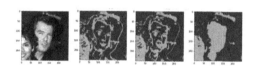

Fig. 5. Optics with different Min_cluster_size applied to the original image.

For the purpose of our study, we decreased the resolution of images by 1/16 and then applied OPTICS for clustering. As shown in Fig. 6, we can get better results by increasing the minimum cluster size and removing unnecessary pixels in our image.

Kmeans. Kmeans is the simplest and most popular unsupervised clustering algorithm. Kmeans algorithm finds "k" number of clusters with their associate centroids and then allocates each point to its nearest cluster. We can use Kmeans clustering to cluster pixels of an image. We flatten the image and consider each pixel as one data point with 3 values. Pixels with similar colors belong to the same cluster. To apply Kmeans, number of clusters is needed. We used Elbow method to find the optimal k for our image. In Fig. 7, we used the labels from Kmeans with k = 4 to create a mask and denoise the images.

Fig. 6. Optics with different applied to the image with low resolution. Left: Min_cluster_size = 0.05, Right: Min_cluster_size = 0.35

Fig. 7. Left to right: Applied Kmeans-K = 5, k = 4, k = 3, Using Kmeans k = 4 to declutter the image

Histogram of the Image. An image histogram is a graphical representation of an image that shows the tonal distribution of the image. In the histogram plot shown in Fig. 8, the "y" axes shows the number of pixels in each tone. Images with a plain background have remarkably high values for the background color. The purpose of this study is to remove the tones with high counts from the image. We manually checked the histogram of each image and removed the tones with high frequency (See Fig. 9).

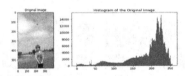

Fig. 8. Left: Original image, Right: histogram of the Image.

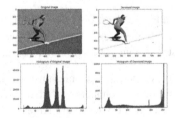

Fig. 9. Histograms of original image versus the denoised one

4 Results

4.1 Training Using Different Dataset

In this study, we have implemented YOLOv4 on two different frameworks, Darknet and TensorFlow, and investigated impacts of the decluttering methods on the accuracy of the models. It is worth noting that the decluttering method was applied to both the training and the test set. We have also examined impacts of different augmentation methods on face detection accuracy.

To train the darknet we used NVIDIA Tesla P100 GPU in Google Colab. We have trained the Darknet-based YOLOv4 model with different combination of datasets, including Wider face, LFW, combination of Wider-Face & LFW, and combination of Wider-Face & LFW & COCO non-face images. For all the models we have used transfer learning - pre-trained weights: yolov4.conv.137 from MS COCO from YOLOv4 original GitHub repository.

To evaluate the effect of our algorithm, we used following measures: Precision, Recall, F1-score, True positive or TP (where the model correctly predicts the positive class), False positive or FP (where model incorrectly predicts the positive class), False Negative of FN (where the model incorrectly predicts the negative class), True Negative or TN (where the model correctly predicts the negative class), Average IoU (Intersection over union is the method to evaluate the accuracy of the predicted bounding boxes in respect to ground truth), and mAP@0.5 (mean average precision with IoU larger than 0.5).

Results of the Darknet-based YOLOv4 model, which was trained with Wider face dataset, has been captured in Table 1. This table also shows the impacts of the input size on performance of the model. As it is shown, input size of 608 × 608 has 8.82% higher accuracy at mAP@0.50. This means the predicted bounding boxes are closer to ground truth. As it is shown in Fig. 10, this model detects faces with high confidence score.

Table 1. Training darknet using Wider Face dataset

Dataset	Input size	Precision	Recall	F1-score	TP	FP	FN	Average IoU	mAP @0.50
Wider face	416	0.66	0.58	0.62	18533	9673	13320	48.88%	59.35%
Wider face	608	0.72	0.65	0.69	20799	7910	11054	54.57%	68.17%

For our second training model, we have trained the model with image size of 608 × 608 for 6000 epochs using the LFW dataset. The model achieved better results when testing on the LFW test set as shown in Table 2 and it achieved higher Precision, higher recall, lower false detection as well as lower true predictions. On the other side, it did not perform well when testing on random images from the Wider face dataset (See Fig. 11)

In our third training model, we combined LFW and Wider face dataset and trained the model for 3000 epochs. By combining these two datasets, we improved our detection

Fig. 10. A sample face detection using a model trained with Wider Face dataset.

Table 2. Training Darknet using LFW dataset

Dataset	Input size	Precision	Recall	F1-score	TP	FP	FN	Average IoU	mAP @0.50
LFW	608	0.89	0.98	0.93	3090	3653	79	48.88%	98.30%

performance as listed in Table 3. The third model had higher true positive and provides better prediction and could detect mush more faces in images. An example of the model detection has been shown in Fig. 12.

Fig. 11. Samples of face detection of Wider face images using the model trained with Lfw dataset.

Table 3. Training darknet using LFW + Wider Face dataset

Dataset	Input size	Precision	Recall	F1-score	TP	FP	FN	Average IoU	mAP @0.50
LFW + WF	416	0.6	0.63	0.62	21990	14439	13032	45.20%	61.95%

Fig. 12. Training the model with different datasets. Left: Lfw, middle: Wider Face, right: Lfw + Wider Face.

In order to measure specificity of the models and to evaluate the model performance when handling images with distractions on diverse backgrounds, we have randomly chosen 1000 images from COCO dataset with no human face. The results of the test have been captured in Table 4. When testing COCO images, we found that the model is detecting animal faces, food images, or small objects, as human faces as shown in Fig. 13.

Table 4. Results of test on 1000 images from coco dataset

Dataset	False positive	True negative	Specificity
WF	80	920	92
LFW	11	989	98.9
LFW + WF	80	920	92

Fig. 13. Samples of false detections

To fix false detection of animal faces, we trained the Darknet model by adding distractions to our training and validation dataset. We added 7500 images from COCO dataset without any human in the image. 6000 images have been added to the train set and 1500 to the validation set (see Table 5). After adding coco images to LFW and Wider face the number of false detections decreased by 70 as shown in Table 6. The new model was not detecting any animal faces or foods as human faces. The false positives were a few sculptures faces and a few exceedingly small and blurry teddy bear faces (See Fig. 14).

Table 5. Training darknet using LFW, Wider face dataset and 6000 images from coco dataset

Dataset	Input size	Precision	Recall	F1-score	TP	FP	FN	Average IoU	mAP @0.50
LFW + WF + COCO	416	0.67	0.63	0.65	21997	10643	13025	51.63%	63.8%

By using a combination of images from the three different datasets we tested our model's detection on challenging UFDD dataset.

As presented in Fig. 15 our model performed well. UFDD dataset contains a lot of distraction that cause other models to have a high false positive rate which was not

Table 6. Results of test on 1000 images from coco dataset

Dataset	False Positive	True Negative	Specificity
LFW + WF + COCO	10	990	99

Fig. 14. Samples of false detections

Fig. 15. Result of detection of our model on images from UFDD dataset

the case for our model. As shown in distraction image in Fig. 15, unlike other models mentioned in [44] we only have one false detection in this image. Our model was able to detect faces in the background that were not even labeled in UFDD dataset (see Fig. 16).

Fig. 16. Example of detecting faces in the background.

4.2   Effect of Image Augmentation

In order to assess the impact of augmentation, we used YOLOv4 in TensorFlow framework. We trained the TensorFlow model on Ubuntu 20.04 using NVIDIA GeForce 1070 GPU. We used the weights from our trained model on Darknet using Wider face dataset for transfer learning and only trained the model for a few hundred epochs each time. In the first few training sessions, we did not apply any data augmentation. Later, for the second round we applied two random shifts to images from the LFW dataset while keeping the entire bounding box in the image and applied improved mosaic to random images to see how they affect the results. As shown in Table 7, we were able to improve the specificity when testing 1000 COCO images by around 70%. We improved our results further by adding some distraction images from COCO to the training set and were able to decrease the number of false detections from 21 to 5.

Table 7. Results of test on 1000 images from coco dataset

Dataset	FP	TN	Specificity
LFW	721	279	27.9
LFW + applied shift and mosaic augmentation	21	979	97.9
LFW + applied shift and mosaic augmentation + added distraction images	5	995	99.5

4.3 Effect of Image Enhancement and Image Decluttering

In order to test image decluttering, we used the OPTICS method to declutter images from COCO dataset and measured the impact of decluttering using the Darknet-Based model and TensorFlow based model. As it is shown in Table 8, the Specificity improved around 2%.

Table 8. Results of detection using original and denoised test set

Dataset	Test set	TP	FP	FN	Recall	Precision
LFW + Wider Face + coco	Original	211	8	7	96.79	96.35
LFW + Wider Face + coco	Decluttered	205	3	13	94.04	98.56
LFW	Original	38	2	180	17.43	95
LFW	Decluttered	36	1	182	16.51	97.3

Since decluttering improved Specificity, we have also investigated the confidence score of the detected faces. In Fig. 17 we have captured the distribution of the confidence scores. In both plots we can see the number of detections with higher confidence score is increased and number of detections with lower scores is decreased.

Figure 18 compares the results of both models and, as clear, there is a slight improvement. After applying decluttering, the average confidence scores get higher, and the standard deviation gets lower. To further investigate, we chose 250 random images from the COCO dataset that contained one or more faces for testing and used two different training sets. First, we used Wider face dataset and second, we randomly applied image

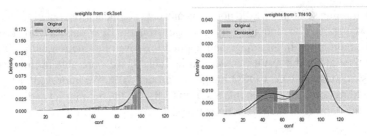

Fig. 17. Confidence score histogram of detected faces Left: Darknet weights, Right TensorFlow Weights

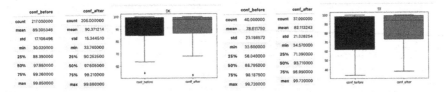

Fig. 18. Left to Right: Darknet: Confidence score of all detected faces in original test set, confidence score of all detected faces in Decluttered test set, Boxplot, TensorFlow: confidence score of all detected faces in original test set, Confidence score of all detected faces in Denoised test set, Boxplot

processing and image decluttering on the training images. We have tested the model in five different conditions, which are: 1) original images, 2) Decluttered images, 3) Apply CLAHE on original images before detection, 4) Apply CLAHE on denoised images and 5) Change brightness of denoised images and apply CLAHE. For all the tests we used score threshold of 0.3.

Test results have been captured in Table 9. As it can be seen, FP and FN are higher for the tests with pre-processing. To address this issue, we added decluttering and CLAHE preprocessing and trained the model.

Table 9. Test results with Wider Face training set

Train set	Test set	TP	FP	FN	Recall	Specificity
Wider Face	Original	522	102	101	83.79	83.65
Wider Face	Decluttered	513	91	110	82.34	84.93
Wider Face	Clahe	508	86	115	81.54	85.52
Wider Face	Decluttered + Clahe	496	89	127	79.61	84.79
Wider face	Decluttered + Brithness + Clahe	501	100	122	80.42	83.36

Comparing the results of the two Table 10 and Table 9, it can be implied that preprocessing improves the specificity, and decrease False positives by 30%. In both tests,

Table 10. Test results after adding some preprocessed images to training set

Train set	Test set	TP	FP	FN	Recall	Specificity
Wider Face + preprocessing + decluttering	Original	517	95	106	82.99	84.48
Wider Face + preprocessing + decluttering	Decluttered	505	83	118	81.06	85.88
Wider Face + preprocessing + decluttering	Clahe	509	84	114	81.7	85.83
Wider Face + preprocessing + decluttering	Decluttered + Clahe	497	80	126	79.78	86.14
Wider Face + preprocessing + decluttering	Decluttered + Brithness + Clahe	494	79	129	79.29	86.21

with and without decluttered, the average confidence score decreased. The main reason of this decrease was the higher number of new detected faces with lower confidence score. If we do not consider the new detections, the average confidence score of the true detections is higher when testing the decluttered images, and the confidence score of the false detections is lower when testing the decluttered images.

Figure 19 shows examples of detection improvement after applying image enhancements before running the detection. Figure 20 demonstrates the impacts of decluttering. As clear, the images on the left detect one more face in comparison to the original image after decluttering. There are also some cases that the confidence score of the detection decreased after applying decluttering. Further investigation is required to identify the reason for these cases (see Fig. 20).

Fig. 19. Example of effect of image enhancement on face detection.

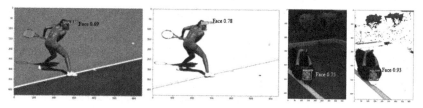

Fig. 20. Examples of effect of the decluttering on face detection.

5 Conclusion

The purpose of this study is to improve the results of YOLOv4 object detection and specifically face detection. We studied the effect of applying different data augmentation and image enhancement methods. We chose and modified exciting methods to apply the most suitable data augmentation for face detection problem. By applying the modified data augmentation and image enhancement we improved the detection probability of YOLOv4 by 70%. We also proposed image decluttering techniques to further improve the accuracy and the average confidence value of detected faces by YOLOv4 in various images. In the future studies, we are planning to investigate the effect of our proposed method in wider selection of images.

References

1. Girshick, R., Donahue, J., Darrell, T., Malik, J.: Rich feature hierarchies for accurate object detection and semantic segmentation. In: Proceedings of the IEEE Conference on Computer Vision and Pattern Recognition, pp. 580–587 (2014)
2. Girshick, R.: Fast R-CNN. In: Proceedings of the IEEE International Conference on Computer Vision, pp. 1440–1448 (2015)
3. Ren, S., He, K., Girshick, R., Sun, J.: Faster R-CNN: towards real-time object detection with region proposal networks. In: Advances in Neural Information Processing Systems, vol. 28 (2015)
4. Redmon, J., Divvala, S., Girshick, R., Farhadi, A.: You only look once: unified, real-time object detection. In: Proceedings of the IEEE Conference on Computer Vision and Pattern Recognition, pp. 779–788 (2016)
5. Redmon, J., Farhadi, A.: YOLO9000: better, faster, stronger. In: Proceedings of the IEEE Conference on Computer Vision and Pattern Recognition, pp. 7263–7271 (2017)
6. Liu, W., et al.: SSD: single shot multibox detector. In: Leibe, B., Matas, J., Sebe, N., Welling, M. (eds.) Computer Vision, vol. 9905, pp. 21–37. Springer, Cham (2016). https://doi.org/10.1007/978-3-319-46448-0_2
7. Bochkovskiy, A., Wang, C.Y., Liao, H.Y.M.: Yolov4: optimal speed and accuracy of object detection. arXiv preprint https://arxiv.org/abs/2004.10934 (2020)
8. LeCun, Y., Bottou, L., Bengio, Y., Haffner, P.: Gradient-based learning applied to document recognition. Proc. IEEE **86**(11), 2278–2324 (1998)
9. Bengio, Y., et al.: Deep learners benefit more from out-of-distribution examples. In: Proceedings of the Fourteenth International Conference on Artificial Intelligence and Statistics, pp. 164–172. JMLR Workshop and Conference Proceedings, June 2011
10. Krizhevsky, A., Sutskever, I., Hinton, G.E.: ImageNet classification with deep convolutional neural networks. In: Advances in Neural Information Processing Systems, vol. 25 (2012)
11. Wu, R., Yan, S., Shan, Y., Dang, Q., Sun, G.: Deep image: scaling up image recognition. **7**(8). arXiv preprint https://arxiv.org/abs/1501.02876 (2015)
12. Zhong, Z., Zheng, L., Kang, G., Li, S., Yang, Y.: Random erasing data augmentation. In: Proceedings of the AAAI Conference on Artificial Intelligence, vol. 34, no. 07, pp. 13001–13008 (2020)
13. Deng, J., Dong, W., Socher, R., Li, L.J., Li, K., Fei-Fei, L.: ImageNet: a large-scale hierarchical image database. In: 2009 IEEE Conference on Computer Vision and Pattern Recognition, pp. 248–255. IEEE (2009)
14. DeVries, T., Taylor, G.W.: Improved regularization of convolutional neural networks with cutout. arXiv preprint https://arxiv.org/abs/1708.04552 (2017)

15. Singh, K.K., Yu, H., Sarmasi, A., Pradeep, G., Lee, Y.J.: Hide-and-seek: a data augmentation technique for weakly-supervised localization and beyond. arXiv preprint https://arxiv.org/abs/1811.02545 (2018)
16. Chen, P., Liu, S., Zhao, H., Jia, J.: Gridmask data augmentation. arXiv preprint https://arxiv.org/abs/2001.04086 (2020)
17. Zhang, H., Cisse, M., Dauphin, Y.N., Lopez-Paz, D.: mixup: beyond empirical risk minimization. arXiv preprint https://arxiv.org/abs/1710.09412 (2017)
18. Yun, S., Han, D., Oh, S.J., Chun, S., Choe, J., Yoo, Y.: Cutmix: regularization strategy to train strong classifiers with localizable features. In: Proceedings of the IEEE/CVF International Conference on Computer Vision, pp. 6023–6032 (2019)
19. Hao, W., Zhili, S.: Improved mosaic: algorithms for more complex images. In: Journal of Physics: Conference Series, vol. 1684, no. 1, p. 012094. IOP Publishing (2020)
20. Wei, Z., Duan, C., Song, X., Tian, Y., Wang, H.: Amrnet: Chips augmentation in aerial images object detection. arXiv preprint https://arxiv.org/abs/2009.07168 (2020)
21. Deng, J., Guo, J., Ververas, E., Kotsia, I., Zafeiriou, S.: Retinaface: single-shot multi-level face localisation in the wild. In: Proceedings of the IEEE/CVF Conference on Computer Vision and Pattern Recognition, pp. 5203–5212 (2020)
22. Simonyan, K., Zisserman, A.: Very deep convolutional networks for large-scale image recognition. arXiv preprint https://arxiv.org/abs/1409.1556 (2014)
23. Szegedy, C., Vanhoucke, V., Ioffe, S., Shlens, J., Wojna, Z.: Rethinking the inception architecture for computer vision. In: Proceedings of the IEEE Conference on Computer Vision and Pattern Recognition, pp. 2818–2826 (2016)
24. Najibi, M., Samangouei, P., Chellappa, R., Davis, L.S.: SSH: single stage headless face detector. In: Proceedings of the IEEE International Conference on Computer Vision, pp. 4875–4884 (2017)
25. Zhang, S., Zhu, X., Lei, Z., Shi, H., Wang, X., Li, S.Z.: S3FD: single shot scale-invariant face detector. In: Proceedings of the IEEE International Conference on Computer Vision, pp. 192–201 (2017)
26. Gidaris, S., Komodakis, N.: Object detection via a multi-region and semantic segmentation-aware CNN model. In: Proceedings of the IEEE International Conference on Computer Vision, pp. 1134–1142 (2015)
27. Maini, R., Aggarwal, H.: A comprehensive review of image enhancement techniques. arXiv preprint https://arxiv.org/abs/1003.4053 (2010)
28. Rustagi, S., Tuteja, T., Sharma, V., Gangwar, V., Parihar, A.S.: Comparative study of various image enhancement techniques based on retinex theory and fuzzy logic. In: 2018 Second International Conference on Electronics, Communication and Aerospace Technology (ICECA), pp. 464–469. IEEE (2018)
29. Hemalatha, V., Selvapriya, P.B., Maheswari, K.C.: An inclusive analysis on various image enhancement techniques. IJMER **4**(12), 1–6 (2014)
30. Farbiz, F., Menhaj, M.B., Motamedi, S.A., Hagan, M.T.: A new fuzzy logic filter for image enhancement. IEEE Trans. Syst. Man Cybern. Part B (Cybern.) **30**(1), 110–119 (2000)
31. Shen, R., Cheng, I., Basu, A.: QoE-based multi-exposure fusion in hierarchical multivariate Gaussian CRF. IEEE Trans. Image Process. **22**(6), 2469–2478 (2012)
32. Singh, K., Kapoor, R.: Image enhancement via median-mean based sub-image-clipped histogram equalization. Optik **125**(17), 4646–4651 (2014)
33. Suthaharan, S., Zhang, Z.: Exploration of intelligent techniques for image filtering. In: Proceedings of the 1998 Second IEEE International Caracas Conference on Devices, Circuits and Systems, ICCDCS 98, (Cat. No. 98TH8350), pp. 211–216. IEEE (1998). On the 70th Anniversary of the MOSFET and 50th of the BJT

34. Hemalatha, G., Sumathi, C.P.: Preprocessing techniques of facial image with Median and Gabor filters. In: 2016 International Conference on Information Communication and Embedded Systems (ICICES), pp. 1–6. IEEE (2016)
35. Singh, K.B., Mahendra, T.V., Kurmvanshi, R.S., Rao, C.R.: Image enhancement with the application of local and global enhancement methods for dark images. In: 2017 International Conference on Innovations in Electronics, Signal Processing and Communication (IESC), pp. 199–202. IEEE (2017)
36. Gonzalez, R.C., Woods, R.E.: Digital Image Processing. Pearson, London (2002)
37. Wang, C.Y., Liao, H.Y.M., Wu, Y.H., Chen, P.Y., Hsieh, J.W., Yeh, I.H.: CSPNet: a new backbone that can enhance learning capability of CNN. In: Proceedings of the IEEE/CVF Conference on Computer Vision and Pattern Recognition Workshops, pp. 390–391 (2020)
38. He, K., Zhang, X., Ren, S., Sun, J.: Spatial pyramid pooling in deep convolutional networks for visual recognition. IEEE Trans. Pattern Anal. Mach. Intell. **37**(9), 1904–1916 (2015)
39. Liu, S., Qi, L., Qin, H., Shi, J., Jia, J.: Path aggregation network for instance segmentation. In: Proceedings of the IEEE Conference on Computer Vision and Pattern Recognition, pp. 8759–8768 (2018)
40. Redmon, J., Farhadi, A.: Yolov3: an incremental improvement. arXiv preprint https://arxiv.org/abs/1804.02767 (2018)
41. Learned-Miller, E., Huang, G.B., RoyChowdhury, A., Li, H., Hua, G.: Labeled faces in the wild: a survey. In: Kawulok, M., Celebi, M., Smolka, B. (eds.) Advances in Face Detection and Facial Image Analysis, pp. 189–248. Springer, Cham (2016). https://doi.org/10.1007/978-3-319-25958-1_8
42. Yang, S., Luo, P., Loy, C.C., Tang, X.: Wider face: a face detection benchmark. In: Proceedings of the IEEE Conference on Computer Vision and Pattern Recognition, pp. 5525–5533 (2016)
43. Lin, T.Y., et al.: Microsoft COCO: common objects in context. In: Fleet, D., Pajdla, T., Schiele, B., Tuytelaars, T. (eds.) Computer Vision, vol. 8693, pp. 740–755. Springer, Cham (2014). https://doi.org/10.1007/978-3-319-10602-1_48
44. Nada, H., Sindagi, V.A., Zhang, H., Patel, V.M.: Pushing the limits of unconstrained face detection: a challenge dataset and baseline results. In: 2018 IEEE 9th International Conference on Biometrics Theory, Applications and Systems (BTAS), pp. 1–10. IEEE (2018)

Context-Switching Neural Node
for Constrained-Space Hardware

Yassen Gorbounov[1]([X]) [iD] and Hao Chen[2] [iD]

[1] New Bulgarian University and MGU "St. Ivan Rilsky", Sofia, Bulgaria
gorbounov@gmail.com
[2] China University of Mining and Technology, Xuzhou 221000, People's Republic of China
hchen@cumt.edu.cn

Abstract. Artificial neural networks are a mathematical abstraction that models the nerve cells and their connections in the biological brain. Their use to solve a wide range of nonlinear problems in the field of approximation, machine learning, and artificial intelligence may require significant computing power. This requires the search for approaches to more efficient use of hardware resources. The article describes an early stage in the development of an optimized neural network designed for use on hardware with constrained resources, but with the ability to run parallel algorithms. Circuits that meet these requirements are the field programmable gate arrays. In the research an approach is proposed to significantly reduce the amount of logic used by contextually switching the weight matrices and the matrices of the activation functions which will result in reducing the number of network layers. This suggests the ability to create more affordable and smarter devices without compromising performance significantly.

Keywords: Artificial neural network · Contextual switching · Programmable logic

1 Introduction

Despite the high level of technological development nowadays, there is still nothing more perfect than nature in terms of the ability to recognize images and situations, decision-making under conditions of uncertainty, adaptation to changing environments, and the efficient use of energy. Unequivocal examples in this regard are, on the one hand, the ability to orient, the speed of reaction, and the path that an insect can travel in relation to its weight, and, on the other hand, the complex organizational structure of organisms such as bees and ants [22]. At the bottom of all this is the nervous system, the functioning of which people try to recreate through various mathematical approaches. One possible apparatus are the artificial neural networks [15], which are an attempt to simulate the interaction and collaboration of a large group of nerve cells. In purely mathematical terms, neural networks have been considered by [21] as a universal approximator. The ultimate goal of these models is to create a technical device capable of training and making decisions similar to the human brain.

© ICST Institute for Computer Sciences, Social Informatics and Telecommunications Engineering 2022
Published by Springer Nature Switzerland AG 2022. All Rights Reserved
T. Zlateva and R. Goleva (Eds.): CSECS 2022, LNICST 450, pp. 45–59, 2022.
https://doi.org/10.1007/978-3-031-17292-2_4

To solve a real problem, artificial neural networks consist of many neural models (cells), arranged in a multilayer structure. There are many different and quite complex models of neural networks [26]. Some topologies such as Convolutional Neural Networks (CNN) [13], Recursive Neural Networks (RNN) [3], Generative Adversarial Networks (GAN) [27] and many others, are aimed at processing non-digital and unstructured data such as text, image and speech. However, if analog methods of implementation [5, 24] are excluded, in their deep essence, all structures and algorithms for building artificial neural networks work with digital and structured data. Analog methods and features of different network architectures, as well as solving specific examples, are not the subject of this paper and therefore they are not discussed here. However, it is clear that the improvement of artificial neural networks increases the level of complexity of the mathematical apparatus used. This leads to a number of problems in their practical implementation, mainly related to the work with floating point arithmetic and the high-speed exchange of large volumes of data. As a result, the requirements for digital circuits in terms of their speed, reduction of energy consumption and augmenting the degree of integration are increasing. Despite the increase in the number of cores and thus in the performance of modern processors, and the proliferation of highly optimized software approaches for small devices such as TinyML [23, 28], today more and more programmable logic circuits such as Field Programmable Gate Arrays (FPGA) are used. They are characterized by high operating frequencies, the possibility of multiple reprogramming, but most of all the ability to perform parallel algorithms [4, 8, 12]. This property is architecturally inherent and is their undeniable advantage over conventional microprocessors and microcontrollers.

In recent research from Princeton University [14] a multiplexing technique called DataMUX is proposed. It allows the neural network to analyze multiple data feeds nearly simultaneously by multiplexing the inputs and the outputs. The authors conducted their experiments in the Python language. Although they claim to potentially prune the numbers of configuration parameters by more than 90 percent, the architecture of their neural network remains unchanged. The current research article takes different approach. It presents an early stage in the development of an optimized neural network designed for use on hardware with limited resources, but with the possibility of running algorithms in parallel. Among the circuits with such capabilities are the lower-end FPGAs. An approach to significantly reduce the amount of logic used is proposed, which is expected that when the artificial neural network is trained in advance, the tasks using this category of reprogrammable logic will be performed without compromising performance. This means creating more affordable and smarter devices.

The remainder of this work is organized as follows: At first in chapter "Architecture of the artificial neuron," it is described the digital implementation of a possible basic model of an artificial neuron. Discussed are its main building block and occupied resource. Next, the proposed new method for sharing resources and reducing the total number of neurons in the neural network is presented in the chapter "Context switching approach". Guidelines for future development and improvement are given in chapter "Future work". The chapter "Conclusions" summarizes the results.

2   Architecture of the Artificial Neuron

In biological nerve cells, signals are exchanged through the axon with the aid of a synaptic structure that passes an electrical or chemical signal from a source neuron to a group of target neurons. A target neuron can have many inputs (dendrites) that can connect to many other neurons. The soma (cell body) contains a nucleus whose function is to sum all the inputs and to compute their overall "influence" weight. This signal is then processed by an activation function. If the result is above a given threshold the neuron fires, thus spreading the nerve signal to other neurons. This way a quite complicated network is organized. The process of learning consists of strengthening or weakening connections between neurons. This process inspired the creation of artificial neural networks, which are the basis of modern disciplines such as deep learning (DL), machine learning (ML), artificial intelligence (AI), autonomous decision-making systems, image recognition, and many applications in robotics, including also much simpler tasks such as function approximation.

This section discusses the working principle and building blocks of an elaborated artificial neuron. In [17–20] an attempt in that direction is already made but it has several major drawbacks. The presented neuron model is built up by using solely the schematic approach which means that arbitrary change in its function requires a significant redesign of the device and makes it hardly portable between different programmable logic families and manufacturers. This approach is especially problematic in regards to the activation function because it consumes most of the logic gates resources of the device. In addition, this model contains excessive code converter modules used for signed arithmetic operations, and it cannot be configured in terms of altering the bit width of the inputs, the outputs, or the internal bus organization. The lack of versatility limits its adaptability and applications.

The proposed device is devoid of these shortcomings and is significantly optimized in terms of performance and resources. The Verilog hardware description language (HDL) has been used for the synthesizable description of the design, and the Spartan series FPGA from Xilinx (now AMD) has been used as a target platform.

The structure of the proposed artificial neuron is given in Fig. 1. In analogy with the biological neuron, the cell nucleus is represented by the adder, which sums up the input signals x_i multiplied by the weighting factors w_i and some correction factor b called the bias. The obtained sum is submitted to an activation function, which sets the trigger threshold. The learning process consists in training the neural network over a training set according to different algorithms, but finally, it ends up in memorizing optimal values of the weighting factors and the bias. The weights can be either positive or negative. Negative weights reduce the value of the output, and positive weights increase it. The above said means that the hardware implementation requires signed floating-point arithmetic. FPGA circuits do not have built-in floating-point units (FPU) so they do not support the floating-point (FP) standard IEEE-754 [10] by default. In order to use the FP arithmetic, a dedicated submodule can be synthesized but it will add an unnecessary burden to the overall complexity and will negatively impact the size of the design and the speed of execution.

To overcome this the proposed design is using signed fixed-point arithmetic. This can be easily done by using the shift operation for upscaling and downscaling the FP

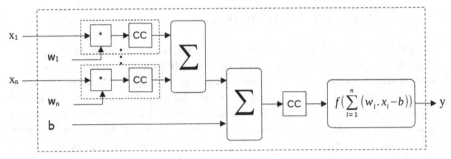

Fig. 1. Block diagram of the artificial neuron.

number with numbers multiples of the powers of two. Due to the signed numbers and to simplify the design of the adder the product from the multiplication of the input signals by the weights can be converted to two's complement code with the aid of the code converter modules (CC). Another possibility is to use a signed multiplier which will decrease the processing delay. However, the CC block should be used for the output of the adder before it is fed to the activation function due to the fact that it takes part in the addressing of the look-up table (LUT) that holds the description of that activation function. All the weights, the bias, and the activation function are stored in a Block RAM memory (BRAM). The proposed architecture follows the principles of regularity, modularity, and hierarchy [7]. That means that it is divided into subordinate modules and submodules and it is uniform, so modules can be easily reused.

2.1 Signed Multiplier

The inputs that enter the artificial neuron need to be multiplied by the weight coefficients before they are fed to the adder. There exist many algorithms to do so such as the Dadda multiplier, Wallace tree, parallel multipliers [9], Karatsuba algorithm [6, 11], and its generalization, the Toom–Cook (Toom-3) [1] or Fourier transform, all of which can be successfully used. In the proposed neuron model the behavioral description of the signed multiplier is chosen due to its simplicity and because the Spartan-6 FPGA family has a high ratio of embedded DSP modules to logic, making it ideal for math-intensive applications. It is equipped with up to 180 DSP48A1 slices and each one contains a built-in 18×18 bit two's complement multiplier capable of operating at frequencies of up to 390 MHz. The Verilog description of the configurable signed multiplier together with a substantial part of the register-transfer level (RTL) view and the simulation results are shown in Fig. 2.

The module is designed to be parameterizable so that the width of the operands can be configured by changing the parameter N.

```
module smult #(parameter N = 8)
(   input signed [N-1:0] A,
    input signed [N-1:0] B,
    output signed [2*N-1:0] M
);
    assign M = A * B;
endmodule
```

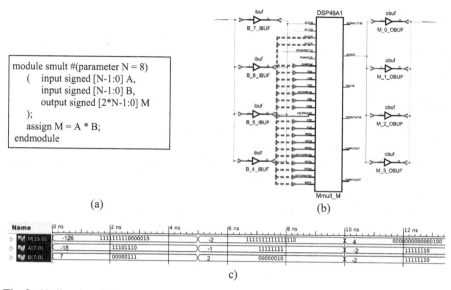

(a)   (b)

Name	0 ns	2 ns	4 ns	6 ns	8 ns	10 ns	12 ns
M[15:0]	-126	111111110000010	-2	1111111111111110	4	000000000000100
A[7:0]	-18	11101110	-1	11111111	-2	11111110
B[7:0]	7	00000111	2	00000010	-2	11111110

c)

Fig. 2. Verilog description (a), partial RTL view showing the DSP48A1 slice after synthesis (b), and simulation (c) of the work of the signed multiplier.

2.2 Code Converter

The output of the second adder of the neuron has to be converted in two's complement form. This is done on the basis of a modified adder (MA) (see Fig. 3).

Cin	B	A	Cout	S
0	0 → 0	0	0	0
0	0 → 0	1	0	1
0	1 → 0	0	0	0
0	1 → 0	1	0	1
1	0 → 0	0	0	1
1	0 → 0	1	1	0
1	1 → 0	0	0	1
1	1 → 0	1	1	0

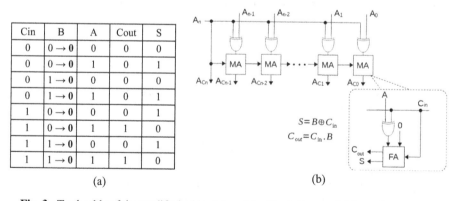

(a)   (b)

$$S = B \oplus C_{in}$$
$$C_{out} = C_{in} . B$$

Fig. 3. Truth table of the modified adder (a), and the block diagram of the code converter.

The design of the code converter is implemented by modifying a simple full adder where one of the operands is set firmly to 0, and the carry-in bit is set to logic 1. The conversion from a positive to a negative number and vice versa is done in two's complement form by using one and the same algorithm, which consists of two main steps: 1) inverting all of the bits to get the one's complement code, and 2) adding a one to the inverted result. The sign is presented with the left-most bit (MSB) which is a 0 for positive numbers and a 1 for negative ones. The exclusive OR gate in the figure serves the purpose of a controllable inverter. The negation of the bits or addition of a 1 is done by the left-most bit (MSB) of the number to be converted which is *An*.

2.3 Adding Device

Besides the built-in functional modules of the FPGA there are many architectures to build a binary adder such as the Carry Skip Adder, Carry Save Adder and Carry Select Adder (CSA), Pre-Fix Adder (PFA), Pipelined Parallel Adder (PPA), etc. that are well described in the literature [2, 7, 9]. Here a Carry-Lookahead Adder (CLA) has been implemented because its performance improves for larger bit-widths while preserving simplicity. The architecture of the adder is divided into groups of four bits and provides a way to determine the carry-out signal as soon as it becomes known to the group. For this purpose, two signals are generated (1):

$$\begin{aligned} g(A, B) &= A.B \\ p(A, B) &= A + B \end{aligned} \tag{1}$$

The "*generate*" (*g*) appears if the addition of two bits leads to a carry, regardless of whether the input *Cin* is set. The "*propagate*" (*p*) appears if the addition of two bits results in a carry when the *Cin* input is set but does not result in a carry if the *Cin* input is not set. Therefore, the carry out of a group can be obtained by (2):

$$C_{out(i)} = A_i.B_i + (A_i + B_i).C_{in(i)} \tag{2}$$

There are two adders in the artificial neuron (see Fig. 1). The block diagram of that portion of the circuit is shown in Fig. 4.

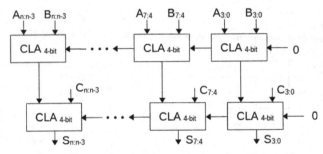

Fig. 4. Block diagram of the 3-input adder based on CLA architecture.

The inputs A and B are in two's complement form and connect to the outputs of the multipliers. The input C connects with the bias which is converted before it is stored in the memory. The output of the adder S is also in two's complement form.

2.4 Activation Function

The activation function is the output stage of the neuron and determines whether it fires or not. It adds nonlinearity to the neuron's function, otherwise, it would be no different than a linear regression model. Non-linear activation functions allow for backpropagation as the derivative is related to the input and thus it makes it possible to have better solution prediction based on the weights of the inputs. There is a great variety of activation functions depending on the purpose of the neural network. Some of the most common types are briefly summarized in Fig. 5.

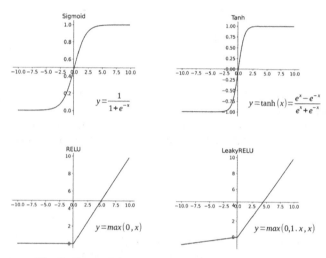

Fig. 5. Some of the most common activation functions.

The sigmoid activation function is differentiable and provides a smooth gradient. It is suitable for predicting probabilities. The sigmoid outputs values between 0 and 1 based on real value on the input. The hyperbolic tangent function (tanh) is similar to the sigmoid but its output is in the range of -1 to 1. The hyperbolic tangent output is centered across the zero. This function is mostly used in the hidden layers of the neural network. The Rectified Linear Unit (ReLU) activation function allows for back-propagation while keeping computational efficiency because only some neurons are activated. The Leaky ReLU improves the ReLU function by adding a small positive slope in the negative area. It enables backpropagation for negative input values.

The computation of the corresponding activation function in real-time may pose a challenge as it can consume significant logic resources. It is much more convenient to compute it off-line in advance and next fill-in a memory array. The Verilog code snippet that implements the reading from the BlockRAM memory is shown in Fig. 6.

A single BlockRAM in the Spartan-6 FPGA can store up to 18K bits of data, and the FPGA has a total of 268 blocks. The memory can be used in either single-port or dual-port mode having independent bit-widths in two-port configuration [25]. That amount of memory and the proposed Verilog code allows for storing more than one look-up table into a single BlockRAM. The left term [dataWidth-1:0] describes the memory width and

```
reg [dataWidth-1 : 0] mem [2**xWidth-1 : 0];
reg [xWidth-1 : 0] out;

initial
  begin
    $readmemb("actfunc.mif",mem);
  end
```

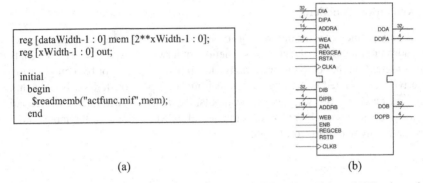

(a)   (b)

Fig. 6. Verilog description for reading from the BlockRAM memory (a), and RTL view of the instantiated RAMB16BWER memory module.

the right term [2**xWidth-1:0] is the memory depth. Using some simple arithmetic, it is possible to calculate the separate memory spaces allocated for each LUT. The input file "actfunc.mif" is an ASCII text memory initialization file (MIF) that specifies the initial content of a memory block. It can be generated in advance by using software tools such as a Matlab or Python script.

2.5 Synthesized Device

The RTL view of the synthesized artificial neuron model is shown in Fig. 7. The SADDER block denotes the signed adder since it sums the weighed inputs and the BADDER is the one that adds the bias which value is taken from a look-up table. The SIGMOID module contains the activation function look-up table.

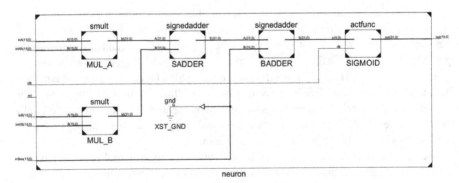

Fig. 7. RTL view of the synthesized artificial neuron model.

After compiling the design, the device usage statistics is generated (see Table 1).

Table 1. Device usage statistics.

Device utilization summary	Target Device: xc6slx75t-3fgg676		
Logic utilization	Used	Available	Utilization
Number of slice registers	5	93296	0.01%
Number of slice LUTs	149	46648	0.32%
Number of fully used LUT-FF pairs	5	149	3.36%
Number of bonded IOBs	97	348	27.87%
Number of BUFG/BUFGCTRLs	1	16	6.25%
Number of DSP48A1s	2	132	1.52%

Based on the elaborated design a simple neural network for applications such as color recognition can be built. An example of a suitable structure is shown in Fig. 8.

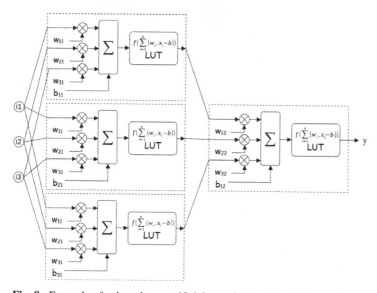

Fig. 8. Example of a three-layer artificial neural network with four neurons.

The processing effort of this simple three-layer neural network is 4 neurons, 12 signed multiplications, 12 additions (using 4 four-input adders), and 4 sigmoid activation functions. The first layer in fact represents the inputs and has no associated weights. It can be easily deduced that the processing effort will rise dramatically for a real neural network. Just to visualize the idea, a network with 76 neurons is shown in Fig. 9. This network has 5 layers with 20 neurons in each hidden layer and 16 neurons in the output layer. The number of multiplications can be calculated using (3):

$$N_{mult} = \sum_{i=1}^{N-1} (N_i . N_{i+1}) \qquad (3)$$

In this equation N is the number of layers and Ni is the corresponding layer. In this case the network has 1280 multiplications and 76 activation functions. Obviously, there exist many more complicated structures. For the implementation of such a structure a bigger FPGA is to be used which means higher price, and higher power consumption.

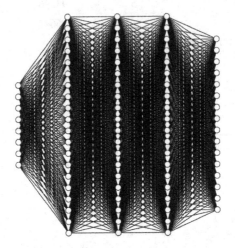

Fig. 9. Example of a five-layer artificial neural network with 76 neurons (generated with [16]).

3 Context Switching Approach

From the topology of the artificial neural network described in the previous section it can be seen that the network consists of a large amount of repeated structures – neurons, weights and biases (in the sense of repeating amounts of memory), and activation functions. Having a look at the network in Fig. 10 the mathematical description of the inputs of each layer can be derived (4–6).

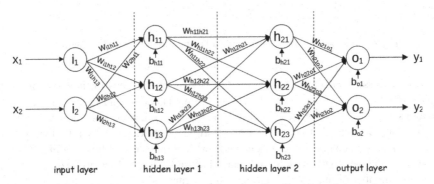

Fig. 10. Description of the connections in a four-layer neural network.

$$
\begin{pmatrix} h_{11} \\ h_{12} \\ h_{13} \end{pmatrix} = \begin{pmatrix} w_{i1h11} \ w_{i2h11} \\ w_{i1h12} \ w_{i2h12} \\ w_{i1h13} \ w_{i2h13} \end{pmatrix} \begin{pmatrix} i_1 \\ i_2 \end{pmatrix} + \begin{pmatrix} b_{h11} \\ b_{h12} \\ b_{h13} \end{pmatrix}
$$

$$
= \begin{pmatrix} w_{i1h11} \cdot i_1 + w_{i2h11} \cdot i_2 + b_{h11} \\ w_{i1h12} \cdot i_1 + w_{i2h12} \cdot i_2 + b_{h12} \\ w_{i1h13} \cdot i_1 + w_{i2h13} \cdot i_2 + b_{h13} \end{pmatrix}
$$

(4)

$$
\begin{pmatrix} h_{21} \\ h_{22} \\ h_{23} \end{pmatrix} = \begin{pmatrix} w_{h11h21} \ w_{h12h21} \ w_{h13h21} \\ w_{h11h22} \ w_{h12h22} \ w_{h13h22} \\ w_{h11h23} \ w_{h12h23} \ w_{h13h23} \end{pmatrix} \begin{pmatrix} h_{11} \\ h_{12} \\ h_{13} \end{pmatrix} + \begin{pmatrix} b_{h21} \\ b_{h22} \\ b_{h23} \end{pmatrix}
$$

$$
= \begin{pmatrix} w_{h11h21} \cdot h_{11} + w_{h12h21} \cdot h_{12} + w_{h13h21} \cdot h_{13} + b_{h21} \\ w_{h11h22} \cdot h_{11} + w_{h12h22} \cdot h_{12} + w_{h13h22} \cdot h_{13} + b_{h22} \\ w_{h11h23} \cdot h_{11} + w_{h12h23} \cdot h_{12} + w_{h13h23} \cdot h_{13} + b_{h23} \end{pmatrix}
$$

(5)

$$
\begin{pmatrix} o_1 \\ o_2 \end{pmatrix} = \begin{pmatrix} w_{h21o1} \ w_{h22o1} \ w_{h23o1} \\ w_{h21o2} \ w_{h22o2} \ w_{h23o2} \end{pmatrix} \begin{pmatrix} h_{21} \\ h_{22} \\ h_{23} \end{pmatrix} + \begin{pmatrix} b_{o1} \\ b_{o2} \end{pmatrix} =
$$

$$
\begin{pmatrix} w_{h21o1} . h_{21} + w_{h22o1} . h_{22} + w_{h23o1} . h_{23} + b_{o1} \\ w_{h21o2} . h_{21} + w_{h22o2} . h_{22} + w_{h23o2} . h_{23} + b_{o2} \end{pmatrix}
$$

(6)

With letters i, h, w, and o they are denoted the number of the neuron, and the ingoing and outgoing signals related with that neuron, all following from the figure. Letter b stands for the bias.

If the layer with the most neurons and, accordingly, the largest multiple of weight matrices is chosen, then a single structure could be obtained that can be multiplied as many times as the number of layers. For the layers with a smaller number of neurons, the weighting coefficients for the missing neurons will be set to 0. The network gets the unified type shown in Fig. 11.

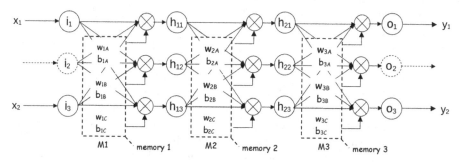

Fig. 11. Unified multi-layer structure of the neural network.

In the newly obtained structure, M1, M2, and M3 denote the matrices that unite all the weighted inputs for the neurons in each layer according to the right-hand side of

Eqs. (4–6). Taking this into consideration a single layer of the neural network can be represented as in Fig. 12.

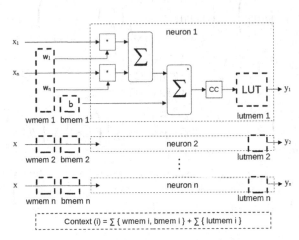

Fig. 12. Memories in the structure of a layer.

It can be seen that there are three types of memories in this structure –the weights (*wmem*), the biases (*bmem*), and the activation functions (*lutmem*). In fact, for a given network the processing elements (the neurons) have one and the same computational function, and only their configuration parameters (weights and biases) change. Moreover, the layers are connected in series so that the inputs of each layer depend on the outputs of the previous layer. In a real network, this serial dependence allows for pipelining the computation chain. It should be noted, however, that the number of layers is not that high compared to the number of neurons in a layer. Therefore, a neural network can be constructed with a single layer by simply changing the memory (context) and switching it over time. This concept is depicted in Fig. 13.

The proposed structure contains only a single computation (neuronal) layer. In this case, the "layers" differ in time, not in space. The outputs of the layer are processed by the activation functions for each neuron. They are stored in a single BlockRAM memory but occupy different memory sub-spaces. The content of the activation functions LUT can be the same or can be different for each layer depending on the type of the neural network which means that another memory sub-space is to be selected. Next, the result is stored in a register file whose purpose is to serve as a buffer for the next stage (in time). For all the layers except the last one, the buffered result is fed to the inputs of the same neuron column with the only difference that they are multiplied by weights and biases matrices from the new context – time $t + 1$. The outputs of the last layer become the outputs of the network, which is made possible with the aid of a demultiplexer. The context switching over time and the selection of the demultiplexer channels is controlled by the context switching finite state machine (FSM) whose function is very close to that of a counter. Since in a trivial neural network the inputs of each layer depend on the results from the processing of the previous one, it should be concluded that the time

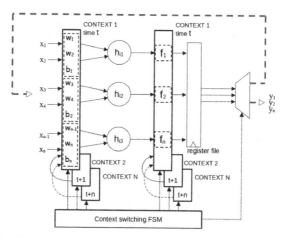

Fig. 13. Context switching organization of a single-layer neural network.

penalty, i.e. the increase in network latency will not increase significantly. This is a matter of a large volume of experiments, which are a subject of future work.

4 Future Work

The proposed new organizational approach to the structure of neural networks provides a very wide field for scientific research. The subject of future work is the construction of a multilayer neural network and the conduct of experimental comparisons of network performance, built in a classical way and through the proposed single-layer contextually switched topology. It is expected that the quality of the new network will be comparable in terms of time and it will be much better in terms of hardware resources used compared to other artificial neural networks. In addition, as future work, it is proposed to extend the presented approach in the direction of a time-multiplexed network built with only one neuron.

5 Conclusion

A new approach for building a high-performance neural network structure with only a single layer of neurons was proposed in the research article. It is based on a switching context method that employs the sharing of resources and leads to reducing the total number of neurons in the neural network. Although in an early stage, the proposed method is viable and opens a wide field for scientific research. This method will allow the development of optimized neural networks for use on hardware with constrained resources but without compromising with the computational performance.

Acknowledgments. This article is written in relation to contracts between the China University of Mining and Technology, New Bulgarian University, and the University of Mining and Geology "St. Ivan Rilski" on the subjects "Study of the control elements of a switched reluctance motor"

(MEMF-170/09.05.2022), "Joint Research and Development of key technologies for autonomous control systems", and "Construction of International Joint Laboratory for new energy power generation and electric vehicles".

References

1. Bodrato, M.: Towards optimal Toom-Cook multiplication for univariate and multivariate polynomials in characteristic 2 and 0. In: Carlet, C., Sunar, B. (eds.) Arithmetic of Finite Fields, vol. 4547, pp. 116–133. Springer, Cham (2007). https://doi.org/10.1007/978-3-540-73074-3_10
2. Chen, Y., Xie, X., Song, L., Chen, F., Tang, T.: A survey of accelerator architectures for deep neural networks. Engineering **6**(3), 264–274 (2020). ISSN: 2095-8099, https://doi.org/10.1016/j.eng.2020.01.007
3. Chinea, A.: Understanding the principles of recursive neural networks: a generative approach to tackle model complexity. In: Alippi, C., Polycarpou, M., Panayiotou, C., Ellinas, G. (eds.) Artificial Neural Networks, vol. 5768, pp. 952–963. Springer, Heidelberg (2009). https://doi.org/10.1007/978-3-642-04274-4_98
4. Cieszewski, R., Linczuk, M., Pozniak, K., Romaniuk, R.: Review of parallel computing methods and tools for FPGA technology. Proc. SPIE – Int. Soc. Opt. Eng. **8903**(1), 890321 (2013). https://doi.org/10.1117/12.2035385
5. Draghici, S.: Neural networks in analog hardware - design and implementation issues. Int. J. Neural Syst. **10**(01), 19–42 (2000). https://doi.org/10.1142/S0129065700000041
6. Fields WAIFI 2007 Proceedings, Madrid, Spain, pp. 116–133, LNCS 4547 (2007)
7. Harris, D., Harris, S.: Digital Design and Computer Architecture, 2nd edn. Morgan Kaufmann, Elsevier (2013). ISBN 978-0-12-394424-5
8. Hassanein, A., El-Abd, M., Damaj, I., Rehman, H.: Parallel hardware implementation of the brain storm optimization algorithm using FPGAs. Microprocess. Microsyst. **74**, 103005 (2020). https://doi.org/10.1016/j.micpro.2020.103005
9. Hennessy, J., Patterson, D.: Computer Architecture: A Quantitative Approach. Morgan Kaufmann, Elsevier (2012). ISBN: 978-8178672663
10. IEEE Std 754-2019, IEEE Computer Society 2019. IEEE Standard for Floating-Point Arithmetic IEEE STD 754-2019, pp. 1–84 (2019). ISBN 978-1-5044-5924-2
11. Karatsuba, A.: The complexity of computations. In: Proceedings of the Steklov Institute of Mathematics, vol. 211, pp. 169–183 (1995). Translation from Trudy Mat. Inst. Steklova, pp. 186–202
12. Kastner, R., Matai, J., Neuendorffer, S.: Parallel Programming for FPGAs, The HLS Book. arxiv e-prints, https://doi.org/10.48550/arXiv.1805.03648 (2022)
13. Khan, A., Sohail, A., Zahoora, U., Qureshi, A.S.: A survey of the recent architectures of deep convolutional neural networks. Artif. Intell. Rev. **53**(8), 5455–5516 (2020). https://doi.org/10.1007/s10462-020-09825-6
14. Murahari, V., Carlos, J., Yang, R., Narasimhan, K.: DataMUX: Data Multiplexing for Neural Networks (2022). https://doi.org/10.48550/arXiv.2202.09318
15. Mutihac, R.: Mathematical modeling of artificial neural networks. In: Dopico, J., Calle, J., Sierra, A. (eds.) Encyclopedia of Artificial Intelligence, pp. 1056–1063 (2019). ISBN: 13: 9781599048499, https://doi.org/10.4018/978-1-59904-849-9.ch156
16. NN-SVG. https://alexlenail.me/NN-SVG/index.html. Accessed 30 Apr 2022
17. Pavlitov, K., Gorbounov, Y.: Multiplier based on the Xilinx Spartan II programmable logic family. E+E J. Sofia (2004). ISSN 0861-4717

18. Pavlitov, K., Gorbounov, Y.: Programmable logic in electromechanics. Technical University of Sofia (2007). ISBN 978-954-438-645-0
19. Pavlitov, K., Gorbounov, Y.: TanSig non-linear converter based on Xilinx's Spar-tan II programmable logic family. E+E J. 3–4, Sofia (2005). ISSN 0861-4717
20. Pavlitov, K.: Application of programmable logic circuits for implementation of artificial neural networks. E+E J. 9–10, Sofia 33–38 (2007). ISSN: 0861-4717
21. Poggio, T., Girosi, F.: Networks for approximation and learning. Proc. IEEE **78**(9), 1481–1497 (1990)
22. Quevillon, L., Hanks, E., Bansal, S., et al.: Social, spatial, and temporal organization in a complex insect society. Nat. Sci. Rep. **5**, 13393 (2015). https://doi.org/10.1038/srep13393
23. Ray, P.: A review on TinyML: state-of-the-art and prospects. J. King Saud Univ. – Comput. Inf. Sci. **34**(4), 1595–1623 (2022). https://doi.org/10.1016/j.jksuci.2021.11.019
24. Siegelmann, H., Sontag, E.: Analog computation via neural networks. Theor. Comput. Sci. **131**(2), 331–360 (1994). https://doi.org/10.1016/0304-3975(94)90178-3
25. Spartan-6 FPGA Block RAM Resources User Guide, UG383 (v1.5), 8 July 2011. www.xilinx.com. Accessed 01 Mar 2022
26. Van Veen, F., Leijnen, S.: The Neural Network Zoo, The Asimov Institute (2019). https://www.asimovinstitute.org/neural-network-zoo/. Accessed 01 Mar 2022
27. Wang, Z., She, Q., Ward, T.: Generative adversarial networks in computer vision: a survey and taxonomy. ACM Comput. Surv. **54**, 1–38(2020). ISSN: 0360-0300
28. Warden, P., Situnayake, D.: TinyML. O'Reilly Media, Sebastopol (2019). ISBN 9781492052043

Region-Based Multiple Object Tracking with LSTM Supported Trajectories

Manish Khare[1(✉)], Manan Mapara[1], Noopur Srivastava[2], and Bakul Gohel[1]

[1] DA-IICT, Gandhinagar, Gujarat, India
mkharejk@gmail.com, {201911031,bakul_gohel}@daiict.ac.in
[2] Shri Ramswaroop Memorial University, Lucknow-Deva Road, Barabanki, Uttar Pradesh, India
noopurs6@gmail.com

Abstract. Object Tracking is the growing field in computer vision with its demands in various areas in monitoring and surveillance. Areas of surveillance can be improved with proper and efficient trackers that can ensure people's safety on roads, the safety of children in school, and in many other areas. Object tracking is a super-set of elements object classification, object detection, etc. Most of the work done consists of tracking based on visual features, so we have worked on region-based features. In this context, a method is proposed for tracking, based on region features extracted with the help of intersection over union and prediction of trajectories with the help of LSTM in case of occlusion. Comparison for the same is being carried out with the traditional centroid tracking algorithm.

Keywords: Multi-object tracking · LSTM · Dataset · Object detection

1 Introduction

Object tracking is detecting the object in a video, i.e. consecutive frames of images. It can be stated as tracking the object's trajectory throughout the sequences in which it is detected. Object tracking is the second stage, but the primary stage is object detection, so better detection accuracy will lead to better trajectory tracing. Object tracking is growing day by day. It is being used in several areas such as CCTV monitoring, traffic control, and self-driven vehicles to provide a good driving experience avoiding accidents with pedestrians and other objects on the streets. The naive idea is to use template matching throughout the video sequence to track a single object, which can be done using standard convolutional neural networks. Object detection is the classical problem of computer vision which is divided into two parts object classification and object localization i.e. finding the location of an object in the image. Object classification identifies the presence of an object in the image but fails when there are multiple objects present in the image.

Object localization is the process of enclosing the identified object with the help of a bounding box. The bounding box is a rectangle with four parameters: centre, height, width, and the class of objects, i.e., the enclosed object belongs, e.g. car, person. Going through the literature in object detection and object tracking, the depth of the problem, its

T. Zlateva and R. Goleva (Eds.): CSECS 2022, LNICST 450, pp. 60–72, 2022.
https://doi.org/10.1007/978-3-031-17292-2_5

importance, and the challenges were understood, which are open for research. Most of the work done in this domain involves standard deep learning and computer vision methodologies, mainly focusing on visual features. The growing demand for object tracking in traffic monitoring, CCTV surveillance, pedestrian detection shows an opportunity for research in this Area. It is being found that the accuracy of the tracker solely depends on object detection. So the main goal is proposing a method of tracking with proper object detection with region-based features, i.e. visualizing the effect of region-based features for tracking.

There are several challenges in multiple object tracking, but those to be considered of higher importance are occlusion handling and identifying objects in the required frame of reference. In this context, the problem of occlusion is tackled in the case of region-based analysis. Tracking of person takes place with the help of region they occupy in the respective frames and predicting the missing frames with the help of LSTM models, i.e. dealing with the case of occlusion.

The organization of the paper is as follows: Sect. 2 contains related work on Multiple object tracking. Section 3 presents the proposed methodology. Section 4 presented experimental results and analysis. Section 5 presents the conclusions and future work of the study.

2   Related Work

The goal of tracking is achieved by proper object detection; two methods used for object detection [8] are YOLO [9] and Faster R-CNN [10]. As YOLO is the state-of-the-art detection method, we have used it for detection purposes. Nig et al. [6] mainly discusses the idea of object tracking with the help of YOLO and LSTM [7] to preserve location histories. It works efficiently in both the temporal and spatial domains, but the prime focus is on the spatial domain to solve occlusion and motion blur issues. YOLO is used in the first stage for feature extraction and LSTM in the second stage for sequence processing. The algorithm is deep in both senses, spatial and temporal. It uses 4096 visual features, so it is a fusion of high-level visual features and location histories.

Yilmaz et al. [16] published a survey on object tracking, which discusses the state-of-the-art tracking methodologies and newly emerging trends. The first use of object tracking is in gesture recognition, and we can identify gestures with the help of contour detection and convexity defects. The bottom-up approach to designing an object tracker is discussed, starting from object representation, feature extraction/selection, object detection, and object tracking. Object representation is formulating an object in terms of points, contours, etc., and the kind of object representation is selected based on application. Feature selection is essential to identify the object because if accurate features are not obtained, the object might not be adequately detected in further processing. Color, edges, optical flow, and texture are the four kinds of features. The next stage is object detection. The techniques used are point detectors such as SIFT [13], background subtraction, and segmentation. The final stage is object tracking and is being divided into three categories: point tracking and kernel and silhouette tracking. All three methods are differentiated on the type of their object enclosing.

If many shapes are present, one should opt for silhouette tracking, while kernel tracking is best if motion is of significant concern. Chen et al. [4] discussed the idea of intelligent mobility applications in traffic places. A comparison between Yolo and SSD is being made in the first part on datasets that contains a traffic environment. In the second part, distance estimation is done using the mono depth algorithm, an un-supervised CNN approach, and outputs a disparity map. Accurate disparity maps are obtained in the case of VGG as compared to ResNet. However, only obtaining the disparity maps is of no use as in most cases, the relation between the objects in the image and disparity maps is significantly less. So disparity maps are combined with the object detection approaches, which generate bounding boxes around detected objects. The main aim was to develop pedestrian tracking to avoid accidents.

YOLO v3 [5] turned out to be better than SSD on data that is highly filled up with objects in case of object detection. Tang et al. [14] discussed the idea of tracking multiple people with a graph-based approach. The main idea is that the person with an almost similar appearance in object detection may not be the same. Deep net-works are trained to re-identify the person with the help of lifted multi-cut problems multicut problems comprised of regular and lifted edges. Regular edges are the node connections that comprise the feasible solution, while lifted edges are long-range in-formation that connects nodes without changing the feasible solutions. Two objects can be placed in a single cluster if there exists a path between them. The primary goal of this paper is the re-identification of the object (person).

Tracking by detection is the idea of detecting objects and then associating those detections. The simple track by detection method does not handle the problem of occlusion. So there needs to be some relation between consecutive frames so that the object does not lose out to occlusion. To avoid the loss of objects, mean shift was used by searching over a larger region of interest using similarity measures. In contrast, the method of optical flow uses the idea of constant velocity and predict the trajectory. However, both methods are computationally costly and not able to per-form well in case of occlusion. On the other hand, deep sort [15] uses a Kalman filter for linear trajectory prediction and then associates the object with target and predict-ed trajectory with the help of a deep association metric.

The idea of centroid tracking [12, 17] is the traditional method that does not use visual features and only works with the help of region-based features, i.e. Euclidean distance. The first step is object detection over all frames and initialization of object list with objects of frame-1 and computing centroids of all the objects. The second step is the association based on Euclidean distance for objects of frame-2 onwards. So centroids for the objects of the current frame are computed, and then the Euclidean distance between the object list and current objects is being performed. The one which satisfies the threshold distance turns out to be the associated object in the object list. If the threshold distance is not satisfied, then a new object is created. After object association centroids of all the objects are updated, the same procedure continues for all other frames.

3   Proposed Methodology

The simple IOU-based method applies IOU [11] only in consecutive frames and tries to find the association, but this leads to loss of objects in high number. As the traditional method is centroid tracking, we have tried to overcome all the drawbacks of the traditional method in our proposed method. Two methods are proposed for the same.

3.1 Proposed Method 1

Here, we set a goal to track objects based on their region over the frames and propose the methodology for multiple object tracking, specific person. The whole idea is divided into: Detection, Association, Trajectory prediction, Combining the frames, and association of Ids.

3.1.1 Object Detection

YOLO v4 [3] is used for object detection over all the frames. For YOLO v4, the standard weights of the paper that work over the coco dataset are used. A video sequence comprises 1000 frames, then on all 1000 frames, Yolo is applied, and the respective bounding box is obtained for the objects in every frame. As an output, we get objects of every class, but the main concern is person class, so we threshold the image with confidence as 25% and object class as a person. Figure 1 shows object thresholding, and Fig. 2 shows Object detection in consecutive frames.

(a) Unthresholded Image   (b) Thresholded Image

Fig. 1. Object thresholding

(a) Objects in Frame 1   (b) Object in Frame 2

Fig. 2. Object detection

3.1.2 Object Association

For association, we use the thresholded images and initialize the object list with objects of frame-1. After that, every object in frame-2 is associated with all the objects from the object list. However, the occlusion coefficient is kept as 15. As we are dealing with the problem of occlusion, we have defined the term occlusion coefficient. The occlusion coefficient is the numerical difference between the current frame and the frame of the object which is being associated. E.g., The current frame is 50, and the object list contains 15 objects and their trajectories among different frames. So, all the detected objects of frame-50 will be associated with those objects from the object list whose last trajectory has a frame difference of less than or equal to 15, like object-15 has the last trajectory of frame-40. It will be accepted while object-10 has the last trajectory of frame-25, then it will be rejected for the association.

The frame selected for the association will be the frame of the last trajectory in the object list. The Current frame is 50, but the object frame is 47; the association will be performed on frame-47 with bounding box coordinates. The intersection over union for all eligible objects will be calculated.

$$IOU = \frac{Area}{(Area + Area1 + Area2)} \tag{1}$$

In Eq. (1), Area is the intersection of two bounding boxes, and Area 1 is the unique region of bounding box 1 and Area 2 is the unique region of bounding box 2. After calculating it, the maximum intersection over union will be taken for the association.

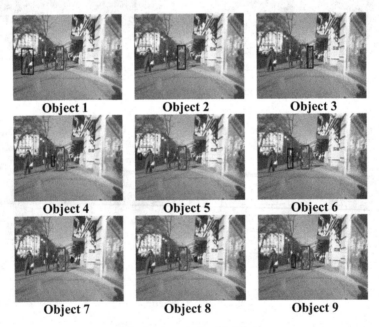

Fig. 3. Association of objects

If the maximum value is less than 20%, then a new object will be created; else, it will be appended to the corresponding object with maximum intersection over the union. Keeping the threshold of 20% is that the IOU takes place in the frame of the object list, not in the current frame. So there are high chances that the shift might have occurred between the objects as the occlusion coefficient is kept as 15. Association can be well understood from Fig. 3. The green bounding box is the object to be associated, while the red bounding box is the object from the object list. The best association is found with object-2, as shown in Fig. 3(b). Here both the green and the red bounding box completely overlapped with an IOU of 91%, while the association with all other objects is 0 or some other value less than 91% making them false associations.

After performing association, we get a list of all objects with their trajectories. However, as YOLO v4 is a robust detection algorithm, there are chances that an object has multiple bounding boxes in the same frame; in that case bounding box of greater height is considered, and the other one is discarded.

3.1.3 Trajectory Prediction

As we have kept the occlusion coefficient as 15, there are chances that when the object is occluded in some frames, we will not have trajectories of that frame, so those trajectories are to be predicted. Two LSTM models of look back 1 and 3 are trained over trajectories of 570 different objects for predicting the trajectories.

For object's we have trajectories in the frame-70, 72, 74, 75, 76, 77. From this, we have two trajectories missing in frames 71 and 73. So trajectory for frame 71 will be predicted with a look back 1 with frame 70, and for prediction of frame 73, the previous frames are more than two, so in that case, the prediction will take place with a look back at 3 with frames 70, 71, 72. The trajectory list is updated after every prediction.

By proposed method-1, all the drawbacks of centroid tracks were cleared, but ID generation was a bit higher, so to reduce the number of ID's proposed method-2 is given which is a slight modification of proposed method-1 and reduces ID up to a certain extent.

3.2 Proposed Method 2

In this method, the complete architecture is kept the same as proposed method-1; only a single change is done when creating new objects. When the *IOU* turns out to be less than the threshold, we search those objects whose Euclidean distance is less than 50. If the search gives 0 objects, we create a new object; otherwise, we compute the difference between Euclidean distance and IOU of all objects whose Euclidean distance is less than 50. Append operation is being performed, i.e. appending trajectory to the object with whom the difference turned out to be minimum; by this, we avoided creating a new object. So proposed method-2 is an improvised version of proposed method-1, which gave better results with fewer IDs.

Figure 4 shows the image flow diagram, and Fig. 5 shows the block diagram, and from both figures proposed approach can be understood pictorially.

Let say two centroids are (x_1, y_1) and (x_2, y_2). Euclidean distance between them is computed as

$$e1 = \sqrt{(x_1 - x_2)^2 + (y_1 - y_2)^2} \tag{2}$$

The minimum value object is being selected for association using threshold check. Threshold check is the difference between IOU and Euclidean distance and is computed as $(|e1 - IOU|)$ for every object where $\max(IOU) \leq 20\%$.

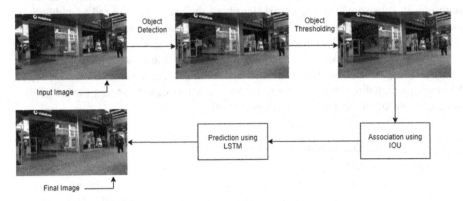

Fig. 4. Image flow diagram

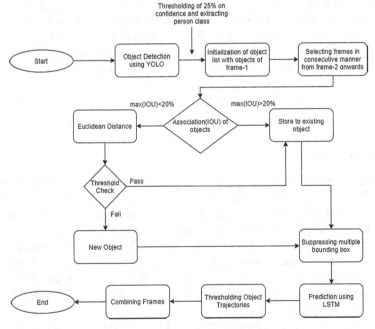

Fig. 5. Block diagram of the proposed method

4 Evaluation and Dataset Used in Experiments

Evaluation is being carried out with the help of standard CLEAR MOT [2] metrics. Some evaluations which we have used in our experimentation are given below:

MOTP: Mean error between the measurements obtained and the ground truth pro-vided. Less the value better the results and can also be represented in percentage by deducting the MOTP from 1 and multiplying by 100. In the case of percentage representation, the higher the value better is the result.

Matches: Object matches between the ground truth and measurement in every frame. The higher the number, was better the result.

Mismatches: Identity mismatch between ground truth and measurement. So a swap of identity in a single frame will lead to 2 mismatches. Lower the number better the result.

False Negatives: Un-identification of the ground truth object in measurement. i.e. the ground truth object is present but in measurement is not identified. Lower the number better the result.

False Positives: False identification of the ground truth object in measurement. i.e. the ground truth object is not present, but in measurement, it is identified. Lower the number better the result.

Object Count and ID: The total number of objects detected in all the frames while ID is the object identity among the total number of objects.

In this work, the MOT15 dataset [1] is used. It contains colored video sequences with different resolutions ranging from standard to full HD. The reason behind choosing this dataset is that it is filmed with both static and moving cameras with a prime focus on pedestrians on the streets. Video sequences with ground truth data are provided for evaluation. Table 1 shows the details of the dataset.

Table 1. Video details of 2D MOT15 dataset

	Video Name	Resolution	Number of frames
1	ADL-Rundle-6	1920 × 1080	525
2	ADL-Rundle-8	1920 × 1080	654
3	ETH-Bahnhof	640 × 480	1000
4	ETH-Pedcross2	640 × 480	837
5	ETH-Sunnyday	640 × 480	354
6	KITTI-13	1242 × 375	340
7	KITTI-17	1224 × 370	145
8	PETS09-S2L1	768 × 576	795
9	TUD-Campus	640 × 480	71
10	TUD-Stadtmitte	640 × 480	179
11	Venice-2	1920 × 1080	600

All experiments and results have been carried out on Google collab GPU. LSTM model is trained with 5 inputs; 4 inputs of the bounding box, i.e. x-center, y-centre, height, width, and 5th input is the frame's aspect ratio. Parameters for lookback = 1 are kept as epochs = 30, optimizer = adam, batch size = 128, loss = mean absolute percentage error, and.

3 Stacked LSTM units while for lookback = 3 only batch size = 64 is changed. Loss curves for lstm models are shown in Fig. 6.

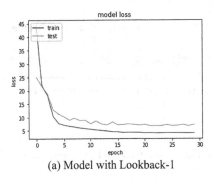

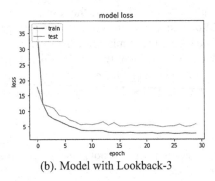

(a) Model with Lookback-1   (b). Model with Lookback-3

Fig. 6. Loss curve for LSTM model

5 Experimental Results and Analysis

We have experimented on standard publicly available datasets as mentioned in Table 1. We have compared both proposed methods with centroid tracking methods. Here, we presented qualitative and quantitative results for one video (ETH-Bahnhof Dataset), as discussed in Table 1. We have shared results for other videos on the website https://sites. google.com/site/mkharejk/research due to page restriction as per conference guidelines.

Experiment 1: ETH-Bahnhof Dataset
The ETH-Bahnhof dataset contains 1000 frames with a resolution of 640 × 480. Experimental results for Centroid tracking and both proposed methods are given in Figs. 7, 8, and 9. Quantitative evaluation values are given in Table 2.

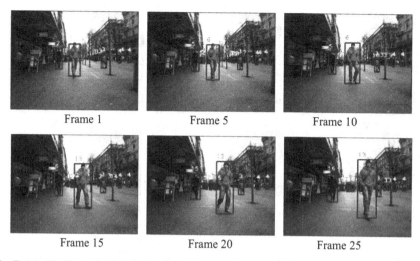

Fig. 7. Multi-object tracking results for ETH-Bahnhof video sequence using centroid tracking

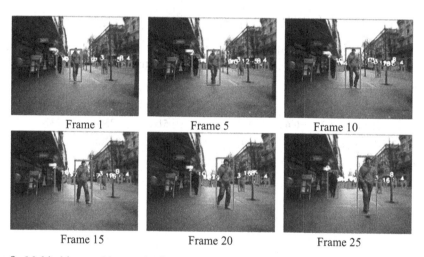

Fig. 8. Multi-object tracking results for ETH-Bahnhof video sequence using proposed method 1

From Fig. 7, we can see that the same object is losing its id as it moves forward. In frame-1, the object is labelled as id-1, in frame-5,10 labelled as id-6, and in frames 15,20,25 labelled as 13. Another evident issue is that the nearby objects have been labelled as the same object. From Fig. 8, we can see that the drawbacks of the traditional method shown in Fig. 7 are entirely resolved. From Fig. 9, we can see that proposed method 2 outperformed in comparison to proposed method 1. From the frames, we can see that occlusion is tackled well in the proposed method and fewer id switches.

We can see from Table 2 that both proposed methods have outperformed the baseline method while proposed approach-1 has also outperformed proposed approach-2 - 4

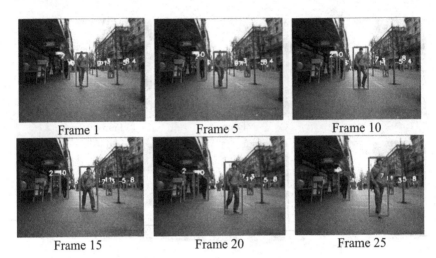

Frame 1   Frame 5   Frame 10

Frame 15   Frame 20   Frame 25

Fig. 9. Multi-object tracking results for ETH-Bahnhof video sequence using proposed method 2

Table 2. Quantitative analysis of ETH-Bahnhof video sequence

		MOTP	ID	False positive	False negative	Matches	Mismatches
Proposed method-1	Threshold-0	0.69	444	14710	7216	454	**28**
	Threshold-15	0.72	216	11565	5335	2335	**252**
	Threshold-25	**0.6**	169	10430	**5162**	**2508**	237
Proposed method-2	Threshold-0	**0.6**	97	**7599**	5822	1848	**104**
	Threshold-15	0.61	81	8363	6683	987	**47**
	Threshold-25	0.61	**72**	8300	6794	876	**36**
Centroid tracking		**0.63**	**950**	**12310**	**7579**	**91**	**40**

metrics (MOTP, False Negative, Matches, Mismatches) out of 6 favoured proposed approach-1.

Please visit my website https://sites.google.com/site/mkharejk/research, on which we shared all other video sequence experimental results and quantitative performance measures values.

By analyzing different video sequences and the nature of individual objects, we figured out that an object is occluded up to 15 frames in standard cases, so the occlusion coefficient is kept as 15. Trials have been carried out with different occlusion coefficients. However, as we increase the value of the occlusion coefficient, the number of object detection remains the same. However, the unique id association count reduces, which increases the false entries, i.e. different objects given the same id.

A similar observation is being drawn from the case of the IOU threshold being kept as 20%. The reason behind keeping it 20% is that in the worst case, the difference between the current frame and the object frame is 15, which can be associated, so there would be a deviation in the object's position. However, as the threshold is 20%, there are fewer chances of missing out on the object.

Thresholding of trajectories used in proposed methods keeps only those whose trajectory length is more significant than the threshold, i.e. for threshold-0, all objects will be considered. In contrast, threshold-5 objects with trajectory lengths greater than 5 will be considered. In general, on increasing the threshold, a positive sign is developed in MOTP, ID, False positives, False Negatives, and Matches while the negative sign for Mismatches.

The key factors were the IOU threshold, trajectory threshold, and the occlusion coefficient in the architecture, so they can be summarized as follows.

$$IOU\ Threshold\ \alpha\ \frac{1}{Result} \tag{3}$$

$$Occulusion\ Coefficient\ \alpha\ \frac{1}{Results} \tag{4}$$

$$Trajectory\ Threshold\ \alpha\ Results \tag{5}$$

We can see that the IOU threshold and occlusion coefficient inversely affects the result while the trajectory threshold directly affects the result.

6 Conclusions and Future Directions

This work mainly focused on the idea of region-based multiple object tracking. So we proposed two methods to deal with this, which gave better results than the traditional method of region-based analysis. The proposed method is extending the evaluation metric IOU for tracking. Method examination is carried out using a mot-precision, false positives, false negatives, matches, mismatches, and ids. The algorithm's efficacy cannot be decided from a single metric, so we have taken the metrics count to favor the algorithm. All drawbacks of the standard method are resolved by occlusion tackling, a high number of ids and the same id to different objects in the same frame. All metrics have outperformed the traditional method in various videos tested. The problem of occlusion is being tackled up to a certain extent. For a steady object, occlusion is tackled well without loss of id and trajectory, while in the case of moving object, the trajectory is not lost, but the id switch takes place after some frames.

Both the proposed methods have outperformed the traditional method, but out of the 11 video sequences, an observation can be derived as follows. Proposed Approach-1 works well in case of more number frames. Proposed Approach-2 works well in case of less number of frames and works well where frames are more as well object crossings are high in number.

As the goal is to tackle the tracking problem with a region-based approach without taking into consideration the visual features, this work can be extended to tackle the problem of id switches in case of occlusion of moving objects by associating occlusion coefficient with some other parameter that deals with the region of interest.

Acknowledgment. This work was supported by the Science and Engineering Research Board (SERB), Department of Science and Technology (DST), New Delhi, India, under Grant No. CRG/2020/001982.

References

1. Taixe, L.I., Milan, A., Reid, I., Roth, S., Schindler, K.: MOTChallenge 2015: towards a benchmark for multi-target tracking. https://arxiv.org/abs/1504.01942 (2015)
2. Rainer, S., Bernadin, K.: Evaluating multiple object tracking performance: the CLEAR MOT metrics. EURASIP J. Image Video Process. **2008**, 10 (2008). Article No. 246309, https://doi.org/10.1155/2008/246309
3. Bochkovskiy, A., Wang, C.Y., Liao, H.Y.M.: Yolov4: optimal speed and accuracy of object detection https://arxiv.org/abs/2004.10934 (2020)
4. Chen, Z., Khemmar, R., Decoux, B., Atahouet, A., Ertaud, J.Y.: Real time object detection, tracking, and distance and motion estimation based on deep learning: application to smart mobility. In: Proceeding of Eighth International Conference on Emerging Security Technologies (EST) (2019)
5. Kathuria, A.: What's new in yolo v3? (2018). https://towardsdatascience.com/yolo-v3-obj ect-detection-53fb7d3bfe6b
6. Ning, G., et al.: Spatially supervised recurrent convolutional neural networks for visual object tracking. In: Proceeding of IEEE International Symposium on Circuits and Systems (2017)
7. Olah, C.: Understanding LSTM networks (2015). https://colah.github.io/posts/2015-08-Und erstanding-LSTMs/
8. Zhao, Z.Q., Zheng, P., Xu, S.T., Wu, X.: Object detection with deep learning: a review. IEEE Trans. Neural Netw. Learn. Syst. 30(11), 3212–3232 (2019)
9. Redmon, J., Divvala, S., Girshick, R., Farhadi, A.: You only look once: unified, real-time object detection. In: Proceeding of IEEE Conference on Computer Vision and Pattern Recognition, pp. 779–788 (2016)
10. Ren, S., He, K., Girshick, R., Sun, J.: Faster R-CNN: towards real-time object detection with region proposal networks. IEEE Trans. Pattern Anal. Mach. Intell. 39(6), 1137–1149 (2017)
11. Rosebrock, A.: Intersection over union (IOU) for object detection (2016). https://www.pyi magesearch.com/2016/11/07/intersection-over-union-iou-for-object-detection/
12. Rosebrock, A.: Simple object tracking with opencv (2018). https://www.pyimagesearch.com/2018/07/23/simple-object-tracking-with-opencv/
13. Singh, A.: A detailed guide to the powerful sift technique for image matching (with python code) (2019). https://www.analyticsvidhya.com/blog/2019/10/detailed-guide-powerful-sift-technique-image-matching-python/
14. Tang, S., Andriluka, M., Andres, B., Schiele, B.: Multiple people tracking by lifted multicut and person re-identification. In: Proceeding of IEEE Conference on Computer Vision and Pattern Recognition, pp. 3701–3710 (2017)
15. Wojke, N., Bewley, A., Paulus, D.: Simple online and realtime tracking with a deep association metric. In: Proceeding of IEEE International Conference on Image Processing, pp. 3645–3649 (2017)
16. Yilmaz, A., Javed, O., Shah, M.: Object tracking: a survey. ACM Comput. Surv. 38(4), 13–es (2006)
17. Zhang, R., Ding, J.: Object tracking and detecting based on adaptive background subtraction. Procedia Eng. **29**, 1351–1355 (2012)

An Approach to Software Assets Reusing

Olena Chebanyuk[1,2(✉)] [ID]

[1] Department of Informatics, New Bulgarian University, Sofia, Bulgaria
Chebanyuk.olena@gmail.com
[2] Software Engineering Department, National Aviation University, Kyiv, Ukraine

Abstract. The modern software development methodologies require systematic reuse of software assets. It is expected that reuse becomes a cause of reducing efforts. From the other hand, nowadays reuse procedure is connected with plenty of problems and risks, for example, how to choose the best software asset from the set of available for reuse? What criterion should be considered to estimate internal structure of software asset? How to perform such an operation quickly and effectively? Paper proposes the approach allowing predicting estimation of effectiveness for further reuse of software asset. Approach is based on matching software assets to requirement specification considering their semantic attributes, namely OCL expressions. Software asset is associated with some problem domain process through keywords. Points of requirement specification are associated with the same keywords and completed by OCL expressions. Similarity of requirement specification and software assets from repository is defined by means of comparing corresponding keywords and OCL expressions. Model for approximate comparison of OCL expressions and its estimation are proposed. Evaluation of the proposed approach according to IBM reuse maturity model is represented.

Keywords: Software product lines · Constraint modeling and languages · AGILE · Model-driven development · OCL · Domain engineering

1 Introduction

Successful software development process today needs following to many business requirements, for example low code, speed development, reducing of development costs, high quality of code and others. Answer to it – organization of development process involving techniques that satisfy to the next requirements: (i) software assets reuse; (ii) high levels of software development processes maturity; (iii) automatization of routine activities in software development processes.

One of the ways to answer to these business requirements is involving activities of asset-based development into modern software development methodologies, such as Test-Driven Development, Behavioral-Driven Development, and Software Product Line approaches [4].

Approaches and tools for static code analysis and generation of static UML diagrams from source code aimed to discover only structure of the source code.

T. Zlateva and R. Goleva (Eds.): CSECS 2022, LNICST 450, pp. 73–83, 2022.
https://doi.org/10.1007/978-3-031-17292-2_6

Questions about semantic are solved mentally and require much time in case of big amount of software assets under search area. Procedure of searching software assets may take much time and, then to become unsuccessful. In addition, absents of strict criteria how to estimate results of searching may be cause for different developers to give different answers to question: "Is found software asset suitable for reuse?".

Further results of reuse search are also may be unpredictable. Similar situations are related to reuse problems for other types of assets, such as test suites test cases, interface prototypes, database models, UML (or BPMN) diagrams [15].

2   Review of Papers

Strategy of related papers review is based on matching papers to Reuse Maturity Model, proposed by IBM [4]. Graphical representation of Reuse Maturity Model looks like a matrix. Each row corresponds to maturity level of CMMI model [6], and its cells explain activities of stakeholders [4].

Researches aimed to perform software assets analysis according to different levels of CMMI, are concentrated on several areas:

- analysis of requirement specification by means of natural languages analysis techniques [9, 15];
  There are reuse approaches containing:

  1. Ontology-based approach to search similar requirements analyzing texts of requirement specification [16];
  2. Investigating of human factor influences in considering requirement specifications for specific areas [12].

- analysis of the software assets' structure with the aim to discover their functionality [14];
- techniques and approaches to describe software asset semantic using analytical apparatus [1].
  There are reuse approaches containing:

  1. System of elements to represent assets' features (their structure and semantic);
  2. A set of requests to recognize assets' features [7].
  3. Complex rules, expressions, and patterns for representation of reuse asset structure [8, 11].
  4. Approaches related to using ontologies

- flexible approaches that are based on using intermedia analytical languages to explain semantic of software asset [2].
  There are reuse approaches containing:

  1. Designing of new reuse approaches that are based on new transformation rules containing specific facts about concrete domains [3];

2. Modification of software designing technologies

Literature review gives the ground to formulate research task – to propose an approach for software assets reuse based on analysis both semantic attributes of requirement specification and software assets.

3 Task and Research Questions

Task: to propose the approach for estimating effectiveness of software assets reuse based on comparison of semantic attributes of software assets and requirement specification. Keywords in natural language and OCL expressions [13] are chosen as semantic attributes. In forward engineering activities, semantic attributes are prepared in requirement analysis. In reverse engineering activities, semantic attributes are prepared when software asset repository is composed.

Research Questions (RQs)

RQ1: Propose a structure for software assets repository. Aim of repository is to systemize information about assets for further reuse. Assets that are gathered in repository related to concrete problem domain.

RQ2: Propose a structure of requirement specification, which summarizes requirements description and semantic attributes of requirements.

RQ3: Develop a comparison algorithm for matching semantic attributes of repository assets and software requirement specification.

RQ4: Propose a model for approximate comparison of semantic attributes allowing comparing semantic of requirement specification and assets from repository (define criterion for full and approximate matching of OCL expressions).

RQ5: Perform an experiment, verifying proposed approach and comparison model.

4 Proposed Approach

Proposed approach is divided into three stages:

– domain analysis - when repository of software assets is designed;
– requirement analysis - when semantic attributes of requirement specification are composed;
– comparison of semantic attributes - when decision about reuse of software module is performed.

1. Domain analysis.

   1.1. A problem domain tree, containing description of problem domain processes, sub-processes and keywords, is designed. See first two rows of the Table 1.

Table 1. Structure of repository tree for software assets

Problem domain processes and sub-processes	Keywords (kw)	Software asset name and links of software assets textual description	OCL expressions
Name of the process1	*kw1,* *kw2,* *kwn*		
Name of the sub-process1 (process1.1)	*kw1.1,* *,...,* *kw1.m*		

1.2. A repository tree of assets for considering problem domain is designed. Structure of repository tree is represented in the Table 1.

2. Requirement analysis.

2.1. A requirements specification with detailed description of the software project is designed.

2.2. Semantic attributes of requirement specification are prepared performing the next steps:

- expressions containing limitations in natural language are defined;
- OCL constraints for these limitations are designed.
- proper keywords from problem domain tree are selected;

Table 2 proposes the structure of requirement specification table with semantic attributes of requirements.

Table 2. Structure of requirement specification table with semantic attributes of requirements

Requirement specification (RQ) code	RQ description and limitations in natural language	Selected keywords from problem domain tree	OCL expressions
...	...	...	...

3. Comparison of semantic attributes from requirement specification and assets repository.

3.1. The common keywords for repository tree and requirement specification are defined. (Comparing proper rows from Table 1 and Table 2).

3.2. Corresponding OCL expressions are compared using a model for approximate comparison of OCL expression.

3.3. Comparison results are analyzed. Then decision about selection software assets from repository for the further reuse is made.

5 Model for Approximate Comparison of OCL Expressions

5.1 Graph Representation of OCL Expression

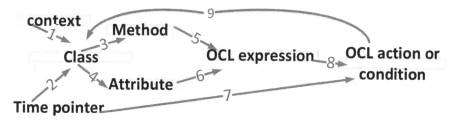

Fig. 1. Graph representation of OCL expressions

In order to describe rules for approximate comparison of OCL expressions, OCL expression is represented as a directed graph (Fig. 1). Developed scheme is based on graph representation of UML diagrams [3].

Possible variants of OCL graph vertexes meanings (Fig. 1) according to OCL standard [13].

Time pointer = {pre, post, inv} - keywords from [11].

Class = {self (keyword from [13], *class name}.*

OCL expressions = {select, exists, forAll, other keywords from [11]}.

OCL action or condition = {or, and, true, false, other keywords from [11]}.

Method – a signature of class method.

Attribute – a name and type of class attribute.

As a result of OCL expressions analysis (Fig. 1) several types of OCL were defined. Aim of the proposed classification is to define *key vertexes of OCL graph* that are important for approximate comparison. Due to limited size of paper, *only several types of OCL expressions* are considered.

OCL Expressions of the First Type
General graph representation of the OCL expression is defined by the following:

$$(contex, 1, class), \; (class, 3, method) \tag{1}$$

Graph representation of the OCL expression, marked by green color, is defined by following (Fig. 1):

(context, 1, sensor), (sensor, 3, isActive(b:action):boolean)

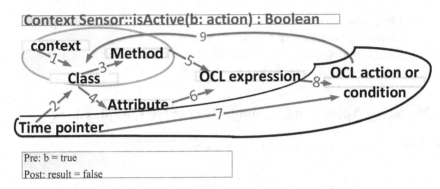

Pre: b = true
Post: result = false

Fig. 2. Examples of OCL expressions representation

OCL Expressions of the Second Type

General graph representation of the OCL expressions, marked by red color, is defined by the following (Fig. 2):

$$(Time\ pointer, 7,\ OCL\ action\ or\ condition) \qquad (2)$$

Graph representation of the OCL expression, marked by red color, is defined by following (Fig. 2):

$(pre, 7, b = true),(post, 7, result = false)$

Complex OCL Expressions

Lets' start from the example considering RQ description in natural language –
If sensor is active it is turned off.

Context Sensor::isActive(b: action): Boolean

pre: b = true.
post: result = false.

OCL expression is composed of OCL expressions of the first and second types (1) and (2).
If one OCL expression contains more than one string or represent different types of OCL expressions, it is a *complex OCL expression.*

OCL Expressions of the Third Type

Lets' start from the example considering RQ description in natural language –
If current user is registered, he obtains an access to database through network.

context Network

inv:self.dbAccess.users- > includes(self.currentUser)

General graph representation of these OCL expressions is defined by the following:

$(Context, 1, class)$, $(Class, 4, Attribute)$, $(Attribute, 6, OCL expression)$,

$(OCL expression, 8, OCL action)$ (3)

OCL Expression of the Fourth Type

Lets' start from the example considering RQ description in natural language.

In order to obtain access to network resource user must get a proper permissions before.

context Network::authenticate (c:Credentials)

pre: self.dbAccess.users- > contains(u - > u.c = c);

It is complex OCL expression. The first sting is OCL expression of the first type (1). The second string represents OCL expression of the fourth type. General graph representation of the OCL expressions is defined by following:

$(Time\ pointer, 2, Class)$, $(Class, 4, Attribute)$, $(Attribute, 6, OCL expression)$,

$(OCL expression, 8, OCL condition)$ (4)

Analysis of other types of OCL expressions is made by the same principle.

Proposed graph model (Fig. 1) is extensible. In order to consider different types of OCL expressions new vertexes and edges may be added.

In addition, graph representation idea may be used to describe other string-based query expressions (For example LINQ, SQL queries, predicate logic expressions or other types of query expressions).

5.2   Model for Approximate Comparison of OCL Expressions

1. Two OCL expressions are parsed to components in accordance with graph represent tation (1)–(4).
1. Types of these OCL expressions are defined. In order to perform this task graph representation of the considering OCL expression are compared with defined types of OCL expressions (1)–(4).
2. If two OCL are the same type, their graph representations are compared.
3. Comparison results are estimated for equality using proposed comparison model.

Comparison model is based on calculating values of weight coefficients that aimed to answer the question – What is the distance between two OCL expressions?

Value of weight coefficient shows "the importance" of some part of OCL expressions for approximate comparison. Those parts of OCL expressions that play more important role in comparison (from the authors' experience) are assigned to greater values of weight coefficients.

Proposed *principles of weight coefficients* assigning and criteria of approximately equality for OCL expressions are also *flexible*. Recommendations are grounded on empirical experience of authors. They were gathered while working in different projects performing semantic analysis of different assets. Area of authors' activities is monitoring of local networks security and game development area.

Estimation of the Proposed Model. Performing authors' projects, more than 50 OCL expressions were prepared manually to test proposed approach. In order to perform approximate comparison, activities similar to described in this chapter were done. For all OCL expressions analysis of human comparison and formal calculations are matched. It is the ground of idea that comparison model is valid and may be used for other OCL experiments.

6   Evaluation of the Proposed Approach

On order to estimate an effectiveness of the represented approach and measure maturity of reuse process it is proposed to use asset reuse strategy [3, 5]. Asset reuse strategy proposes to estimate effectiveness of reuse approaches calculating parameters important for return of investment (ROI) activities.

Estimation process is based on calculating time coefficients measuring "time ratio" between ROI operations of the represented approach and ad-hoc level processes (the first level of reuse maturity model).

In order to make evaluation process more accurate our team have chosen one more approach for comparison. It corresponds to the five maturity reuse level [7]. Part of our team tried to design domain models, represented as class diagrams, performing activities similar to [11]. It was an attempt to design new domain models reusing some entities of existing software assets (sending QVT-R requests to existing elements of class diagrams).

In order to explain the idea of evaluation process ROI parameter: "amount of time spent to learn information about asset" from asset reuse strategy is considered [5]. Table 3 represents time coefficients for different components of this parameter (The first row of the Table 3). Numbers in the title of the Table 3 (1, 4, and 5) correspond to maturity levels of reuse model.

Time coefficients (rows 4 and 5) show the percent of time economy for proposed approach (Sect. 3) and in comparison with the first maturity level.

Table 3. Time coefficients for estimation parameter "amount of time spent to learn information about asset"

Level of maturity	t(i)	1	4	5
Is asset about problem domain?	t1	1	-	0.1 0.2
What is the solution that is provided?	t2	1	0.1	0.07
What other assets can be used in conjunction with this asset?	t3	1	-	0.1 0.2
What constraints are placed on your project after you have used the asset?	t4	1	0.1	0.08

Cells, marked by green, correspond to maturity levels of time coefficients (t1–t4) for the proposed approach.

Cells, marked by yellow correspond to maturity levels of time coefficients (t1–t4) for the ad-hoc approach.

7 Conclusion

Paper proposes flexible approach for estimation of effectiveness for software assets reuse by means of comparison of semantic attributes for requirement specification and software assets. Keywords from natural language and OCL expressions play role of semantic attributes. Keywords serve as pointers allowing performing quick matching of problem domain processes and requirement specification. They help to reduce a number of OCL expressions to be compared (see case study, Table 6). OCL expressions play roles of «semantic hashes» representing characteristics of software requirements (or software assets from repository tree) and expressed by means of formal language.

Proposed approach extends traditional using of OCL expressions as part of meta-models for class diagrams analysis [5]. OCL is chosen for the proposed approach because it is widespread language of OMG standard and OCL plug-ins are integrated into many software tools used for software designing [8].

Consider other flexibilities of the proposed approach.

Area - *changing of semantic attributes.* The answer is that matching procedure may be changed in several directions:

- graph representation of OCL expression may be modified (Fig. 1);
- constituents of OCL expressions and weight coefficients' may be changed (Table 3) [13];
- calculation schemas for estimation for approximate equality may be modified;
- OCL may be changed to other graph-compatible notations for representation of semantic attributes (Table 1 and Table 2) (LINQ, SQL, predicate logic expressions) [10].
- instead of keywords in natural languages their hashes, or vector of synonyms may be used.

Main idea of represented approach (see Sect. 4) is to propose a flexible "way of thinking" in mentioned directions aimed to organize reuse of software assets considering their semantic attributes.

Proposed approach is related to Software Product Line techniques and requires extra efforts to perform domain analysis activities (Table 2). Analysis of procedures aimed to process software assets repositories shows that for large repositories search of information takes a long time and requires large amount of resources. Comparison of keywords allows saving search time for large repository. (For example, when repository contains more than 1000 software assets. Such a repository is used in authors' case study). Software assets are reused with optimized search and estimation procedures.

References

1. Abbas, M., Rioboo, R., Ben-Yelles, C.B., Snook, C.F.: Formal modeling and verification of UML Activity Diagrams (UAD) with FoCaLiZe. J. Syst. Archit. **1**(14), 101911 (2021)
2. Bjørner, D.: Domain engineering. In: Boca, P., Bowen, J., Siddiqi, J. (eds.) Formal Methods: State of the Art and New Directions, pp. 1–41. Springer, London (2010). https://doi.org/10.1007/978-1-84882-736-3_1
3. Chebanyuk, O., Palahin, O., Markov, K.: Domain engineering approach of software requirement analysis. Проблеми програмування **2–3**(2020), 154–172 (2020)
4. Gnatyuk, S., Kinzeryavyy, V., Stepanenko, I., Gorbatyuk, Y., Gizun, A., Kotelianets, V.: Code obfuscation technique for enhancing software protection against reverse engineering. In: Hu, Z., Petoukhov, S.V., He, M. (eds.) AIMEE2018 2018. AISC, vol. 902, pp. 571–580. Springer, Cham (2020). https://doi.org/10.1007/978-3-030-12082-5_52
5. DeCarlo, J., et al.: Strategic Reuse with Asset-Based Development, vol. 15. IBM Corporation, Riverton (2008)
6. Validating and exploring characteristics of UML model elements (2015). https://www.ibm.com/docs/en/rational-soft-arch/9.7.0?topic=models-validating-uml-model-elements
7. Ferdinansyah, A., Purwandari, B.: Challenges in combining agile development and CMMI: a systematic literature review. In: 2021 10th International Conference on Software and Computer Applications, pp. 63–69 (2021)
8. Habeh, O., Thekrallah, F., Salloum, S.A., Shaalan, K.: Knowledge sharing challenges and solutions within software development team: a systematic review. In: Al-Emran, M., Shaalan, K., Hassanien, A.E. (eds.) Recent Advances in Intelligent Systems and Smart Applications. SSDC, vol. 295, pp. 121–141. Springer, Cham (2021). https://doi.org/10.1007/978-3-030-47411-9_7
9. Kopetzki, D., Lybecait, M., Naujokat, S., Steffen, B.: Towards language-to-language transformation. Int. J. Softw. Tools Technol. Transf. **23**(5), 655–677 (2021). https://doi.org/10.1007/s10009-021-00630-2
10. Lami, G., Gnesi, S., Fabbrini, F., Fusani, M., Trentanni, G.: An automatic tool for the analysis of natural language requirements. Informe técnico, CNR Information Science and Technology Institute, Pisa, Italia, Setiembre (2004). https://openportal.isti.cnr.it/data/2004/150653/2004_150653.pdf
11. OMG standard Object Constraint Language 2.3.1 Access mode (2011). https://www.omg.org/spec/OCL/2.3.1/About-OCL/
12. Nestererenko, К., Rahulin, S., Sharabaiko, A.: Human factor in the quality improvement system of aircraft maintenance. Системи управління, навігації та зв'язку. **1**(59), 41–45 (2020). https://doi.org/10.26906/SUNZ.2020.1.041

13. Pérez, B., Porres, I.: Reasoning about UML/OCL class diagrams using constraint logic programming and formula. Inf. Syst. **81**, 152–177 (2019)
14. Silva, A.R., Savić, D.: Linguistic patterns and linguistic styles for requirements specification: focus on data entities. Appl. Sci. **11**(9), 4119 (2021). https://doi.org/10.3390/app11094119
15. Quinton, C., Vierhauser, M., Rabiser, R., Baresi, L., Grünbacher, P., Schuhmayer, C.: Evolution in dynamic software product lines. J. Softw.: Evol. Process **33**(2), e2293 (2021)
16. Tkachenko, O., Tkachenko, K., Tkachenko, O.: Designing complex intelligent systems on the basis of ontological model. In: Proceedings of the Third International Workshop on Computer Modeling and Intelligent Systems (CMIS-2020), Zaporizhzhia, Ukraine, 27 April 27–1 May 2020, P. 266–277 (2020)

Methodological Creation of HDRI from 360-Degree Camera - Case Study

Maria Peteva[⊠]

New Bulgarian University, Ul. "Montevideo" 21, Sofia, Bulgaria
lintch.co@gmail.com

Abstract. Panoramic imagery has been used in a variety of ways in many industries - cinema, architecture, entertainment. With the steady rise of 360-degree images and VR, the creation of realistic environments for industry purposes has come even close to CG artists. 360-degree cameras have enabled users to take even more control of lightning and HDRI in their own hands by creating their own images. This paper focuses on the process of creating an HDRI through a 360-degree camera within a commercial price rate while also investigating artifacts and errors during the process.

Keywords: 360-degree images · HDRI · Cubemap

HDRI has been established in many Medias as a must-have. High Dynamic Range Image (HDRI) is a 360-degree image that is wrapped around an image plane for lighting and background purposes. HDRI are easy to add in an environment and create realistic lightning in computer graphics. They are widely used for 3D visualizations in the entertainment industry - movies, animation, games, and in architecture, interior design and many more. The best way to describe an HDRI in plain terms is as a scene captured not as a two dimensional surface, but a spherical interactive surface, where the viewer is set in the middle of a sphere. The main difference between normal 360-degree pictures and HDRI is that HDRI is a technique where multiple images are taken in the same environment and then combined into a single spherical image. Such an image has a higher dynamic range of luminosity and contains more information about the lighting than a normal photograph. The HDRI than can be used for realistic rendering purposes. Using a 360-degree camera to create an HDRI has proved to be even more easy and effective than creating an HDRI from multiple images. 360-degree cameras have approved over the century and now have the needed specifications for creating a good HDRI. In this paper, we are going to review the process of creating an HDRI using a 360-degree camera.

1 360-Degree Cameras

360 degree cameras have become household objects that consumers could afford. 360-degree cameras did not only come with easy ways to take photographs, but with free software to ensure the images were easy to download, review, edit, stitch and export. 360-degree cameras are easy to carry and use. Manufacturers gave the users and CG artists

T. Zlateva and R. Goleva (Eds.): CSECS 2022, LNICST 450, pp. 84–91, 2022.
https://doi.org/10.1007/978-3-031-17292-2_7

the opportunity to create their own HDRI for multiple purposes be it professional or entertaining. This paper concentrates on the specifics and performance of a commercial 360-degree camera and the creation of HDRI by using the Q00Cam 8K 360-degree camera created by Kandoo.

From 2020 to 2022, the main manufacturers of 360-degree cameras for commercial use have changed the number of cameras, and managed to develop more models with even more characteristics. When a consumer buys the camera, it comes with free apps for easily controlling the camera from your phone. The software for image manipulation still has something to be desired from but it accommodates the basic needs for exporting a good image. The software has a huge limitation in color correction and exposure settings. However the specifications of a 360-degree camera come very close to a professional camera and ideally it is what a user needs for a good HDRI. From 2020 to 2022, GoPro has switched from only two 360-degree cameras to five. Theta has also switched from two cameras produced in 2020 to seven. Insta 360 have not changed the number of cameras they have produced - still at five, but all of their models have improved. Kandoo, which is the manufacturer of the camera used for this process, have not changed the number of cameras they produced, however they also manufacture professional cameras - and they have added one more professional camera to the three they already had. Major companies associated with 360-degree cameras you can see in Table 1 below.

Table 1. 360-degree camera changes of models from 2020 to 2022.

	2020	2022		2020	2022
Go Pro	Go Pro Max	Hero 10 – Creators Edition	Theta	Ricoh Theta V	Theta Z1
	Go Pro Fusion	Hero 10		Ricoh Theta Z1	Theta X
		Hero 9			That V
		Hero 8			Theta SC2
		Max			Theta S
Insta 360	One R	One RS			Theta SC
	One X	One X			Theta m12
	EVO	One X2	Kandoo	QooCam 8K	QooCam 8K
	One	Evo		QuoCam Fun	QooCam Fun
	NanoS	Go 2		QooCam	Qoocam
		Nano S	Kandoo Professional	Obsidian Go	Obsidian Pro
Insta 360 Professional	Pro 2	Pro 2		Obsidian S	Obsidian R

(*continued*)

Table 1. (*continued*)

	2020	2022		2020	2022
	Pro	Pro		Obsidian R	Obsidian S
	Titan	Titan			Obsidian Go
Samsung	Samsung Gear (2017)	Samsung Gear (2017)			
Vuze	Vuze XR	Vuze XR			
	Vuze+	Vuze+			
	Vuze	Vuze			

2 Methodology

HDRI stores the three value colors of RGB scale with floating point precision, which means the brightness is recorded in each color pixel. It contains 32 bits per pixel per channel which is more than the traditional 8-bit image. When we talk about using a 360-degree camera to produce an HDRI image, what we need to accomplish is to take several RAW pictures with different ISO - sensitivity to light and different EV - exposure value or the amount of light radiation in an image. Both of which are available in range even in a low budget 360 camera. The specifications of the Kandoo 8K camera can be viewed on Table 2.

Table 2. Specifications and features in QooCam 8k.

ISO	Shutter			White Balance	EV – Exposure value	
100	1	1/80	1/640	Auto	−2	0
200	1/1.3	1/100	1/800	Underwater	−1.7	0.3
400	1/1.6	1/120	1/1000	Incandescent	−1.3	0.7
800	1/2	1/160	1/1600	Florescent	−1	1
1600	1/2.5	1/200	1/2000	Daylight	−0.7	1.3
3200	1/3	1/250	1/3200	Cloudy	−0.3	1.7
6400	1/10	1/320	1/4000			2
	1/30	1/400	1/5000			
	1/60	1/500	1/6400			

In terms of compression, we can always downscale from an upscale resolution, QuoCam 8k camera provides a 7680 by 3840, 12 bit DNG (RAW), Raw+ photo (16bit). DNG stands for Digital Negative Image. DNG images are easier to edit than Raw images. From the parameters even the quality given from this 360-degree camera is as standart as a professional camera. The various combinations between parameters ensures the capture of a good HDRI image. The two most important aspects of HDIR are dynamic range of the image and high resolution. Dynamic range is an indication of the contrast in an image - the more contrast there is the better the HDRI would look. To compress a good HDRI you need at least from 5 to 12 images for indoor shooting and 5 do 22 for outdoor shooting. These images are a combination of EV and Shutter speed, however, images with EV = 0 are considered a well-exposed image (Bloch 2012). To start off the process, the first picture we take needs to be almost black with a EV -2 and shutter speed 1/8000. The formula on the dependency between EV and shutter speed you can view on Fig. 1(a). In the equation, F is the relative aperture of the lens and Δt is the exposure time. (Do 2016) and the visual representation of such an image can be viewed below on Fig. 1(b).

(a)

$$EV = log_2 \frac{F^2}{\Delta t}$$

(b)

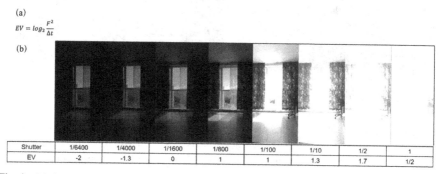

Shutter	1/6400	1/4000	1/1600	1/800	1/100	1/10	1/2	1
EV	-2	-1.3	0	1	1	1.3	1.7	1/2

Fig. 1. (a) A measurement of exposure value (EV). (b) Images captures with QooCam8K with different EV and shutter speed.

Due to the huge variety of options between the Shutter and the EV presented in the 360-degree camera on Fig. 1(b) only a sample of the different exposure settings are presented. The most important example of this picture taking is the huge difference between EV of 1, taken with different Shutter speeds - 1/100 and 1/10 - the difference is noticeable in Fig. 1(b) above.

3   Stitching Issues

This far we have managed to talk only about the principles of making a good HDRI from a photographer point of view. However there are other problems that could occur when using a 360-degree camera - these problems are mostly motivated by stitching issues, distortion awareness and unwanted artifacts in the image (See and Cheok 2015).

Image stitching and 360-degree stitching is the technology of overlapping images to generate a wider panoramic image. Stitching issues occur because of field of view limitations (FOV limitations). 360-degree cameras use two fisheye lenses, on each side of the device, each capturing a 180-degree angle of view. The two hemispherical images are then stitched together to produce a 360-degree spherical view. To portrait a stitching issue we can view Fig. 2. To eliminate the issues of potential flows in the image and to extend to the HDRI, a seamless method is endorsed. 360-degree cameras have closed-loop stitching - each image is aligned, deformed and projected onto a spherical surface. The software Kandoo uses to stitch together a 360-degree image is based on optical flow. The best way to describe optical flow is through image motion. In videos or animation, a series of images set one after another create a motion, between frames we have a small time step. Optical flow is a technique that calculates the velocity of points within the different frames – but it calculates the point's direction of motion. It is just one of the many algorithms used for stitching images (Lyu et al. 2019).

Fig. 2. Unstitched image taken from QooCam 8k.

Because optical flow calculates not only what is inside the image, but also estimates the camera parameters with great accuracy, the issues with stitching, even in a low-budget camera are few and even non-existing. Most issues of stitching occur while taking 360-degree videos.

4   Parallax Errors

Parallax errors are displacements that appear in the image due to different viewing angles. Due to the 180 fish lenses of the camera, these errors occur especially if the 360-degree camera is too close to the ground. As you can see in Fig. 3, on a tile floor, the parallax error is quite visible. This is why 360-degree photographs are taken using a tripod with approximate height next to a human height. HDRI are effectively positioned in the middle of a sphere, the world position set at (0, 0, 0, 0), so the position of the camera will match the world position in a third-party software. Knowing this while taking a 360-degree camera is customary to turn one of the two lenses to any important part of the environment you are taking. A lens being perpendicular to an object minimizes parallax error.

Having gathered a variety of images taken with a range of shutter speed and EV, the images are ready to be compressed into an HDRI. The Kandoo Studio application can retrieve and re-render the information taken from the camera - stitch from separate lens images and use optical flow to stitch them together into one panoramic image, creating a new image. In this step we can choose the size of the new image. High resolution ensures less distortion of the image, precise shadows and crisp and sharp image. To avoid pixilation in the final image, especially since HDRI is visible in the background for rendering purposes. A third-party software is needed to compress the images into

Fig. 3. Parallax error.

one HDRI with a 32-bit channel. This step will not be described in depth in this article but will be set aside for more in depth study in future work.

However the compression of the HDRI and the stitching are two separate steps which can be taken vice-versa. Lens images can be run by a third-party software and compressed into HDRI before being re-rendered as a whole image by the Kandoo software. It is arguable if images that are first re-rendered through Kandoo are not losing some of their quality as a RAW image as any interaction would further take some quality from the original render.

While testing the HDRI in Unity engine by implementing it on a spherical surface a few artifacts on the top and the bottom of the sphere. Figure 4. Increased number of polygons added to the sphere do not clean the artifact and with a VR headset the errors were even easier to spot.

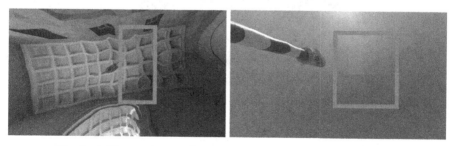

Fig. 4. Artifacts at the top of two HDR images captures in Unity Engine.

5 Results

The best method to cope with these errors is to convert the HDRI into a cubemap, also called skybox. The cubemap method uses six cube faces to fill the whole sphere. Figure 5(a) 360-degree images or HDRI are largely used when the environment needs to be projected onto an object - to stimulate reflections and light. However to make an environment with minimal performance cost and no such errors, developers use the cubemap as a neat solution. Cubemaps are created by six seamless textures with a left, front, right, back, top and bottom texture. Figure 5(b). The illusion of a HDRI stays intact since the center of the engine and the cube remain the same and the cubemap sustains the sharpness of the image without any distortions. Figure 5(c) gives us how a cubemap looks inside the Unity engine. The only part of the image that could occur as an "error" is the shadow the tripod has left on the ground in the HDRI. In a clean HDRI, especially one used as a cubemap. The solution is to clean the image of the shadow using various retouching methods by a third-party application.

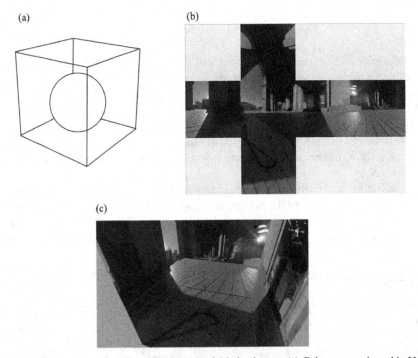

Fig. 5. (a) Cubemap surrounding HDRI. (b) Unfolded cubemap (c) Cubemap as viewed in Unity engine.

References

See, Z.S., Cheok, A.D.: Virtual reality 360 interactive panorama reproduction obstacle and issue. Virtual Reality **19**(2), 71–81 (2015)

Bloch, C.: The HDRI Handbook 2.0: High Dynamic Range Imaging for Photographers and CG Artists. Rocky Nook, Inc. (2012)

Li, J., Yu, K., Zhao, Y., Zhang, Y., Xu, L.: Cross-reference stitching quality assessment for 360° omnidirectional images. In: MM 2019: Proceedings of the 27th ACM International Conference on Multimedia, pp. 2360–2368. October 2019

Lyu, W., Zhaou, Z., Chen, L., Zhou, U.: A survey on image and video stitching. Virtual Reality Intell. Hardw. 1(1), 55–83 (2019)

Akenine-Moller, T., Haines, E., Hoffman, N., Pesce, A., Iwanicki, M., Hillaire, S.: Real-Time Rendering, 4th edn. CRC Press, Boca Raton (2018). ISBN 978-1-1386-2700-0

Do, T.: Development of a tool to create hdri-environments used for rendering. Department of Design Sciences, Master thesis, Lund University (2016)

Bioinformatics: Model Selection and Scientific Visualization

Metodi Traykov[1]([✉]) [iD], Radoslav Mavrevski[2] [iD], Slav Angelov[1] [iD],
and Ivan Trenchev[3] [iD]

[1] New Bulgarian University, Sofia, Bulgaria
mtraykov@nbu.bg, slav_angelov@abv.bg
[2] South-West University "Neofit Rilski", Blagoevgrad, Bulgaria
radoslav_sm@abv.bg
[3] University of Library Studies and Information Technologies, Sofia, Bulgaria

Abstract. Bioinformatics is an interdisciplinary field that develops methods for understanding biological data and solving different bioinformatics problems. Therefore, mathematical models and computer modeling are widely used tools in bioinformatics. Using them, we can analyze different biological systems, predict the outputs from biological processes, or develop new experimental cases for some bioinformatics problems. Therefore, the choice of the optimal mathematical model is essential. The main feature of the selected model must be to provide a balance between the goodness of the data fitting and the model complexity. This article aims to summarize and show the basic criteria for model selection in bioinformatics to develop a reliable approach for predicting different relationships in bioinformatics. In addition, we will briefly describe the application of computer modeling in the analysis of the results obtained by optimal mathematical models for problems in bioinformatics, such as protein folding problems, which is an analysis of biological structures, model selection, bioinformatics. (Review article).

Keywords: Computer modeling · Mathematical models · Model selection · Bioinformatics

1 Introduction

The basics of bioinformatics have been laid in the early 1960s of the last century when the scientists try to study the properties of the protein sequences through complex computational methods, such as de novo sequence assembly or substitution models. The main aim of bioinformatics researches is to propose different methods and models for describing different processes in living organisms, but how to determine which method or model is optimal and how to represent its results. The answers to these questions are in statistics (model selection) and computer modeling (optimizations and computer graphics) [1–4].

The application of nonlinear regression techniques to describe experimental data is widespread across wide areas of bioinformatics. The problem of selecting an "optimal"

© ICST Institute for Computer Sciences, Social Informatics and Telecommunications Engineering 2022
Published by Springer Nature Switzerland AG 2022. All Rights Reserved
T. Zlateva and R. Goleva (Eds.): CSECS 2022, LNICST 450, pp. 92–101, 2022.
https://doi.org/10.1007/978-3-031-17292-2_8

model is a fundamental problem in analyzing experimental data in bioinformatics. If we have a set of competitive mathematical models, we may use different statistical information criteria to find the model that approximates the data better, the so-called model selection process, and data fitting in the statistic. These statistical information criteria are an attractive way for model selection [1, 3–10].

To find an "optimal" model in a set of candidate models, we can use different fitting approaches, such as the least-squares (LS) method and robust (stable) regression (RR), available in more statistical software packages [7]. Akaike's information criterion (AIC) and Bayesian Information Criterion (BIC) are well-known in the literature, as criteria for evaluating models from different classes [7, 10].

Therefore, using the mentioned above criteria we may determine the optimal model in a set of mathematical models for a specific task. For example, there are many mathematical models to solve the Protein folding problem, i.e. to find the protein's tertiary structure, using its primary structure (the sequence of amino acids) [11–16]. Using model selection criteria we may find the optimal model for this problem, but the question with the visualization of the results that the model will generate is still open. The visualization of the results for the protein folding problem is not so easy, because there are many approaches and models to solve the problem, such as the HP protein folding model, and they lead to different kinds of results. This is the reason to have little information about the visualization of these results in model selection [17].

2   Methods

2.1   Fitting Experimental Data

The finding of the individual "optimal" model for a specific class of tasks, can be made using the least-squares method or robust regression fitting by GraphPad Prism, Origin, SPSS, Matlab, or other statistical software (see Fig. 1) [7, 9, 10].

The purpose of the least-squares method is to minimize the sum of squares of the deviations between the points and the curve [5]. The deviations are the distances between Y-values.

2.2   Model Selection Criteria

AKAIKE'S Information Criterion (AIC). The goal of this criterion is to select a model that minimizes the negative probability of penalizing. To achieve this the criterion uses the number of the parameters in the models. It is one of the most commonly used criterion:

$$AIC = \begin{cases} n * \ln\left(\frac{RSS}{n}\right) + 2 * k, \ \frac{n}{k} \geq 40 \\ n * \ln\left(\frac{RSS}{n}\right) + 2 * k + \frac{2*k*(k+1)}{n-k-1}, \ \frac{n}{k} < 40 \end{cases} \tag{1}$$

- Residual Sum of Squares (RSS) – the sum of the squares of deviations of each data point from the curve of the selected "optimal" model;
- k – the number of the parameters mapped by the regression plus 1;

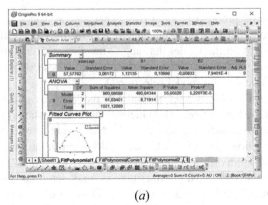

(a)

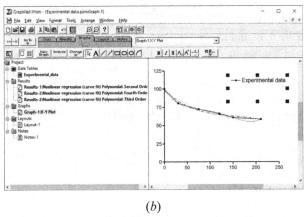

(b)

Fig. 1. Examples for fitting experimental data by least squares method using Origin (a) and GraphPad Prism (b)

- n – the size of the sample.

Bayesian Information Criterion (BIC). BIC has the highest posterior probability. It is similar to AIC [5, 6]. The main difference between AIC and BIC is in the coefficient multiplied by the number of parameters. This coefficient determines how strongly the criteria will penalize large models:

$$BIC = n * \ln\left(\frac{RSS}{n}\right) + k * \ln(n). \qquad (2)$$

The meaning of RSS, n, and k is the same as in the previous model (AIC). Therefore, based on the above definitions, we may say that:

1. The AIC criterion does not depend directly from the sample size.
2. The model that minimizes the BIC criterion will has the highest posterior probability.
3. The BIC criterion penalizes the studied models more than AIC at an increasing number of parameters.

We may conclude that the models selected through BIC will be more parsimonious than those selected through AIC.

Software for Calculating the AIC and BIC Criteria. Below you may see the graphical user interface of a program for the calculation of both criteria (AIC and BIC), according to the mentioned above formulas. We developed this program, and it is described in details in [7]. Figure 2 shows the option in the program for calculating the AIC criterion.

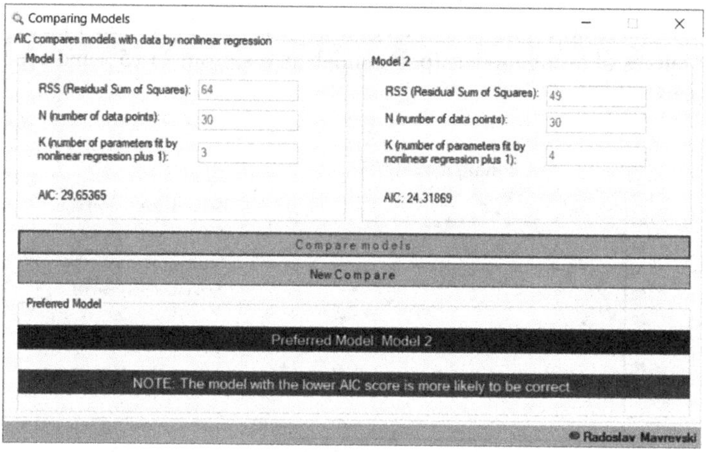

Fig. 2. Calculating the AIC criterion, using the "Comparing Models" software.

2.3 HP Protein Folding Model

The simplest and most used model for protein folding problem is the Hydrophobic-Hydrophilic/Polar model. This model divides the 20th amino acids in the human body into two groups, namely Hydrophilic (H) or Hydrophilic/Polar (P). The process of folding an amino acids sequence in a 2D or 3D lattice leads to a self-avoiding walk, where the main aim is to maximize the number of neighboring H amino acids that are not adjusted in the primary sequence. This is also known as optimal conformation.

The model can be summarized as follow:

Maximize

The contacts between the Hydrophilic amino acids (H-H contacts).
subject to

1. (Connectivity) Every two amino acids that are neighboring in the protein's sequence must occupy neighboring cells in the lattice.
2. (Non-overlapping) Two amino acids cannot share the same cell in the lattice.
3. (Assignment) Each amino acid must occupy exactly one cell in the lattice.

It is proven (using different criteria, such as biological, mathematical, and statistical) that the HP protein folding model is an optimal model and leads to an optimal solution for protein folding problem in 2D or 3D lattices [13, 18, 19].

3 Results and Discussion

The least-squares method is most widely used in different fields of bioinformatics. The model selection criteria can ignore both the statistical adequacy and the reliability of the conclusions about the problem. For this reason, the assessment needs to be made, based on more than one model selection criterion. The next figure (see Fig. 3) shows an example of curves of fitting models (polynomial curves, from 2 to 5°) and experimental data (30 points).

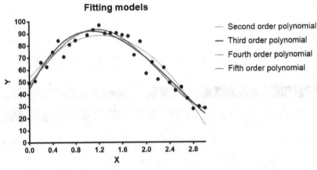

Fig. 3. Curves of fitting models (polynomials curves, from 2 to 5°) and experimental data (30 points)

Generally, the AIC and/or BIC criteria are very appropriate methods in order to select an "optimal" model with the smallest mean square error. Both criteria will choose the optimal model that has the relatively same error for each experimental data point. The criteria will return as result a value that represents a compromise between the complexity of the model (the number of parameters) and the accuracy (Table 1).

Table 1. Model selection (assessment) from different classes by **AIC** and **BIC**

Polynomial class model	Number of data points	Number of parameters	AIC value	BIC value
Second degree	30	3	128.93	132.94
Third degree		4	118.47	122.97
Fourth degree		5	**117.08**	**121.84**
Fifth degree		6	120.35	125.07

3.1   HP Protein Folding Model

There are many models to solve the protein folding problem, as we mentioned above. We may find the optimal model for this problem, using different criteria (such as AIC or BIC) and approaches (statistically, mathematical, biological, and so on.). Once we identify the optimal model, we may solve it, using optimization software (such as CPLEX or GUROBI) or implementing it in an application. In most cases the models for solving the protein folding problem generate the results as numbers, 2D or 3D coordinates of the amino acids, after that we need any additional software to draw the obtained protein conformation. The figure (see Fig. 4) below shows software with the name "HP Folding Visualization" (developed and presented by us) for visualization of a solution for the protein folding problem in the 2D HP lattice model [17].

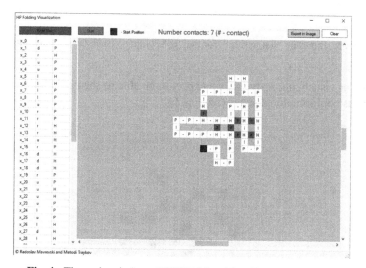

Fig. 4. The main window of "HP Folding Visualization" software.

Figure 5 shows the results (the input data for the "HP Folding Visualization" software), obtained by the selected model (2D HP lattice model) for the problem.

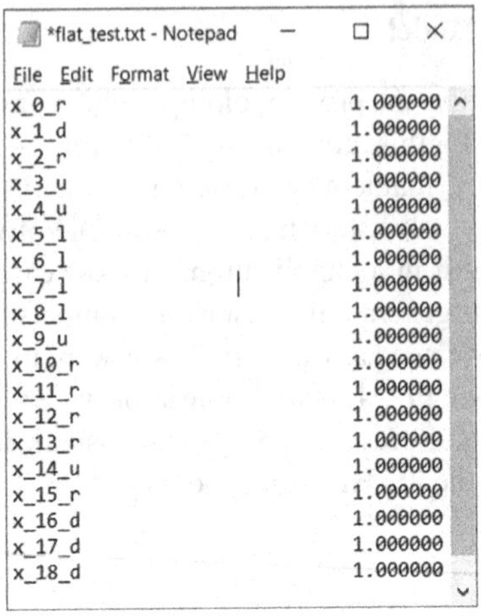

```
*flat_test.txt - Notepad
File Edit Format View Help
x_0_r       1.000000
x_1_d       1.000000
x_2_r       1.000000
x_3_u       1.000000
x_4_u       1.000000
x_5_l       1.000000
x_6_l       1.000000
x_7_l       1.000000
x_8_l       1.000000
x_9_u       1.000000
x_10_r      1.000000
x_11_r      1.000000
x_12_r      1.000000
x_13_r      1.000000
x_14_u      1.000000
x_15_r      1.000000
x_16_d      1.000000
x_17_d      1.000000
x_18_d      1.000000
```

Fig. 5. Input file "flat_test.txt" for the "HP Folding Visualization" software.

Using our visualizing software, we expect to be able to shed light on the nature of these various conformational states (see Fig. 6).

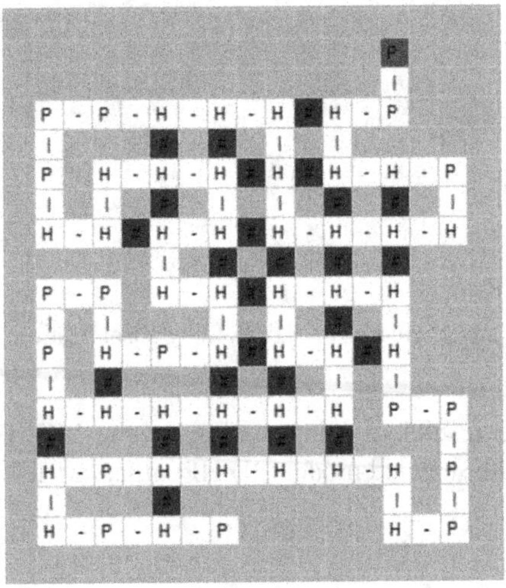

Fig. 6. Visualization of obtained solution for protein with a length of 60 amino acids (27 H-H contacts).

The next figure (see Fig. 7) shows optimal solutions in 3D. The results were obtained using an algorithm, based on HP folding model and described in [20]. The 3D visualization software follows the same approach as in the "HP Folding Visualization" software.

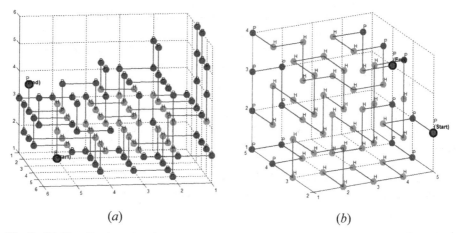

(a)   *(b)*

Fig. 7. 3D Visualization of optimal solutions for protein folding problem: (a) 102 amino acids, (b) 60 amino acids (MATLAB).

Figure 8 shows a visualization of results obtained by the 3D HP off-lattice model for the problem.

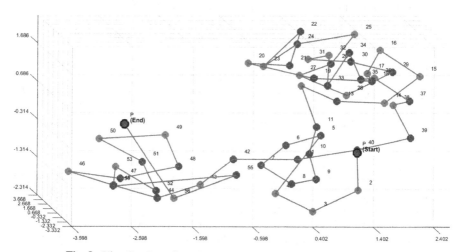

Fig. 8. Visualization of results in 3D HP off-lattice model (MATLAB).

4 Conclusions

Usually, finding a specific model in a set of models can be done through various fitting methods, e.g. the least-squares method (the most widely used) or robust fitting. Based on the results described in Sect. 3 (section "Results and Discussion") we may conclude:

1. The AIC criterion leads to relatively well results for samples with small sizes. The criterion is inconsistent.
2. The BIC criterion has poor performance in samples with small sizes, but it is consistent. This criterion leads to better results when we increase the sizes of the samples.

Generally, the current results suggest the use of the AIC criterion in the model selection process for samples with small sizes and the BIC criterion for larger samples. However, we recommend using both criteria for a more accurate assessment.

About the visualization, in the protein folding problem, developed by us visualization software are potential tools that can be helpful to study in details the folding trajectories and the number of contacts between amino acids in protein folding.

References

1. Acquah, H.: Comparison of Akaike information criterion (AIC) and Bayesian information criterion (BIC) in selection of an asymmetric price relationship. J. Dev. Agric. Econ. **2**, 1–6 (2010)
2. Ahn, S.J.: Geometric fitting of parametric curves and surfaces. J. Inf. Process. Syst. **4**, 153–158 (2008)
3. Akaike, H.: A new look at the statistical model identification. IEEE Trans. Autom. Control **19**, 716–772 (1974)
4. Bickel, P., Zhang, P.: Variable selection in nonparametric regression with categorical covariates. J. Am. Stat. Assoc. **87**, 90–97 (1992)
5. Burnham, P., Anderson, D.: Model Selection and Multimodel Inference, 2nd edn. Springer-Verlag, New York (2002). https://doi.org/10.1007/b97636
6. Joseph, B., Nicole, L.: Methods and criteria for model selection. J. Am. Statist. Assoc. **99**, 279–290 (2004)
7. Mavrevski, R.: Selection and comparison of regression models: estimation of torque-angle relationships. C. R. Acad. Bulg. Sci. **67**, 1345–1354 (2014)
8. Dzimbova, T., Sapundzhi, F., Pencheva, N., Milanov, P.: Computer modeling of human delta opioid receptor. Int. J. Bioautom. **17**, 5–16 (2013)
9. Mavrevski, R., Milanov, P., Traykov, M., Pencheva, N.: Performance comparison of model selection criteria by generated experimental data. In: ITM Web of Conferences, vol. 16 (2018) https://doi.org/10.1051/itmconf/20181602006
10. Mavrevski, R., Traykov, M., Trenchev, I., Trencheva, M.: Approaches to modeling of biological experimental data with graphpad prism software. Wseas Trans. Syst. Control **13**, 242–247 (2018)
11. Ahn, N., Park, S.: Finding an upper bound for the number of contacts in hydrophobic-hydrophilic protein structure prediction model. J. Comput. Biol. **17**, 647–656 (2010)
12. Alberts, B., Bray, D., Johnson, A., et al.: Essential Cell Biology: An Introduction to the Molecular Biology of the Cell. Garland Science Publishing, New York (1998)
13. Berger, B., Leighton, T.: Protein folding in the hydrophobic-hydrophilic (HP) is NP-complete. J. Comput. Biol. **5**, 27–40 (1998)
14. Carr, R., Hart, W., Newman, A.: Discrete optimization models for protein folding. Technical report SAND2002. Sandia National Laboratories (2003)
15. Chen, M., Huang, W.: A branch and bound algorithm for the protein folding problem in the HP lattice model. Genomics Proteomics Bioinf. **3**, 225–230 (2005)

16. Chandru, V., Rao, M., Swaminathan, G.: Protein folding on lattices: an integer programming approach. IIM Bangalore Research Paper No. 199 (2004)
17. Mavrevski, R., Traykov, M.: Visualization software for hydrophobic-polar protein folding model. Sci. Vis. **11**(1), 11–19 (2019)
18. Dill, K.A.: Theory for the folding and stability of globular proteins. Biochemistry **24**, 1501–1509 (1985)
19. Dill, K.A., Bromberg, S., Yue, K., et al.: Principles of protein folding. A perspective from simple exact models. Protein Sci. **4**, 561–602 (1995)
20. Yanev, N., Traykov, M., Milanov, P., Yurukov, B.: Protein folding prediction in a cubic lattice in hydrophobic-polar model. J. Comput. Biol. **24**, 412–421 (2017)

Estimating COVID Case Fatality Rate in Bulgaria for 2020–2021

Latchezar Tomov[1]([⊠]) [iD], Hristiana Batselova[2] [iD], and Tsvetelina V. Velikova[3] [iD]

[1] Department of Informatics, New Bulgarian University, 1618 Sofia, Bulgaria
lptomov@nbu.bg
[2] Department of Epidemiology and Hygiene, University Hospital "Saint George", Medical University, 6000 Plovdiv, Bulgaria
dr_batselova@abv.bg
[3] Department of Clinical Immunology, University Hospital Lozenetz, Sofia University St. Kliment Ohridski, 1407 Sofia, Bulgaria
Tsvelikova@medfac.mu-sofia.bg

Abstract. We estimate the case fatality rate from COVID-19 with our method by age groups for three waves - September 2020 to January 2021 (wild type), February 2021 to May 2021 (alpha), and July 2021 to January 2022 (delta). We use linear regression with optimal lag with 21 days moving averaging to correct for reporting delays. We take the coefficient from the regression as the case fatality ratio. We unite the lower age groups into one to achieve a good correlation. We have new cases by age group and deaths by age group and sex. Our results indicate that the delta variant is more severe than alpha, and this is enough to outweigh any improvements in treatment since the first major wave, 14.08.2020–01.01.2021.

Keywords: COVID-19 · Case fatality rate · Delta wave · Statistics · Linear regression

1 Introduction

1.1 The COVID-19 Global Pandemic

At the end of 2019, the first reports of clusters of pneumonia with unknown etiology appeared in Wuhan City, Hubei Province of China. Many of the patients were linked with a wet seafood market where other wildlife species were also sold. An unknown virus was isolated from all the patients, and molecular analysis has proven that the pathogen was a new coronavirus (CoV). The scientist first named it 2019-nCoV, and the name of the disease was given by WHO- COVID-19. The virus was widespread and, from an outbreak in Wuhan, turned into a public health emergency of international concern [1].

For decades Coronaviruses have been known to be a high pandemic risk. SARS-CoV-2 is the ninth coronavirus known to be a pathogen to humans and the seventh identified in the last 20 years [2]. All human coronaviruses are proven to be with zoonotic origins. The emergence of SARS-CoV-2 had many similarities to SARS-CoV that appeared

T. Zlateva and R. Goleva (Eds.): CSECS 2022, LNICST 450, pp. 102–115, 2022.
https://doi.org/10.1007/978-3-031-17292-2_9

among humans in Foshan, Guangdong province, China, in November 2002 and again in Guangzhou, Guangdong province, in 2003 [3].

All of these SARS-CoV emergence cases among humans were linked to markets where live animals were sold, particularly civets and raccoon dogs [4], and were also sold live in Wuhan markets in 2019 [5] and are known to be a host of SARS-CoV-2 [6, 7].

COVID-19 is an infectious respiratory illness caused by the severe acute respiratory syndrome–coronavirus 2 (SARS-CoV-2) [8]. Since May 2022 WHO reported 512,607,587 confirmed cases of COVID-19, including 6,243,038 deaths [9]. The median incubation period of COVID-19 ranges from 5 to 6 days [10].

COVID-19 can affect any age group, and all humans are susceptible. However, the risk for severe disease is higher in the elderly and patients with comorbidities such as cardiovascular disease, diabetes mellitus, chronic respiratory disease, hypertension, and cancer can experience worse outcomes [11]. Therefore, the consequences of the infection depend on the interplay between the viral and immune mechanisms [10].

1.2 The COVID-19 Pandemic in Bulgaria

The first person to test positive for SARS-2-COV was on 08.03.2020 [12]. The Bulgarian government acted swiftly before the clusters transitioned into diffusion, thus stopping the first wave [13]. The first wave started in the middle of August - there was a transient spike in June and July due to the ending of lockdown and temporarily removing all measures on the 15th of June [14], coupled with holiday migrations from the big cities towards the countryside and the Black sea coastline. The seasonal autumn wave accelerated when schools opened with very few measures and was reversed after the gradual transition towards online education in schools [15]. The second wave started on 01.01.2021 and was driven by a new variant, called "alpha", which soon became dominant. The third wave was driven by the Delta variant and infected and killed the most people – almost 40% of all deaths from these three waves are from the third one – the three large waves took approximately 8000,10000 and 12000 each with 200 000,220 000 and over 300 000 infected. A crude estimate of overall mortality risk shows 4%, 4.5% and 4%, which could lead to an incorrect assessment of risks for the waves. That's why we need a better estimation of the Case Fatality Rate (CFR, %), separate for all waves and age groups. Furthermore, different age groups have different average lags between infection and death, which introduces variance in an estimation method, that only incorporates single lag.

2 Methods

We have data from the open portal for new cases by age groups since 06.06.2020 [16] and data for new deaths by age groups since 09.03.2020 [16, 17]. The data between 09.03.2020 and 5.6.2020 is gathered and prepared manually from the coronavirus website by Ralitza Ilieva-Markova, our assistant.

Several different methods for estimating case fatality rate (CFR,%) exist. Possibly the simplest is to get the ratio between deaths and the new cases with some lag and obtain a function with varying values at varying moments of time. Its mean value could be used for the case fatality ratio [18]. Another approach is to use a linear or polynomial regression [19]. This crude case fatality ratio has some limitations - it does not disseminate by risk factors such as age, sex, and comorbidities. For such purposes, a much more sophisticated method is employed in various risk calculators in the UK, for example [20]. Time series analysis is also a viable option that can be scaled for more detailed or limited data [21]. These models are useful for predicting actual mortality during a particular wave but do not give a single value for CFR by age group. A single value is more valuable in communication with authorities when discussing policies to prevent or mitigate a pandemic and its subsequent medium and long term effects on the public health an the public health system.

Furthermore, the adjustment of lags of predictors is not an automated procedure. We need an estimate for CFR by age for the different waves, driven by different conditions such as different infected populations, different variants, etc. This way, we can compare the variants and their "burden" in the first approximation. Our data for Bulgaria is very limited - no detailed info for comorbidities of the deceased, no sex for the infected, comorbidities of infected, no seroprevalence study, etc. We do not need a complicated method for CFR analysis, so we use simple linear regression. What is new is our algorithm, because we identified waves by objective markers such as the effective reproductive number and/or changepoint analysis. We also used the sample cross-correlation function to extract the optimal lag (with the highest correlation between new cases and deaths) for the deceased. We used the coefficient of the linear regression for our case fatality ratio. We applied a longer moving average with a 21-day-period both to the new cases by age group and the deceased by age group to correct for noise from random delays and periodicity in reporting on a weekly basis. This is the largest possible n-weekly period that does not alter the dynamics of the processes. We use the Robert Koch formula for the effective reproductive number R_t [22] - we don't need a more complicated method for our goals. We use the non-commercial software GNU Octave for our purpose.

The defining criteria for waves are formed from a minimum value of calculated R_t in proximity or coinciding with changepoints. Analysis of regime change from [13]- Fig. 1. This is not yet fully automated criteria since there are multiple local extrema of calculated R_t (Fig. 2) in the period between two waves and, in some cases, more than one changepoint. However, this could be automated as *"the last local minima in R_t in the proximity of changepoint before a prolonged period of $R_t > 1$"* (the length of the period being at least twice longer than the longest period before two successive local extrema in the "in-between" zone, also the "proximity" needs to be quantified). The three waves according to these criteria are Wave 1: 14.08.2020– 01.01.2021, Wave 2: 02.01.2021–30.06.2021, and Wave 3: 01.07.2021–27.12.2022.

3   Results and Discussion

In the period 2020–2021, there were three major waves of this pandemic, attacking different subpopulations with different age and comorbidities. Although we do not have access to the data for comorbidities, they strongly correlate with age. We believe that estimating the case fatality rate has some meaning, especially for pandemic control policies and healthcare management, due to the exponential nature of the hospitalization risk and the different CFR in different waves. There are more suitable models to predict deaths from new cases, and we explored some of them in previous publications [21]. However, having a single number per age group is useful in forming policies and communicating risks towards the general population and the responsible government officials in charge of these policies.

The results from our almost completely automated procedure are shown for the three waves in Table 1, 2 and 3, respectively, and in Figs. 3, 4 and 5 (Wave 1), Figs. 6, 7 and 8 (Wave 2), Figs 9, 10 and 11 (Wave 3). In Tables 1, 2 and 3, we give the estimated CFR for 10 different models - the linear regression coefficient for each age group, their p values, their t-stats and the RMSE of the linear regressions, showing how close are the actual death counts to the model fit. We give two of the models in Fig. 13–14 as examples – the fit for age group 70–79 for the first wave an 90+ for the third wave. The comparisons of the three waves (Fig. 12) show several interesting results:

- The risk of death exponentially increases with age up to 70 years of age, after which there is saturation. This could have several different explanations, one of which is the lower probability of surviving 80+ years of age with many comorbidities and the lack of control for such in our research due to lack of data.
- The delays between new cases and deaths from wave 2, driven mostly by variant alpha, are decreased compared to the first wave, driven by the wild-type virus. This indicates increased severity and corresponds to anecdotal evidence from doctors in Bulgaria's COVID wards and research [23].
- Adjusted R^2 for Wave 2 is smaller than in the other waves, reflecting more dispersion around the maximum correlation – the maximum correlation with the optimal lag is not as high due to substantial contributions from other lags – or the deaths are more spread out in time than in the other waves. A single number here captures the mortality risk a bit worse than in the other waves.
- Despite the increased severity of alpha, the estimated case fatality rate is substantially lower than in Wave 1. This could be explained by the substantial increase in testing (this is case fatality rate, not infection fatality rate) and/or by improvements in treatment, but also partially with the smaller correlations in model estimation (hidden mortality risks)
- Delay for children is substantially higher, and mortality risks are considerably lower. However, a good model fit was successful only for the first wave. This could also be due to a change in reporting of deaths (listing the comorbidities as a primary cause of death).
- Delta showed CFR, similar to the first wave despite increased testing and improved treatment protocol, but early signs of an overburdened hospital system [24]. There were also substantial reinfections that work towards decreased CFR [25]. The Delta wave also happened in a partially vaccinated population [26]. This indicates significantly increased severity of the Delta variant, which as a hypothesis needs additional research to support it.

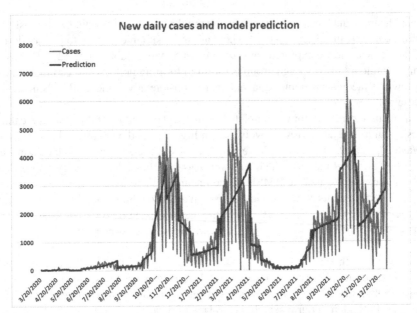

Fig. 1. Model prediction of COVID-19 daily cases with automatic detection of regime changes and stochastic modeling of trajectories [13]. The points of discontinuity refer to regime changes.

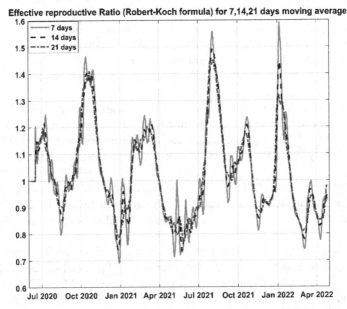

Fig. 2. Effective reproduction ratio, estimated by the formula of Robert Koch institute with 4 days of the incubation period for moving average of daily cases with periods of 7,14 and 21 days.

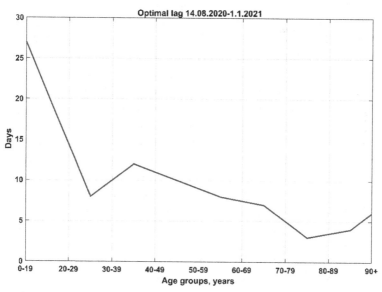

Fig. 3. Optimal lag of sample cross-correlation between new cases and deaths per age group for Wave 1.

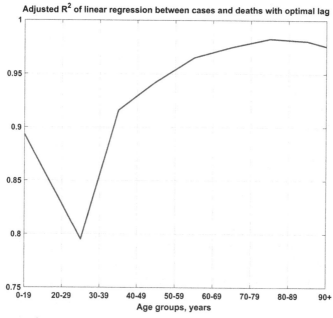

Fig. 4. Adjusted R^2 of the linear regression between new cases and deaths with optimal lag per age group for Wave 1.

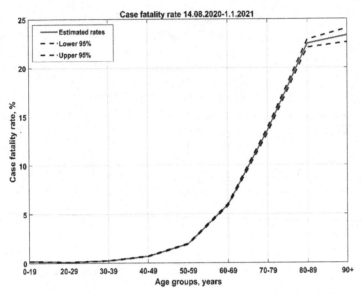

Fig. 5. Estimated case fatality rate and 95% confidence intervals as the coefficient from linear regression with optimal lag per age group for Wave 1.

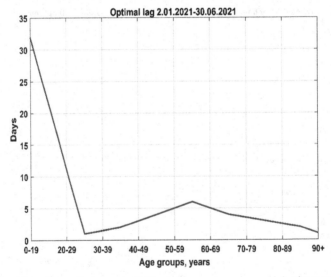

Fig. 6. Optimal lag of sample cross-correlation between new cases and deaths per age group for Wave 2.

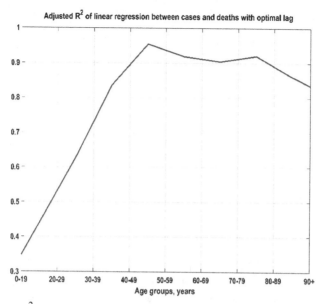

Fig. 7. Adjusted R^2 of the linear regression between new cases and deaths with optimal lag per age group for Wave 2.

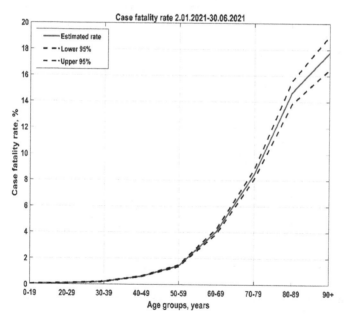

Fig. 8. Estimated case fatality rate and 95% confidence intervals as the coefficient from linear regression with optimal lag per age group for Wave 2.

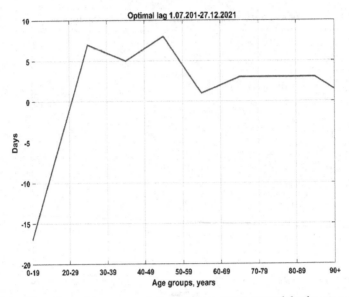

Fig. 9. Optimal lag of sample cross-correlation between new cases and deaths per age group for Wave 3.

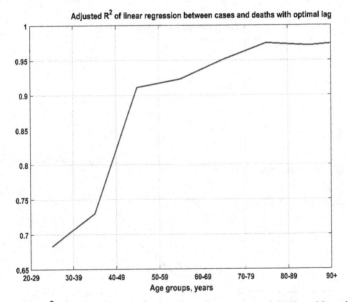

Fig. 10. Adjusted R^2 of the linear regression between new cases and deaths with optimal lag per age group for Wave 3.

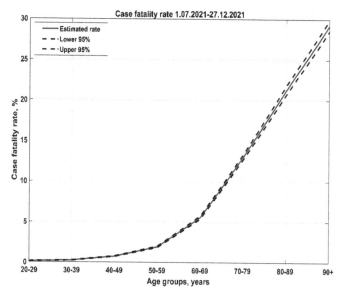

Fig. 11. Estimated case fatality rate and 95% confidence intervals as the coefficient from linear regression with optimal lag per age group for Wave 2.

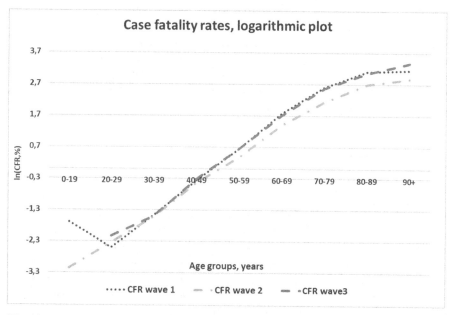

Fig. 12. Comparison of the estimated case fatality rates for the three waves (logarithmic plot).

Table 1. Estimated CFR and model parameters for Wave 1

Age group	CFR,%	T-stat	P value	RMSE
0–19	0.185343422487180	38.9110979328123	1.30817035064048e−76	0.021732
20–29	0.0814640663243919	18.2326275468917	1.09988316471984e−38	0.055223
30–39	0.230159017738559	38.7935582526591	1.92310126757591e−76	0.144791
40–49	0.689188248236168	53.6055189594344	9.84784198059810e−95	0.379568
50–59	1.93038503082146	92.9271625360074	5.23345933982721e−127	0.633749
60–69	5.93965884283796	105.184425073305	2.20675477239857e−134	1.452484
70–79	13.5895553151869	92.9362143877190	5.16418027007381e−127	2.218877
80–89	22.4676792760740	108.672603974902	2.49925803109170e−136	1.061962
90+	23.3160356243301	64.6250278180166	1.38759960707132e−105	0.167789

CFR: ...Case Fatality Rate..........; RMSE: ......Root Mean Square Error.......

Table 2. Estimated CFR and model parameters for Wave 2.

Age group	CFR,%	T-stat	P value	RMSE
0–19	0.0422356296567256	9.79693481057488	2.22851007371688e−18	0.021509
20–29	0.0956918315236564	17.2611764374006	8.70168515847137e−40	0.063986
30–39	0.217996100910862	30.2424115433259	7.80149815693797e−72	0.151505
40–49	0.638694058840290	60.9730277484419	9.46038326682465e−121	0.277128
50–59	1.44984967745342	44.9122024954124	1.09579425737544e−98	0.899099
60–69	4.07056706902815	41.0765543261353	2.01408414848497e−92	2.681178
70–79	8.45935083431752	45.4107576525972	1.81346937173692e−99	3.646795
80–89	14.7076759170350	33.2386618263124	5.15824052965261e−78	2.81023
90+	17.7741156731515	27.3619701862002	1.72506047259888e−65	0.32967

CFR: ...Case Fatality Rate..........; RMSE: ......Root Mean Square Error.......

Table 3. Estimated CFR and model parameters for Wave 3.

Age group	CFR,%	T-stat	P value	RMSE
0–19	-	-	-	-
20–29	0.118384398162955	19.6531966249049	1.83592637752605e−46	0.094262
30–39	0.223735563220952	22.0294355443674	9.96578783625195e−53	0.281782
40–49	0.729399256401650	42.8391931708295	1.09018475772862e−95	0.556642
50–59	1.90537446158302	46.3166942774476	3.14992631355092e−101	1.164027
60–69	5.52926275243861	58.9483408966994	9.98593754990433e−119	2.371468
70–79	12.9733371591063	82.6712913696373	6.11083999904439e−144	3.00583
80–89	21.2299468812402	77.3111919608126	6.73558995179243e−139	1.906377
90+	29.2022949933292	85.5649458137322	1.55419014993249e−146	0.210967

CFR: ...Case Fatality Rate..........; RMSE: ......Root Mean Square Error.......

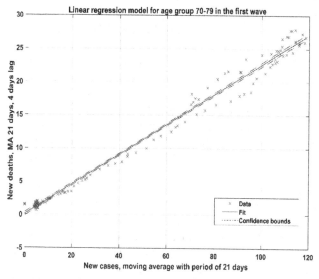

Fig. 13. Example of linear regression model, generated by our algorithm – linear regression for age group 70–79 years old with lag of 4 days.

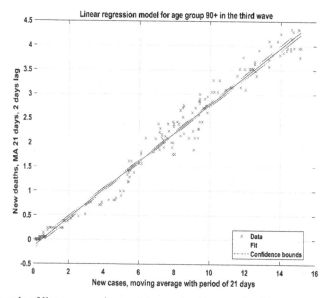

Fig. 14. Example of linear regression model, generated by our algorithm – linear regression for age group 90+ years old.

4   Conclusion

The goal of this research is to compare case fatality rates of different covid-19 waves by age groups in order to obtain first approximation of the burden of different waves in terms of lethality. There are other models, that the authors use to predict deaths by age groups, and to predict excess mortality, but they are not easy to communicate to authorities – there is need of single number for CFR instead of complicated model, to compare visually the different waves and to assist in development of new policies. For this reason, a broader spectrum of models, methods and algorithms needs to be employed, to deliver the messages with the adequate level of complexity to policymakers. This method is not new, its implementation is novel – using optimum lags for different age groups from cross-correlation analysis, and application of larger periods for smoothing of data due to large delays of reporting of deaths an weekly periodicity. More complex models (part of ongoing research) are used to detect the start and the end of different waves.

Our results indicate that the delta variant is more severe than alpha, which is enough to outweigh any improvements in treatment since the first significant wave. The crude methods of estimation give higher burden of the alpha wave, because they do not adjust by age. The larger absolute number of deaths during the alpha wave was from the significant increase of the proportion of people over 60 years old. Furthermore, low vaccination coverage and lack of effective measurements led to more significant waves. Additionally, we confirmed that the CFR is valuable parameter to evaluate, follow up and compare waves by age groups.

References

1. Sun, J., et al.: COVID-19: epidemiology, evolution, and cross-disciplinary perspectives. Trends Mol. Med. **26**(5), 483–495 (2020). ISSN 1471-4914
2. Lednicky, A., et al.: Emergence of porcine delta-coronavirus pathogenic infections among children in Haiti through independent zoonoses and convergent evolution. medRxiv (2021). https://doi.org/10.1101/2021.03.19.21253391
3. Xu, R.H., et al.: Epidemiologic clues to SARS origin in ChinaEmerg. Infect. Dis. **10**, 1030–1037 (2004)
4. Guan, Y., et al.: Isolation and characterization of viruses related to the SARS coronavirus from animals in southern China. Science **302**, 276–278 (2003)
5. Close, R.H., et al.: Epidemiologic clues to SARS origin in China. Emerg. Infect. Dis. **10**, 1030–1037 (2004)
6. Freuling, C.M., et al.: Susceptibility of raccoon dogs for experimental SARS-CoV-2 infection Emerg. Infect. Dis. **26**, 2982–2985 (2020)
7. Edward, C., et al.: The origins of SARS-CoV-2: a critical review. Cell **184**(19), 4848–4856 (2021)
8. Dhar Chowdhury, S., Oommen, A.M.: Epidemiology of COVID-19. J. Dig. Endosc. **11**(1), 3–7 (2020). https://doi.org/10.1055/s-0040-1712187
9. https://covid19.who.int. WHO Coronavirus (COVID-19) Dashboard. Accessed 06 May 2022
10. Linton, N.M., Kobayashi, T., Yang, Y.: Incubation period and other epidemiological characteristics of 2019 novel Coronavirus infections with right truncation: a statistical analysis of publicly available case data. J Clin Med. **9**(02), E538–E538 (2020)
11. Wu, Z., McGoogan, J.M.: Characteristics of and important lessons from the Coronavirus disease 2019 (COVID-19) outbreak in China: summary of a report of 72 314 cases from the Chinese Center for Disease Control and Prevention. JAMA 2020;(e-pub ahead of print). doi https://doi.org/10.1001/jama.2020.2648

12. https://bnr.bg/post/101237668/potvardeni-sa-dva-sluchaa-na-koronavirus-v-balggaria. Accessed 06 May 2022
13. Tchorbadjieff, A., Tomov, L.P., Velev, V., Dezhov, G. Manev, V., Mayster, P.: On regime changes of Covid-19 outbreak. J. Appl. Stat. (2020, under review)
14. https://news.lex.bg/%D0%BF%D1%80%D0%B5%D0%BC%D0%B8%D0%B5%D1%80%D1%8A%D1%82-%D1%81%D0%BB%D0%B5%D0%B4-15-%D1%8E%D0%BD%D0%B8-%D0%BE%D1%82%D0%BF%D0%B0%D0%B4%D0%B0%D1%82-%D0%B2%D1%81%D0%B8%D1%87%D0%BA%D0%B8-%D0%BC%D0%B5/. Accessed 06 May 2022
15. Tomov, L., Lazova, S., Velikova, T.S., Batselova, Hr.: Epidemiology of COVID-19 spread in Bulgaria. In: National Cardiologic Conference on Covid-19, Bulgaria, 19–20th November (2021). https://doi.org/10.13140/RG.2.2.12061.18403
16. https://data.egov.bg/data/resourceView/8f62cfcf-a979-46d4-8317-4e1ab9cbd6a8. Accessed 06 May 2022
17. http://coronavirus.bg. Accessed 06 May 2022
18. Baud, D., Qi, X., Nielsen-Saines, K., Musso, D., Pomar, L., Favre, G.: Real estimates of mortality following COVID-19 infection. Lancet Infect Dis. **20**(7), 773 (2020) https://doi.org/10.1016/S1473-3099(20)30195-X. PMID: 32171390; PMCID: PMC7118515
19. Suleiman, A.A., Suleiman, A., Abdullahi, U.A., Suleiman, S.A.: Estimation of the case fatality rate of COVID-19 epidemiological data in Nigeria using statistical regression analysis. Biosaf. Health, 3(1), 4–7 (2021), Öztoprak et al., COVID-19: Turkey's epidemiology; March 2020.https://doi.org/10.14744/ejmo.2020.60998
20. Hippisley-Cox, J., Coupland, C.A., Mehta, N., Keogh, R.H., Diaz-Ordaz, K., Khunti, K., et al.: Risk prediction of covid-19 related death and hospital admission in adults after covid-19 vaccination: national prospective cohort study. BMJ, **374**, n2244 (2021) https://doi.org/10.1136/bmj.n2244
21. Tomov, L., Tchorbadjieff, A., Angelov, S.: Age-specific mortality risk from Covid-19 in Bulgaria. Comput. Sci. Educ. Comput. Sci. (2021, accepted)
22. Georg, Q.: The reproduction number and its measurement. A critique of the Robert Koch Institute. (2020). https://doi.org/10.13140/RG.2.2.29012.83849
23. Grint, D.J., et al.: Severity of SARS-CoV-2 alpha variant (B.1.1.7) in England. Clin Infect Dis. (2021). Ciab754
24. Tomov, L.P., Batselova, H.M., Velikova, T.V.: COVID-19 Delta wave caused early overburden of hospital capacity in the Bulgarian healthcare system in 2021. Healthcare **10**(4), 600 (2022). https://doi.org/10.3390/healthcare10040600
25. Marinov, G.K., Mladenov, M., Rangachev, A., Alexiev, I.: SARS-CoV-2 reinfections during the first three major COVID-19 waves in Bulgaria. https://doi.org/10.1101/2022.03.11.22271527
26. https://vaccinetracker.ecdc.europa.eu/public/extensions/covid-19/vaccine-tracker.html#uptake-tab. Accessed 06 May 2022

Pregnancy Outcomes in Women with Pregestational Diabetes

Linpeiyu Ji[1] (ID), Zhaoyu Li[1,3] (ID), Mary Lucas[1,4] (ID), Irena Vodenska[2] (ID),
Lou Chitkushev[1] (ID), and Guang Lan Zhang[1(✉)] (ID)

[1] Department of Computer Science, Metropolitan College, Boston University, Boston,
MA 02215, USA
guanglan@bu.edu
[2] Administrative Sciences Department, Metropolitan College, Boston University, Boston,
MA 02215, USA
[3] Krieger School of Arts and Science, Johns Hopkins University, Baltimore, MD 21218, USA
[4] College of Computing and Informatics, Drexel University, Philadelphia, PA 19104, USA

Abstract. Using data from the Truven Health Analytics MarketScan Databases,
we study the characteristics of pregnant patients with pregestational diabetes and
their pregnancy outcomes. We investigate whether there is a significant difference
in pregnancy outcomes between women who have pregestational diabetes and
those who don't. We find that patients with pregestational diabetes stay hospitalized longer and that pregestational diabetes is associated with a higher risk of
delivering high birth weight babies and preeclampsia.

Keywords: Pregestational diabetes · Preeclampsia · Preterm delivery · High
birth weight · Cesarean delivery

1 Introduction

The ACOG (the American College of Obstetricians and Gynecologists) December 2018
practice bulletin pointed out that pregestational diabetes is one of the most challenging
complications of pregnancy. It not only requires frequent monitoring and medication
adjustments for the mother but also increases the risk of maternal and fetal complications
[1]. From 3.1% to 6.8% of women of reproductive age have diabetes, with pregestational
diabetes observed in 1–2% of all pregnancies [1]. Pregestational diabetes is associated
with multiple adverse pregnancy outcomes such as preeclampsia, macrosomia, cesarean
delivery, preterm delivery, congenital malformation, and glucose tolerance [2].

We retrospectively studied pregnant patients with pregestational diabetes and their
pregnancy outcomes. We compared them with those of pregnant patients without pregestational diabetes in 2008 using the Truven Health MarketScan Commercial Claims and
Encounters Database. The questions underlying our study are: 1) Is there a significant difference in pregnancy outcomes between women who have pregestational diabetes compared to those who don't? 2) Do patients with pregestational diabetes stay hospitalized
longer than those without diabetes?

T. Zlateva and R. Goleva (Eds.): CSECS 2022, LNICST 450, pp. 116–125, 2022.
https://doi.org/10.1007/978-3-031-17292-2_10

2   Material and Methods

The dataset used for this study was the Truven Health MarketScan Commercial Claims and Encounters Database, which records health insurance plan enrollment and captures person-specific, clinical utilization expenditure across inpatient, outpatient, and prescription drug services on millions of individuals (active employees and dependents, early (non-Medicare) retirees and dependents, and COBRA continues annually, covered by over 100 health plans and self-insured employers. Each inpatient admission record includes the principal diagnosis and up to fourteen secondary diagnosis codes, and each outpatient record includes the principal diagnosis and up to two secondary diagnosis codes. The diagnoses were coded in ICD-9-CM codes (International Classification of Diseases, 9th revision, Clinical Modification) before 2015.

We focused on pregnancy resulting in live births in 2008. Women 12 to 55 years old with continuous health insurance coverage for at least 12 months before and two months after the live birth were included in the study. The year 2008 inpatient visits of admission type 3 (maternity and newborn) and outpatient service data from January 1st, 2007 to February 28th, 2009 were used in the study. As shown in Fig. 1, after applying the specified study eligibility criteria, we ended up with 5437 patients in Group 1 (no pregestational diabetes) and 731 patients in Group 2 (with pregestational diabetes). The ICD-9-CM codes used in the study are listed in Table 1. All data analysis was carried out using the Python programming language.

We first compared the characteristics of the two groups of patients, including their age distribution and length of stay. We then assessed four adverse outcomes: preeclampsia, preterm delivery, high birth weight, and cesarean delivery. We used risk ratio (RR) to describe the relative risks of the four adverse outcomes between the two groups. The risk ratio, also called relative risk, is defined as the ratio of the probability of an outcome in an exposed group to the probability of the outcome in an control group [5]. We calculated it by dividing the risk (cumulative incidence) in Group 2 by the risk in Group 1,

$$\text{Risk Ratio} = \frac{\text{CIe}}{\text{CIc}} \tag{1}$$

where CIe is the cumulative incidence in the exposed group (Group 2) and CIc is the cumulative incidence in the control group (Group 1).

118   L. Ji et al.

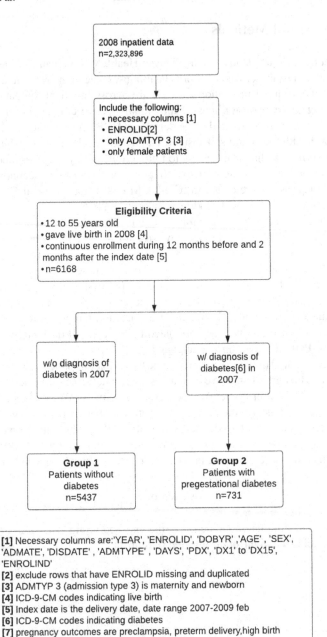

Fig. 1. Flowchart for the patient selection process.

Table 1. The ICD-9-CM codes used to identify various conditions and outcomes [4].

Category	Description	ICD-9-CM codes
Pregnancy type	Live birth, term delivery	645, 650, 766.2, 649.8, 765.29
	Live birth, preterm delivery	765.0, 765.1, 644.21, 765.20, 765.21, 765.22, 765.23, 765.24, 765.25, 765.26, 765.27, 765.28
	Live birth, unknown timing of delivery	V39, 650, V30, V279, V270
	Preeclampsia	642.4, 642.5, 642.6, 642.7
	High birth weight	766.0, 766.1, 775.0, 656.6, 653.5
	Cesarean delivery	V39.01, V37.01, V30.01, V31.01, 669.70, 669.71
Diabetes	Diabetes	250, 357.2, 362.0, 648.0, 366.41

3 Results

The study populations included 6168 pregnant women, with 5437 (88.15%) in Group 1 (without pregestational diabetes) and 731 (11.85%) in Group 2 (with pregestational diabetes). As shown in Table 2, the minimal length of stay was one day, and the median was two days for both groups. Most patients, 80% in Group 1 and 78% in Group 2, stayed 1–3 days in the hospital. No significant difference in the distribution of length of stay was observed between the two groups. The median patient age of both groups was 30, with most patients aged 21 to 40. No significant difference in the age distribution was observed either.

We performed summary statistics on the principal diagnosis and listed the top 20 reasons for hospitalization in Table 3. The top eight reasons were the same for the two groups. More than half of Group 2 patients experienced early onset of delivery (ICD-9-CM code 644.21), compared to over one-third of Group 1 patients. It indicates that patients with pregestational diabetes were more likely (12.75% higher frequency) to have early onset of delivery. Patients with pregestational diabetes were also more likely to have premature rupture of membranes (3.65% higher frequency for ICD-9-CM code 658.11) and abnormality in fetal heart rate or rhythm (2.86% higher frequency for ICD-9-CM code 659.71).

As shown in Table 4, pregestational diabetes was associated with a higher risk of delivering high birth weight babies (RR = 1.49). Pregestational diabetes did not affect the risk of preterm delivery and cesarean delivery. As shown in Table 5, pregestational diabetes was associated with a higher risk of preeclampsia (RR = 1.29) and did not affect the risk of preterm delivery. The numbers of high birth weight babies and cesarean delivery were too small to interpret meaningfully.

Table 2. Comparative analysis of the patient age and length of stay between the two groups.

		Group 1		Group 2	
		Counts	Percentages	Counts	Percentages
Length of stay	1–3 days	4372	80.41%	572	78.25%
	4–7 days	716	13.17%	107	14.64%
	8–20 days	237	4.36%	41	5.61%
	21–50 days	78	1.44%	8	1.09%
	51–170 days	33	0.62%	3	0.41%
	Mean	3.82		3.71	
	Median	2		2	
	Min	1		1	
	Max	169		122	
Age distribution	Age 12–20	407	7.49%	43	5.88%
	Age 21–30	2539	46.70%	355	48.56%
	Age 31–40	2354	43.30%	312	42.68%
	Age 41–50	134	2.46%	20	2.74%
	Age 51–55	3	0.06%	1	0.14%
	Mean	29.98		29.98	
	Median	30		30	
	Min	12		15	
	Max	54		54	

We studied the length of stay for pregnancies associated with high birth weight and preeclampsia. Among those suffering from preeclampsia, a higher proportion of women with pregestational diabetes had extended stays – around 22% in Group 2 stayed 1–3 weeks compared to 10% in Group 1. Among those who delivered high birth weight babies, a higher proportion of women with pregestational diabetes had extended stays- around 20% in Group 2 stayed 1–7 weeks compared to 6% in Group 1 (Fig. 2).

Table 3. The top 20 principal reasons for hospitalization sorted by their frequencies in Group 1.

	ICD-9-CM Codes	Description	Group1 freq.	Group2 freq.	Group 1%	Group 2%
1	64421	Early onset of delivery delivered with or without antepartum condition	2066	370	37.87%	50.62%
2	65811	Premature rupture of membranes delivered	450	87	8.25%	11.90%
3	66411	Second-degree perineal laceration with delivery	329	53	6.03%	7.25%
4	66401	First-degree perineal laceration with delivery	261	52	4.78%	7.11%
5	65101	Twin pregnancy delivered	216	25	3.96%	3.42%
6	65971	Abnormality in fetal heart rate or rhythm delivered with or without antepartum condition	157	42	2.88%	5.74%
7	650	Normal delivery	142	26	2.60%	3.56%
8	65821	Delayed delivery after spontaneous or unspecified rupture of membranes delivered	125	22	2.29%	3.01%
9	64251	Severe pre-eclampsia with delivery	121	18	2.22%	2.46%
10	64241	Mild or unspecified pre-eclampsia with deliver	98	27	1.80%	3.69%

(continued)

Table 3. (*continued*)

	ICD-9-CM Codes	Description	Group1 freq.	Group2 freq.	Group 1%	Group 2%
11	65961	Other advanced maternal age delivered with or without antepartum condition	91	15	1.67%	2.05%
12	66331	Other and unspecified cord entanglement without compression complicating labor and delivery delivered	77	8	1.41%	1.09%
13	65421	Previous cesarean delivery with delivery with or without antepartum condition	75	13	1.37%	1.78%
14	64891	Other current conditions classifiable elsewhere of mother with delivery	68	12	1.25	1.64%
15	64231	Transient hypertension of pregnancy with delivery	67	12	1.23	1.64%
16	65801	Oligohydramnios delivered	58	12	1.06%	1.64%
17	65261	Multiple gestation with malpresentation of one fetus or more delivered	53	0	0.97%	0%
18	65651	Poor fetal growth affecting management of mother delivered	52	10	0.95%	1.37%
19	65451	Cervical incompetence with delivery	44	9	0.81%	1.23%

(*continued*)

Table 3. (*continued*)

	ICD-9-CM Codes	Description	Group1 freq.	Group2 freq.	Group 1%	Group 2%
20	64421	Early onset of delivery delivered with or without antepartum condition	2066	370	37.87%	50.62%

Table 4. The relative risk of adverse outcomes of pregnancies complicated by pregestational diabetes compared to normal pregnancy. The numbers were counted by checking the outcomes in all diagnosis codes.

	Group 1		Group 2		Risk ratio(RR)
	Counts	Percentages	Counts	Percentages	
Preeclampsia	498	9.15%	73	9.99%	1.091
Cesarean delivery	296	5.44%	37	5.06%	0.949
High birth weight	50	0.92%	10	1.37%	1.49
Preterm delivery	5050	92.88%	703	96.16%	1.03

Table 5. The relative risk of adverse outcomes of pregnancies complicated by pregestational diabetes compared to normal pregnancy. The numbers were counted by checking the outcomes in the principal diagnosis code.

	Group 1		Group 2		Risk ratio(RR)
	Counts	Percentages	Counts	Percentages	
Preeclampsia	265	4.87%	46	6.29%	1.29
Cesarean delivery	7	0.13%	2	0.27%	2.07
High birth weight	13	0.24%	1	0.14%	0.58
Preterm delivery	2100	38.62%	275	37.62%	0.97

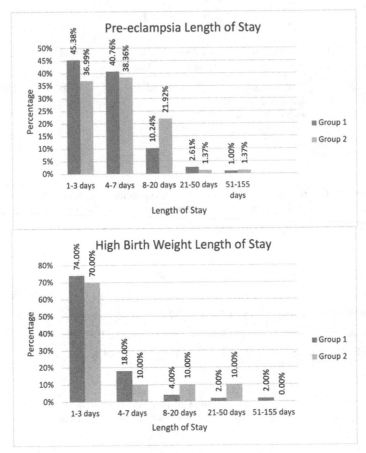

Fig. 2. The length of stay for pregnancies associated with preeclampsia and high birth weight by checking the outcomes in all diagnosis codes.

4 Conclusion

Based on the analysis of more than 6,000 pregnancies that resulted in a live birth in 2008, we concluded that pregestational diabetes is associated with a higher risk of delivering high birth weight babies and preeclampsia. High birth weight is associated with a higher risk of long-term health, including higher death rates from prostate cancer and possibly breast cancer [6]. Preeclampsia is among the top six causes of maternal mortality in the United States (US) and is associated with perinatal morbidity and mortality. The incidence of preeclampsia in the US has increased dramatically over the past twenty to thirty years [7]. We did not find significant differences between the risks of preterm delivery and cesarean delivery in the two groups. Higher proportions of women with pregestational diabetes had extended stays in hospital compared to those without pregestational diabetes.

Our result differed from a previous study of pregnancy outcomes in adolescent patients [4]. Kohn and coauthors reported that pregestational diabetes was associated with an increased risk for high birth weight babies, preeclampsia, preterm delivery, and cesarean delivery [4]. In the future study, we plan to expand the study population by including pregnancy data from multiple years and extend the scope by studying healthcare expenditure data and other pregnancy-related complications.

References

1. American College of Obstetricians and Gynecologists: ACOG practice bulletin no. 201: pregestational diabetes mellitus. Obstet. Gynecol. **132**(6), e228–e248 (2018)
2. Newman, C., et al.: Diabetes care and pregnancy outcomes for women with pregestational diabetes in Ireland. Diabetes Res. Clin. Pract. **173**, 108685 (2021)
3. Casson, I.F.: Pregnancy in women with diabetes – after the CEMACH report, what now?, pp. 481–484 (2021)
4. Kohn, J.R., Rajan, S.S., Kushner, J.A., Fox, K.A.: Outcomes, care utilization, and expenditures in adolescent pregnancy complicated by diabetes. Pediatr. Diabetes **20**(6), 769–777 (2019)
5. Hoppe, F.M., Hoppe, D.J., Walter, S.D.: Odds ratios deconstructed: a new way to understand and explain odds ratios as conditional risk ratios. J. Clin. Epidemiol. **82**, 87e93
6. Law, C.M.: Significance of birth weight for the future. Arch. Dis. Child Fetal Neonatal Ed. **86**(1), F7-8 (2002)
7. Shih, T., et al.: The rising burden of preeclampsia in the United States impacts both maternal and child health. Am. J. Perinatol. **33**(04), 329–338 (2016)

Real-Time and Near-Real-Time Services in Distributed Environment for IoT – Edge – Cloud Computing Implementation in Agriculture and Well-Being

Rossitza Goleva[1]([⊠])[iD], Radosveta Sokullu[2][iD], Vassil Kadrev[3], Alexandar Savov[4], Svetoslav Mihaylov[5], and Nuno Garcia[6][iD]

[1] New Bulgarian University, Montevideo str. 21, Sofia, Bulgaria
rgoleva@gmail.com
[2] Ege University, Izmir, Turkey
radosveta.sokullu@ege.edu.tr
[3] New Bulgarian University, Montevideo str. 21, Sofia, Bulgaria
[4] Comicon Ltd., Sofia, Bulgaria
savov@comicon.bg
[5] New Bulgarian University, Sofia, Bulgaria
[6] Computer Science Department of the University of Beira Interior, Covilhã, Portugal
ngarcia@di.ubi.pt

Abstract. Well-being and agriculture works of people living not only in villages but also in towns nowadays, the healthy living environment at home, in the park, in the sports center, at work, local and remote monitoring of different parameters of the body, house, garden, the greenhouse is a matter of increased interest from families. Regardless of the size of the family, garden, villas, and fields, there is a need for support of integrated smart services in real-time and near-real-time forming an adaptable family software-defined Personal Enhanced Living Environment 4.0 network configurable on the top of the existing public and private infrastructure. The scale of the network, the variety of Internet of Things parts, and the distributed edge and cloud computing services that are fragmented nowadays need to be integrated. The raw data created, data storage and data processing require a common edge-to-dew-to-fog-to-cloud approach and clear correlation to the related sectors such as water, land, house, factory, environment, parks, and infrastructure management. In this paper, an integrated approach toward services for different types of users based on the previously defined scenarios is presented. The services are software-defined and use existing infrastructure orchestrated resources that are unified, and allocated appropriately to support the functional and non-functional requirements. Private and public parts of the data, data flows, data space, and capacity for processing are considered.

Keywords: Sensors · Data sharing · Edge · Dew · Fog · Cloud computing technologies · Smart agriculture · Smart cities · Smart home · Smart well-being

T. Zlateva and R. Goleva (Eds.): CSECS 2022, LNICST 450, pp. 126–141, 2022.
https://doi.org/10.1007/978-3-031-17292-2_11

1 Introduction

Nowadays the work of the so-called smart systems is specific with its fragmentation. Regardless of using cloud services and the Internet of Things (IoT), devices the applications are separated and do not exchange data with few exceptions. The requirements of the market for an integrated simple and highly customizable service for a Personal Enhanced Living Environment are high. However, the Personal Enhanced Living Environment 4.0 should be integrable, sharing, importing, and exporting data with a clear view of the privacy of the data. It is also expected to be distributed by nature and uses: 1) local, smart dust level computing facilities like gateways and controllers for different sensor devices at home, park, field, and factory; 2) dew computing level facilities such as home computers, tablets, smartphones; 3) fog computing facilities formed by the regional data centers; 4) cloud computing facilities formed by the global data centers [1]. In many papers, the smart dust and dew computing levels are covered by the common term edge computing. In some papers, even fog computing infrastructure is considered as part of the edge. The distribution of the data, data flows, clear identification of the private and public data, resources to be used at different computing levels, and orchestration and sharing of these resources are a matter of intensive development [2]. The new paradigm of distributed resources orchestration is expected to allow fully distributed processing of the data and better utilization of the network nodes.

Well-being is a term that is considered often to be related to the Body Area Networks and body monitoring in general. However, in the context of this work, the term is enhanced with new features related to the living environment, and many things known as home automation, building automation, and smart agriculture. Smart environments and smart cities influence the complexity of the services prepared for the well-being platforms. Very often such platforms are also considered to be data-driven [3, 4], i.e., changing behavior depending on the data.

Another important point in the creation of the services for the Personal Living Environment 4.0 is the distinction between the real-time and near-real-time services for the customers. The term real-time is tricky and is interpreted by different authors differently. In this paper, there is a definition of services based on a clear explanation of the real-time requirements with a limit of round trip delay of 150 ms. This is the perception of the human beings for the delay. One could say that a service is offered in near-real-time when the round trip delay is close to 150 ms, i.e. up to one second. All services with a round trip delay bigger than one second are considered to be working in non-real-time.

Finally, the new services could not be developed without the digitalization of sectors that feed the Personal Enhanced Living Environment 4.0 with multidisciplinary data. However, many of the sectors are still too fragmented and use proprietary technology solutions.

The structure of this paper contains a literature review of the recent papers in the field, a clear classification of the end-users of the platforms and expected services, classification of the services based on the functional and non-functional requirements and scenarios investigated, possible network architecture and technologies to be implemented and preliminary results in the controlled and real environment.

2 State of the Art

The new term Personal Enhanced Living Environment 4.0 that is proposed in this paper is an extension of the previously well-defined platforms for Enhanced Living Environment, Ambient Assisted Living, and Personal Defined Networks. Many details of such a platform are already defined and worldwide experimented. However, the existence of a sustainable and customizable integrated solution is still missing. The main problems are the fragmentation of the business, different levels of digitalization of the sectors, the use of too many proprietary solutions, and the lack of appropriate data sharing rules between systems and platforms.

In this paper, there is a trail to integrate different proprietary and non-proprietary solutions, create circumstances for data sharing, distributed resource orchestration, and allocation, and distributed data storage and processing.

The integration of the agriculture and living environment will require the use of short-range and long-range sensor technologies. Data collected is often missing, corrupted, or late and appropriate processing could suffer from the lack of data and processing capacity.

The existence of Long Range (LoRa) sensor technology is already proven to be implementable in the open space environment like sea coast, crop fields, meadows, forests, rivers, and smart cities [5]. The range of the technology is about 40 km. However, the limits in the power of transmission have happened to shorten this distance. This is the case in Europe. To avoid the development of infrastructure in rural places or in places where installation is almost impossible, part of the equipment and especially the gateways and controllers are developed to fly on drones or be carried by mountain vehicles, or transported by boats, or trucks.

The efficiency of the sensor implementations in agriculture is of vital importance as it reflects the water use and reuse, smart ways to grow crops and manage the production, prediction of possible disasters, and ways to avoid disasters, i.e., making the agriculture more sustainable [6, 7]. A rich analysis of the possible scenarios in smart agriculture could be seen in [8]. The work combines the use of different fixed and mobile approaches for data collection, the possibility to monitor different parameters of the crops, and has an implementation of artificial intelligence in data processing. The proposed in this paper modular approach to making the gateways interoperable with multiple sensor technologies at the same time is more universal. A similar approach toward smart agriculture is also presented in [9].

A rich analysis of the climate influence on smart agriculture is presented in [10]. The vast implementation of artificial intelligence in data processing and data correlation is well demonstrated.

The problems in the typical living environments seem not to be similar to the ones in smart agriculture [11, 12]. In many cases, the sensors are working in short range and the transmission power could be limited easily. However, when the Personal Enhanced Living Environment 4.0 is distributed towards the parks, public transport, yards, and shops the problem with infrastructure interoperability, the distance of the transmission and collection and sharing of different types of data is again a matter of high importance. The aim is also to go further and create a cooperative solution for living and working environments as they could not be separated so easily during the last pandemic years because most of the people work from home.

The problems in urban environments as in smart cities [13] are in the existence of too many and highly dependable parameters of different systems that could be analyzed. This creates circumstances for the use of multiple often diverse solutions. An approach to the data analyses is presented in [14]. The approaches require often the processing of the images obtained from different sources and careful correlation between the data obtained from the image analyses as seen in [15].

Work with medical devices, the necessity to use the network for healthcare is analyzed in many papers over the last decade such as [16]. Implementation of machine learning in activity recognition is demonstrated in [17]. Enhanced Living Environment platform architecture and testing could be seen in [18] and [19]. General approaches to the definition of IoT scenarios are taken into consideration in [20].

3 Users' Requirements

The requirements of the users towards their personal defined network are usually high and depend very much on the culture, background, traditions, and habits of the people. The living and working environment is always expected to be comfortable and to consider additional features of life and work. The personal environment is part of the living and working environment of the people in the house and colleagues in the office. Therefore, data sharing and data correlation between different parameters need special consideration. The idea for Enhanced Personal Living Environment 4.0 is presented in Fig. 1. The proposal is to create a circumstance for the use of the integrated approach from any place and at any time, i.e., transparent in space and time.

Recently, thanks to the vast digitalization of different sectors and increased use of IoT and cloud computing in houses, companies, parks, and factories it is possible to define and specify the requirements and main functions of platforms such as Living Environment 4.0, Working Environment 4.0, Personal Living Environment 4.0. The requests from the market for such a service are high. However, the solutions offered are still fragmented and proprietary by design without an appropriate level for data sharing and data correlation.

Many of the services in the Personal Enhanced Living Environment 4.0 have to work in real-time, while quite a big amount of services also work in near-real-time. The meaning of these terms depends very much on the context to be implemented. For example, the alarms for falling, fires, floods, and high personal temperatures are expected to be created and processed in real-time. Parameters like temperature in the garden, soil humidity, and particle matters in the room and street might be detected and monitored in near-real-time. It is important to mention that in many cases the limit of 150 ms is relaxed. There are many examples such as Voice over IP communication, sensors-to-cloud communication, sensor-to-server communication where the limit could be up to 5 s, and even more. Many IoT implementations when the sensors are sleeping exchange the data within the intervals of 5 s due to the specific features of the technology.

Fig. 1. The idea of the enhanced personal living environment 4.0.

All services need to be supported transparently in space and time using standard interfaces, protocols, and data formats, i.e., Wi-Fi, 3G, 4G, Ethernet, 5G interfaces, MQTT (Message Queuing Telemetry Transport), or similar protocols, and JSON (JavaScript Object Notation) or other similar data formats.

4 Primary, Secondary, and Tertiary Users

The classification of the users is an important issue as they will require different functionality and be implemented over different infrastructure facilities and resources. From the point of the service use, one may distinguish three types of users: primary, secondary, and tertiary.

Primary users are direct users of the services provided. These are people and their living and working environment. They also have:

- Their own Personal Enhanced Living Environment for the body
- Optional Personal Enhanced Living Environments of their relatives/ patients for the doctors and caring people, customers for management of specified part of the data
- House living environment access
- Garden living environment access
- Working living environment access
- School/shops, other public places living environment access
- Car/ infrastructure living environment access

Primary users could support:

- Partial orchestration of resources
- Import of common data
- Export of part of their private data

Secondary users have the same functionality as the primary users having additionally the possibility to extend the monitored devices and persons such as family members, colleagues, places, environment, and devices. Secondary users have:

- Their Enhanced Living Environment
- Personal Enhanced Living Environments of their relatives/ patients for the doctors and caring people, customers for management of specified part of the data
- House living environment
- Working living environment
- Car/public transport infrastructure living environment

Secondary users should support also data sharing on their data and the data of the monitored people and network places.

Tertiary users have additional roles in configuration management, support, insurance management, social analyses, medical data analyses, and public services analyses made for the communes, governmental and non-governmental organizations. Their network should support;

- Their Enhanced Living Environment
- Personal Enhanced Living Environments of their customers for configuration, statistics, management, monitoring of part of the data
- Infrastructure use and resources orchestration
- Infrastructure development
- Definition and specification of policies for infrastructure development and use of data

Tertiary users share data on the infrastructure, many types of publicly available data for the climate, infrastructure, facilities, utilities, community policies, etc.

5 Scenarios Implemented at IoT Level

Last decade many scenarios on the IoT level have been implemented in diverse fields and sectors. In [21] and [22] there is a detailed scenarios' specifications for the home, person, and garden management. All scenarios are explored in a real environment. Scenarios are classified here for simplicity and used for the service creation process as well.

Groups of scenarios to be implemented in the Personal Enhanced Living Environment 4.0 platform are classified shortly in next sections.

5.1 House Automation Management, Office/ Factory Building Automation Management, Crops Management in the House, in the Greenhouse

Common devices to be implemented in the house and garden could be summarised as doors and windows guarding, security systems, and utility devices for electricity, water, and gas supply. The results expected are data and appropriate visualization of the data for monitoring and management as well as setting of appropriate alarms for power failures, fire, flooding, gas leakage, etc. Implementation of the machine learning on the data collected at dew, fog, and cloud computing level could lead to the prediction of alarms and raising/decreasing of alerting level to the end-users.

Many parts of the rooms in the houses and offices and halls in the factories could be a matter of passive and active monitoring and management as lamps, recuperators, heaters, coolers, humidifiers, dehumidifiers, purifiers, curtains, windows, doors, sockets, air quality sensors, and many others.

5.2 Crops Management in the Yard, in the Park, in the Fields

People in the villages, people living in the houses with yeards grow different crops. The Personal Enhanced Living Environment 4.0 implementation needs to be extended by IoT solutions for crop management in short and long distances. The water supply system may work depending on the environmental conditions such as sunlight, rain, the humidity of the air, soil, type of the soil, type of crops, and many others. Water sources need additional management for the levels, capacities, number of pumps, electricity supply, type of sensors and actuators implemented, etc. Additionally, the monitoring services could be optimized based on machine learning and passive/active on-site experiments. The aim is to optimize the use of energy, water, and electricity and reach an efficient and sustainable solution that is specific for every customer and climate zone.

5.3 Healthcare Scenarios

Scenarios for healthcare implement sensors for both parameters measurements and management as well as the definition of different levels of notifications, messaging, alarms, and reports of the person under care. Types of the sensors could be classified into sensors for the body parameters (blood sugar, temperature, skin resistance, activity) and actuators for management such as panic cords, voice commands, noise sensing, alert levels, etc.

6   Functional and Nonfunctional Requirements of the Personal Enhanced Living Environment 4.0

The data collected from different parts of the distributed environment could be a matter of additional analyses and additional functions could be defined accordingly.

The main functional requirements of the Personal Enhanced Living Environment 4.0 could be summarized as:

- measuring data
- monitoring data
- reporting data
- storing data
- processing data
- correlation of data
- visualization of data
- export of data
- import of data
- transformation of data
- verification of data
- validation of data
- comparison of data
- prediction of events
- analyses of events
- creation of alarm
- notification
- acknowledgment requests
- request for data
- hiding private data
- sharing public data
- collection of resources
- orchestration of resources
- allocation of resources
- unification of resources
- release of resources

Non-functional requirements could be summarised as making the Personal Enhanced Living Environment 4.0:

- adaptable and scalable
- identifying resources
- having policies for resource allocation and release
- keeping the performance parameters

- identifying the missing data, missing parameters, and missing parts of the infrastructure
- being capable to perform a self-test of the infrastructure
- having self-configuration capabilities.

7 Services for Primary, Secondary, and Tertiary Users

Services for the primary, secondary, and tertiary end-users are different. While the basic services are directly related to the functional requirements the added value monolithic services are combining many features and functions with the data from the existing infrastructure. Therefore, some additional services could be defined as additional functions of the platforms such as:

- Analyses of the efficiency of the electricity use
- Redistribution of the electricity using predefined algorithms or machine learning algorithms
- Security smart service
- Added value smart service for the garden and crop fields that are specific to the crops and environment
- Additional services for the thermal comfort of the crops in the greenhouses
- Value-added service for the light control
- Value-added service for the air quality
- Smart care adaptable services controlling medicines, body parameters, additional prescriptions, activities, training, dietary prescriptions
- Value-added multicast services for alarms and alerts
- Services for the control of the swarm behavior

In Fig. 2 the main menu for the main agriculture management service is shown. There are submenus for the management of the greenhouse, irrigation system, water supply basin, greenhouse heating system, environmental parameters for the yard, and the technical parameters of the sensor IoT network. In the figure, the Signal-to-Noise Ratio (SNR) and Received Signal Strength Indication (RSSI) are related to the quality of wireless connection to the sensors.

In Fig. 3 the submenu for the greenhouse is presented with measurements of the temperature and relative humidity (SM or soil moisture in the figure).

Services for the secondary users are enhanced by possibilities to:

- add additional persons for monitoring
- drop persons for monitoring
- add a place for monitoring
- drop a place for monitoring
- activate/ deactivate service
- share data

- define policies for data sharing
- import data
- perform additional data visualization and analyses
  manage alarms and events
- implement machine learning for the prediction of events

Services for the tertiary users are mostly related to the:

- data visualization
- data correlation
- data collection
- data analyses
- policy definitions
- policy implementation
- data validation
- data sharing
- correlation between the data and legislation
- service adaptivity and sustainability
- service scaling

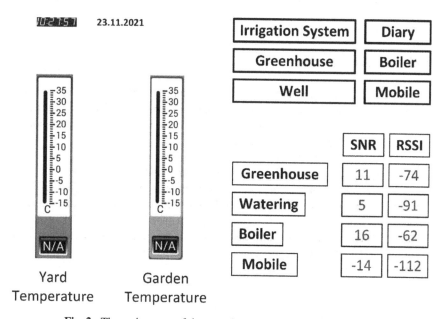

Fig. 2. The main menu of the greenhouse IoT system management.

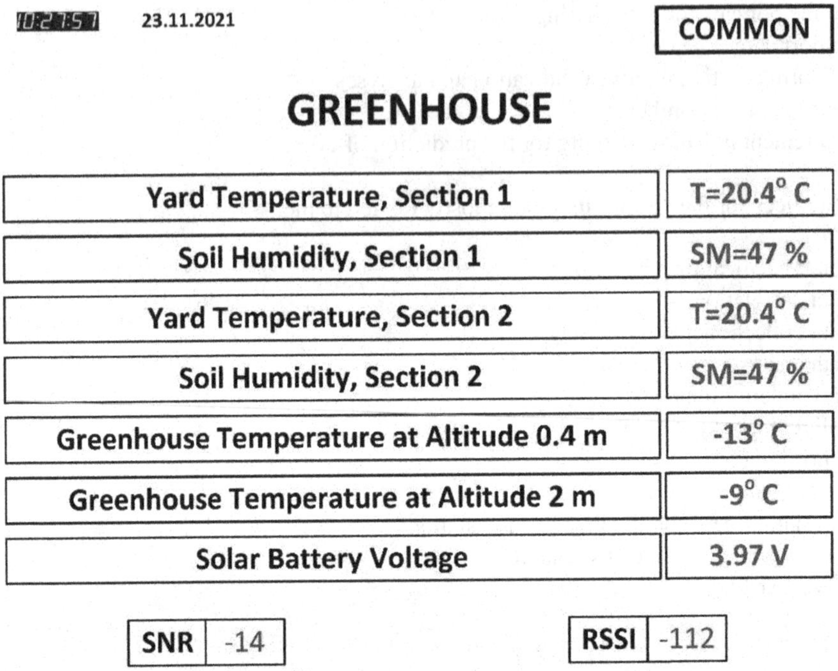

COMMON

GREENHOUSE

Yard Temperature, Section 1	T=20.4° C
Soil Humidity, Section 1	SM=47 %
Yard Temperature, Section 2	T=20.4° C
Soil Humidity, Section 2	SM=47 %
Greenhouse Temperature at Altitude 0.4 m	-13° C
Greenhouse Temperature at Altitude 2 m	-9° C
Solar Battery Voltage	3.97 V

SNR	-14		RSSI	-112

Fig. 3. Greenhouse submenu.

8 Network Architecture

The network infrastructure is heterogeneous and supports both functional and non-functional requirements for the services. The adaptivity and the performance of the services depend very much on the existing infrastructure. The main home implementation with ZigBee and EnOcean sensors is presented in Fig. 4.

The edge/smart dust-to-dew-to-fog-to-cloud computing is presented by sensors, gateways, controllers, local servers, and Internet connectivity.

The software-defined and personal-defined networks on the top of the existing infrastructure have an interface locally or through the Internet using fixed or mobile devices. Data flows, data storage, and data processing are distributed among network devices.

Figure 5 presents an automation infrastructure for the greenhouse, water irrigation, water supply, boiler for water heating, and mobile computing devices.

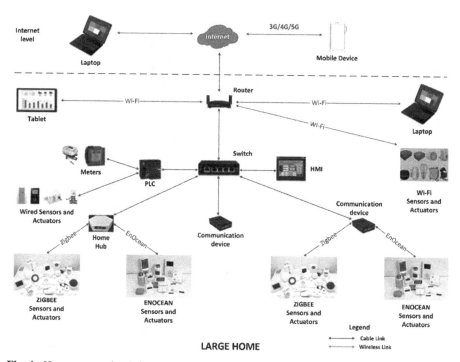

Fig. 4. Home automation infrastructure (PLC - Programmable Logic Controller, HMI – Human-Machine Interface),

The presented Personal Enhanced Living Environment 4.0 platform has currently more than 500 sensors of different types and technologies, fixed and mobile gateways, some of them flying on a drone, controllers, and local and remote servers for data storage and processing. It is capable to raise alarms, uses the algorithms with the parameters obtained by the machine learning algorithms, monitors the infrastructure for its performance parameters such as batteries levels, link quality (Fig. 6), telegrams delays, telegram losses, validates the vitality of the data collected and is capable to predict some events as increased consumption, non-typical behavior, the necessity for reaction, lack of notifications and many others.

There is a need to mention explicitly that the validity of the data from sensors and removal of the outliers in the time series obtained from the sensors is also an important topic. It is expected that the data acquisition algorithms and machine learning classification algorithms could support the creation of a valid data sets at the edge. Creation of ontologies like SAREF (Smart Applications REFerence) and woking on a common data representation formats like JSON (JavaScript Object Notation) aim to support the standardization process of the data representations, flows and storing and enforce the data sharing.

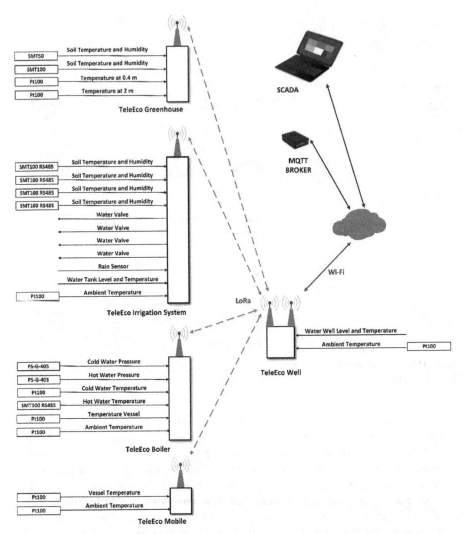

Fig. 5. Garden automation (SCADA - Supervisory control and data acquisition).

Reservation of the connections is another important issue in the technologies presented. Most of the sensors are working in multicasting mode or in a mesh retransmission mode. This is the natural sensor technologies way to support connectivity reservation. Some of the sensors are working in point-to-point mode. There is no reservation in the connections in these cases. However, the variety of the sensors, the multivariate analyses, the data dependencies and/or machine learning and data acquisition algorithms are capable to solve the problem of missing data.

There is yet another way to support data reservation on the fly using so-called peer ports at application layer. The technology is implementatble at the edge, fog of cloud computing level.

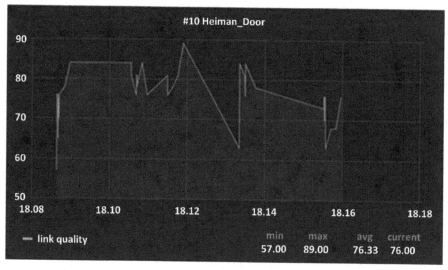

Fig. 6. Link quality to the sensor of a door, SNR between 6:08 and 6:18 pm.

9   Conclusions and Future Work Plans

Services in the Personal Enhanced Living Environment 4.0 have been highlighted and classified towards primary, secondary, and tertiary end-users, real-time and non-real-time performance, and distributed orchestration of the data at the smart dust, dew, fog, and cloud computing. All services are based on the experimented scenarios and added value services have been identified based on the results from real environment implementations. The aim is to create more smart services based on machine learning algorithms that could predict events and manage risks in the distributed environment and implement also the distributed resource orchestration.

The analyses continue with a more accurate estimation of the storage capacity, data flows and traffic of data flows, data processing requirements at edge/fog/cloud level and possible mapping to the resource allocation algorithms to make the services more sustainable.

Acknowledgments. This work is developed under support of multiple projects as: a) 2020–2021 Research and Development of Prototype of Multifunctional IIo LPWAN Communication Model for Wireless Data Transmission of Ecological Parameters Using Sensors – TeleEco, National Innovation Fund, Bulgaria; b) 2020–2024, CA19130 - Fintech and Artificial Intelligence in Finance - Towards a transparent financial industry, https://www.cost.eu/actions/CA19130/; c) 2018–2021, Theoretical Models for Digital Agriculture Development, National Fund for Research, Bulgaria; d) 2018–2019, 5P, Research and Development of a Prototype of the Platform for Continuous Monitoring of Vital Parameters and Processes, National Innovation Fund, Bulgaria; e) 2017–2019, European Civil Protection and Humanitarian Aid Operations, Advanced systems for prevention & early detection of forest fires 2016/PREV/03 (ASPIRES), granted by European Commission; f) 2013–2017, COST Action IC1303, Algorithms, Architectures and Platforms for Enhanced Living Environments (AAPELE), vice chair, granted by European Commission; g) 2022 Flying Forest Fire Fighting, Open Call project to Innovation Boosted by Small Flying Objects (UFO), granted by European Commission; h) 2022 Prototype Design of the LoRa® Repeater for Unified Signals and Channel Selection Management (LIOREPLICON), National Innovation Fund, Bulgaria.

References

1. Goleva, R., Mihaylov, S.: European Catalogue of ICT Water Standards and Specifications, p. 128. https://ec.europa.eu/digital-single-market/en/news/european-catalogue-ict-water-standards-and-specifications; https://op.europa.eu/es/publication-detail/-/publication/36d88e41-d6c3-11ea-adf7-01aa75ed71a1/language-es, https://doi.org/10.2759/39178, ISBN 978-92-76-17850-7. Last update: 5 August 2020, Shaping Europe's digital future, REPORT / STUDY, Team responsible, Smart Mobility and Living (Unit H.5), Directorate-General for Communications Networks, Content and Technology (European Commission) (2020)
2. Goleva, R., Asenova, P., Mihaylov, S., Siderov, D., Kadrev, V.: Sensor2Fog2Cloud2Application Platform for Smart Agriculture and Water Management. In: International Conference on Computer Science and Education in Computer Science CSECS 2020, Sofia, 5 Sept. 2020, ISSN 1313-8624, p. 5 (2020)
3. Saiz-Rubio, V., Rovira-Más, F.: From smart farming towards agriculture 5.0: a review on crop data management. J. of Agronomy **10**, 207 (2020). https://doi.org/10.3390/agronomy10020207, www.mdpi.com/journal/agronomy
4. Anikwe, C.V., et al.: Mobile and wearable sensors for data-driven health monitoring system: State-of-the-art and future prospect. J. Expert Systems with Applications **202**, 117362, ISSN 0957-4174 (2022). https://doi.org/10.1016/j.eswa.2022.117362. https://www.sciencedirect.com/science/article/pii/S095741742200714X
5. Peinl, P., Goleva, R., Ackoski, J.: Advanced system for the prevention and early detection of forest fires (ASPires). In: The35th ACM/SIGAPP Symposium on Applied Computing (SAC '20), March 30-April 3, Brno, Czech Republic. ACM, New York, NY, USA, 4, pp. 1200–1203 (2020). https://doi.org/10.1145/3341105.3374052
6. Roy, R., Aslekar, A.: IoT in farm productivity enhancement. In: International Conference on Decision Aid Sciences and Applications (DASA), pp. 1034–1039 (2022). https://doi.org/10.1109/DASA54658.2022.9765273
7. Basu, B., Kal, S., Ghosh, U., Datta, R.: SoftDrone: softwarized 5G assisted drone networks for dynamic resource sharing using machine learning techniques. J. Comp. Electri. Eng. **101**, 107962, ISSN 0045-7906 (2022). https://doi.org/10.1016/j.compeleceng.2022.107962
8. Elsayed Said Mohamed, E.S., Belal, A.A., Abd-Elmabod, S.K., El-Shirbeny, M.A., Gad, A., Zahran, M.B.: Smart farming for improving agricultural management. The Egyptian J. Remote Sensing and Space Sci. **24**(3 and Part 2), 971–981, ISSN 1110-9823 (2021). https://doi.org/10.1016/j.ejrs.2021.08.007
9. Quy, V.K., et al.: IoT-enabled smart agriculture: architecture, applications, and challenges. Appl. Sci. **12**, 3396 (2022). https://doi.org/10.3390/app12073396
10. Rosenstock, T.S., Nowak, A., Girvetz, E. (eds.): The Climate-Smart Agriculture. Papers Published by Springer International Publishing (January 2019). https://doi.org/10.1007/978-3-319-92798-5, ISBNs 978-3-31-992797-8, 978-3-31-992798-5
11. IC1303 – Algorithms: Architectures and Platforms for Enhanced Living Environments (AAPELE) (2021). https://www.cost.eu/actions/IC1303/
12. Dobre, C., Ganchev, I., Garcia, N., Goleva, R.: Introduction to enhanced living environment. In: Goleva, R., Ganchev, I., Dobre, C., Garcia, N., Valderrama, C. (eds.) Enhanced Living Environments: From Models to Technologies. The Institution of Engineering and Technology, pp. 1–20, ISBN: 978-1-78561-211-4 (2017)

13. Wu, M., Yan, B., Huang, Y., Sarker, M.N.I.: Big data-driven urban management: potential for urban sustainability. Land 2022 **11**, 680 (2022). https://doi.org/10.3390/land11050680
14. Mavrevski, R., Milanov, P., Traykov, M., Pencheva, N.: Assessment of different model selection criteria by generated experimental data. WSEAS Transactions on Computers, ISSN / E-ISSN: 1109-2750 / 2224-2872, vol 16, Art. #30, pp. 260–268 (2017)
15. Laskov, L.M.: Methods for document image de-warping. Astronomical and Astrophysical Transactions (AApTr), Cambridge Scientific Publishers **30**(4), 511–522 (2020)
16. Ivanov, I.E., Gueorguiev, V., Georgieva, D., Nenova, M., Ivanov, B.: Risk-based testing approach for medical devices software. In: Proceedings of the Technical University – Sofia **70**(4), 41–48, ISSN 1311-0829 (2020). https://doi.org/10.47978/TUS.2020.70.04.025
17. Zdravevski, E., et al.: Improving activity recognition accuracy in ambient assisted living systems by automated feature engineering. IEEE Access J. **PP**(99), 5262–5280 (2017). https://doi.org/10.1109/ACCESS.2017.2684913
18. Goleva, R., et al.: AALaaS and ELEaaS Platforms. In: Goleva, R., Ganchev, I., Dobre, C., Garcia, N., Valderrama, C. (eds.) Enhanced Living Environments: From Models to Technologies. The Institution of Engineering and Technology, pp. 207–243, ISBN: 978-1-78561-211-4 (2017)
19. Autexier, S., et al.: End-Users AAL and ELE Service Scenarios in Smart Personal Environment. In: Goleva, R., Ganchev, I., Dobre, C., Garcia, N, Valderrama, C. (eds.) Enhanced Living Environments: From Models to Technologies. The Institution of Engineering and Technology, pp. 101-131, ISBN: 978-1-78561-211-4 (2017)
20. Simeonova, T.: Development of Internet of Things. Monography. Aseventsi Publisher, Sofia, p. 362, ISBN 978-619-7586-25-1 (2021)
21. 2GreenHome web page: https://2greenhome.com/en/smart-home/. Accessed May 2022
22. Goleva, R., Kadrev, V., Savov, A., Koleva, Z., Draganov, P., Mihaylov, S.: Scenarios to use sensors in agriculture, home, office, well-being. In: International Conference on Computer Science and Education in Computer Science CSECS 2021, Sofia, p. 7, ISSN 1313-8624 (18 Sept. 2021). https://www.ceeol.com/search/article-detail?id=978468

On a Class of Minihypers
in the Geometries PG(r, q)

Ivan Landjev[1]([✉]), Emilyan Rogachev[2], and Assia Rousseva[2]

[1] New Bulgarian University, 21 Montevideo Str., 1618 Sofia, Bulgaria
i.landjev@nbu.bg
[2] Faculty of Mathematics and Informatics, Sofia University,
5 J. Bourchier Blvd., 1164 Sofia, Bulgaria
rogachev@uni-sofia.bg, assia@fmi.uni-sofia.bg

Abstract. We characterize all minihypers with parameters ($v_3 + 2v_2, v_2 + 2v_1$) in the geometries PG(r, q). Apart from the trivial ones which are the sum of a plane and two lines, we construct several sporadic minihypers in the geometries PG(r, q) with $q = 3$ and $q = 4$.

Keywords: Liear codes · Minihypers · Griesmer bound

1 Introduction

We begin by introducing two geometric objects that are equivalent to linear codes. Let PG(r, q) be the r-dimensional projective geometry over $\mathbb{F}_q$ and denote the set of its points by $\mathcal{P}$. A multiset of points in PG(r, q) is a mapping $\mathcal{K} : \mathcal{P} \to \mathbb{N}_0$, i.e. a mapping which assigns to every point a non-negative integer called its multiplicity. This mapping is extended additively to the subsets of $\mathcal{P}$: for every $X \subseteq \mathcal{P}$ we set $\mathcal{K}(X) = \sum_{P \in X} \mathcal{K}(P)$.

A multiset $\mathcal{K}$ in PG(r, q) is called an (n, w)-arc in PG(r, q) if (i) $\mathcal{K}(\mathcal{P}) = n$, (ii) $\mathcal{K}(H) \leq w$ for every hyperplane H in PG(r, q), and (iii) $\mathcal{K}(H_0) = w$ for some hyperplane H_0. Similarly, a multiset $\mathcal{K}$ in PG(r, q) is called an (n, w)-minihyper (also (n, w) blocking multiset) if it is a multiset with (i) $\mathcal{K}(\mathcal{P}) = n$, (ii) $\mathcal{K}(H) \geq w$ for every hyperplane H in PG(r, q), and (iii) $\mathcal{K}(H_0) = w$ for some hyperplane H_0. The notion of a minihyper was introduced by N. Hamada in connection with the so-called main problem in coding theory stated below. For more details one should consult the survey [1] and the references there.

Linear codes, arcs and minihypers are in some sense equivalent to linear codes.

Theorem 1. *The existence of the following objects is equivalent:*

(1) a linear $[n, k, d]_q$-code with the property that in any generator matrix has at most t identical columns;

(2) an ($n, n - d$)-arc in PG($k - 1, q$) with maximal point multiplicity t;

T. Zlateva and R. Goleva (Eds.): CSECS 2022, LNICST 450, pp. 142–153, 2022.
https://doi.org/10.1007/978-3-031-17292-2_12

(3) *a* $(tv_k - n, tv_{k-1} - n + d)$*-minihyper in* $PG(k - 1, q)$ *with maximal point multiplicity* $\leq t$.

We consider the so-called main problem in coding theory (cf. [2]) which is to optimize one of the three main parameters of a linear code given the other two. In this paper, we focus on the problem of determining the minimal length n of a linear code of fixed dimension k and fixed minimum distance d over the field with q elements. This value is commonly denoted by $n_q(k, d)$. There exists a natural lower bound on $n_q(k, d)$ – the so-called Griesmer bound:

$$n_q(k, d) \geq \sum_{i=0}^{k-1} \lceil \frac{d}{q^i} \rceil. \tag{1}$$

The RHS in the above inequality is denoted by $g_q(k, d)$. Linear codes with parameters $[n, k, d]_q$ of length $n = g_q(k, d)$ are called Griesmer codes. Arcs and minihypers associated with linear Griesmer codes are called Griesmer arcs, resp. Grismer minihypers.

In this paper, we adopt the geometric point of view and deal with minihypers. Our main result is the characterization of the minihypers with parametes $(v_3 + 2v_2, v_2 + 2v_1)$ in the geometries $PG(r, q)$ for all r and all prime powers q. Here v_s denotes the Gaussian coefficient $v_s = \dfrac{v^s - 1}{v - 1}$. Minihypers with the above parameters are Griesmer minihypers. This can be shown by a straightforward calculation. This characterization we give is used further in the nonexistence proof for some hypothetical Griesmer codes [6]. The motivation for this investigation cam from the recent research on the exact values of $n_3(6, d)$ carried out in [8–11].

2   Preliminaries

In this section, we present some basic definitions and facts in the geometries $PG(k - 1, q)$. Since in coding theory the letter k denotes the dimension of the linear codes, we consider the associated minihypers as multisets in the $(k - 1)$-dimensional projective geometry $PG(k - 1, q)$.

For a given (n, w)-arc $\mathcal{K}$ in $PG(k - 1, q)$, we denote by $\gamma_i(\mathcal{K})$ the maximal multiplicity of an i-dimensional flat in $PG(k - 1, q)$, i.e. $\gamma_i(\mathcal{K}) = \max_\delta \mathcal{K}(\delta)$, $i = 0, \ldots, k-1$, where δ runs over all i-dimensional flats in $PG(k-1, q)$. If $\mathcal{K}$ is clear from the context we shall skip the name of the arc and shall write simply γ_i.

For an (n, w)-minihyper $\mathcal{K}$ in $PG(k - 1, q)$ we denote by $\beta_i(\mathcal{K})$ the minimal multipliciuty of an i-dimensional flat in $PG(k-1, q)$: $\beta_i(\mathcal{K}) = \min_\delta \mathcal{B}(\delta)$, where δ runs over all i-dimensional flats.

Let C be a Griesmer $[n, k, d]_q$-code. Denote by $\mathcal{K}$ the $(n, n-d)$-arc associated with C. Then using a similar argument as in the geometric proof of the Griesmer bound we get that

$$\gamma_i = \sum_{j=k-1-i}^{k-1} \lceil \frac{d}{q^j} \rceil. \tag{2}$$

If $\mathcal{B} = \gamma_0 - \mathcal{K}$ then $\beta_i = \gamma_0 v_{i+1} - \gamma_i$.

Below we give without proof several classical results for linear codes, and th related arcs and minihypers.

Theorem 1 *(H. N. Ward, [12]).*

(1) Let C be an $[n, k, d]$ Griesmer code over $\mathbb{F}_p$, p a prime. If p^e divides d, then p^e is a divisor of C.

(2) Let $\mathcal{K}$ be a Griesmer (n, w)-arc in $PG(k-1, p)$, p a prime, and let $w \equiv n$ (mod p^e). Then for every hyperplane $\mathcal{K}(H) \equiv n$ (mod p^e), that is p^e is a divisor of $\mathcal{K}$.

(3) Let $\mathcal{B}$ be a Griesmer (n, w)-minihyper in $PG(k-1, p)$, p a prime, and let $w \equiv n$ (mod p^e). Then for every hyperplane $\mathcal{B}(H) \equiv n$ (mod p^e), that is p^e is a divisor of $\mathcal{B}$.

An (n, w)-arc $\mathcal{K}$ in $PG(k-1, q)$ is called extendable if there exists an $(n+1, w)$-arc $\mathcal{K}'$ in $PG(k-1, q)$ with $\mathcal{K}'(P) \geq \mathcal{K}(P)$ for every point P of $PG(k-1, q)$. Similarly, an (n, w)-miihyper $\mathcal{B}$ in $PG(k-1, q)$ is called reducible if there exists an $(n-1, w)$-minihyper $\mathcal{B}'$ in $PG(k-1, q)$ with $\mathcal{B}'(P) \leq \mathcal{B}(P)$ for every point P of $PG(k-1, q)$. The next statement is the geometric version of Hill and Lizak's extension result [3,4]. Below we state the exetnsion theorem of Hill and Lizak in several formulations.

Theorem 2 *(Hill-Lizak, [3,4]).*

(1) Let C be an $[n, k, d]_q$-code with $\gcd(d, q) = 1$ and with all weights congruent to 0 or d mod q. Then C is extendeable to an $[n+1, k, d+1]_q$-code.

(2) Let $\mathcal{K}$ be an (n, w)-arc in $PG(k-1, q)$ with $(n-w, q) = 1$, such that the multiplicities of all hyperplanes are n or w modulo q. Then $\mathcal{K}$ is extendable to an $(n+1, w)$-arc.

(3) Let $\mathcal{B}$ be an (n, w)-minihyper in $PG(k-1, q)$ with $(n-w, q) = 1$, such that the multiplicities of all hyperplanes are n or w modulo q. Then $\mathcal{B}$ can be reduced to an $(n-1, w)$-minihyper.

Further, we give a more elaborate extension (reducibility) condition found by Hitoshi Kanda [5] which applies only for codes over the field with three elements.

Theorem 3 *(H. Kanda, [5]).*

(1) Let C be an $[n, k, d]_3$ code with $(d, 3) = 1$ such that $A_i = 0$ for all $i \not\equiv 0, -1, -2$ (mod 9). Then C is doubly-extendable.

(2) Let $\mathcal{K}$ be an (n, w)-arc in $PG(k-1, 3)$. Assume that for every hyperplane H $\mathcal{K}(H) \equiv n, n+1, n+2$ (mod 9). Then $\mathcal{K}$ can be extended to an $(n+2, w)$-arc.

(3) Let $\mathcal{B}$ be an (n, w)-minihyper in $PG(k-1, 3)$. Assume that for every hyperplane $\mathcal{B}(H) \equiv n, n+1, n+2$ (mod 9). Then $\mathcal{B}$ can be reduced to an $(n-2, w)$-minihyper.

The following argument will be used several times in this paper. Let $\mathcal{B}$ be an (n, w)-minihyper in $PG(k-1, q)$. Fix an i-dimensional flat δ in $PG(k-1, q)$, with $\mathcal{B}(\delta) = t$. Let further π be a j-dimensional flat in $PG(k-1, q)$ of complementary dimension, i.e. $i + j = k - 2$ and $\delta \cap \pi = \varnothing$. Define the projection $\varphi = \varphi_{\delta, \pi}$ from δ onto π by

$$\varphi: \begin{cases} \mathcal{P} \setminus \delta \to \pi \\ Q \quad\ \to \pi \cap \langle \delta, Q \rangle. \end{cases} \tag{3}$$

This means that every point Q of $PG(k-1, q)$, which is not in δ, has as an image the point which is the intersection of π and the subspace generated by δ and Q. Here $\mathcal{P}$ denotes the pointset of $PG(k-1, q)$. Note that φ maps $(i + s)$-flats containing δ into $(s-1)$-flats in π. Given a set of points $F \subset \pi$, we define the induced minihyper $\mathcal{B}^\varphi$ by

$$\mathcal{B}^\varphi(F) = \sum_{\varphi_{\delta, \pi}(P) \in \mathcal{F}} \mathcal{B}(P).$$

We shall exploit the observation that if F is an f-dimensional flat in π then $\mathcal{B}^\varphi(F) \geq \beta_{f+i+1} - t$.

3 The Characterization of $(v_3 + 2v_2, v_2 + 2v_1)$-minihypers in $PG(r, q)$, $q \geq 5$

Let $\mathcal{B}$ be a $(v_3 + 2v_2, v_2 + 2v_1)$-minihyper in $PG(3, q)$, $q \geq 5$. Note that $(v_3 + 2v_2, v_2 + 2v_1) = (q^2 + 3q + 3q, q + 3)$. The restriction $\mathcal{B}|_H$ of $\mathcal{B}$ to a minimal plane is a $(v_2 + 2v_1, v_1) = (q + 3, 1)$-plane blocking set. For $q \geq 5$, blocking sets with these parameters are the sum of a line and two points.

Fix a minimal plane π_0 and a 1-line L in it. Denote by π_i, $i = 0, \ldots, q$, all planes through L. The planes π_i are all minimal since $1 + (q+1)(q+2) = q^2 + 3q + 3$. Consider a projection φ from the 1-point on L. Set $L_i = \varphi(\pi_i)$. Clearly, the lines L_i are of type $(0, q + \epsilon_0^{(i)}, \epsilon_1^{(i)}, \ldots, \epsilon_q^{(i)})$ with $\sum_j \epsilon_j^{(i)} = 2$.

Denote by X the set of points in the projection plane of multiplicity $q + \epsilon$. First we shall assume that not all points of X in the projection plane are collinear. Note that no four of these points are collinear. Otherwise, there exists a point P and three lines M_1, M_2, M_3 through P that do not contain points of multiplicity $q + \varepsilon$. Now we have

$$3 \cdot 2 + 2q \geq \sum \mathcal{B}^\varphi(M_i) \geq 3(q + 2),$$

a contradiction.

If at most three of the points from X are collinear (call this line M) then the same argument gives that all the remaining points on M are 2-points. Consider a 2-point P on M and call the two lines without points from X by M_1 and M_2. Now for the lines M_i we have

$$2 \cdot 2 + 2 \cdot 3 + (q - 3) \cdot 0 \geq \mathcal{B}^\varphi(M_1) + \mathcal{B}^\varphi(M_2) \geq 2(q + 2),$$

a contradiction.

If q is odd, there exist three collinear points in X. Therefore all the points from X are collinear. If $q \geq 8$ is even it is possible that the points in X and the common point of the lines L_i form a hyperoval. Then an external point to the hyperoval is incident with $q/2 \geq 4$ external lines and for the external lines through an external point we get again $2 \cdot q/2 + 2q \geq q/2(q+2)$, which is a contradiction. Hence in all cases the points from X are collinear. This implies that $\mathcal{B}$ is the sum of a plane and a $(2v_2, 2v_1)$ which is known to be the sum of two lines (cf. [7]).

The above argument proves the following result.

Theorem 4. *Every $(v_3 + 2v_2, v_2 + 2v_1)$-minihyper in $PG(3, q)$, $q \geq 5$ is the sum of a plane and two lines.*

The same theorem is true for minihypers with the same parameters in geometries of larger dimension.

Theorem 5. *Every $(v_3 + 2v_2, v_2 + 2v_1)$-minihyper in $PG(r, q)$, $r \geq 3$, $q \geq 5$ is the sum of a plane and two lines.*

Proof. We shall prove this result by induction on r. The first step in the induction is provided by Theorem 4.

Denote by $\mathcal{B}$ a minihyper in with parameters $(v_3 + 2v_2, v_2 + 2v_1)$ in $PG(r, q)$. Since the projection from a 0-point is again a minihyper with the same parameters in $PG(r-1, q)$, and since such a minihyper is the sum of a plane and two lines we have that the admissible hyperplane multiplicities for $\mathcal{B}$ are contained in the set

$$\{3, q+3, 2q+3, 3q+3, q^2+q+3, q^2+2q+3, q^2+3q+3\}. \tag{4}$$

Consider a hyperline S in $PG(r, q)$ of multiplicity 1. Let the point of multiplicity 1 in S be denoted by P. Denote by H_i the hyperplanes through S. The restriction of $\mathcal{B}$ to each H_i is the sum of a line L_i and two further points (which also might lie on L_i).

First let us assume that the lines L_i are not coplanar. In such case there exists a hyperline T in $PG(r, q)$ which is not blocked by the set $\cup L_i$. Denote by F_i the hyperpalnes through T. One of them meets $\cup L_i$ in one point and the remaining q meet $\cup L_i$ in $q+1$ points. Since each hyperplane is to be blocked . $q+3$ times we need $(q+2) + q \cdot 2 = 3q + 2$ additional points. But outside $\cup L_i$ we have just $2q + 2$ points which is a contradidiction. Hence the lines L_i are coplanar and $\cup L_i$ is a plane.

Since the admissible multiplicities of hyperplanes are in the list (4), we have that $\mathcal{B}$ is the sum of a line and a $(2v_2, 2v_1)$-minihyper. This proves the result since the latter is the sum of two planes.

For $(v_3 + 2v_2, v_2 + 2v_1)$-minihypers in $PG(3, q)$, where $q = 3$ or 4, the situation is more complicated. It is studied in the next two sections.

4   (21, 6)-minihypers in PG(3, 3)

Each line in PG(3, 3) has to blocked at least once. This implies that the restriction of a (21, 6)-minihyper to a plane is a line plus two points, or a projective triangle (a quadrangle plus two of its diagonal points). Moreover the maximal point multiplicity is 3.

Let $\mathcal{B}$ be a (21, 6)-minihyper (w.r.t. hyperplanes) in PG(3, 3). By Theorem 1 the possible multiplicity of a hyperplane is 0 (mod 3), i.e. these belong to $\{6, 9, 12, 15, 18, 21\}$. Moreover, a hyperplane of multilicity ≥ 15 does not have 0-points. Otherwise, an easy counting gives $|\mathcal{B}| \geq 15 + 9 \cdot 1 = 24 > 21$ (since each line through the 0-point outside the plane should be blocked). Hence if $\mathcal{B}$ has a hyperplane of multiplicity at least 15 then it is the sum of a plane and a (8, 2)-minihyper which in turn is the sum of two lines [1, 7].

It remains to consider (21, 6)-minihypers with hyperlanes of multiplicity 6, 9, 12. Note that 9- and 12-planes cannot have points of multiplicity 3. Consequently, $\mathcal{B}$ also does not have a point of multiplicity 3. For the spectrum of $\mathcal{B}$ we have

$$
\begin{aligned}
a_6 + \quad a_9 + \quad a_{12} = & \quad 40 \\
6a_6 + \quad 9a_9 + 12a_{12} = & \quad 273 \\
15a_6 + 36a_9 + 66a_{12} = & 840 + 9\lambda_2
\end{aligned}
$$

whence

$$
a_6 = 30 + \lambda_2, \ a_9 = 9 - 2\lambda_2, \ a_{12} = 1 + \lambda_2.
$$

Note that there cannot be a point-plane pair (P, π) with P a 2-point, π – a 12-plane, and $P \notin \pi$. Indeed, all lines through a 0-point in π must be blocked exacly once, while one of them is blocked twice (because of the 2-point). Hence all 2-ponts are in the intersection of all 12-planes. This implies that $\lambda_2 \leq 3$. The cases $\lambda_2 = 3$ or 2 are ruled out by an easy countnig of the multiplicities of the four (resp. three) 12-planes through the common line containing the 2-points. In the case $\lambda_2 = 1$, an easy counting gives that the two 12-planes meet in a 5-line, and that the other two planes through this 5-line are 6-planes.

Let us first consider the case $\lambda_2 = 1$. The two 12-planes have four 0-points in common: two in each of the 12-planes. The two 0-points in each of the 12-planes are collinear with the 2 point. Moreover the plane defined by the four 0-points in the 12-planes is a 6-plane consisting of four 1-points and one 2-point; the 1-points in this plane are collinear. This determines $\mathcal{B}$ uniquely.

Indeed, select five points P_1, P_2, P_3, P_4, Q in general position. The point $R = P_1 P_2 \cap P_3 P_4$ is the 2 -point; the line QR is the 5-line which is the common line of the 12-planes $\pi_0 = \langle P_1, P_2, Q \rangle$, $\pi_1 = \langle P_3, P_4, Q \rangle$. Let the other two planes through QR are π_2 and π_3. They are 6-planes. The 1-points off QR in π_2 and π_3 define the 4-line in the plane $\langle Q, P_1, P_2 \rangle$.

It remains to consider the case when $\lambda_2 = 0, a_{12} = 1$. Denote the unique 12-plane by π_0, and by P the 0-point in π_0. There are nine 1-points outside π_0. Assume these nine points and the point P form a cap. Then a tangent plane to this cap in a point different from P must be a 5-plane, which is impossible.

Hence there exist three collinear 1-points outside π_0 , P_1, P_2, P_3 say. Denote the fourth point on this line by Q_1; clearly $Q_1 \in \pi_0$.

Set $\pi_1 = \langle P, P_1, Q_1 \rangle$, and let π_2 and π_3 be the other other planes through PQ_1. Denote the other two points on PQ_1 by Q_2 and Q_3. It is easily checked that the remining six points of $\mathcal{B}$ are on two lines in π_2 and π_3, respectively, that meet π_0 in Q_2 and Q_3, respectively.

It is easily checked that this configuration is unique. We can sum up these observation in the following theorem.

Theorem 6. *A* $(21,6)$-*minihyper in* $PG(3,3)$ *is one of the following:*

(1) the sum of a plane and two lines.
(2) a minihyper with $\lambda_2 = 1$, $a_{12} = 2$;
(3) a minihyper with $\lambda_2 = 0$, $a_{12} = 1$.

Corollary 7. *There exist five* $(21,6)$-*minihypers (up to isomorphism).*

The five minihypers of the three possible types described in Theorem 6 are presented graphically on the pictures below. The doublecircled nodes represent 2-points (Figs. 1, 2 and 3).

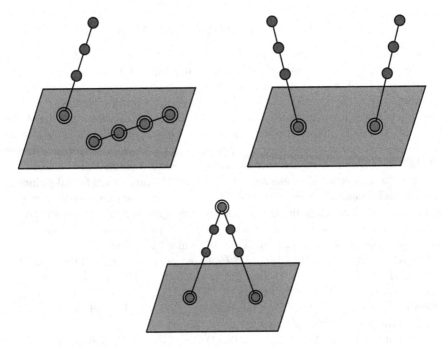

Fig. 1. $(21,6)$-minihypers in $PG(3,3)$ of type (1)

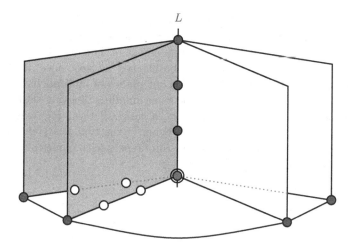

Fig. 2. $(21, 6)$-minihypers in PG$(3, 3)$ of type (2)

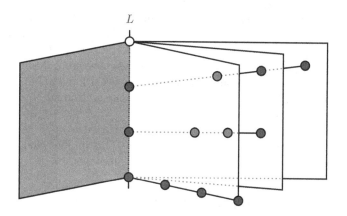

Fig. 3. $(21, 6)$-minihypers in PG$(3, 3)$ of type (3)

5 $(31, 7)$-minihypers in PG$(3, 4)$

In this section we characterize the $(v_3 + 2v_2, v_2 + 2v_1)$-minihypers in PG$(3, 4)$.

Theorem 8. *A $(31, 7)$-minihyper in PG$(3, 4)$ is one of the following:*

(1) the sum of a plane and two lines.
(2) a minihyper with $\lambda_3 = 1$; it is a cone with vertex the 3-point and base curve
  – a Baer subplane.

Proof. Let $\mathcal{B}$ be a $(31,7)$-minihyper in $PG(3,4)$. The restriction of $\mathcal{B}$ to a plane is either the sum of a line and two points or a Baer subplane.

By a result of Ward [12] which is a refinement of Theorem 1 all planes have odd multiplicity. Since each line has to be blocked at least once, a plane with 0-points has at most 15 points. This rules out planes of multiplicity 17 and 19.

Furthermore 21-planes are impossible since an affine blocking set has at least 13 points which gives $|\mathcal{B}| \geq 21 + 13 = 34$, a contradiction. The existence of a plane with at least 23 points gives a minihyper of the type described in (1).

Hence we have to characterize just the minihypers with planes of multiplicity 7, 11, 15. For the spectrum of $\mathcal{B}$ we have

$$
\begin{aligned}
a_7 + \quad a_{11} + \quad a_{15} &= 85 \\
7a_7 + 11a_{11} + 15a_{15} &= 651 \\
21a_7 + 55a_{11} + 105a_{15} &= 2325 + 16\lambda_2 + 48\lambda_3
\end{aligned}
$$

whence

$$
a_7 = 75 + \lambda_2 + 3\lambda_3, \; a_{11} = 6 - 2\lambda_2 - 6\lambda_3, \; a_{15} = 4 + \lambda_2 + 3\lambda_3.
$$

A 15-plane is (i) the sum of three concurrent lines; (ii) the sum of three non-concurrent lines (iii) the complement of an oval.

In case (iii) the planes through a 3 line must be all 7-planes and hence the minihyper should be projective, i.e. $\lambda_2 = \lambda_3 = 0$. On the other side through a 5-line there is one further 15-plane whence $a_{15} = 7$, a contradiction.

In case (ii) we get easily $\lambda_2 = 3$ since all planes through a 3-line without 0-points should be 7-planes without 0-points. On the other hand a 7-line is incident with two further 15-planes, and each of them has one additional 2-point, whence $\lambda_2 \geq 5$, a contradiction.

In case (i), it is easily seen that $\lambda_3 = 1, \lambda_2 = 0$. Hence $a_7 = 78, a_{11} = 0, a_{15} = 7$. In addition all 7-planes should be Baer planes. This implies that $\mathcal{B}$ is a cone with vertex the 3-point and base curve – a Baer subplane.

6 $(22,6)$-minihypers in $PG(3,3)$

The goal here is to prove that every $(22,6)$-minihyper in $PG(3,3)$ is reducible to a $(21,6)$-minihyper.

Denote by $\mathcal{B}$ a minihyper in $PG(3,3)$ with parameters $(22,6)$. Counting arguments give that for every plane π, it holds $\mathcal{B}(\pi) \in \{6,7,\ldots,22\}$. Morover we have the following lemma.

Lemma 9. *Let $\mathcal{B}$ be a $(22,6)$-minihyper in $PG(3,3)$. If π is a hyperplane of multiplicity $\mathcal{B}(\pi) = 22 - 3i - j$, $i \in \{0,\ldots,5\}$, $j \in \{0,1,2\}$ then $\mathcal{B}|_\pi$ is a $(22 - 3i - j, 6 - i)$ minihyper*

Corollary 10. *A $(22,6)$-minihyper in $PG(3,3)$ does not have 11-plane. An 8-plane in such a minihyper is the sum of two lines.*

As in the previous subsection, a 14-plane does not have 0-points. If $\mathcal{B}(\pi) \geq 15$ for some plane π then it is the sum of a plane and a $(9, 2)$-minihyper in $PG(3, 3)$. The latter is the sum of two lines and point [1]. This implies that in this case $\mathcal{B}$ is reducible.

Next we tackle the case when $a_{14} > 0$.

Lemma 11. *There exists no $(22, 6)$-minihyper in $PG(3, 3)$ with a 14-plane.*

Proof. Since a 14-plane does not have 0-points, it has one 2-point and twelve 1-points, and spectrum $a'_4 = 9$, $a'_5 = 4$. Morover all planes different from the 14-plane have multiplicity at most 10. We have the following equations for the spectrum of $\mathcal{B}$:

$$\sum a'_i = 40 \tag{5}$$

$$\sum i a'_i = 286 \tag{6}$$

$$\sum \binom{i}{2} a'_i = 924 + 9\lambda'_2 + 27\lambda'_3 \tag{7}$$

which, taking into account that $a'_{14} = 1$ implies

$$a_8 + 3a_9 + 6a_{10} = 20 + 9\lambda'_2 + 27\lambda'_3. \tag{8}$$

Now we count the contributions to the LHS of (8) of the planes through the different lines in the 14-plane. For a 4-line this contribution is 0 since a 8-plane does not have a 4-line (it is the sum of two lines and has just 2-, 5- or 8-lines). For a 5-line this contribution is at most 6. Hence (8) implies

$$20 + 9\lambda'_2 + 27\lambda'_3 \leq 9 \cdot 0 + 4 \cdot 6 = 24.$$

This implies $\lambda'_2 = \lambda'_3 = 0$, which is a contradiction because we have at least one 2-point (the one in the 14-plane).

Finally, we are going to rule out the existence of 8-planes in $\mathcal{B}$. Then $\mathcal{B}$ will be reducible by the lemma of Hill and Lizak. Let us note that if π is an 8-plane then $\mathcal{B}|_\pi$ is the sum of two lines and has one of the two spectra:

$(A)\ a'_8 = 1, a'_2 = 12, \lambda'_2 = 4;\quad (B)\ a'_5 = 2, a'_2 = 11, \lambda'_2 = 1.$

Again from (5), we have

$$a_8 + 3a_9 + 6a_{10} + 15a'_{12} + 21a'_{13} = 48 + 9\lambda'_2 + 27\lambda'_3. \tag{9}$$

Lemma 12. *There exists no $(22, 6)$-minihyper in $PG(3, 3)$ with a 8-plane.*

Proof. 1) Assume there exists an 8-plane with spectrum (A), and let us count the contribution of the planes through the lines in the 8-plane to the left-hand side of (9). The maximal contribution through the 8-line is 57, while the comaximal contribution through a 2-line is 1. Hence we have (since $\lambda'_2 \geq 4$)

$$70 = 1 + 1 \cdot 57 + 12 \cdot 1 \geq 48 + 9\lambda'_2 + 27\lambda'_3 \geq 48 + 9 \cdot 4 = 84,$$

a contradiction.

2) The same argument for an 8-plane with spectrum (B) gives

$$66 = 1 + 2 \cdot 27 + 11 \cdot 1 \geq 48 + 9\lambda'_2 + 27\lambda'_3, \tag{10}$$

whence $\lambda'_2 = 1$ or 2, $\lambda'_3 = 0$.

Assume $\lambda'_2 = 2$. Then in (10) we have equality and the spectrum of $\mathcal{B}$ is

$$a'_{13} = 2, a'_{10} = 2, a'_8 = 12, a'_6 = 24.$$

Since the largest cap in $PG(3,3)$ has 10 points, there exist three 8-planes sharing a common line which is forced to be a 2-line. This is clearly impossible since then we have:

$$|\mathcal{B}| \geq 3 \cdot 8 + 6 - 3 \cdot 2 = 24 > 22.$$

Now assume $\lambda'_2 = 1$. We get from (10) that $a'_{13} \geq 1$. But $a'_{13} \geq 2$ is impossible since two 13-planes should meet in a line of multiplicity at least 6. This is a contradiction since we have just one 2-point. Hence $a'_{13} = 1$. But there must be a plane of multiplicity (otherwise, we have again a contradiction to (10)).

Now denote by π_o the 13-plane, by π_1 – the 12-plane. These two should meet in a 5-line which contains the 2-point P. The two remaining planes through L, π_2 and π_3 say, are 6-planes. Denote by R_1 (resp. R_2) the 1-point in π_2 (resp. π_3) outside L. Furthermore, let Q_0 be the 0-point in π_o, and Q_1, Q_2 – the two 0-points in π_1. As before Q_1Q_2 is incident with P and so the plane $\langle Q_0, Q_1, Q_2 \rangle$ is incident with the point P.

Now assume there exists a 10-plane, δ say. This plane should meet π_o and π_1 in 5-lines (through P), and it should contain also R_1 and R_2. The line Q_0Q_1 contains one of the points R_1, R_2, R_1 say, since it should be blocked at least once. By a similar argument, Q_0Q_2 contains R_2. But now we have that $\langle Q_0, Q_1, Q_2 \rangle \cap \delta$ contains P, R_1, and R_2, whence $\langle Q_0, Q_1, Q_2 \rangle \equiv \delta$, which is clearly impossible. So far, we have shown that $\mathcal{B}$ contains no 10-plane. It remains to use (10) once more to get

$$57 + 48 + 9\lambda'_2 \leq 1 + 1 \cdot 24 + 1 \cdot 19 + 11 \cdot 1 = 55,$$

a contradiction.

Theorem 13. *A $(22,6)$-minihyper in $PG(3,3)$ is reducible.*

Using similar arguments it can proved that the same result holds for arbitrary 3-dimensional geometries.

Theorem 14. *Every $(v_3 + 2v_2 + v_1, v_2 + 2v_1)$-minihyper in $PG(3, q)$, $q \geq 3$, is reducible.*

Acknowledgments. The first author was supported by the Strategic Development Fund of the New Bulgarian University and by the Bulgarian National Science Research Fund under Contract KP-06-32/2 - 07.12.2019. The second author was supported by the Research Fund of Sofia University under Contract 80-10-177/27.05.2022 and by the Bulgarian National Science Research Fund under Contract KP-06-32/2 - 07.12.2019. The third author was supported by the Research Fund of Sofia University under Contract 80-10-52/10.05. 2022.

References

1. Hamada, N.: A characterization of some $[n, k, d; q]$-codes meeting the Griesmer bound using a minihyper in a finite projective geometry. Discrete Math. **116**, 229–268 (1993)
2. Hill, R.: Optimal linear codes. In: Mitchell, C. (ed.) Cryptography and Coding II. Oxford Univ, pp. 75–104. Press, Oxford (1992)
3. Hill, R.: An extension theorem for linear codes. Des. Codes Cryptogr. **17**, 151–157.11111 (1999)
4. Hill, R., Lizak, P.: Extensions of linear codes. In: Proceedings IEEE International Symposium on Information Theory, Whistler, Canada, p. 345 (1995)
5. Kanda, H.: A new extension theorem for ternary linear codes and its application. Finite Fields Appl. **67**, 1017111 (2020). https://doi.org/10.1016/j.ffa.2020.101711
6. Landjev, I., Rogachev, E., Rousseva, A.: On ternary codes and blocking sets in PG(r, q), manuscript
7. Landjev, I., Vandendriesche, P.: A study of (xv_t, xv_{t-1})-minihypers in PG(t, q). J. Combin. Theory Ser. A **119**, 1123–1131 (2012)
8. Maruta, T., Oya, Y.: On optimal ternary linear codes of dimension 6. Adv. Math. Comm. **5**(3), 505–520 (2011)
9. Sawashima, T., Maruta, T.: Nonexistence of some ternary linear codes with minimum weight-2 modulo 9, Adv. Math. Comm. (2022). (to appear)
10. Takenaka, M., Okamoto, K., Maruta, T.: On optimalnon-projective termary linear codes. Discrete Math. **308**, 842–854 (2008)
11. Yoshida, Y., Maruta, T.: Ternary linear codes and quadrics. Electronic J. Combin. **16**, #R9 (2009)
12. Ward, H.N.: Divisibility of codes meeting the Griesmer bound. J. Comb. Theory Ser. A **83**(1), 79–93 (1998)

Integer Sequences in the HP Model of Dill

Slav Angelov[✉][iD] and Latchezar Tomov[iD]

New Bulgarian University, Sofia, Bulgaria
{sangelov,lptomov}@nbu.bg

Abstract. We examine a sequence that we derive from Dill's hydrophobic-polar protein folding model in a two-dimensional square lattice. This sequence already exists as A248333 in the OEIS, but the information is scarce. We construct two more sequences not previously listed in the OEIS, A342711 and A342712. Thanks to the perspective given us by Dill's model, we find relationships between sequences 248333, A240025, A000267, A342711, A342712, 000027, and A000217. We use the newly found relationships to obtain an explicit formula for the nth member of A248333 and a formula for the nth member of its partial sums, A342712. Moreover, we find an explicit formula for the nth member of A342711 and present an alternative proof for the nth member of A000267.

Keywords: Dill's HP model · Square lattice · Quarter square · Spiral · Positive integer sequence

1 Introduction

The sequence that we are going to discuss is listed in the OEIS [4] as A248333, first documented by Wesley Hurt in 2014. The first terms of the sequence are as follows:

$$0, 0, 0, 0, 1, 1, 2, 2, 3, 4, 4, 5, 6, 6, 7, 8, 9, 9, 10, 11, 12, 12, 13, 14, 15, 16, 16, 17, 18, 19,$$
$$20, 20, 21, 22, 23, 24, 25, 25, 26, 27, 28, 29, 30, 30, 31, 32, 33, \ldots.$$

Sequence A248333 emerges while trying to count the total number of squares that are formed while adding adjacent points on a square lattice. The complete idea behind the creation of the sequence can be seen in Fig. 1.

Hurt noticed that the pattern fails to add a square for $n > 0$ if n is of the form $k^2 + 1$ (A002522) or $k^2 - k + 1$ (A002061). This is all that was known till now. We will continue this paper by presenting a slightly different way of deriving A248333. This will help us to obtain an explicit formula for the nth member of the sequence and a formula for the sum of the first n members. Moreover, we will derive and analyze some other sequences related to A248333.

© ICST Institute for Computer Sciences, Social Informatics and Telecommunications Engineering 2022
Published by Springer Nature Switzerland AG 2022. All Rights Reserved
T. Zlateva and R. Goleva (Eds.): CSECS 2022, LNICST 450, pp. 154–167, 2022.
https://doi.org/10.1007/978-3-031-17292-2_13

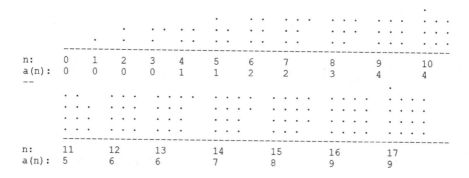

n:	0	1	2	3	4	5	6	7	8	9	10
a(n):	0	0	0	0	1	1	2	2	3	4	4

n:	11	12	13	14	15	16	17
a(n):	5	6	6	7	8	9	9

Fig. 1. Counting the squares while observing the added points.

2 Deriving the Sequence

In order to present the new approach for deriving A248333, we will make a brief introduction to a problem in biology. We may observe the proteins as the building blocks of the living organisms. Each protein consists of a strictly determined sequence of amino acids (there might be some additions to the protein's structure, but we will ignore them for simplicity). If we put a sequence of amino acids in a liquid environment, it will always take one and the same shape in space. This shape determines the unique properties of each protein. If the biologists have an away to determine what will be the shape based on the amino acid sequence, this will help them to create methods against incurable diseases. The problem is that finding a protein structure is not an easy task. Dill was one of the first scientists who proposed a possible approach to the protein structure problem, see paper [2]. He noticed that some of the amino acids are hydrophilic (H) while the rest are hydrophobic (P). Then he classified all of the main amino acid types into the two mentioned groups. Thus, a protein can be observed as a finite strictly determined sequence of Hs and Ps, we will refer to them as HP-sequences. Dill observed HP-sequences in a square lattice where he claimed that to obtain the protein structure, we need to locate the HP-sequence in a way that maximizes the number of *contacts* between the Hs. We say that there is a *contact* if two Hs are adjacent on the lattice and are not next to each other on the HP-sequence. The described model is called hydrophobic-polar protein folding model (HP model).

Finding the maximum number of contacts in the HP model is an NP-hard task even on a two-dimensional square lattice. Thus, many heuristic algorithms were created, see papers [1,5–8], and many others. In general, the upper bound for the possible number of contacts on a two-dimensional square lattice is equal to $2 \times min\{ODD, EVEN\}$, where ODD is the total number of Hs in the chosen HP-sequence that are on odd positions (respectively for $EVEN$). This boundary is exploited by the theory, e.g., see this article [3]. The upper bound is obtained thanks to the fact that it is not possible to realize a contact between Hs that are both odd or both even on a square lattice. In order to refine the upper bound for specific cases, we examined HP-sequences that are entirely from Hs. We maximized the total number of contacts by putting HP-sequences of size n in the form of a spiral, see Fig. 1. We noted that the total number of contacts for a spiral with n elements corresponds to the nth member of A248333. This is not an unexpected fact, if we observe carefully, we see that counting contacts in the spiral is equivalent to counting squares while adding points like Hurt did, see Fig. 1.

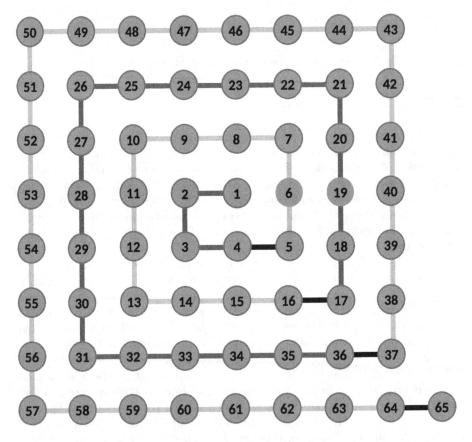

Fig. 2. Aminoacid chain on a square lattice ordered in the form of a spiral.

3   Definitions and Lemmas

We analyzed some structures in the spiral in Fig. 2 to help us for the further analysis in this work. We defined these structures in the next several definitions and described some of their properties.

Definition 1. *We distinguish* layers *in the spiral.* Layer 1 *includes the elements indexed by 1, 2, 3, and 4 in the spiral.* Layer 2 *includes the elements that fully surround* Layer 1, *i.e.,* 4, 5, 6,...,16. Layer 3 *includes the elements that fully surround* Layer 2, *and so on. We denote* Layer N *by* L_N.

In Fig. 2, layers are easily distinguishable thanks to the colors blue and red, the back color shows the transition between the layers. Note that each layer is in the form of a square. We examined some properties of the newly defined layers.

Lemma 1. *The number of elements in the Nth layer are $8N - 4$.*

Proof. The number of elements in each layer is as follows:

1. $4 \to 4 + 0 \times 8$;
2. $12 \to 4 + 1 \times 8$;
3. $20 \to 4 + 2 \times 8$;
4. $28 \to 4 + 3 \times 8$;
5. ...

Let the observed relations hold for Layer N, so we have $4 + 8(N-1)$. If we observe Fig. 2, we see that the elements in each layer form a square. If we transpose the sides of this square to the upper layer, we will need to add exactly 4 more elements to complete the upper layer, and we have duplicated the elements in each corner of the previous layer. Thus, the total number of elements added is 8. For Layer N+1, we have $(4 + 8(N - 1)) + 8 = 4 + 8N$. The expected formula for Layer N+1 is $4 + 8N$, and is identical to the obtained one. We proved the lemma by induction. The only think left is to simplify the formula for Layer N: $4 + 8(N - 1) = 8N - 4$.

Lemma 2. *The total number of contacts in the Nth layer with the previous ones is $C(L_N) = \#L_N - 4 = 8(N - 1)$, $N > 1$.*

Proof. Note that the elements in L_N do not form a contact only at the beginning, and on the three consecutive corners of the square, the total number is 4. If we denote the total number of contacts in L_N by $C(L_N)$, we have $C(L_N) = \#L_N - 4 = 8(N - 1)$. The only exception is Layer 1, where we have only one contact, and it is with itself.

Definition 2. *A* level *in the spiral is a structure that includes all of the layers till the index of the level. We denote the Nth level by Lv_N or Level N, and by $Lv(n)$ the maximum possible level which has elements less than n.*

Level 1 consists of Layer 1; Lv_2 consists of L_1 and L_2; Lv_3 consists of L_1, L_2, and L_3; and so on.

Lemma 3. *The number of elements $\#Lv_N$ in the Nth level is $(2N)^2$.*

Proof. The number of elements in the Nth level is equal to the sum of the elements in all of the layers in this level:

$$\#Lv_N = \sum_{i=1}^{N}(8i - 4) = 8\sum_{i=1}^{N} i - 4N = 8\frac{N(N+1)}{2} - 4N = 4N^2.$$

Lemma 4. *The total number of contacts in the Nth level is $C(Lv_N) = (2N - 1)^2$.*

Proof.

$$C(Lv_N) = \sum_{i=1}^{N} C(L_i) = \sum_{i=1}^{N} (8(i-1)) + 1 = 8 \sum_{i=1}^{N} i - 8N + 1 =$$

$$= 8 \frac{N(N+1)}{2} - 8N + 1 = 4N^2 - 4N + 1 = (2N - 1)^2.$$

Corollary 1. *The total number of contacts in the Nth level is equal to the sum of the first m odd numbers, where $m = 2N - 1$.*

Proof. We will use the following well-known formula $1+2+3+5+\ldots+(2m-1) = m^2$. It states that the sum of the first m odd numbers is equal to the square of their number. We can use $m = 2N - 1$ to obtain the desired result.

Lemma 5. *The maximum possible level $Lv(n)$ of a given integer n is equal to $\lfloor \frac{\sqrt{n}}{2} \rfloor$, function $\lfloor \ldots \rfloor$ is the floor function.*

Proof. Note that the expression $\lfloor \frac{\sqrt{n}}{2} \rfloor$ gives an integer for $n = 4N^2$, $N \in N$ even without the floor function, this happens when n coincides with the number of elements in a level, see Lemma 3. Let observe the case where $n = \#Lv_N + e$ is between Lv_N and Lv_{N+1}:

$$4N^2 < n < 4(N+1)^2 \leftrightarrow \frac{\sqrt{4N^2}}{2} < \frac{\sqrt{n}}{2} < \frac{\sqrt{4(N+1)^2}}{2} \leftrightarrow N < \frac{\sqrt{n}}{2} < N+1.$$

Thus, we obtain N if we use $\lfloor \frac{\sqrt{n}}{2} \rfloor$ for any n between $4N^2$ and $4(N+1)^2$.

4   Some Other Related Sequences

We, again, observe Fig. 2. Let observe the spiral from the beginning layer by layer, and put 1 where the aminoacids do not form a contact with the previous layer, and 0 elsewhere. We will obtain the following sequence:

$$n = 1, 2, 3, 4, 5, 6, 7, 8, 9, 10, 11, 12, 13, 14, 15, 16, 17, 18, 19, 20, 21, 22, 23, 24, \ldots$$
$$a(n) = 1, 1, 1, 0, 1, 0, 1, 0, 0, 1, 0, 0, 1, 0, 0, 0, 1, 0, 0, 0, 1, 0, 0, 0, \ldots$$

We denote this sequence by A_0, and its nth member by $A_0(n)$. The nth member of sequence A_0 corresponds to the $n - 1$th member of sequence A240025 in the OEIS (small difference in the indexing). We keep our indexing because it better reflects the framework of the HP model that we are using.

If we observe the partial sums of A_0, we will obtain the following sequence:

$$n = 1, 2, 3, 4, 5, 6, 7, 8, 9, 10, 11, 12, 13, 14, 15, 16, 17, 18, 19, 20, 21, 22, 23, 24, \ldots$$
$$a(n) = 1, 2, 3, 3, 4, 4, 5, 5, 5, 6, 6, 6, 7, 7, 7, 7, 8, 8, 8, 8, 9, 9, 9, 9, \ldots$$

Let denote this sequence by S_{A_0} and its nth member by $S_{A_0}(n)$. The nth member of sequence S_{A_0} corresponds to the $n - 1$th member of sequence A000267 in the OEIS.

Now, if we observe the partial sums of S_{A_0}:

$$n = 1, 2, 3, 4, 5, 6, 7, 8, 9, 10, 11, 12, 13, 14, 15, 16, 17, 18, 19, 20, 21, \ldots$$
$$a(n) = 1, 3, 6, 9, 13, 17, 22, 27, 32, 38, 44, 50, 57, 64, 71, 78, 86, 94, 102, 110, 119, \ldots$$

Let denote this sequence by SS_{A_0} and its nth member by $SS_{A_0}(n)$. The nth member of sequence SS_{A_0} corresponds to the $n - 1$th member of sequence A342711 in the OEIS.

Finally, we will denote our initial sequence A248333 by A and its nth member by $A(n)$. While observing the partial sums of A, we obtain the following sequence:

$$n = 1, 2, 3, 4, 5, 6, 7, 8, 9, 10, 11, 12, 13, 14, 15, 16, 17, 18, 19, 20, 21, 22, \ldots$$
$$a(n) = 0, 0, 0, 1, 2, 4, 6, 9, 13, 17, 22, 28, 34, 41, 49, 58, 67, 77, 88, 100, 112, 125, \ldots$$

We denote this sequence by S_A and its nth member by $S_{A(n)}$. Sequence S_A corresponds to A342712 in the OEIS.

5   Some Explicit Formulas for the Presented Sequences

Proposition 1. *The nth member of sequence S_{A_0} is estimated by the following formula:*

$$S_{A_0}(n) = 3N + q - 1 + \left\lceil \frac{\sqrt{n}}{2} \right\rceil,$$

where:

1. $N = \left\lfloor \frac{\sqrt{n}}{2} \right\rfloor$;
2. $q = \left\lfloor \frac{n - 4N^2}{2N + 1} \right\rfloor$.

The function $\lfloor \ldots \rfloor$ is the floor function, and the function $\lceil \ldots \rceil$ is the ceil function.

Proof. Sequence A_0 highlights the elements that do not form a contact in the spiral, see Fig. 2, we have 1 there, 0 if there is a contact. Note that A_0 is 1 only on the three of possible four formed corners of a layer (each layer has a square form) of the spiral, and at the first element of the next layer. We represent n as $n = \#Lv_N + R$, where $\#Lv_N = Lv(n)$ is the number of elements of the maximum level which has elements less than n, and $R = n - N$ is what is left from n. Sequence S_{A_0} represents the sum of the first n members of A_0. Let $n = \#Lv_N$, $N = 1, 2, \ldots$. Then $S_{A_0}(n) = 4N - 1$ - for each layer we have 1 four times, in the Nth layer 3 times. Let $n \neq \#Lv_N$. Then $n = \#Lv_N + R$, $0 < R < \#L_{N+1}$. We need to determine the ones in R. The elements in R are part from Layer $N + 1$. Each layer can be observed as a square with 4 sides, each side has $\frac{\#L_{N+1}}{4} = 2N + 1$ elements (we used Lemma 1). We have one 1 at the end of each side. The total number of sides that are covered by the elements of R is equal to R divided by the number of elements in one of the sides of Layer N which is $\left\lfloor \frac{R}{2N+1} \right\rfloor = \left\lfloor \frac{n-4N^2}{2N+1} \right\rfloor$. Thus, we obtained $S_{A_0}(n) = 4N - 1 + \left\lfloor \frac{n-4N^2}{2N+1} \right\rfloor$. Because there is one additional 1 at the beginning of Layer $N + 1$, we must correct the formula by replacing "1" with $F = \left\lfloor N + 1 - \frac{\sqrt{n}}{2} \right\rfloor$. The fix F is 1 only if n coincides with the number of elements of a level, i.e., $R = 0$, it is 0 in all other cases. We simplified F by using the following link between the floor and ceil functions: $\lfloor -a \rfloor = -\lceil a \rceil$.

$$F = \left\lfloor N + 1 - \frac{\sqrt{n}}{2} \right\rfloor = N + 1 + \left\lfloor -\frac{\sqrt{n}}{2} \right\rfloor = N + 1 - \left\lceil \frac{\sqrt{n}}{2} \right\rceil.$$

$$S_{A_0}(n) = 4N - 1 + \left\lfloor \frac{n-4N^2}{2N+1} \right\rfloor - F = 3N + q - 1 + \left\lceil \frac{\sqrt{n}}{2} \right\rceil.$$

Theorem 1. *An explicit formula for the nth member of sequence S_{A_0} is as follows:*

$$S_{A_0}(n) = \lceil 2\sqrt{n} \rceil - 1,$$

where the function $\lceil \ldots \rceil$ is the ceil function.

Proof. We count the number of ones in each level in the context of sequences A_0 and S_{A_0}:

1. The total number is 3;
2. The total number is $3 + 4$;
3. The total number is $3 + 2 \times 4$;
4. The total number is $3 + 3 \times 4$;
5. ...

By induction (we skip the induction phase for clarity, see the proof of Lemma 1 for a similar approach), we obtain the following formula for Layer N: $3 + 4(N-1)$. Now, $\#Lv_N = 4N^2$. Thus, $n = 4N^2$, and $N = \frac{\sqrt{n}}{2}$. Finally, $S_{A_0}(n) = 3 + 4(\frac{\sqrt{n}}{2} - 1) = 2\sqrt{n} - 1$. The final expression is not always an integer because n cannot always coincide with $\#Lv_N$. However, if we round it to the upper integer, we will obtain the desired result: $S_{A_0}(n) = \lceil 2\sqrt{n} - 1 \rceil = \lceil 2\sqrt{n} \rceil - 1$. Now, we will show that the derived express for $S_{A_0}(n)$ is equivalent to the expression in Proposition 1:

$$\lceil 2\sqrt{n} \rceil - 1 \overset{?}{=} 3N + q - 1 + \left\lceil \frac{\sqrt{n}}{2} \right\rceil \Leftrightarrow \left\lceil \frac{4\sqrt{n}}{2} \right\rceil \overset{?}{=} 3N + q + \left\lceil \frac{\sqrt{n}}{2} \right\rceil. \tag{1}$$

From Lemma 5, we have that $\lfloor \frac{\sqrt{n}}{2} \rfloor = N \Rightarrow \frac{\sqrt{n}}{2} = N + r, 0 \le r < 1$. We substitute the derived expression for $\frac{\sqrt{n}}{2}$ in (1):

$$\left\lceil \frac{4\sqrt{n}}{2} \right\rceil \overset{?}{=} 3N + q + \left\lceil \frac{\sqrt{n}}{2} \right\rceil \Leftrightarrow \lceil 4(N + r) \rceil \overset{?}{=} 3N + q + \lceil N + r \rceil. \tag{2}$$

Additionally, using Lemma 3, we can express n by $n = N^2 + R, R < 4(2N + 1)$. Let observe $R = 4(2N + 1)$. Then $n = (N + 1)^2$, and it coincides with the next level. If we observe $q = \left\lfloor \frac{n-4N^2}{2N+1} \right\rfloor$ (see Proposition 1), we note that:

- $q = 0$, $0 \leq R < 2N + 1$;
- $q = 1$, $2N + 1 \leq R < 2(2N + 1)$;
- $q = 2$, $2(2N + 1) \leq R < 3(2N + 1)$;
- $q = 3$, $3N + 1 \leq R < 4(2N + 1)$;
- $q = 4$, $R = 4(2N + 1)$.

Finally, we need to obtain a relationship between R and r based on $\frac{\sqrt{n}}{2}$:

- For $R = 0$, we have $\frac{\sqrt{n}}{2} = \sqrt{\frac{n}{4}} = \sqrt{\frac{4N^2 + 0}{4}} = N + 0 = N + r$, $r = 0$;

- For $R = 2N + 1$, $\sqrt{\frac{n}{4}} = \sqrt{\frac{4N^2 + 2N + 1}{4}} = \sqrt{N^2 + \frac{N}{2} + \frac{1}{16} + \frac{1}{16}}$
  $= \sqrt{(N + \frac{1}{4})^2 + \frac{1}{16}} > N + \frac{1}{4} = N + r$, $r = \frac{1}{4}$;

- For $R = 2(2N + 1)$, $\sqrt{\frac{n}{4}} = \sqrt{\frac{4N^2 + 2(2N+1)}{4}} = \sqrt{N^2 + N + \frac{1}{4} + \frac{1}{4}}$
  $= \sqrt{(N + \frac{1}{2})^2 + \frac{1}{4}} > N + \frac{1}{2} = N + r$, $r = \frac{1}{2}$;

- For $R = 3(2N + 1)$, $\sqrt{\frac{n}{4}} = \sqrt{\frac{4N^2 + 3(2N+1)}{4}} = \sqrt{N^2 + \frac{6N}{4} + \frac{9}{16} + \frac{3}{16}}$
  $= \sqrt{(N + \frac{3}{4})^2 + \frac{3}{16}} > N + \frac{3}{4} = N + r$, $r = \frac{3}{4}$;

- For $R = 4(2N + 1)$, we have $\frac{\sqrt{n}}{2} = \sqrt{\frac{n}{4}} = \sqrt{\frac{4N^2 + 4(2N+1)}{4}} = N + 1 = N + r$, $r = 1$.

So, we obtained the following relationships:

- $n = 4N^2 + R$, $0 \leq R < 2N + 1 \Rightarrow \frac{\sqrt{n}}{2} = N + r$, $0 \leq r \leq \frac{1}{4}$;
- $n = 4N^2 + R$, $2N + 1 \leq R < 2(2N + 1) \Rightarrow \frac{\sqrt{n}}{2} = N + r$, $\frac{1}{4} < r \leq \frac{1}{2}$;
- $n = 4N^2 + R$, $2(2N + 1) \leq R < 3(2N + 1) \Rightarrow \frac{\sqrt{n}}{2} = N + r$, $\frac{1}{2} < r \leq \frac{3}{4}$;
- $n = 4N^2 + R$, $3(2N + 1) \leq R < 4(2N + 1) \Rightarrow \frac{\sqrt{n}}{2} = N + r$, $\frac{3}{4} < r < 1$.

Now, from Expression 2, we can check $\lceil 4(N + r) \rceil \overset{?}{=} 3N + q + \lceil N + r \rceil$:

- For $n = 4N^2 + R$, $0 \leq R < 2N + 1$, we have $4N + 1 \overset{?}{=} 3N + 0 + N + 1 = 4N + 1$;
- For $n = 4N^2 + R$, $2N + 1 \leq R < 2(2N + 1)$, we have $4N + 2 \overset{?}{=} 3N + 1 + N + 1 = 4N + 2$;
- For $n = 4N^2 + R$, $2(2N + 1) \leq R < 3(2N + 1)$, we have $4N + 3 \overset{?}{=} 3N + 2 + N + 1 = 4N + 3$;
- For $n = 4N^2 + R$, $3(2N + 1) \leq R < 4(2N + 1)$, we have $4N + 4 \overset{?}{=} 3N + 3 + N + 1 = 4N + 4$;
- For $n = 4N^2 + R$, $R = 4(2N + 1)$, we have $n = 4(N + 1)^2$. This means that n coincides with the next level, and the equality is true.

Thus, the expressions in Proposition 1 and Theorem 1 are equivalent.

Corollary 2. *An explicit formula for the nth member of A000267 is as follows:*

$$A000267(n) = \lceil 2\sqrt{n + 1} \rceil - 1,$$

where the function $\lceil \dots \rceil$ is the ceil function.

Proof. It directly follows from the relationship between S_{A_0} and $\underline{A000267}$, S_{A_0} $(n) = A000267(n-1)$.

Lemma 6. *The nth member of $\underline{A248333}$ can be expressed thanks to sequence S_{A_0}:*

$$A(n) = n - S_{A_0}(n) = \underline{A000027} - \underline{A000267}(n-1).$$

Proof. First, note that $A(n) = n$ if each consecutive element adds a contact. Second, correct that expression by subtracting the cases where there are no contacts, they are $S_{A_0}(n)$ by definition (see how we defined A_0 and S_{A_0}).

Proposition 2. *An explicit formula for the nth member of $\underline{A248333}$ is as follows:*

$$A(n) = n - 3N - q + 1 - \left\lceil \frac{\sqrt{n}}{2} \right\rceil,$$

where:

1. $N = \left\lfloor \frac{\sqrt{n}}{2} \right\rfloor$;
2. $q = \left\lfloor \frac{n-4N^2}{2N+1} \right\rfloor$.

The function $\lfloor \ldots \rfloor$ is the floor function, and the function $\lceil \ldots \rceil$ is the ceil function.

Proof. It directly follows from Proposition 1 and Lemma 6.

Theorem 2. *An explicit formula for the nth member of $\underline{A248333}$ is as follows:*

$$A(n) = \lfloor (\sqrt{n}-1)^2 \rfloor = n + 1 - \lceil 2\sqrt{n} \rceil,$$

where the function $\lfloor \ldots \rfloor$ is the floor function, and the function $\lceil \ldots \rceil$ is the ceil function.

Proof. We can derive this formula by induction in a similar way like in the pretext of Theorem 1. We can see that the expression in Theorem 2 is equivalent to the expression in Proposition 2 by the following:

$$n + 1 - \lceil 2\sqrt{n} \rceil \overset{?}{=} n - 3N - q + 1 - \left\lceil \frac{\sqrt{n}}{2} \right\rceil \Leftrightarrow \lceil 2\sqrt{n} \rceil \overset{?}{=} 3N + q + \left\lceil \frac{\sqrt{n}}{2} \right\rceil.$$

Thus, we ended with the already proved equality in the proof of Theorem 1.

We can use Theorem 2 to obtain the nth partial sum $SS_{A_0}(n)$ of sequence $\underline{A248333}$:

$$SS_{A_0}(n) = \sum_{i=1}^{n}(i + 1 - \lceil 2\sqrt{i} \rceil) = \frac{n(n+3)}{2} - \sum_{i=1}^{n}(\lceil 2\sqrt{i} \rceil). \tag{3}$$

The problem is that in (3), for a large n, it will be a time-consuming procedure to estimate $\sum_{i=1}^{n}(\lceil 2\sqrt{i} \rceil)$. We treat this problem by introducing an explicit formula for $SS_{A_0}(n)$ without long sum of squared ns that should be rounded to the upper integer.

Theorem 3. *The nth member of sequence SS_{A_0} can be obtained by the following formula:*

$$SS_{A_0}(n) = 4nN - \frac{16}{3}N^3 - 2N^2 + \frac{N}{3} - \frac{q(q+1)}{2}(2N+1) + q(n - 4N^2 + 1),$$

where:

1. $N = Lv(n) = \left\lfloor \frac{\sqrt{n}}{2} \right\rfloor$,

2. $q = \left\lfloor \frac{n-4N^2}{2N+1} \right\rfloor$.

Proof. We can split any integer n into $n = \#Lv(N) + (n - \#Lv(N))$. Then, we can observe $SS_{A_0}(n)$ in the following way:

$$SS_{A_0}(n) = SS_{A_0}(\#Lv(N)) + S_{A_0}(\#Lv(N)) \times (n - \#Lv_N) + E(n), \quad (4)$$

where $N = Lv(n)$; $S_{A_0}(\#Lv(N))$ is the value of sequence S_{A_0} for the complete Level N; the expression $S_{A_0}(\#Lv(N)) \times (n - \#Lv_N)$ shows what is accumulated after the complete Level N; and the function $E(n)$ is what left to add in order to obtain $SS_{A_0}(n)$.

$$E(n) = \begin{cases} \varepsilon(N,0) & \text{if } 4N^2 < n < 4N^2 + 1(2N+1); \\ 2\varepsilon(N,1)+ \\ +1(2N+1)+1 & \text{if } 4N^2 + 1(2N+1) \leq n < 4N^2 + 2(2N+1); \\ 3\varepsilon(N,2)+ \\ +1(2N+1)+1+ \\ +2(2N+1)+1 & \text{if } 4N^2 + 2(2N+1) \leq n < 4N^2 + 3(2N+1); \\ 4\varepsilon(N,3)+ \\ +1(2N+1)+1+ \\ +2(2N+1)+1+ \\ +3(2N+1)+1 & \text{if } 4N^2 + 3(2N+1) \leq n < 4(N+1)^2. \end{cases}$$

where $\varepsilon(N,q) = n - 4N^2 - q(2N+1)$, $q = \left\lfloor \frac{n-4N^2}{2N+1} \right\rfloor$, is what is left from n when we omit the elements in the complete Level N, and the elements that cover the complete sides from layer $N+1$ in the spiral. To understand better $E(n)$, see Fig. 3.
We generalize $E(n)$ in the following way:

$$E(n) = (q+1)\varepsilon(N,q) + \sum_{i=0}^{q} q(2N+1) + q = (2N+1)\frac{q(q+1)}{2} + q + (q+1)\varepsilon(N,q).$$

$$E(n), \qquad 4N^2 \le n \le 4(N+1)^2$$

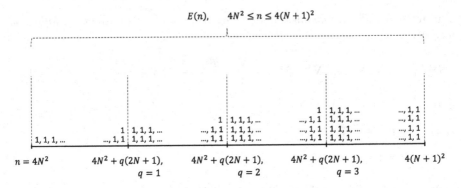

Fig. 3. The relationship between $E(n)$ and n.

Now, we obtain the expression for $E(n)$ when $n = \#Lv(N+1)$, i.e., $n = 4(N+1)^2$, it is equivalent to $E(n)$ where $q = 3$, fixed Level N, and $\varepsilon(N, q) = 2N + 1$. We have:

$$E(\#Lv(N+1)) = 6(2N+1) + 4(2N+1) + 3 = 20N + 13. \qquad (5)$$

We want to obtain the sum of the elements of S_{A_0} in Layer $N + 1$, we will denote by $SS_{A_0}(L_{N+1})$. We skip $SS_{A_0}(\#Lv(N))$ in Expression 4, use Expression 5, and obtain:

$$SS_{A_0}(L_{N+1}) = S_{A_0}(\#Lv(N)) \times (n - \#Lv_N) + E(\#Lv(N+1)).$$

After we apply Proposition 1 to $S_{A_0}(\#Lv(N))$, we obtain the following expression:

$$SS_{A_0}(L_{N+1}) = (4N - 1) \times (n - \#Lv_N) + E(\#Lv(N+1)).$$

Note that $\#L_{N+1} = n - \#Lv_N$, $Lv(n) = N + 1$:

$$SS_{A_0}(L_{N+1}) = (4N - 1) \times \#L_{N+1} + E(\#Lv(N+1))$$
$$= (4N - 1)4(2N + 1) + 20N + 13 = (4(N+1) - 5)4(2(N+1) - 1) + 20(N+1) - 7.$$

Now, we substitute $N+1$ with N. We expand the brackets and obtain $SS_{A_0}(L_N)$:

$$SS_{A_0}(L_N) = 32N^2 - 36N + 13.$$

Finally, note that $SS_{A_0}(\#Lv_N) = \sum_{i=1}^{N} SS_{A_0}(L_i)$. Then:

$$SS_{A_0}(\#Lv_N) = \sum_{i=1}^{N}(32i^2 - 36i + 13) = 32\sum_{i=1}^{N}i^2 + 36\sum_{i=1}^{N}i + \sum_{i=1}^{N}13$$

$$= 32\frac{N(N+1)(2N+1)}{6} - 36\frac{N(N+1)}{2} + 13N$$

$$= N(N+1)\left(\frac{16}{3}(2N+1) - 18\right) + 13N = N(N+1)\left(\frac{32}{3}N - \frac{38}{3}\right) + 13N$$

$$= \frac{N}{3}(32N^2 - 6N + 1).$$

We use that $\sum_{i=1}^{N} i^2 = \frac{N(N+1)(2N+1)}{6}$ which are the *square pyramidal numbers*, A000330. One thing that left is to further simplify the expression for $E(n)$:

$$E(n) = (2N+1)\frac{q(q+1)}{2} + (q+1)\varepsilon(N,q) + q$$

$$= (2N+1)\frac{q(q+1)}{2} + (q+1)(n-4N^2 - q(2N+1)) + q$$

$$= (2N+1)\frac{q(q+1)}{2} - (2N+1)q(q+1) + (q+1)(n-4N^2) + q$$

$$= (n-4N^2)(q+1) - (2N+1)\frac{q(q+1)}{2} + q$$

$$= n - 4N^2 - (2N+1)\frac{q(q+1)}{2} + q(n-4N^2+1).$$

Finally, we simplify the whole formula:

$$SS_{A_0}(n) = SS_{A_0}(\#Lv(N)) + S_{A_0}(\#Lv(N)) \times (n - \#Lv_N) + E(n)$$

$$= \frac{32}{3}N^3 - 2N^2 + \frac{N}{3} + (4N-1)(n-4N^2) + E(n)$$

$$= \frac{32}{3}N^3 - 2N^2 + \frac{N}{3} + 4nN - n - 16N^3 + 4N^2 + E(n)$$

$$= 4nN - n - \frac{16}{3}N^3 + 2N^2 + \frac{N}{3} + n - 4N^2 - (2N+1)\frac{q(q+1)}{2} + q(n-4N^2+1)$$

$$= 4nN - \frac{16}{3}N^3 - 2N^2 + \frac{N}{3} - (2N+1)\frac{q(q+1)}{2} + q(n-4N^2+1).$$

Lemma 7. *The relationship between the sum of the first n elements of sequence A and the sum of the first n elements of sequence S_{A_0} is as follows:*

$$S_A(n) = \frac{n(n+1)}{2} - SS_{A_0}(n) = \underline{A000217}(n) - \underline{A342711}(n-1).$$

Proof. From Lemma 6, we have $A(n) = n - S_{A_0}(n)$. Then $S_A(n) = \sum_{i=1}^{n} i - \sum_{i=1}^{n} S_{A_0}(i) = \frac{n(n+1)}{2} - SS_{A_0}(n)$. A well-known fact is that the nth member of the triangular numbers, A000217, is equal to $\frac{n(n+1)}{2}$.

Theorem 4. *The nth member of sequence S_A has the following explicit formula:*

$$S_A(n) = \frac{n(n+1)}{2} - 4nN + \frac{16}{3}N^3 + 2N^2 - \frac{N}{3} + \frac{q(q+1)}{2}(2N+1) - q(n-4N^2+1),$$

where:

1. $N = Lv(n) = \left\lfloor \frac{\sqrt{n}}{2} \right\rfloor$,

2. $q = \left\lfloor \frac{n-4N^2}{2N+1} \right\rfloor$.

Proof. The stated formula directly follows from Lemma 7 and Theorem 3.

6   Application

Let, again, observe the HP model of Dill. A well-known fact is that the maximum number of contacts of one protein sequence S of Hs and Ps cannot exceed $2 \times min(ODD(S), EVEN(S))$, where $ODD(S)$ is the number of Hs with odd index in S and $EVEN(S)$ is the number of even Hs. We will refer to this limit of contacts as *the standard threshold for the number of contacts*. The standard threshold is used as a stop in the heuristic algorithms, which are designed to optimize the number of contacts (an NP-hard task). In his work [2], Dill states that while maximizing the number of contacts, we obtain a compact core in the protein. Let observe a sequence of only Hs. We assume that the maximum number of contacts on a square lattice is obtained when the sequence of Hs is in a square shape. If this holds, then following the analysis in this paper, we have that the maximum number of contacts of a sequence with size n, which has only Hs, is equal to the nth member of A248333. Thus, any protein sequence of size n cannot exceed $n + 1 - \lceil 2\sqrt{n} \rceil$ contacts, see Theorem 2. We will refer to this limit of contacts as *the absolute threshold for the number of contacts*. Note that the absolute threshold depends only on the length of the protein sequence, not on the inner structure of the protein (Ps and Hs). Moreover, for a sequence with only Hs, the standard threshold will never be reached (for even n, this threshold assumes n contacts, but they are less in the spiral). Thus, the absolute threshold can be used as a more precise estimate for the maximum number of contacts in the cases where we have protein sequences that consist dominantly of Hs. Finally, we can further refine the absolute threshold if we observe the position of the Ps in the spiral and in other conformations of the sequence that form a square shape, e.g., to prune the Ps on both sides in order to obtain smaller sequence's length n.

7   Summary

In this paper, we observed A248333 from a slightly different angle - we noticed the sequence while trying to deal with a problem in the Dill's hydrophobic-polar protein folding model on a two-dimensional square lattice. This point of view, a geometrical one, allowed us to distinguish several more integer sequences and to show their geometrical interpretation. We investigated the relationships between them, which led us to explicit formulas for their nth members (including A248333). Moreover, we stated shorter explicit formulas for the nth members of A248333 and A000267 (for this sequence, we presented an alternative prove to an existing formula) and managed to prove them. Moreover, we obtained an explicit formula for the nth partial sum of A248333, sequence A342712 in the OEIS. Finally, we gave a possible application of the explicit formula for the nth member of sequence A248333.

References

1. Chen, M., Huang, W.: A branch and bound algorithm for the protein folding problem in the HP Lattice Model. Genomics Proteomics Bioinf. **3**(4), 225–230 (2005). https://doi.org/10.1016/S1672-0229(05)03031-7
2. Dill, K.: Theory for the folding and stability of globular proteins. Biochemistry **24**, 1501–1509 (1985). https://doi.org/10.1021/bi00327a032
3. Hart, W., Istrail, S.: Robust proofs of NP-hardness for protein folding: general lattices and energy potentials. J. Comput. Biol. **4**, 1–22 (1997). https://doi.org/10.1089/cmb.1997.4.1
4. Sloane, N., et al.: The on-line encyclopedia of integer sequences (2018). https://oeis.org
5. Thachuk, C., Shmygelska, A., Hoos, H.: A replica exchange Monte Carlo algorithm for protein folding in the HP model. BMC Bioinf. **8**, 342–362 (2007). https://doi.org/10.1186/1471-2105-8-342
6. Traykov, M., Angelov, S., Yanev, N.: A new heuristic algorithm for protein folding in the HP model. J. Comput. Biol. **23**, 662–668 (2016). https://doi.org/10.1089/cmb.2016.0015
7. Yanev, N., Traykov, M., Milanov, P., Yurukov, B.: Protein folding prediction in a cubic lattice in hydrophobic-polar model. J. Comput. Biol. **24**(5), 412–421 (2017). https://doi.org/10.1089/cmb.2016.0181
8. Yanev, N., Milanov, P., Mirchev, I.: Integer programming approaches to HP folding. Serdica J. Comput. **5**, 359–366 (2011). http://hdl.handle.net/10525/1633

Challenges and Opportunities in ESG Investments

Irena Vodenska[1,4(✉)], Risto Trajanov[2], Lou Chitkushev[3], and Dimitar Trajanov[3,4]

[1] Administrative Sciences Department, Metropolitan College, Boston University, Boston, MA, USA
vodenska@bu.edu
[2] Rice University, Houston, TX, USA
risto.trajanov@rice.edu
[3] Computer Science Department, Metropolitan College, Boston University, Boston, MA, USA
ltc@bu.edu, dimitar.trajanov@finki.ukim.mk
[4] Faculty of Computer Sciences and Engineering, Ss. Cyril and Methodius University, Skopje, Republic of Macedonia

Abstract. Environmental, Social, and Governance (ESG) criteria gain increasing attention by governments and corporations to assess how advanced countries and companies are with sustainability. The adoption of the ESG in-vestment approach addresses risk management issues and sets goals to-ward more responsible behavior. Sustainable development goals adopted by the United Nations in 2015 include a call for action to end poverty, save the planet, and ensure peace and prosperity for all by 2030. This paper studies advanced machine learning methodologies to assess, analyze, and suggest improvements in corporate behavior to comply with global sustainable development goals.

Keywords: ESG (Environmental · Social · And Governance) Investments · Machine learning · AI-based systems · Sustainable development · Financial and economic stability

1 Introduction

In the past, considerations about the environmental, social, and governance (ESG) aspects have been limited to specific interest groups concerned with ethical and socially responsible investing. More recently, ESG is becoming an integral part of investment considerations by the broader investment community. Table 1. Examples of ESG Issues (source: www.albertgoodman.co.uk) shows examples of ESG issues considered in environmental, social, and governance areas, including Greenhouse gas emissions, employment rights, and ethics in business. The importance of ESG factors is global, a responsibility not only of corporations but countries themselves. The awareness of today's investment community about the "dangerous human interference with the climate system" was built on The United Nations Framework Convention on Climate Change (UNFCCC), signed by 154 countries at the Earth Summit held in Rio de Janeiro in June 1992. The

T. Zlateva and R. Goleva (Eds.): CSECS 2022, LNICST 450, pp. 168–179, 2022.
https://doi.org/10.1007/978-3-031-17292-2_14

Kyoto Protocol followed in 1997 and was superseded by the Paris Agreement, which entered into force in 2016. By 2020, the UNFCCC had 197 state parties, and the parties (COP) meet annually to assess progress in dealing with climate change.

Table 1. Examples of ESG Issues (source: www.albertgoodman.co.uk)

Environmental	Social	Governance
Biodiversity loss	Mass migration	Executive compensation
Greenhouse gas emissions	Wealth distribution	Bribery and corruption
Energy efficiency	Access to healthcare	Independent directors
Renewable energy	Workplace health and safety	Ethics in business
Resource depletion	Diversity	Transparent disclosure of ESG criteria
Ocean acidification	Employment rights, child labor, and slavery	Whistle-blowing policies
Ozone depletion	Controversial weapons such as cluster bombs	Implications of business strategy on social and sustainability issues

Todd Stern, the US Climate Change envoy, expressed the challenges with the UNFCCC process, stating: "Climate change is not a conventional environmental issue. It implicates virtually every aspect of a state's economy, making countries nervous about growth and development. This is an economic issue every bit as it is an environmental one." He explained that the United Nations Framework Convention on Climate Change is a multilateral body concerned with climate change and can be an inefficient system for enacting international policy. Because the framework system includes over 190 countries and negotiations are governed by consensus, small groups of countries can often block progress"[1]. Another criticism of the UNFCCC came from the National Geographic magazine, stating: "Since 1992, when the world's nations agreed at Rio de Janeiro to avoid 'dangerous anthropogenic interference with the climate system,' they've met 20 times without moving the needle on carbon emissions. Between 1992 and 2015, we've added almost as much carbon to the atmosphere as we did in the previous century" [1].

A flicker of hope appeared recently during the 26th Annual Summit on Climate Change, COP26. By the end of the COP26[2] meeting in Glasgow in November 2021, 151 countries have submitted their climate plans to reduce their GHG[3] emissions by 2030 to contribute to the goal of limiting the temperature increase to 1.5 degrees Celsius. The world's largest CO2 emitters, US and China, pledged to cooperate more over the decade between 2020 and 2030 to switch to clean energy. Leaders in over 100 countries

---

[1] https://en.wikipedia.org/wiki/United_Nations_Framework_Convention_on_Climate_Change.

[2] COP26 – The 26th United Nations Climate Change Conference Annual Summit held in November 2021 in Glasgow, Scotland. COP stands for "Conference of the Parties.".

[3] GHG – Greenhouse gasses which cause climate change.

covering about 85% of the world's forests promised to stop deforestation by 2030. Financial organizations controlling $130 trillion agreed to back clean technologies such as renewable energy and reduce their financing in fossil fuel burning industries[4].

On March 21, 2022, the US Securities and Exchange Commission (the "SEC") proposed rules governing the "Enhancement and Standardization of Climate-Related Disclosures for Investors"[4]. The proposed rule will require companies to disclose climate-related risks, how material these risks are, and how the risks might affect corporations' business outlook. The United Nations Principles for Responsible Investment (PRI) have been a strong motivating force behind fundamental changes in shaping the decision-making process for investors to actively and explicitly involve ESG considerations to manage portfolio risks better. Societal pressure has been instrumental in implementing ESG factors in shaping corporate behavior.

In this paper, we address the challenges that investors and investment funds face in light of the non-standardized reporting of climate-related risks, the social responsibilities of corporations, and their governance practices. We propose an AI-powered solution to understand the difference between corporate reporting and the public perception of corporate social responsibility. We develop a model to identify these discrepancies based on machine learning approaches, including natural language processing and sentiment analysis of corporate filings with the SEC and mainstream or social media reports.

The rest of the paper is organized as follows: In Sect. 2, we give an overview of responsible investment. In Sect. 3, we present technology-based solutions to improving ESG investment outcomes. In Sect. 4, we describe the future opportunities. In Sect. 5, we present the ExxonMobil ESG-related study, and in Sect. 6, we offer our discussion and concluding remarks.

2 Responsible Investment

ESG is an investment approach that explicitly incorporates the environmental, social, and governance factors in investment decisions, keeping an investment portfolio's long-term return at the forefront [14]. Environmental factors concern the natural world, including using and interacting with renewable and nonrenewable resources. Essential considerations include biodiversity, deforestation, water security, pollution, and climate change. Social factors include human capital management, local communities, Labor Standards, human rights, health and safety, and customer responsibility. Last but not least, the governance factors involve issues tied to the interest of the broader stakeholder community, risk management, corporate governance, anti-corruption, and tax transparency. The ESG investment is a part of investing approaches collectively named responsible investment [12]. To invest responsibly means to intend to impact the environment or society positively. Being socially responsible considers the issue of sustainability in the investment decision-making thinking about green investment, such as allocating capital to assets that mitigate climate change or biodiversity loss [11]. Social investment

---

[4] COP26: What was agreed at the Glasgow climate conference? https://www.bbc.com/news/science-environment-56901261.

intends to address social challenges faced by the bottom of the pyramid (BOP)[5] [15]. The responsible investment framework is built around the UN Sustainable Development Goals (SDGs)[6], shown in Fig. 1. UN Sustainable Development Goals, defined in 2015, at the 70th anniversary of the foundation of the United Nations, addressing global challenges such as poverty, inequality, environmental issues, peace, and justice.

Fig. 1. UN sustainable development goals, defined in 2015, at the 70th anniversary of the foundation of the United Nations

To enhance investment philosophy and measure companies' impact on global development goals, the mapping of the SDGs to the companies' ESG indicators could be performed [16]. The proposed mapping of SDG to ESG is shown in Fig. 2. Mapping the SDGs across the three ESG factor groups (SDGs that appear more than once are relevant across two or even all three groups) [16]. SDGs that appear more than once are relevant across two or even all three factors.

3   Technology-Based Solutions for ESG Investment Outcomes

When considering ESG investments, portfolio managers look into companies or funds with high ESG ratings. Several companies, including MSCI, S&P, Sustainalytics, CDP, ISS, Bloomberg, and others, provide ESG ratings [13]. However, the consensus level regarding the ratings is relatively low, making ESG-focused investments challenging.

Existing solutions from technology-based providers offer insights into how companies can improve their ESG index or score and get a better overall view of their index of sustainability [6]. The insights are generated by building a specific model for the company based on accessing, organizing, and analyzing relevant company files. Another interdisciplinary, analytical solution to increasing the ESG transparency is to provide

---

[5] BOP refers to the poorest 2/3 of the economic human pyramid including more than four billion people leaving in poverty.

[6] https://sdgs.un.org/goals.

Fig. 2. Mapping the SDGs across the three ESG factor groups (SDGs that appear more than once are relevant across two or even all three groups) [16].

datasets of raw ESG indicators. This solution involves collecting company data from various sources, such as company documents, news, social media, and alternative data sources. The data can then be used either in a row format or in a more insightful report based on collaboration between data scientists and high-level investor knowledge of market insights and company ESG involvement. This model offers excellent synergetic and profitable cooperation for influencing corporate behavior and contributing to enhanced sustainability and financial stability.

Machine learning and AI-based solutions can contribute to the meaningful representation of each company's most critical ESG factors [5, 18]. Dashboards can effectively emphasize corporate dedication to ESG factors by comparing annual reports and company-related news about ESG actions. The dashboard would extract and visualize the overall corporate commitment and involvement in ESG causes. The insight is generated by collecting every data point for the company from internal and external sources and giving more profound insight into the company sustainability index. The AI-based solution could model dynamic changes and go beyond ESG reporting by providing a future estimated outlook on corporate ESG risks [5, 17]. On the other hand, the AI-based solution could offer positive impacts indices and explainable results from machine learning analysis and extract insights about how social and environmental trends will impact the company. A similar study could offer insights into how negative scenarios (e.g., climate or social disasters) will affect the company's future and determine its resilience to adverse events.

4 Future Opportunities

Research shows a significant upward trend of institutional investors in the last fifteen years, directing funds toward ESG-related investments and funds. In 2005, institutional investors held $1.5 trillion in ESG-based funds, while by 2020, the level of ESG-based assets quadrupled to reach $6.2 trillion [3]. This trend is a solid indicator of the need to develop reliable tools to distinguish between the companies and funds that are genuinely ESG-related and the companies involved in "Greenwashing." We believe that the trend shown in Fig. 4 will rise even faster if investors can determine whether a company or a fund is taking steps to improve its ESG profile with high confidence (Fig. 3).

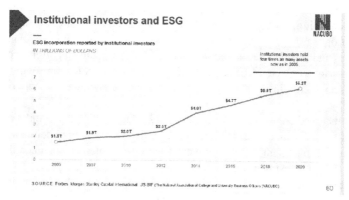

Fig. 3. Institutional investor funds directed towards ESG-related investments and funds [3].

The challenges with ESG Data create opportunities for interdisciplinary approaches to developing and offering tools for disentangling the information from the noise in reporting ESG metrics and unraveling the truth about corporate dedication and actions toward becoming more socially responsible. The newly developed methodologies could measure the "environmental legitimacy" of the corporations and offer evidence of "Greenwashing," a term describing companies that are "talking the talk, but not walking the walk."

To provide a good understanding of Greenwashing, we need to collect and analyze a large amount of data, including market-based and specific company-based data. We consider different data sources combining specific corporate news articles, company filings, and alternative data sources. The main challenge of data gathering is that high-quality data sources are often proprietary and inaccessible. Hence, we focus on publicly available data from reputable data sources. One of the most valuable data sources in the US is the SEC's Electronic Data Gathering, Analysis, and Retrieval[7], which contains all company filings of publicly-traded companies on the stock exchanges. Using these documents, we can identify companies' perspectives on their involvement in ESG-related actions.

---

[7] EDGAR. US Securities and Exchange Commission (Filings & Forms) https://www.sec.gov/edgar.shtml.

In addition to companies' perspectives offered in their annual reports, we collect media-based stories to obtain an enhanced insight into the public perception of companies' ESG involvement. We intend to gather corporate news articles from various media websites, such as GDELT, Google RSS services, and Yahoo Finance news. We also consider social media portals such as Reddit and Twitter as supplementary data. These two platforms offer APIs that give access to their content, accessible under certain limits. We also use APIs like Yahoo finance which provide financial information about a company like stock prices, trading volumes, and ESG risk scores.

Before offering any Machine Learning, Artificial Intelligence, or other technological solution in finance, a crucial part of our research is to understand the regulatory environment and the repercussions of technology-based solutions within the securities and investment regulatory framework. Another important aspect is finding definitions and rules for determining ESG-related metrics used as benchmarks for company ESG rankings. The European Union and the United States have issued guidelines about greenhouse gas emissions and carbon neutralization diversity. These documents offer recommendations about various aspects of ESG, explaining considerations for improving corporate ESG rating, and outlining sanctions for the company's negative impacts on specific aspects of ESG.

One of the challenges in tackling the ESG-related challenges and determining whether companies' trajectories are improving or deteriorating is to define a taxonomy of words that will represent the main topics of our environmental, social, and corporate governance (ESG) investment research.

We establish a list of words and phrases that can be used when searching for relevant news articles, social media posts, and regulatory mandated corporate disclosure documents.

We finally connect the search terms and phrases with selected corporations to extract information such as the frequency of co-occurrence between the company names and a set of ESG terms. We then map out the sentiments for the extracted text to understand the relationship between ESG-related topics and companies. This information gives us a timestamp with frequencies and sentiments where we observe the company's good or bad ESG decisions. We could then overlap the frequency and sentiment graphs with the stock price return information to relate the ESG (qualitative) and the price (quantitative) indicators of company performance.

5 Case Study: ExxonMobil

In this section, we present a case study about ExxonMobil (EM) as a representative company of the energy sector. We perform and explain an end-to-end process of the ESG-related reporting and news about EM corporate behavior.

Firstly, we gathered the data needed for the analysis by developing crawlers that accumulate data into our datasets from alternative sources and company filing reports. As sources for the alternative data, we use Google RSS news feed, GDELT, and Yahoo Finance API. We collect specific news that is related to targeted ESG topics. We extract the news based on co-occurrence between the company we analyze and the topics we predefine (ex. Exxon climate change). We store the news title, content, date, domain site, and search query metadata. We then store the company documents gathered through the portal of the US Securities and Exchange Commission (the "SEC").

We filter and preprocess the news considering the frequency of appearances of our customized taxonomy words. Based on a predefined minimum word occurrence threshold, we classify the company news as ESG related or not. After filtering the news, we calculate the news sentiment by using a predefined Hugging Face pipeline, "sentiment-analysis." The pipeline creates the embeddings, and afterward, leveraging the transformer architecture, it calculates the test sentiment scores between -1 (most negative) and 1 (most positive). We define a threshold for the certainty of the sentiment and classify the news as positive if the sentiment score is above 0.7. We classify the news as negative if the sentiment score is below -0.7.

For a better insight into the results, we create several charts for the short-term sentiment data collected between 05/01/2022 and 06/15/2022. Using the frequency of appearances of our taxonomy words, we map the values on the chart and color them by their sentiment, with red representing a negative and green expressing a positive sentiment, as shown in Fig. 4. The line indicates the frequency of the term present in the news. We repeat this analysis for the three ESG categories: environmental, social, and corporate governance.

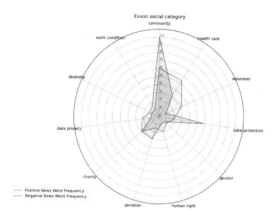

Fig. 4. Sentiment on words in the news in the social category from 05/01/2022 to 06/15/2022

As shown in Fig. 4, ExxonMobil has more negative than positive news related to community behavior. On the other hand, they have more positive than negative news for health care, volunteering, and their involvement in human rights movements.

In Fig. 5, we observe the number of appearances of the term "ESG" in the news with negative and positive sentiments. The red bar indicates the number of occurrences of "ESG" in the news with negative sentiment related to EM for the week starting with the date on the x-axis. The green bar indicates the appearance of the "ESG" word in the news with positive sentiments.

Relation Extraction helps extract meaningful connections between entities from unprocessed texts and use the relations to create a Knowledge Base. Using this method, we generate a Knowledge Graph (Fig. 6) from the text in Def 14A, a proxy statement

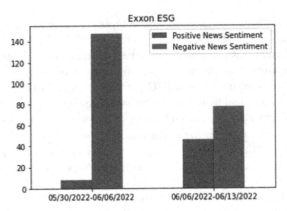

Fig. 5. Sentiment of the news where ESG was mentioned aggregated weekly.

filed by EM for 2022. The model has detected that, in their proxy statement (Def 14A), EM specifies that they are founders of an organization called Alliance to End Plastic Waste Figure.

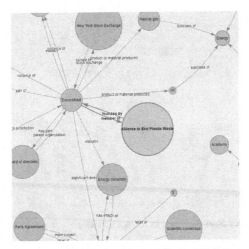

Fig. 6. Knowledge Graph generated by the text from EM's Def 14A (Proxy Statement) filing for 2022, related to Plastic-based Pollution

To compare this graph with the news, we create a knowledge graph from the news gathered by the "Exxon Alliance to end Plastic Waste" query, shown in Fig. 8, where we could detect a potential greenwashing. We find a connection between a parent organization, "American Chemistry Council," and "Lobbying." (Fig. 7)

We then create a Knowledge Graph from the news results of the search query "American Chemistry Council Lobbying," shown in Fig. 8. The news that resulted in the relationship between American Chemistry Council and Lobbying has a headline: "Oil-backed trade group is lobbying the Trump administration to push plastics across Africa" [2].

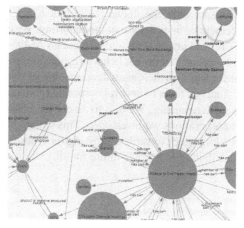

Fig. 7. Knowledge Graph generated from the news results by the search query: "Exxon Alliance to end Plastic Waste"

The news is indicative of the lobbying activities of EM aiming to proceed with using plastic products, which is adverse to environmental issues and corporate governance.

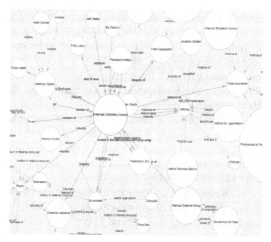

Fig. 8. Knowledge Graph created by searching the news related to "American Chemistry Council Lobbying."

6 Discussion and Conclusion

This paper analyzes the challenges investors face in selecting ESG investments in their quest to impact environmental, social, and governance matters positively. While the corporations are required to disclose their actions and describe their contribution to becoming more socially responsible, the challenges include a lack of standard in reporting and a lack of enforcement of fines in case of misreporting. We offer an insight into a significant issue of ESG-related investments and propose an AI-based, machine learning solution to identify corporations that do not behave responsibly besides reporting their dedication to ESG-related matters in their annual reports. We use Natural Language Processing and Sentiment Analysis tools to unravel corporate (company-based) and media (public-based) reporting discrepancies. We aim to assess the ESG risk and understand the business outlook of corporations we investigate. This study intends to increase corporate responsibility in taking steps towards improving their positive impact on society and the environment contributing to a better future for all.

References

1. Kunzig, R.: Fresh Hope for Combating Climate Change. National Geographic (2015). https://www.nationalgeographic.com/magazine/article/climate-change-issue-intro-essay Accessed 01 June 2022
2. Howard, E.: Oil-backed trade group is lobbying the Trump administration to push plastics across Africa: The American Chemistry Council also pushed back against new global rules that will restrict the flow of plastic waste to the global south, Unearthed. 30 August 2022
3. An introduction to ESG investing: An overview of environmental, social, and governance (ESG) investing – NACUBO (https://www.nacubo.org) (August 16 2021)
4. Securities And Exchange Commission: Rules to Enhance and Standardize Climate-Related Disclosures for Investors. Release Nos. 33-11042; 34-94478; File No. S7-10-22 (2022)
5. Sokolov, A., et al.: Building machine learning systems for automated ESG scoring. The Journal of Impact and ESG Investing 1(3), 39–50 (2021)
6. Lokuwaduge, C.S.S., Heenetigala, K.: Integrating environmental, social and governance (ESG) disclosure for a sustainable development: An Australian study. Business Strategy and the Environment 26(4), 438–450 (2017)
7. Daugaard, D.: Emerging new themes in environmental, social and governance investing: a systematic literature review. Accounting & Finance 60(2), 1501–1530 (2020)
8. Taliento, M., Favino, C., Netti, A.: Impact of environmental, social, and governance information on economic performance: Evidence of a corporate "sustainability advantage" from Europe. Sustainability 11(6), 1738 (2019)
9. Barko, T., Cremers, M., Renneboog, L.: Shareholder engagement on environmental, social, and governance performance. Journal of Business Ethics 1–36 (2021)
10. Cunha, F.A.F.S., et al.: Can sustainable investments outperform traditional benchmarks? Evidence from global stock markets. Business Strategy and the Environment 29(2), 682–697 (2020)
11. Kim, S., Yoon, A.: Analyzing Active Fund Managers' Commitment to ESG: Evidence from the United Nations Principles for Responsible Investment. Management Science (2022)
12. Gerard, B.: ESG and socially responsible investment: A critical review. Beta 33(1), 61–83 (2019)
13. Leins, S.: 'Responsible investment': ESG and the post-crisis ethical order. Econ. Soc. 49(1), 71–91 (2020)
14. Zumente, I., Bistrova, J.: ESG importance for long-term shareholder value creation: Literature vs. practice. J. Open Innovation: Technol. Market, and Complexity 7(2), 127 (2021)
15. Brest, P., Born, K.: When can impact investing create real impact. Stanf. Soc. Innov. Rev. 11(4), 22–31 (2013)

16. Berenberg: Understanding the SDGs in Sustainable Investing; Joh. Berenberg, Gossler & Co. KG: Hamburg, Germany (2018)
17. Hello: How Do Jamaicans Say, and Day Pass Planet Fitness Cost. "Trends in AI4ESG: AI for Sustainable Finance and ESG Technology." Science (2022)
18. Selim, O.: ESG and AI: the beauty and the beast of sustainable investing. Sustainable Investing Sustainable Investing A Path to a New Horizon. Routledge, 227–243 (2020)

Education in Computer Science

A Visual Tool to Study Sorting Algorithms and Their Complexity

Tanyo Kostadinov, Ivon Nikolova, Radoslav Radev, Angel Terziev, and Lasko Laskov[(✉)][iD]

Informatics Department, New Bulgarian University, Sofia, Bulgaria
ivonvesko@abv.bg, llaskov@nbu.bg

Abstract. Sorting algorithms are a well-known part of the curriculum in programming courses in the academia. They are taught not only because their numerous applications in practice, but also because they are a good and a comprehensive introduction to the topic of computer algorithms. However, the *asymptotic notation* used to describe algorithm complexity is not intuitive for beginners. A visual tool that demonstrates both the algorithm's steps and its time complexity makes the abstract notion *asymptotic notation* more intuitive, and can improve the learning curve of the students.

Keywords: Algorithms and data structures · Sorting algorithms · Informatics education

1 Introduction

Sorting algorithms have been a subject of extensive study, and an indivisible part of the academia courses of compute programming, and algorithms and data structures [13,19]. Actually, the history of studies of sorting algorithms can be traced back to the beginning of computing around the middle of the 20th century (see for example works [3,6–9]).

Of course, sorting algorithms are an important step in many other methods and algorithms, and different examples can be given on different level of computing and computer science. A basic example is the binary search algorithm that requires data to be sorted [15]. Sorting and ordering of data is a part of complex systems such as relational database management systems [18]. Sorting also is applied in image processing and computer vision methods, as in the case of the implementation of the median filtering [11].

Besides their practical importance, sorting algorithms are often part of a beginner's course in computer algorithms in the academia, since they give a good introduction to the complex topic of computer algorithms as a whole. The objective of sorting is easily defined: implement an algorithm that orders a given sequence in ascending or descending order using a predefined relation among its elements; however, different algorithms may have a significant complexity of

T. Zlateva and R. Goleva (Eds.): CSECS 2022, LNICST 450, pp. 183–195, 2022.
https://doi.org/10.1007/978-3-031-17292-2_15

their definition and may require different skill level in order to be understood. A problem that is easily formulated, and methods of different complexity that are applicable in its solution, open the possibility for creation of a *system of tasks* that can aid the notion formation during the course (for notion formation through a system of tasks see [2] and [14]).

Sorting algorithms are a good starting point to computer algorithms topic, but also they allow the introduction of the complicated notion *algorithm complexity* (see [4]) in a way that is relatively fluent and intelligible for the students in the first and second year of their studies. The understanding of the *asymptotic notation* that is used to denote algorithm complexity, frequently is an obstacle for students in the introductory course of computer algorithms, mainly because of their level of knowledge of calculus and analysis, where this notion comes from. For that reason, usually the notion algorithm complexity is introduced by measuring the execution time of the algorithm implementation running on a concrete computer system, as for example in [10], which helps the intuitive understanding, even though it cannot substitute the analytic complexity derivation.

The above motivates us to develop a software that is able to provide learners with two different visual representations of the sorting algorithms: (i) step-by-step visualization of the algorithm, and (ii) visual representation of the time complexity of the algorithm, compared with the same information for other algorithms in the same package. The graphical user interface of the software enables the experiment with a number of standard sorting algorithms, applied sequences of different data types which allows students to develop a visual concept of both algorithms themselves, and their computational complexity. This visual concept significantly improves the perception of the analytical explanation of the notion asymptotic notation.

This paper is organized as follows. In Sect. 2 we give a brief survey of the algorithms we have currently incorporated in our project grouped by their average-case complexity: square complexity algorithms (Sect. 2.1), and $n \log n$ complexity algorithms (Sect. 2.2). In Sect. 3 we present some details of visualization implementation. Finally, in Sect. 4 we present our conclusions and future work on the project.

2   Some Frequently Taught Sorting Algorithms

In this section we present some of the frequently taught sorting algorithms in an introduction course in computer algorithms, which we have implemented in our visualisation software. We separate the algorithms in two parts: methods that can be classified as square complexity algorithms, and those that can be classified as $n \log n$ complexity algorithms, according to their average-case execution complexity.

2.1   Average-Case Square Complexity Algorithms

Bubble Sort. Bubble sort is a classical square complexity algorithm, that used to be one of the first methods taught in academia programming courses [13,19]. It is relatively straightforward both to understand and implement (see Algorithm 1), and yet many studies prove that is inefficient, even for a "slow" sorting algorithm (see [1]).

Bubble sort is invented around the middle of the previous century, and different names were used to refer to it (exchange sorting, or sorting by exchange) [3,6,8]. The first occurrence of the term *bubble sort* can be traced back to 1962 [12], and this is the name with which this algorithm gained popularity.

Algorithm 1. Basic version of the bubble sort, applied on a sequence a.

---

function BUBBLESORT(a)
   $n \leftarrow$ SIZE(a)
   for $i \leftarrow 0$ **to** $n - 2$ **do**
      for $j \leftarrow 0$ **to** $n - j - 2$ **do**
         if $a[j] > a[j + 1]$ **then**
            SWAP($a[j]$, $a[j + 1]$))
         end if
      end for
   end for
end function

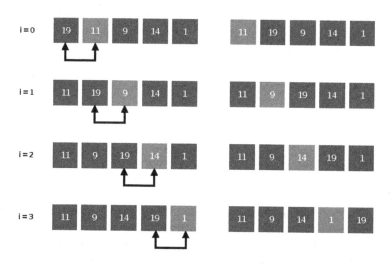

Fig. 1. Execution of the bubble sort algorithm for its first four iterations.

The algorithm works by repeatedly swapping adjacent positions that are not ordered (Algorithm 1). If the first element is greater than the second, it will swap these elements, it will then continue with second and third until the end of the sequence is reached. On each run, the method pushes the largest element to the end of the sequence (see Fig. 1). Also, different variations of bubble sort exist, yet it is easy to be proven that the gained efficiency is not enough to match the performance of selection sort and insertion sort, described further.

For a sequence of n elements, each pass requires $n - i$ comparisons. Then the complexity of the algorithm can be expressed by

$$g(n) = \sum_{i=1}^{n}(n - i) = \frac{n(n - 1)}{2}, \tag{1}$$

where $g(n)$ denotes the number of operations performed by the algorithm. Using big-O notation, the complexity of the bubble sort in the general case is $g(n) \in O(n^2)$, which is also its worst case performance in the case in which the input is sorted in reversed order. Best case may occur, if the sequence is already sorted, and the algorithm may stop after the first pass without a swap (with a slight modification of Algorithm 1).

Selection Sort. Another simple square complexity algorithm, that has been known from the same period as the bubble sort, is the *selection sort* algorithm [6]. Besides its simplicity, it outmatches the bubble sort efficiency, and in many academia courses now-a-days it is preferred as the first example for a sorting method [10].

Algorithm 2. Selection sort, applied on a sequence a. The function MinPos() finds the index of the minimum element in a, starting from position i.

```
function SelectionSort(a)
    n ← Size(a)
    for i ← 0 to n − 2 do
        j ← MinPos(a, i)
        if j ≠ i then
            Swap(a[i], a[j])
        end if
    end for
end function
```

On each step of the main loop of the algorithm (see Algorithm 2) the method selects the minimum element from the current unsorted sub-sequence. It swaps the discovered minimum element with the one on the first position of the sub-sequence (see Fig. 2). The main loop of the algorithm is repeated until the unsorted sequence is two elements big (the index i reaches the element $n - 1$).

On the first iteration, selection sort performs n visits to find the minimum element, and two visits to swap, totally $n + 2$ visits. On the second visit it performs $n + 2 + (n - 1) + 2$ visits, and since all swaps are $(n - 1)$, the total number of operations are (see also [10]):

$$g(n) = n + 2 + (n - 1) + 2 + \ldots + 2 + 2. \tag{2}$$

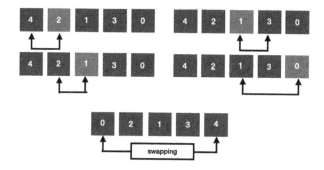

Fig. 2. The first swap operation performed by the selection sort algorithm

Since $\sum_{i=1}^{n} i = \frac{n(n+1)}{2}$:

$$g(n) = \frac{n(n+1)}{2} - 1 + (n-1) \cdot 2 = \frac{1}{2}n^2 + \frac{5}{2}n - 3, \tag{3}$$

and we get that $g(n) \in O(n^2)$.

Insertion Sort. The last square complexity algorithm that we will discuss here is the *insertion sort*. According to Knuth (see [13]), a version of this algorithm called *binary insertion* is mentioned in 1946 by John Mauchly in a legacy publication dedicated on computer sorting.

Algorithm 3. Insert an element x into sorted sequence a with length n.

function INSERT(a, n, x)
  $i \leftarrow n - 1$
  while $i \geq 0$ **and** $a[i] > x$ **do**
    $a[i+1] = a[i]$
    $i \leftarrow i - 1$
  end while
end function

The algorithm is based on a routine (see Algorithm 3) that inserts an entry into a sorted sequence in its correct position. Insertion sort algorithm simply calls the routine INSERT() for all elements of the input sequence consecutively for a subsequence with length 1, 2 until $n-1$, where n is the length of a (see Algorithm 4) (Fig. 3).

In the general case we can assume that half of the elements of a are less than the current element $a[i]$ which implies $i/2$ comparisons on average. Then the total number of comparisons performed by the algorithm are (see also [13]):

$$g(n) = \frac{\sum_{i=1}^{n} i}{2} = \frac{n(n+1)}{4}. \tag{4}$$

Algorithm 4. Insertion sort based on the INSERT() routine.

```
function INSERTSORT(a)
    n ← SIZE(a)
    for i ← 1 to n − 1 do
        INSERT(a, i, a[i])
    end for
end function
```

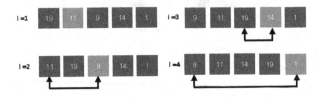

Fig. 3. Four iterations of the insertion sort algorithm.

Again, using asymptotic notation, the complexity is $O(n^2)$, however comparing equations (1), (3) and (4), we see that insertion sort performs better than selection sort, and much better than bubble sort in the general case. Also, different improvements of the algorithm can be applied, which can speed up its average performance (see [13] and [16]). For example, if binary search is used in the inserting routine (Algorithm 3), the complexity of the search of the insert location is reduced to $O(\log n)$. The latter method, called *binary insertion*, also does not solve the problem that the elements of the array must be moved to make space for the element to be inserted.

2.2 Average-Case $n \log n$ Complexity Algorithms

Merge Sort. Merge sort is a classical sorting algorithm that is based on a divide-and-conquer strategy. Maybe the first description of this algorithm can be found in the work of Goldstine and von Neumann [7], where merging procedure is referred to as "meshing". In this work a full explanation and analysis of *bottom-up* version of merge sort that is based on iteration, is given.

Algorithm 5. Recursive top-down version of the merge sort algorithm.

```
function MERGESORT(a, f, t)
    if f = t then
        return
    end if
    m ← (f + t)/2
    MERGESORT(a, f, m)
    MERGESORT(a, m + 1, t)
    MERGE(a, f, m, t)
end function
```

Here we will focus on the more popular contemporary *top-down* approach that uses recursion to be implemented. Often, recursive solutions provide clearer approach to complex problems (see for example [10]), and merge sort implementation is not an exception.

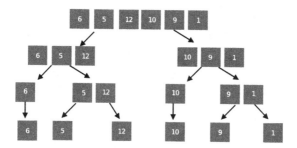

Fig. 4. Merge sort divides by half the sequence recursively until a sequence of length 0 is reached.

In the main function of the algorithm (Algorithm 5), the input sequence is divided by half, and each half is sorted recursively. The trivial case of the recursion is when the divided sequence is of length 0. The sequence that is composed by a single element can be considered sorted by definition. This is the *divide part* of the divide-and-conquer algorithm. An example of this process is given on Fig. 4.

After reaching the bottom of recursion, in the backwards function calls of the recursion, the algorithm performs its *conquer* part using the function MERGE() (see Algorithm 6) that merges two sorted sub-sequences into a resulting sorted sequence. An example of the merging process applied in the backward functions calls of the recursion is given on Fig. 5.

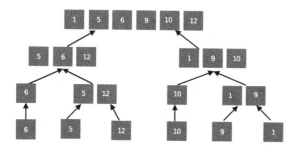

Fig. 5. Backward recursive calls of the merge sort algorithm consecutively merge the sub-sequences using the routine in Algorithm 6.

The complexity of the MERGE() procedure can be evaluated to three visits per single iteration, and hence $3n$ visits totally n iterations. To copy the sorted

Algorithm 6. Merge two sorted sub-sequences with ranges $[f, m]$ and $[m+1, t]$ stored in the same array a.

```
function MERGE(a, f, m, t)
    b is a temporary array
    i ← f, j ← m + 1, k ← 0
    while i ≤ m and j ≤ t do
        if a[i] < a[j] then
            b[k] ← a[i], i ← i + 1
        else
            b[k] ← a[j], j ← j + 1
        end if
        k ← k + 1
    end while
    while i ≤ m do
        b[k] ← a[i]
        i ← i + 1, k ← k + 1
    end while
    while j ≤ t do
        b[k] ← a[j]
        j ← j + 1, k ← k + 1
    end while
    COPY(a, b)
end function
```

sequence from the temporary array the algorithm spends $2n$ visits, and the whole procedure has complexity $5n$ visits.

The complexity of the recursive function MERGESORT() for $n = 2^m$ elements can be evaluated recursively as well (see also [10]):

$$g(n) = g\left(\frac{n}{2}\right) + g\left(\frac{n}{2}\right) + 5n = 2g\left(\frac{n}{2}\right) + 5n \tag{5}$$

and

$$g\left(\frac{n}{2}\right) = 2g\left(\frac{n}{4}\right) + 5\frac{n}{2} \tag{6}$$

then we get:

$$g(n) = 4g\left(\frac{n}{4}\right) + 10n. \tag{7}$$

Finally the above expression for $n = 2^m$:

$$g(n) = 2^m g\left(\frac{n}{2^m}\right) + 5nm = ng(1) + 5nm = n + 5n\log_2 n. \tag{8}$$

Of course, in asymptotic notation the complexity of the merge sort algorithm is written $O(n\log n)$.

Quicksort. Another algorithm that is based on the divide-and-conquer paradigm just like previously discussed merge sort, is the *quicksort* algorithm. It is developed by the British computer scientist Tony Hoare, and published in 1961 [9]. The algorithm originates from the need of fast sorting algorithm during his work on machine translation project for the National Physical Laboratory while he was a visiting student at Moscow State University [17]. Since then the algorithm undergoes various modifications and improvements to become the most notable sorting algorithm, applicable on long input sequences.

Algorithm 7. Main function of the quicksort algorithm. The recursive function gets the input sequence a with the range in the closed interval $[l, r]$.

```
function QUICKSORT(a, l, r)
    if r ≤ l then
        return
    end if
    m ← PARTITION(a, l, r)
    QUICKSORT(a, l, m)
    QUICKSORT(a, m + 1, r)
end function
```

The divide part of the algorithm splits the input sequence recursively in the closed range $[l, r]$ (Algorithm 7). If the range contains one or less elements, the trivial case solution is reached, and the function returns. Otherwise, a function PARTITION() (Algorithm 8) finds the index to split the sequence in the given range. Also, the function PARTITION() ensures that there are no elements leftwards the pivot p at the returned index that are grater than it, and there are no elements rightwards p that are less than it. Then the two parts of the sequence (the one that is less than p, and the one that is greater than p) are partitioned recursively.

Algorithm 8. Basic version of the partitioning routine of the quicksort algorithm which selects as a pivot the first element in the given range.

```
function PARTITION(a, l, r)
    p ← a[l]                          ▷ Pivot value.
    i ← l − 1, j ← r + 1
    while i < j do
        do
            i ← i + 1
        while a[i] < p
        do
            j ← j − 1
        while a[j] > p
        if i ¡ j then
            SWAP(a[i], a[j])
        end if
    end while
    return j
end function
```

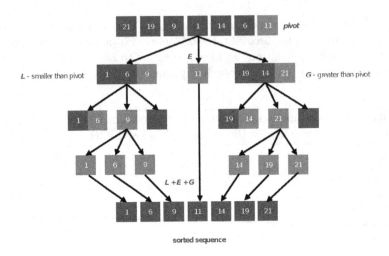

Fig. 6. Partitioning with the last element selected as the pivot.

There are different ways to select the pivot value p in the routine PARTITION(). In the basic version, the first or the last element is selected (on Fig. 6 we show an example with last element as the pivot, while Algorithm 8 is an example of the first element as the pivot). In the *worst case* this could be the maximum or the minimum element in the range, which will lead to square complexity if it is repeated on each recursive call. An improved version of the algorithm uses a random pivot which ensures that the partitioning of the sequence in the range will be roughly equal. In balanced partitioning on each recursive call, the *average-case complexity* of the algorithm can be evaluated in analogy to (5) using the recurrence relation (see [4]):

$$g(n) = O(n) + 2g(\frac{n}{2}), \tag{9}$$

where single call to the QUICKSORT() has complexity $O(n)$ plus the complexity of the two recursive calls. From the *Master Theorem* ([4], p. 94) we know this leads to algorithm average-case complexity $O(n \log n)$.

3   Visual Application Implementation

The software we present here is implemented using the programming language C++ and Qt platform (see [5]) which makes it fully portable on each operating system that is supported by Qt. It is composed by the following main sections:

1. Implementation of the sorting algorithms described in the previous section.
2. Modified versions of the algorithm functions to allow step-by-step algorithm visualization.
3. Timers and a graphical plot of the execution time of each algorithm (see Fig. 7).

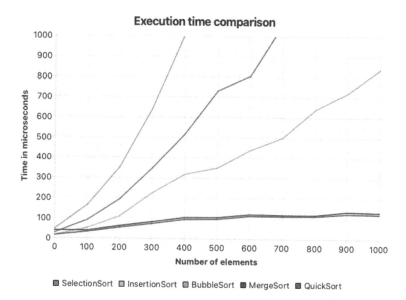

Fig. 7. Plot of the execution time of the examined algorithms produced by our software.

The application allows user to select whether algorithms to be tested on randomly generated sequence, or to load a predefined sequence from a file. Also, the user can select the data type of the input sequences. These two options allow to test sorting algorithms with a broad variety of input data, and also to load data sequences that are extracted from other problems. The latter can demonstrate the efficiency of a given algorithm in the context of a given practical situation.

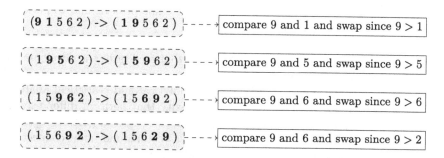

Fig. 8. A fragment of the visualization of the first pass of the bubble sort algorithm.

In order to visualize each step of the sorting algorithms, we use a function call at every key point inside the sorting algorithms and display the changes that have been made so far to the unsorted sequence. The function provides the ability to set different pause times at the different key points. This allows an improved visualization and better understanding of the process of sorting, due to the difference in the way sorting algorithms work and the need of emphasis on some key points more than on others.

On Fig. 8 is given the visualization of the first pass of the bubble sort algorithm. The learner is able to run the algorithm and to monitor each stage of its execution on the selected input sequence.

The plot of the execution time of sorting algorithms give good visual representation of their complexity. For example, on the plot (Fig. 7) it is obvious that the complexity of the bubble sort algorithm can be modelled with a square function. Also, it is easily seen that among square complexity functions the worst performance is given by the bubble sort, selection sort performs significantly better than it, and insertion sort outmatches both of them. The demonstrated experiment clearly shows why bubble sort algorithm is usually ignored in contemporary programming courses.

4   Conclusion

In this paper we present our software tool to visualize sorting algorithms and their complexity. We provide a survey of some of the most frequently taught sorting algorithms in university course, tracing their origins, and providing analytical analyses of their complexity. The complexity of algorithms is an important notion usually presented in the course of computer programming, algorithms and data structures. However, it is not intuitively perceived by the students in the first years of their study because of the complexity of the asymptotic notation.

Our project can improve the intuitive understanding of the complex term complexity of algorithms by providing visual comparison of the execution time of different algorithms (see Fig. 7). Learners can perform experiments with different sequences, both random and predefined. Also, more advanced students can implement another sorting method as part of the same project, and to perform the same experiments with them.

The project is a part of our effort to organize the curriculum using a practical approach that is based on a system of task [14] that facilitates the development of complex notions during the learning process.

As future work we plan to perform both analytical and statistical analysis of algorithms with the same worst-case complexity that perform differently in practice. We also plan to compare the performance of such algorithms applied on different data structures: array based, such as vectors, and node/connection based, such as linked lists. Our software tool will be extended to visualize the execution of other types of algorithms, for example the standard graph algorithms that are taught in the courses of graph theory. Also, our source code is published as an open-source project[1], and can be extended and modified, according to the needs of a particular course.

---

[1]   https://github.com/RitaPlusPlus/sorting.

References

1. Astrachan, O.: Bubble sort: an archaeological algorithmic analysis. SIGCSE Bull. **35**(1), 1–5 (2003)
2. Asenova, P., Marinov, M.: System of tasks in mathematics education. J. Educ. Res. Az Buki National Publishing House Educ. Sci. **62**(1), 52–70 (2019)
3. Bose, R.C., Nelson, R.J.: A sorting problem. J. ACM **9**(2), 282–296 (1962)
4. Cormen, T.H., Leiserson, C.E., Rivest, R.L., Stein, C.: Introduction to Algorithms, 3rd edn. The MIT Press, Cambridge (2009)
5. Eng, L.Z.: Qt5 C++ GUI Programming Cookbook, 2nd edn. PACKT Publishing, Birmingham (2019)
6. Friend, E.H.: Sorting on electronic computer systems. J. ACM **3**(3), 134–168 (1956)
7. Goldstine, H.H., von Neumann, J.: Planning and Coding of Problems for an Electronic Computing Instrument, Part II, vol. 2, pp. 49–66. The Institute for Advanced Study Princeton, New Jersey (1947)
8. Gotlieb, C.C.: Sorting on computers. Commun. ACM **6**(5), 194–201 (1963)
9. Hoare, C.A.R.: Algorithm 64: quicksort. Commun. ACM **4**(7), 321 (1961)
10. Horstmann, C., Budd, T.: Big C++, 2nd edn. Addison-Wesley, Boston (2008)
11. Huang, S., Yang, J., Tang, Y.: A fast two-dimensional median filtering algorithm. IEEE Trans. Acoust. Speech Signal Process. **27**(1), 13–18 (1979)
12. Iverson, K.E.: A Programming Language. John Wiley, Hoboken (1962)
13. Knuth, D.: The Art Of Computer Programming, volume: 3 Sorting and Searching. Addison- Wesley, Boston (1973)
14. Laskov, L.: Introduction to computer programming through a system of tasks. Math. Inf. J. Educ. Res. Az Buki National Publishing House Educ. Sci. **64**(6), 634–649 (2021)
15. Nowak, R.: Generalized binary search. In: 2008 46th Annual Allerton Conference on Communication. Control, and Computing, pp. 568–574. IEEE, Monticello, IL, USA (2008)
16. Sedgewick, R.: Algorithms in C. Addison-Wesley Longman, Boston (2002)
17. Shustek, L.: Interview: an interview with CAR Hoare. Commun. ACM **52**(3), 38–41 (2009)
18. Sumathi, S., Esakkirajan, S.: Fundamentals of Relational Database Management Systems Studies in Computational Intelligence 47. Springer, Heidelberg (2007). https://doi.org/10.1007/978-3-540-48399-1
19. Wirth, N.: Algorithms + Data Structures = Programs. Prentice-Hall, Hoboken (1976)

Database Schemas Used in SQL University Courses – State of the Art

Georgi Tuparov[✉] [ID]

New Bulgarian University, 21 Montevideo str., Sofia 1618, Bulgaria
gtuparov@nbu.bg

Abstract. The body of knowledge in IT courses area includes topics about relational databases in which students have to obtain at least basic knowledge and skills in SQL. Also for the students in the areas of computer science majors SQL is an obligatory part of knowledge and skills. To be effective, SQL training in university courses has to use appropriate case studies (i.e. database schemas) which are semantically clear, simple, and suitable to demonstrate the major SQL functionality not only "on paper" but also in real DBMS environment (or DBMS sandbox). Moreover, the appropriate database state is important to demonstrate understandable results from SQL queries, which can be manually evaluated by students to compare with results of execution in real database environment.

In this paper some popular database schemas and states used in SQL training in university level courses are analyzed from these points of view. For this study, six schemas from popular database books used in university courses are considered. Two major streams in database schemas and states are distinguishable. One is focused on overall solution, that covers database design topics and SQL training, another is focused only on SQL training. It is found that a possible break point between these streams is to use database schema which is complex enough for demonstration of the design process, and after that to use simplified version of the database schema with reduced number of records for SQL training.

Keywords: Database schema · SQL · University courses

1 Introduction

Nowadays more and more students want to obtain knowledge and skills in Information technology (IT) as a part of their academic study. In general, the body of knowledge in IT courses area includes topics about relational databases in which students have to obtain basic knowledge and skills in SQL. For the students in the areas of computer science majors SQL is an obligatory part of knowledge and skills as is stated in ACM Curricula Recommendations [1].

In the last ten years we have a stable trend of rising number of young people in IT majors and minors. Lecturers in the database field now understand that part of the students simply follow the needs of more and more specialists in IT, without being deeply involved in the area. Moreover, contemporary development environments provide very

T. Zlateva and R. Goleva (Eds.): CSECS 2022, LNICST 450, pp. 196–204, 2022.
https://doi.org/10.1007/978-3-031-17292-2_16

rich tools to access, query and maintain relational databases, so students are not aware of the importance of SQL knowledge and skills.

Another general problem in nowadays teaching is that students spend more and more time in social networks preferably using smartphones. They believe that all information needed is available on the Internet and this – in combination with social distancing during COVID-19 crisis, changes the students' perception in ways of learning. In consequence these Internet channels of communication should be used to provide effective learning materials in appropriate formats. Practice during COVID-19 crisis showed that the simple usage of e-learning environments is not enough to increase the effectiveness of teaching and the quality of learning materials is a key point to achieve learning goals.

Focusing on SQL training, students have to be provided with appropriate case studies (i.e. database schemas) which are semantically clear, simple, and can be used to demonstrate the major SQL functionality not only "on paper" but also in real DBMS environment (or DBMS sandbox). Moreover, the appropriate database state is important to demonstrate understandable results from SQL queries, which can be easily evaluated manually by students to compare with results of execution in the DBMS. This will contribute to a deeper understanding of SQL functionality and some side effects in particular SQL implementation. Also, it will be very useful if the database schema used during the semester is used in quizzes and exams, eventually with minor changes.

2 Methodology Used

2.1 Collecting Data and Study Points

For this study six schemas from popular database books used in university courses are considered. Also some good database books are excluded due to lack of case study database schema and/or state used in examples of applying SQL to solve problems.

The database schemas and states study points are:

- Is this a case study in the book? Is the schema used in topics of conceptual modeling, relational model introduction and SQL examples?
- Database schema quality according to good practices – naming of attributes, primary and foreign key used, normalization.
- Is the schema and state usable to demonstrate major SQL functionality?
- Is the schema and state suitable to solve complex SQL queries?
- Is the schema and state useful for manual evaluation of SQL queries?
- Is DDL script provided for practical training?

2.2 Textual Representation of Relational Schemas

In this paper the following textual notation is used to describe relational DB schemas:

- Relation name – first letter is capital, i.e. Person.
- List of attributes are enclosed in parenthesis – (personID, name, phone)
- Primary key attribute is underlined – personID.

- Where FK is a foreign key in R1 relation, R2.PK is referred primary/candidate key i.e. FK → R2.PKey
- If the foreign key is composite, its attributes are enclosed in brackets [], i.e. R1.[FK1, FK2] → R2.[PK1, PK2].

3 Database Schemas and States Included in the Research

3.1 Supplier Database [2]

Supplier database [2] is the case study in the entire book and consists of three relations.

Relation **S** represents suppliers. Each supplier has a unique supplier number (sno), which is the primary key of this relation, and personal data like supplier's name and residence. Also a status value, representing ranking (preference level) among available suppliers is stored in the relation.

Relation P represents parts. Each part has a unique part number (pno), which is the primary key of the relation; and part's description properties like a name, color, weight; and city where the part is stored.

Relation SP represents shipments, which show which part is supplied (or shipped), by which supplier. It is assumed that one supplier can supply/ship a particular part only once. Each shipment has a supplier number (sno), a part number (pno), which are both foreign keys, corresponding to the primary keys of S and P, respectively and quantity of this part being shipped. Primary key is composite (sno, pno).

The database schema described in textual manner mentioned above is presented in Fig. 1:

S (sno, sname, status, city)
P (pno, pname, color, weight, city)
SP (sno->S.sno, pno->P.pno, qty)

Fig. 1. Supplier database schema [2] with foreign keys' references added

Database sample state used in the examples contains 23 records, five in S table, six in P table and 12 in SP table. One supplier doesn't have any shipments.

The database schema and state provided are very suitable to demonstrate full functionality of SQL. Naming conventions like using the same name for foreign key attributes as referred attributes, and database state allow to demonstrate full JOINs functionality. Simplicity of the schema is a problem for creating more complex queries, but is suitable for middle level training. Schema state allows easy manual evaluation of the queries. DDL script is not provided, but it is not a problem to implement database schema and state manually in relational DBMS environment.

3.2 Company Database [3]

Company Database [3] is used as case study in the entire book and implements the following business rules:

- The company has divisions, called departments. Each department has a unique name and number, several locations, and a particular employee who manages the department.
- One department may manage several projects, which are described with a unique project number and name, and location of project activities.
- The database stores each employee's personal data, including Social Security number and employee's supervisor (who is another employee). An employee can be assigned to only one department, but may be engaged in several projects, which may not be managed by the same department.
- The number of hours per week that an employee works on each project is logged into the database.
- The database keeps track of the dependents of each employee for insurance purposes, including each dependent's personal data and relationship to the employee.

Database schema consists of six relations and is presented in textual manner in Fig. 2:

Employee (fname, minit, lname, <u>ssn</u>, bdate, address, sex, salary,
super_ssn -> Employee.ssn, dno -> Department.dnumber)
Department (dname, <u>dnumber</u>, mgr_ssn->Eemployee.ssn, mgr_start_date)
Dept_location (<u>dnumber</u>->Department.dnumber, <u>dlocation</u>)
Project (pname, <u>pnumber</u>, plocation, dnum->Department.dnumber)
Works_on (<u>essn</u>->Employee.ssn, <u>pno</u>->Project.pnumber, hours)
Dependent (<u>essn</u>->Employee.ssn, <u>dependent_name</u>, sex, bdate, relationship)

Fig. 2. Company database schema [3] with foreign keys' references added

The schema represents interesting cases as weak entity type (Dependent relation), self-reference (super_ssn in Employee relation), projection of the composite attribute (fname, minit, lname in Employee relation) and flattening of the multivalued attribute (Dept_location relation). Foreign keys' names follow the conventions for different names with referred attributes.

The database state used in the SQL examples contains 40 records: eight in Employee table, three in Department, six in Projects, 16 in Works_on, and seven in Dependent. DDL script for schema creation and population with data is not provided, but it is not a problem to create a script using the book.

In general, the database schema and state are suitable to present major SQL functionalities, but foreign key naming convention doesn't allow some JOINs to be demonstrated. In fact, the database schema is not so complex, but in combination with the number of the records in the state it makes the manual evaluation of not so complex queries difficult. In this way, the results obtained from SQL query execution in DBMS will be not so easy to understand and check.

3.3 SaleCo Database [4]

SaleCo database [4] is used in the entire book and DDL scrips are provided for MS Access, MS SQL Server, MySQL and Oracle DBMS. The database model implements the following business rules:

- The database keeps data about customers, vendors, invoices and products.
- A customer may have many invoices, but one invoice belongs exactly to one customer.
- An invoice contains one or more invoice lines, and each invoice line belongs exactly to one invoice.
- Each invoice line consists of one product, and a particular product may be part of many invoice (as invoice line).
- A vendor may supply many products. Vendors may be added in the database before supplying any product yet.
- Products may be not supplied by a vendor, but if a product is vendor-supplied, it is supplied by exactly one vendor.

The database schema consists of five relations (Fig. 3):

Customer (cus_code, cus_lname, cus_fname, cus_initial, cus_areacode,
          cus_phone, cus_balance)
Invoice (inv_number, cus_code->Customer.cus_code, inv_date)
Vendor (v_code, v_name, v_contact, v_areacode, v_phone, v_state, v_order)
Product (p_code, p_descript, p_indate, p_qoh, p_min, p_price, p_discount,
          v_code->Vendor.v_code)
Line (inv_number->Invoice.inv_number, line_number, p_code->Product.p_code,
      line_units, line_price)

Fig. 3. SaleCo database schema [4] with foreign keys' references added

The database sample state used in the examples contains 63 records, 10 in Customer table, eight in Invoice table, 11 in Vendor table, 16 in Product table, and 18 in Line table. Part of the customers don't have any invoices; part of the vendors also don't have any product supplied; some of the products are not vendor supplied and/or not ordered yet.

The SaleCo database schema and state are suitable to demonstrate major SQL functionality. Also complex queries can be demonstrated. Although the database schema is not complex, the number of the records in the state makes manual evaluation of complex (and not so complex) queries difficult and the reasons for the results obtained from SQL query execution in DBMS will be not so clear.

3.4 University Database [5]

University database [5] is a case study in the entire book. DDL script is provided for creation of the database, as well as two versions of scripts for population with data – short, used in book examples, and extended with more records. The database model implements the following business rules:

- One instructor belongs to zero or one department and one department may have zero or more instructors.
- One student may enroll in zero or more sections and may be attached to not more than one department. Also students may have advisor (instructor) attached.

- One course may have zero or more sections and may be attached to not more than one department.
- Each course may have zero or more courses as prerequisites.
- One section belongs to exactly one course and exactly one timeslot.

The database schema consists of 11 relations (Fig. 4) with a total of 137 records in the short version of the database state used in illustrative examples in the book:

Classroom (building, room_number, capacity)
Department (dept_name, building, budget)
Course (course_id, title, dept_name->Department, credits)
Instructor (ID, name, dept_name->Department, salary)
Section (course_id->Course.course_id, sec_id, semester, year,
       [building, room_number]->Classroom.[building,room_number], time_slot_id)
Teaches (ID->Instructor.ID, [course_id, sec_id, semester, year]->
       Section.[course_id, sec_id, semester, year])
Student (ID, name, dept_name->Department.dept_name, tot_cred)
Takes (ID->Student.ID, [course_id, sec_id, semester, year]->
       Section.[course_id, sec_id, semester,year], grade)
Advisor (s_id->Student.ID, i_id->Instructor.ID)
Time_slot (time_slot_id, day, start_time, end_time)
Prereq (course_id->Course.course_id, prereq_id->Course.course_id)

Fig. 4. University database schema [5] with foreign keys reference added

The database schema is complex and is not easy to be understood, given the number of relations and complex foreign keys. Composite foreign keys are also not suitable for SQL coding. Moreover, not a single naming convention is used for foreign keys' names – one part follows the convention of the same names, another part – convention of usage of different names with corresponding primary/candidate keys which is a bad practice. Manual evaluation is not easy and in some cases could be not applicable for complex queries.

3.5 Movies DB [6]

Movies database [6] is used as a base case study example in the entire book. In fact, the entire database state is not included in the book and the examples are illustrated by partial states according to particular example. Movies database implements the following business rules:

- One movie is owned by one studio and has one producer.
- One movie star may have roles in zero or more movies.
- A movie executive may be a producer or studio president and has a certificate number.
- A studio may own zero or more movies and has exactly one president.

Database schema (Fig. 5) consists of 5 relations:

Movies (<u>title</u>, <u>year</u>, length, genre, studioName->Studio.name,
producerC#->MovieExec.cert#)
MovieStar (<u>name</u>, address, gender, birthdate)
StarsIn (<u>movieTitle</u>->Movies.title, <u>movieYear</u>->Movies.year,
<u>starName</u>->MovieStar.name)
MovieExec (name, address, <u>cert#</u>, netWorth)
Studio (<u>name</u>, address, presC#->MovieExec.cert#)

Fig. 5. Movies database schema [6] with foreign keys reference added

According to a free accessible DDL file in GitHub [7], the Movies database sample state contains 35 records: 10 in Movie table, five in MovieExec table, seven in MovieStar table, eight in StarsIn table, and five in Studio table. Part of the customers don't have any invoices; part of the vendors also don't have any product supplied; some of the products are not vendor supplied and/or not ordered yet.

Generally, the database schema is simple and understandable. Foreign keys' names don't follow any of the naming conventions, mentioned above, which is a bad practice. The database schema and state allow to demonstrate major functionality of SQL and complex queries can be created. The small number of the records in the state is suitable for manual evaluation of the results.

3.6   SCO Database [8]

SCO database [8] is used as a case study example in the entire book. SCO is an abbreviate for Salespeople-Customers-Orders, which are the names of the relations included in this schema (Fig. 6).

Salespeople (<u>snum</u>, sname, city, comm)
Customers (<u>cnum</u>, cname, city, rating, snum->Salespeople.snum)
Orders (<u>onum</u>, amt, odate, snum->Salespeople.snum, cnum->Customers.cnum)

Fig. 6. SCO database schema [8] with foreign keys reference added

Relation Salespeople denotes suppliers. Each salesperson has a unique number (snum), which is the primary key of this relation; name (sname); rating (rating) in orders; and location (city), where this salesperson resides.

Relation Customers denotes customers. Each customer has a unique number (cnum), which is a primary key of the relation; name (cname); rating (rating), representing some kind of ranking level among available customers; location (city), where this customer resides; and the number of the salesperson (snum) assigned to this customer.

Relation Orders denotes orders placed by the customers and fulfilled by the salespeople. Each order has unique number (onum); number of the customer (cnum), placed the order; number of the salesperson (snum), fulfilled the order; order date (odate); and amount (amt) of the order. It is not obligatory to the customers to place orders only to the salesperson attached.

The SCO database state used in the book examples consists of six records in Sales-people relation, eight records in Customers, and ten records in Orders. A DDL script is not provided, but the creation and population of the database is not a problem, according to its simplicity and small number of records used.

Schema and state are very simple, but suitable for full SQL functionality demon-stration. An interesting point here is a relationship between Salespeople and Customers which allows creation of complex queries too. The simplicity of the schema and state makes manual evaluation very simple and supports better understanding of the results obtained.

4 Discussion

My teaching practice shows that students prefer to execute the SQL query in real DBMS environment (or DBMS sandbox) and after that to check the obtained result manually. Sometimes they don't understand why the obtained result differs from their manual evaluation. This situation makes simplicity of the schema and state a key point in effec-tiveness of SQL training. Another key point is the miniworld [3] presented in the database schema which has to be understandable for the students.

In fact, the database courses don't include only SQL training part, and the usage of one case study during the entire course is very suitable and (possibly) effective. In fact, such kind of overall solution suffer from some weaknesses. In example, to present process of conceptual modeling and relational mapping, a complex case is needed and as result the relational schema designed will be too complex. A good example with real data will fill designed database with many records. In opposite, the database schema and state for SQL training have to be simple and small to be effective for manual evaluation and will increase understanding of SQL semantics and execution.

Four of the discussed database schemas and states [3–6] are used as a case study to represent database design topics and for SQL training. The miniworlds presented in these databases are understandable by the students. Part of them [3, 5] suffer from database schema and state complexity which could reduce the effectiveness of SQL training. In particular, the database schema in [5] is too complex because of the composite foreign keys and could be simplified using surrogate keys in foreign keys constraints. Database schema and state presented in [4, 6] don't have such kind of weaknesses in general.

Database schemas and states presented in [2, 8] are focused mainly on SQL training. The miniworlds presented are simple and the semantic of the queries is easy to understand and manual evaluation is simple. Despite this simplicity, these database schemas and states can be used for training with complex queries.

5 Conclusions

In the books included in this study two major streams in database schemas and states are distinguishable. One is focused on overall solution, that covers database design topics and SQL training, another is focused only on SQL training. As is found in the considered schemas, overall solutions could suffer from complexity when they have to be used for SQL training. In the opposite, schemas focused only on SQL training are too simple for database design and implementation topics. The possible solution is to use miniworld that will produce database schema which is complex enough for demonstration of the design process, and after that to use simplified version of the database schema with reduced number of records for SQL training.

References

1. ACM Curricula Recommendations. https://www.acm.org/education/curricula-recommendations. Accessed 31 May 2022
2. Date, C.J.: SQL and Relational Theory, 3rd edn. O'Reilly Media Inc. (2015)
3. Elmasri, R., Navathe, S.: Fundamentals of Database Systems, 7th edn. Pearson Education (2016)
4. Coronel, C., Morris, S.: Database Systems. Design, Implementation, & Management, 13th edn. Cengage Learning Inc. (2017)
5. Silberschatz, A., Korth, H.F., Sudarshan, S.: Database System Concept, 7th edn. McGraw Hill Education (2020)
6. Garcia-Molina, C., Ullman, J., Widom, J.: Database Systems: The Complete Book, 2nd edn. Pearson Education (2014)
7. GitHub.   https://github.com/stelf/fmi-db/blob/master/scripts/SchemaMovies-MSSQL.sql. Accessed 31 May 2022
8. Gruber, M.: Mastering SQL, Sybex Inc. (2000)

Are Research Universities Meeting
the Educational Challenge of the New Economy?

Tanya Zlateva[(✉)]

Boston University Metropolitan College, Boston, MA 02215, USA
zlateva@bu.edu

Abstract. Rapid technological change is affecting workforce structure and deepening employment polarization. Driven by automation, data science, and increasingly artificial intelligence and cyber-physical systems, new employment opportunities require knowledge and skills in emerging fields or higher technical level that are in short supply in the current workforce. Closing this gap challenges traditional universities to develop diverse portfolios of accessible and affordable programs of industry-relevant content available to working adults for part-time study. As the pace of technological change continues to accelerate and working lifespans continue to increase, successful careers are predicated on lifelong learning, upskilling, and reskilling. Academia, recognizing this challenge, is moving continuing professional education, especially online learning, into the university's core mission. However, there are significant hurdles to integrating online programs into traditional research departments. This paper identifies the main difficulties and proposes approaches for their resolution.

Keywords: Online and hybrid education · Educational modalities · Workforce transformation · Alternative credentials · Job polarization · Artificial intelligence in education · Online at-scale · Continuing education · Professional education

1 Introduction

Academia is confronting a fundamental challenge—creating educational programs and environments for continual, accessible, and affordable learning while preserving the tradition of research and teaching that provides students with the foundational knowledge to last a lifetime. Sparked by the computing revolution of the last century, automation, global networks, data science, and, more recently, artificial intelligence and cyber-physical systems are transforming the economy and the structure of the workforce [1]. While job destruction is not expected to outpace job creation in the next five years, new employment opportunities also require new knowledge and skills, usually at a higher technical level or in an emerging field. Both are in short supply in the current workforce. Technological change, already the highest in history, has continued to increase over the last five years. This trend, along with longer life spans, means that a sustainable career requires continued learning, upskilling, and reskilling to keep pace with the rate

© ICST Institute for Computer Sciences, Social Informatics and Telecommunications Engineering 2022
Published by Springer Nature Switzerland AG 2022. All Rights Reserved
T. Zlateva and R. Goleva (Eds.): CSECS 2022, LNICST 450, pp. 205–212, 2022.
https://doi.org/10.1007/978-3-031-17292-2_17

of change [2]. There is no doubt there is a significant skill gap in the workforce—the question is only about its extent (estimates range from 40% to 70%) and how to address it (a bewildering number of proposals from corporate training to professional certifications and new credentials, to traditional for-credit programs.)

The complexity of the technological and social disruptions does not allow for a single solution. It will require a diverse portfolio of programs of different lengths (intensive short skills program to multiple-year degrees), credentials (certificate, specialization, micro-/nano masters, badges), and modalities (in-person, hybrid, online). However, traditional research universities have little to no experience outside the in-person undergraduate and graduate degrees. The majority of the faculty had no experience with remote learning until the covid-19 epidemic forced transitioning online. The results are mixed. Against this complex background, the inescapable reality remains that the new economy needs a novel educational paradigm, a reimagining of the teaching and learning space to deliver industry-relevant knowledge and skills supporting career success over a working life of more than fifty years.

One source for insights, expertise, and experience for approaching this task are continuing education schools. Their core mission is expanding university access to lifelong learners. Listening to student needs, they have developed professional programs and flexible delivery and emphasized the incorporation of industry tools and approaches in the academic curriculum. In the process, extension schools have accumulated considerable experience in teaching working adults, e.g., by increasing interactivity and developing supporting materials to bridge gaps in prerequisite knowledge. A collaboration between traditional departments and continuing education units that leverages research strengths with flexible, accessible teaching for working professionals would be a powerful approach to creating a new learning space. This paper explores the drivers for the change, the educational need, and the hurdles for achieving a transformation of the traditional university.

2   The Gap Between Educational Need and Availability

To understand the need, nature, and urgency for academic change, we briefly consider the causes driving the restructuring of the workforce from the technology, demographics, and social point of view.

Technology has been the root cause for change, specifically the expansion of computing into (i) automation and robotization of production and (ii) ubiquitous use of analytic and collaboration tools even in traditionally non-technical fields (e.g., managerial tasks, construction work) thanks to the increased ability and ease of processing large amounts of data. As in previous industrial revolutions, existing jobs are destroyed, and new ones are created. But there are two significant differences. First, the pace of change is at a historical high, and with the progressive adoption of artificial intelligence and its integration with physical systems, it will continue to accelerate. Second, unlike previous industrial revolutions that replaced mainly manual labor and created better paying white-collar jobs, the current change affects traditionally safe middle-class occupations such as office work, data entry, paralegal, or, more generally, jobs with well-defined routine activities. In contrast, some low-paid occupations in the service sphere (personal care, security personnel, cleaning services) increased, leading to a more pronounced polarization. The qualifications required for careers in emerging sectors or with highly changed skill profiles are heavily tilted toward data and business analysis, data science, machine learning, and AI, digital strategies and transformation [1, 2].

While demographic factors vary across countries and economies, global life expectancy increased by six years in the twenty pre-covid years. Even with the losses of the last two years, it remains ca. four years higher than in 2000 [3, 4]. Healthy life expectancy exhibits a similar pattern, confirming that people, living longer, healthier lives, need sustainable employment. Country-specific factors may also substantively affect the educational landscape. For instance, in the United States, college enrollments have been declining since 2010, except for graduate professional registrations that increased in the pre-covid years and then held steady [5, 6]. The losses are not uniformly distributed. For-profit universities were the hardest hit, and some smaller liberal colleges faced serious financial problems. However, the overall instability—economic and social—compelled virtually all academic institutions to seek novel programmatic and delivery approaches that will broaden access and expand their student population.

Table 1. .

Economy & Workforce	Higher Education	
Computing, Automation, Data Science, AI, cyber-physical systems	Quantitative Knowledge & Skills, Analytical & Innovative Thinking, Complex Problem Solving, Critical Thinking, Technology Use & Design, Collaboration & Leadership,	
Fastest pace of change in history, and increasing	Continual timely curriculum innovation	Foundational degrees that build disciplinary knowledge to last a lifetime
Longer career lives: 50+ years	Lifelong learning to sustain successful career with variety of program formats (certificates, degrees, badges) and modalities (hybrid, online)	One-time immersive degrees: bachelors and doctoral, more recently master's and some online

←   *Extension Schools*   →   ←   *Traditional Research Departments*   →

Table 1 summarizes the new demands on higher education and how academia is currently meeting them through its traditional and continuing education programs. The main content areas—computing, automation, data science, learning and AI, cyber-physical systems—are all included in the curriculum of both research and extension schools. The difference is in the positioning of the programs. Traditional schools prioritize foundational knowledge and building a deep disciplinary framework to last a lifetime. The premise is that this academic foundation, typically acquired in an immersive learning environment, gives students the ability to stay abreast of their professional field through self-study. In contrast, extension units focus on programs for improving existing skills or providing paths to a new field and a new career. The premise is that there is a need to repeatedly come back to school and engage in a formal learning experience while attending part-time. While the value of an academic foundation is indisputable it is also clear that the program and delivery formats developed for part-time students are better suited to meet the demands of the new economy.

3 Higher Education Response to the Challenge

The educational challenge of the new economy and the danger of social destabilization that can result from continued workforce polarization are well understood in academia. Both research universities and extension schools have rapidly developed, implemented, and tested a variety of educational initiatives. It is worthwhile to explore the differences in approach. Continuing education schools through their immediate and direct contact with professionals understood the learning needs much earlier and became centers for experimentation and innovation for curriculum, formats, and modality. Figure 1 illustrates this trend on the example of Boston University's Metropolitan College. MET was the first to introduce an MS in computer science in the early 1970s, led curricular updates on programming languages (C instead of Pascal, object-oriented programming with C++ then Java) in the 1990s, and after 2000 developed specialized graduate programs in cybersecurity, health informatics, business and data analytics. Program format innovation included the introduction of stackable for-credit certificates in the mid-1990s and non-credit preparatory laboratories in 2015. As early as the mid-1990s the college was offering video-conferencing courses through PictureTel for corporate partners. The first hybrid graduate certificate with 75% online content and video lectures was delivered in 2000, and fully online programs were launched in 2002.

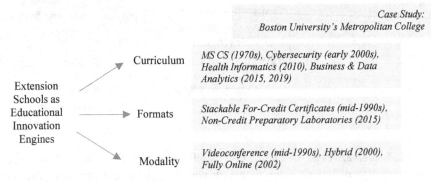

Fig. 1. Educational innovation at Boston University's Metropolitan College

Research departments entered the continuing education space in the early 2000s. The visionary goal of massive open online courses was for free education from the best researchers in the field, available to everybody in the world. It was an explosion of masterly content and creative design, and the world took notice. The first massively open online course (MOOC), an AI course by Sebastian Thrun and Peter Norvig from Stanford, attracted 160,000 students. More courses followed, developed by brilliant scientists and scholars, some reaching half a million students in one session (e.g., Justice by Harvard's Michael Sandel). But soon, two major problems surfaced—(i) completion rates were low, and the majority of students were not from disadvantaged backgrounds but had completed or were in the process of completing a degree; and (ii) the initial business model was unsustainable. A series of adjustments were introduced to address these problems, including low-cost verification certificates, micro- and nano-degree as entry to full degrees, and finally, online for-credit master's degrees (Fig. 2). The tuition of the latter currently ranges from a disruptively low $7,000 to $15,000 (multiple times lower than the in-person version) to a premium of $80,000 to over $110,000 (the same as the in-person version).

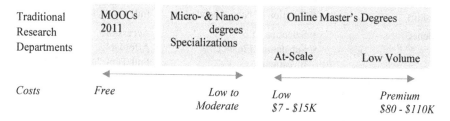

Fig. 2. Evolution of massive open online courses

Both extension schools and research departments have demonstrated a high level of innovation. But it is interesting to note that the style of the innovation is strongly influenced by the institutional culture. Traditional continuing education departments developed programs that directly answered student career needs—emphasizing applications and industry tools and skills, low development cost, and short, affordable programs. The research department approached continuing education as a research project—global vision, emphasis on originality and creativity, consciously disruptive, financial solutions delayed to a later phase.

4 Organizational Hurdles

Recent surveys show that a substantial majority of university leadership support the expansion of continuing education and online programs (e.g., 66% of respondents in a 2021 survey by Modern Campus [7] agree or strongly agree they have support and buy-in to expand from senior leadership.) However, there are serious organizational and cultural hurdles to the faster adoption of continuing education by research departments. Beyond the obvious expansion of educational technologies and support, and adding resources for instructional design and production, there are differences in departmental and faculty priorities, student profile, pedagogy, and program format that are not well understood and therefore not addressed.

Research departments prioritize the creation of new knowledge and expect faculty to devote considerable time to research and scholarship and mentoring doctoral students. Course development and teaching are almost exclusively in the area of research interests of the faculty and primacy is placed on disciplinary depth. Promotion and tenure are strongly dependent on the quality and impact of the publication record. In contrast the deciding factor for continued employment in continuing education units is teaching teaching quality, course updates and curriculum innovation to integrated emerging fields and industry-relevant skills and approaches, and online course development (Table 2).

Table 2. Differences in faculty priorities, student profile, and programs between traditional research departments and continuing education schools

	Traditional research departments	Continuing professional units
Faculty Expectations and Priorities	• Research & Scholarship • Creation of New Knowledge	• Teaching • Industry-Relevant Curriculum
Students	• Selective • Substantial Financial Investment • Full-time Study, (Part-Time Job) • Limited size student body	• Accessible • Affordable • Full-Time Job, Part-Time Study • Large size student body
Curriculum	• Academic Foundational Knowledge Framework • Disciplinary breath & depth	• Applied Knowledge & Skills • Professional tools, applications & techniques
Format & Delivery	• Degrees • On-campus—day • Online, Hybrid	• Degrees, Certificates, • On-campus—eves, weekends • Online, Hybrid

The differences in student profiles can be even starker. Students in traditional research departments are admitted through a rigorous selection process, they attend full-time, are immersed in the academic community, and their main stated goal and responsibility is learning. Continuing education students attend part-time and typically must divide attention between responsibilities for their full-time jobs, family, and learning. A significant percentage are career changer with no prior knowledge of the field they intent to enter. To achieve the same or equivalent learning outcomes for both student populations faculty needs to account for these differences in teaching style and supporting teaching materials, e.g. more extended online materials for prerequisite knowledge for part-time students, more formal guidelines for team and research projects.

Finally, continuing education implies not only flexibility of the delivery modality, but also a range of short programs that can be stand-alone or lead to a degree. The frequency of offering is also important—cohort programs are too rigid, and limiting program start to once or twice per year is insufficient for working adults who often have uneven workload.

5   A Look to the Future

Continuing education has moved into the main mission of the university. It is not yet fully integrated into the fabric of the teaching and learning process, but there is a clear institutional understanding of its strategic significance.

The obstacles to an effective online continuing education operation led and overseen by the research departments are still not well understood and only partially addressed. While it is accepted that faculty needs to be supported by instructional designers, videographers, and developers of graphics and simulations, questions about the level of in-class instructional support are wide open. To give a few prominent examples: Is peer-to-peer grading an adequate substitute for teaching assistants? Is automated grading a sufficient measure for learning? Can AI tools significantly reduce or even eliminate the need for instructor involvement? Georgia Institute of Technology successfully deployed and used "Jill Watson," a virtual teaching assistant and continual free learning resource [7]. However, generic AI tools are limited in number and are not broadly adopted. Answers to the above questions will not be uniform. Schools vary in their academic profile, history, culture, organizational structure, and strategic goals. Each will forge a path to online and continuing education that best fits its profile and resources. But there are some overreaching themes and questions common to all that must be addressed.

Table 3. Continuing education in the mainstream – goals and solutions

Goals	Solutions
• **Meaningful access to faculty for large number of students**? • **Continual curriculum innovation** – new programs in emerging fields & frequent updates of existing curricula with the latest industry tools and approaches • **Extensive hands-on online learning resources** to provide prerequisite knowledge for students with widely diverse background ranging from *recent graduates to seasoned professionals, to career changers with no background in the new field, to practitioners who have been out of school for many years*?	• **From single faculty to teaching teams** • **Collaboration with continuing education departments to leverage experience in teaching working adults** • **Expansion of Teaching Faculty**

Table 3 provides an overview of the goals in bringing continuing education programs into the core educational mission of the university and some solutions for their realization. While a natural extension of the teaching mission the integration of continuing programs in research departments requires significant changes and will have a profound impact on the university as we know it today. The faculty who has been traditionally fully in charge of their course material and teaching will need to transform into leaders of a diverse teaching team including facilitators or section instructors, instructional designers, and administrative support. An expansion of the teaching faculty, needed to manage the large course enrollments, increased the complexity of faculty structure and faculty governance. Developing expertise and experience in teaching part-time students require additional time investments and bridging institutional boundaries. Overall, the expansion is student- and teaching-centered with very limited overlap with the primary research mission. Thus, reconciling demands on faculty time will require creative solutions. However, despite the difficulties, the importance and significance of continuing professional learning for future economic progress and an equitable society remain indisputable.

Acknowledgments. I would like to thank my anonymous reviewers for helping me improve this paper and for raising important issues about preserving the primacy of research and rich multimodal data for extensive analysis.

References

1. Maarten, G., et al.: The impact of technological innovation on the future of work. In: JRC Working Papers Series on Labour, Education and Technology, No. 2019/03, European Commission, Joint Research Centre (JRC), Seville. https://www.econstor.eu/bitstream/10419/202320/1/jrc-wplet201903.pdf. Accessed 22 June 2022
2. The Future of Jobs Report 2020. World Economic Forum. https://www3.weforum.org/docs/WEF_Future_of_Jobs_2020.pdf (October 2020). Accessed 14 May 2022
3. Life expectancy and healthy life expectancy. The Global Health Observatory, World Health Organization. https://www.who.int/data/gho/data/themes/mortality-and-global-health-estimates/ghe-life-expectancy-and-healthy-life-expectancy. Accessed 14 May 2022
4. Effects of covid-19 pandemic on life expectancy and premature mortality in 2020: time series analysis in 37 countries. BMJ. https://www.bmj.com/content/375/bmj-2021-066768. Accessed 14 May 2022
5. National Centers for Education Statistics, Postsecondary Education Enrollments. https://nces.ed.gov/programs/digest/current_tables.asp. Accessed 14 May 2022
6. Fall 2021 Enrollment Report, National Student Clearinghouse. https://nscresearchcenter.org/wp-content/uploads/CTEE_Report_Fall_2021.pdf. Accessed 14 May 2022
7. The State of Continuing Education 2022, Modern Campus. https://resources.moderncampus.com/state-of-ce-2022?__hstc=128368595.7b27d550eef00b5538737e484929b990.1655903745293.1655903745293.1655903745293.1&__hssc=128368595.2.1655903745293&__hsfp=2232108563. Accessed 23 June 2022
8. Watson, J.: A Suite of Learning Tools, Homepage at Georgia Institute of Technology. https://dilab.gatech.edu/a-suite-of-online-learning-tools/. Accessed 14 May 2022

A Collaborative Learning Environment Using Blogs in a Learning Management System

Victor Obionwu[1]($\boxtimes$), David Broneske[2], and Gunter Saake[1]

[1] Otto von Guericke University, Magdeburg, Germany
{obionwu,saake}@ovgu.de
[2] German Centre for Higher Education Research and Science Studies,
Hannover, Germany
broneske@dzhw.eu

Abstract. Over the last decade, we have seen an increasing trend in the development, and adoption of self-paced learning systems in both formal and informal sectors. Our Learning Management system is one such web-based interactive learning system that facilitates the acquisition of structured query language skills. In this pilot study, we extended our LMS teams environment to support more collaborative interactions, and knowledge sharing between learners with a blog feature. Thus allowing learners share their insights and learning experiences and further receive feedback from other learners within the course. To evaluate the effectiveness of our approach, we employed a survey research method and its corresponding evaluations on a selected student population. The evaluation shows that blogs are more effective at conveying one's learning experience compared to the use of chat rooms as learners could progressively restructure, and develop their understanding of every task. Also, the blogging environment allows them understand other students' points of view, thus making them convenient for knowledge acquisition and distribution.

Keywords: Collaborative learning · Educational blogs · Knowledge sharing

1 Introduction

A recent survey on the E-learning market by Global Marketing Insights reveals that the E-Learning Market size crossed USD 250 billion in 2020 and is expected to grow exponentially [1]. There has been a sustained growth in digital education over the years. These platforms not only provide a self-paced learning environment, but also allow learners to restructure their learning and understandings from their peers thus providing a collaborative learning environment with cognitive engagement and social interactions among the learners. Knowledge management and sharing are vital in these learning platforms and it is essential to

T. Zlateva and R. Goleva (Eds.): CSECS 2022, LNICST 450, pp. 213–232, 2022.
https://doi.org/10.1007/978-3-031-17292-2_18

invest time and resources to create an efficient knowledge base that is accessible to all the learners at any time.

Several challenges arise When individuals wish to share knowledge. The sender's perception, and method of transmission may be perceived differently by the receiver, thus resulting in contradictions. Another issue is temporal-spatial issues, where people need appropriate time and location to gather and share knowledge. Before modern communication methods, people needed to gather data and knowledge physically to share it with others, resulting in a time penalty. However, blogs greatly reduce the temporal-spatial aspect of knowledge management and sharing by eliminating the traditional physical proximity requirement for the sender, and receiver [2].

Our Learning Management system, SQLValidator [3] is a web-based interactive tool for learning and practicing structured query language, which is the most commonly used language in database-related courses. The LMS teams feature is dedicated to team collaboration. From the perspective of a student, it aids to fulfill the assigned exercise tasks. In the course of these tasks, students are provided the option of reviewing past query submissions in a bid to foster reflection as they continue working on future tasks. However, solving tasks correctly and completely in itself is not enough for effective learning. Our Literature research showed various methods to present "knowledge sharing" to students as an aid to their learning process and several research articles showed that usage of blogging in education has improved knowledge sharing between individuals.

In all, taking the influence of social networking on students into account, and transferring it to LMS teams via a blog feature, we aim to stimulate more collaboration among student and instructors. This study aims to shed light on the following research questions:

- How blogging within a learning environment helps in efficient knowledge management, sharing, and skill acquisition?
- Which features in blog pages would be effective, encouraging for a learner in finding hints/tips for tasks and expressing themselves?

The paper proceeds as follows. The next section deals with introducing the related background to our work. Section 3 deals with the implementation of blogs in the teams page of Our Learning Management system. Section 4 with an evaluation of the effectiveness of using blogs to support more collaborative interactions, and Sect. 5 concludes with our contributions, and directions for future scope.

2   Literature Research

As stated earlier, our aim is to enhance the current teams environment in the LMS to support more collaborative learning. Collaborative learning is a structured learning technique to allow learners to respond to each other's ideas, designs, or even teach each other [4]. Many researchers embrace collaborative learning theory to offer enhanced learning environments in education systems [4–7]. Smart Collaborative pedagogy directs students and educators in using interactive technology and models [8] to form a collaborative learning environment resulting in improved professional skills through coordination and cooperation in a team consisting of people of the same or different expertise. [6] In traditional classroom learning learners can either produce a proposal/presentation or a report on their learning and it mostly stays between the tutor and the learner [9] or if it is collaborative learning in classrooms then within the team and the tutor. An increase in digital learning has forced researchers to find new ways to reproduce aspects of traditional classroom learning and suit it better to the digital learning environment [10,11]. [6] has assessed key criteria for intelligent collaboration and to provide a better learning environment based on learners' reports and his evaluations. The key criteria are *Transparency, Collective intelligence, Democratized learning, Smartly sharing, Knowledge engagement, and Openness* [6].

A summary of theories behind collaborative learning was described by [4]. [12] mentions "Connectivism" as knowledge distribution traversing among connections i.e.) acquiring knowledge through connections. An important finding during the search on collaborative learning strategies was from [13]. It provides an overview of a collection of research articles relating to the New Generation of Collaborative Learning Systems and the needs of next-generation learning systems. Investigation in [13] reveals the supporting factors of next-generation collaborative learning systems - *Enabling Technologies, Psychological factors, Learning dimension, Knowledge management, Social networking infrastructure.* All these factors were investigated with several dimensions within themselves. Interestingly 3 factors namely Learning dimension, Knowledge management, Social networking infrastructure along with their dimensions suited to our need of enhancing the learning environment in the LMS. Keywords like *E-Feedback micro-blogging management, online communities, Knowledge mobilization, Connectivity Experience* were of our necessities. Also, the classification of collaborative approaches in [4], provided different criteria for collaborative learning techniques in E-learning environments. We picked up factors from each point of view that would suit our need in improving the learning environment in the LMS. From the Purpose View - Debate and discussion, Social networking provides interactions, networking, and collaboration. From the view of Method - Communicating/chatting, sharing links will lead to collaborative interactions. From the tool's view of [4], we picked up - Wikis, Social networking, Content communities, E-learning services, Discussion forums. This led us to think about providing a service within the learning management system to share knowledge with learners and also serve as a knowledge base. Wiki and Blogging models were the first to hit us as they are the most familiar knowledge base and knowledge sharing platforms.

Our search on literature shifted to finding research works on using blogging services in various learning environments and their outcomes. We found several research articles [14–18] using blogs as valuable platforms for constructivist learning and is also suited to support a wide range of educational concepts. To this end, literature research has been carried out to analyze the degree of effectiveness of blogging techniques in collaborative learning environments, along with positive and negative impacts. Apart from that, different features have been remarked within blogging serving different purposes, which are also another direction in our research to augment the learning environment. The vast majority of researches [15,19,20] have been encountered with findings on educational affordances and valuable application methods of blogs within the educational concept.

To begin with, [17] focuses on the effectiveness of blogging application in educational environments based on cognitive and social constructivist thinking, by taking into account the ability of blogs to be customized for supporting various educational activities.

Application of blog technology has been stated as a solution to obstacle factors in individual knowledge sharing, such as human factor, knowledge characteristics, and the spatial and temporal factors by [2], stating the superiority of blog technology as being low-cost, interactive, and open, but most importantly, the main advantage here is in the main target of blogging, which is to share and to facilitate the sharing activities.

While blogging activities are solution-oriented technological advances helping students in collaborative learning and knowledge sharing, the findings are quite divergent in terms of advantageous factors. Preliminary findings by [17] concluded the detrimental effects of blogging as well; for instance, the possibility of students becoming overwhelmed by various topics and concepts causing them to read and contribute rapidly and neglectfully, which in turn may lead to unrelated and not meaningful contributions, by which the effectiveness claim of blogging technology is becoming contradicted.

In the research by [15], the benefits of commenting feature in blogging is stated as the development of interactions between students as well as encouraging and praising each other by guiding on how to solve the problems but searched ways to enhance the self-directed learning skills for students to also coach each other, and by doing so enhancing the value of blogging in a contemporary learning environment.

While analyzing more than 300 cases in form of journal entries and comments by students, [18] concluded that descriptive reflections outnumbered the critical reflections, concluding that most students dedicate time and effort to produce a work in higher quality, knowing that their writing will be presented to an audience. Through the analysis of comments directly from the target audience, [18] highlighted the benefits of blogs as a learning tool in the learning process of students from different aspects.

However, only blogging itself or only Computer-Mediated tools are not enough and appealing from a student perspective in effective learning. This statement is strongly supported by [16], mentioning that instead of replacing the computer-mediated communication (CMC) applications with blogs, prefers integration of blogs in educational contexts to improve the communication environment among students and teachers, believing that would bring more contributions. A summary of important literature is shown in Tables 1 & 2 which covers the summary of the paper, its assessment method, and the type of learning environment.

3 Background

The aim of this study is to improve the collaborative learning aspect in the learning management system by introducing blogs. Therefore, it is essential that we initially cover in detail what these terms are before proceeding with our practical tasks.

3.1 The Learning Management System

Our learning management system features a built-in system to check the syntax and semantics of SQL queries and give feedback to the students accordingly. When a student submits a SQL query with a syntax error, the student is notified that there is a problem with their syntax. In the case of a semantic error, the student is notified of what is required from them and what their code outputs. For example, the result relation may be required to have 2 columns but the students' code may be resulting in a table with 3 columns. This is reflected as such by the learning management system. With this feature, students can check the correctness of their assignments before submitting them. These assignments may be individual or group based assignments. In the case of a group assignment, a page is created for each group, featuring a chat board where students can post their entries as a means of collaboration. When one student submits the assignment, it is submitted for the whole group. Not all students need to anticipate in the submission process. The same goes for editing the code, when a student edits the code, it is visible for the whole group. Here in addition to the team and the chat system, an instructional feedback feature allows the tutor communicate with each team, posting to the chat system together with the students, in addition to this, there is a separate announcement board where the tutor posts task descriptions and students submit their solutions to the respective tasks. To improve the collaborative learning aspect of this tool, we will develop and integrate a blog into the system.

3.2 The Notion of Blogs

A blog can be described as a website in which a blogger or several bloggers can write entries and these entries are ordered chronologically. In the old days one who wanted to blog needed to spend time writing tedious HTML code to own a personal blog. Nowadays people with minimal computer knowledge can effectively use blogs. In education, a blog has several features which make it stand ahead of traditional computer-mediated communication (CMC) technologies [28]. With traditional CMC technology, we can provide students effective and efficient distance learning which enhances collaboration, cooperation, knowledge

Table 1. Summary of important literatures of the study

Ref	Description	Assessment methods	Environment
[9]	Implemented group collaboration, writing progress reports and developing product versions and the online file sharing tool DriveHQ	Students' feedback on collaborative learning and progress report - checking the existence of individual accountability and positive interdependence in the learning environment	Online learning
[21]	Digital group conferences on the group interaction of the students	Analysis of transcripts of conferences and questions to group conferences -Tally, Interviews (NUDIST (Nonnumerical Unstructured Data Indexing, Searching and Theorizing) software to categorize as themes)	Online learning
[7]	Application of different amounts of coercion to the users of Negotiation Tool and testing the effects of three versions of NTool using Kruskal-Wallis tests	Questionnaire (6point Likert Scale), Statistical Analysis (Kruskal-Wallis tests, Spearman test, Mann-Whitney U test), Interviews (recorded, open coding with a focus on formalism and coercion)	Online learning
[18]	Engagement of students in the usage of Social Networking Sites in learning and Blogs as Online Assignment	Qualitative Analysis from students blogs post, comments and interviews	Classroom learning
[22]	A Quantitative research design that uses non-linear regression Partial Least Squares Structural Equation Modelling (PLS-SEM)	Online survey (5 point Likert scale)	Classroom learning
[23]	Measure the effect of the difference between blogs in design (hypertext, super graphics) and form on how students gain knowledge	Pre and Post Knowledge Tests and Quantitative analysis, SPSS	Online learning
[15]	Assessment module in the form of a portfolio comprising of a design diary, peer reviews, interactive pet (requiring 3D object building programming skills)	Thematic analysis from blog corpus. Qualitative content analysis - descriptive statistics (Kurtosis, Skewness), SPSS form inter-rater reliability statistics	Online learning
[24]	A research based on a survey: How the students reacted/perceived the integration of a blog was investigated	A survey (facilitating a 5 point Likert Scale) with data analysis via a t-test, reliability analysis, factor analysis, a series of ANOVAs, and multiple Regression analysis using SPSS 18.0	Classroom learning

Table 2. Summary of important literatures of the study

Ref	Description	Assessment methods	Environment
[25]	The co-relational research design and Examination of the relationship between various pre-service teachers' perceptions and their perceived learning in two courses that incorporated blogging	Three online questionnaires (Collaborative Learning scale, Sense of Community-scale, Perceived Learning scale)	Collaborative learning environment
[26]	Investigation of the influence of the social network's characteristics on students' performance and access to knowledge in learning via blogs	Multiple Online questionnaires - 5 points Likert Scale. Qualitative - Face to Face interviews coded by MAXQDA 18, Open Coding, Category Assignment	Online learning
[27]	Blogging was incorporated into the internship activities of interns. Behavior, perceptions, and processes of blogging among interns was examined from two disciplines and a mixed-method design was used to obtain quantitative and qualitative data through structured interviews and blogging entries	Questionnaires, Telephone interviews [Blogging Behavior (5point Likert scale) - InterQuartile Range, Blogging perception (4 point Scale) - Descriptive statistics (Kolmogorov-Smirnov test, Mann-Whitney test)]. Qualitative Analysis - Nvivo 8 software (Major Themes - cognitive, metacognitive, social and effective)	Online learning
[19]	A framework for educational blogging in the context of teacher education	Exploratory study, Pre-assessment questionnaire (4 point scale), Post-assessment questionnaire (5 point Likert scale), Formal personal interview, Analysis of blogs, and comments using indicators for self-expression and Social support	Online learning

sharing, and exchange of ideas. Students themselves also acknowledge the conclusions of the studies which point out these advantages. Such CMC systems also have limitations. They are not good at motivating students and making them feel engaged in this learning environment. Blogs are a good tool to overcome this challenge [29]. The Simple Syndication (RSS) feature of blogs is pointed out as an improvement to traditional CMC environments. RSS enhances collaboration and knowledge sharing by updating everyone involved with the blog with the relevant information, ensuring engagement which traditional CMC systems often lack. Blogging is also well noted for its ease with which it makes shared data easily available. In traditional CMC environments, there are often many steps/procedures to start using the tool to collaborate and share. Blogs are a lot more flexible in this regard, where even anonymous people may just leave an entry as they wish, meaning a blog is a far more dynamic, efficient, easy to use tool compares to traditional CMCs. A blog also incorporates different types of external media via so-called hyperlinks. This means blogs can incorporate videos, text, and other types of media flexibly and efficiently. The comment/reply feature of blogs can motivate individuals to participate more when they receive comments to their entries from their peers [30,31].

3.3   The Notion of Collaborative Learning

Collaborative learning can be described as a learning setting where students share knowledge, gain knowledge shared by others, express and exchange views and ideas with other students to enhance their overall learning experience [32]. In our study, we will be focusing on online collaborative learning. Collaborative learning systems can be categorized into three types: mirroring systems, meta-cognitive tools, and coaching systems. These systems are further categorized based on their technical aspects such as the type of data they deal with and the high-level representations etc. Another study investigated the issues in the trans-formation of collaborative learning systems in the present day and the dimensions of these issues as well as some scenarios related to these dimensions. [4,13] An important term in our research and development is computer-supported collab-orative learning (CSCL) [33]. The way technology has progressed has made it even more important for individuals to share knowledge and collaborate on their expertise. This term emphasizes the use of technology to enhance the aforemen-tioned concepts of collaborative learning. Two important features of CSCL are noted to be individual accountability and positive interdependence. The first term indicates that every individual comes with their respective set of skills, fields, and knowledge. A promising collaborative learning environment facili-tates the effective deployment and benefiting of this diverse set of knowledge to produce the common goal most effectively [34]. But every individual comes as important here and must contribute accordingly to reach the common goal. This concept of gathering a diverse set of individuals closely around a common goal, pointing out their responsibility motivates everyone to put in their work.

3.4   The SQLValidator

In the SQLValidator architecture, Fig. 1, users access, and interact with the platform via a web interface. The tasks, and submissions components contain all information necessary for its processing. A PHP server mediates between user requests, the databases and the relational database management system [3]. In SQLValidator, there are four main databases:

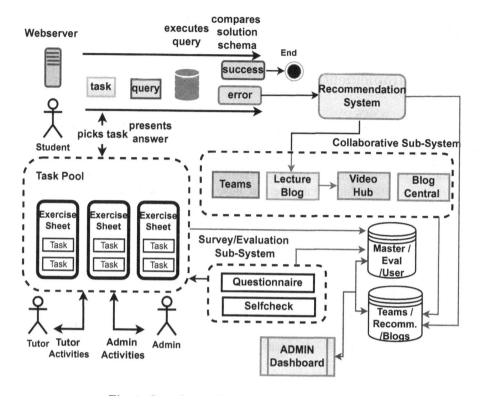

Fig. 1. Granular architecture of the SQLValidator

- `sqlvali_data` contains all relevant data to maintain the organization of the SQLValidator itself, such as user management and task definitions.
- `sqlvali_master` contains all standard tables and data used to perform an evaluation of the user query on the database.
- `user_#` contains physical user-specific slave databases related to the sqlvali_master where the users can perform their own queries.
- `sqlvali_eval` contains all relevant evaluation data to provide a proper basis for analytics.
- `sqlvali_teams` contains all data needed to maintain the team system used for team projects.
- `sqlvali_Recomm` contains the slide recommendation data maintain the team system used for team projects.

Now given that a student with access already picked a task and submitted an answer for the task, as shown in Fig. 1, SQLValidator validates the query for syntactic errors and then compares the resulting schema with a pre-defined solution schema for the particular task. If there is a mismatch between the two schemas, further evaluation is carried out and the cause of the error is returned to the student. The student can then correct and resubmit the query again until the query statement is successfully validated. A record of all last attempts for each individual task is saved on the user's page for that task. For analytic purposes, all submission attempts are saved in the sqlvali_eval database.

4 Blog Implementation

The literature review conducted by [35], highlights blog design, navigation, media use, usability, content, and accessibility as key factors taking into consideration wile designing and developing an educational blog. Navigation was achieved through the menu and links in the header of all pages. We have restricted the media usage to only image files to make it simple. Usability and accessibility are the key criteria in helping users achieve goals efficiently in the context of using the system. Figure 2 shows the use-case diagram that depicts the various use cases, users, and interactions among them.

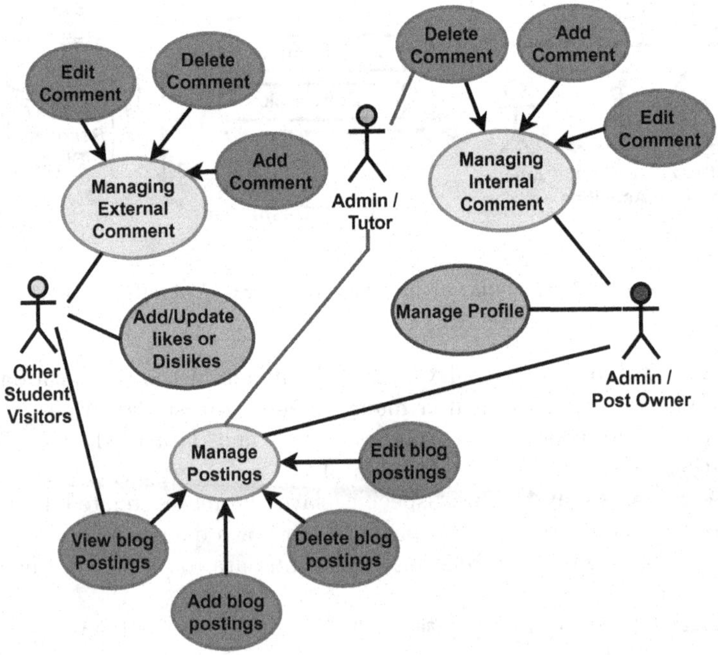

Fig. 2. Use-case diagram

The use case diagram depicts three actors. The owner of a blog post, the other students, and the tutor. The post owner can manage internal comments, which include editing, deleting, and adding comments. The tutor can delete these comments. The other students who are authorized to comment on one's blog post can manage external comments, namely add, edit and delete them. Both the post owner and the other students can manage their profiles. The post

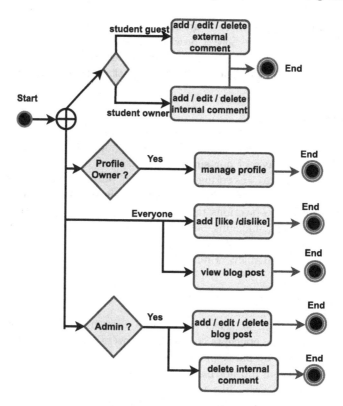

Fig. 3. Activity diagram

owner can manage their posts, namely add, edit and delete them. The other students can only view these.

The activity diagram, Fig. 3, is designed based on the use case diagram, about its constraints. It defines an initial state, from which the user can choose an activity to be performed as a decision node. For example, if the user wanted to manage an external comment, the user must be a student other than a post owner. When an activity is completed, we reach another decision node, asking the user whether they are finished. If not, we return to the initial decision node. To understand every action a user can take and its respective outcomes, we have prepared the activity diagram that depicts user actions and outcomes in Fig. 3. The comment section is available under each blog post to allow discussions related to the respective post. Users can type their comments in the provided box and subsequently post them. If a user wanted to correct a mistake or add more information etc., they have the option of editing their comment. They can also delete their comments. it is also possible to interact with another user's comments. The reply functionality extends this notion further, allowing discussions related to a single comment. Therefore a comment section is a key part of online collaborative learning since it increases collaboration among learners and authors. The author of a post can edit or delete the post is viewed. The author can now edit the contents where a preview of the old attachment is shown so they can decide to update the attachment or not. On confirming we update the table in the database and display the updated post on the index page.

5 Evaluation

A survey research design was used to investigate and get feedback on our system's usability. The basis of our survey was inspired by [24]. We developed a questionnaire relating to answering our research purpose with 5 point Likert scale (Strongly disagree,..Strongly agree) and a few multiple-choice questions. We divided it into three sections namely perception of collaboration, sense of learning and expressing, blogging behavior. We believe each section helps us to quantitatively measure each of our research questions. The questionnaire used can be found from the Table 3, Table 4 & Table 5.

5.1 Evaluation Results

For this pilot evaluation, we selected 21 active users from the 94 students that enrolled in the database concepts course. There were an equal number of males and females and a special participant. Most of the users were between the age of 27–31 and most of them did not have previous experience in using blogs/microblogs. Descriptive Statistics like mean, the standard deviation for the quantitative questions were calculated and added to Table 3, Table 4 & Table 5. No. corresponds to the population and is 21. The vast majority of quantitative replies were 4 and 5 on the scale. Therefore, the standard deviations are fairly small for a vast majority of the questions. There were no questions that were answered mostly negative but there are several questions with mixed replies. A notable

Table 3. Questionnaire

ID	Perception of collaboration	No	Mean	SD
1	I thought the blog was easy to use?	21	4.48	0.79
2	Can you feel a sense of community while learning in this blogging environment?	21	4.14	0.77
3	Blog discussions help me to share my knowledge and experience with my peers easily?	21	4.48	0.66
4	I think that the blog feature will be frequently used by new users	21	4.48	0.66
5	I think that I would need the support of a technical person to be able to use this tutorial	21	2.71	1.24
6	Do you think blogging environment provides an opportunity to improve social skills?	21	4.14	0.71

Table 4. Questionnaire

ID	Sense of learning and expressing	No	Mean	SD
1	Do you feel confident expressing yourself using the blog?	21	4.48	0.79
2	Are you open to debatable learning?	21	4.14	0.77
3	I understand the topic better after reading the blog posts	21	4.48	0.66
4	Blog discussions help me understand other points of view?	21	4.48	0.66
5	Getting to know people of common interests from the profile page is useful?	21	2.71	1.24
6	I find this blogging environment very informative and captivating to read and learn	21	4.14	0.71

Table 5. Questionnaire

ID	Blogging behavior	No	Mean	SD
1	I thought the blog was easy to use?	21	4.48	0.79
2	Can you feel a sense of community while learning in this blogging environment?	21	4.14	0.77
3	Blog discussions help me to share my knowledge and experience with my peers easily?	21	4.48	0.66
4	I think that the blog feature will be frequently used by new users	21	4.48	0.66
5	I think that I would need the support of a technical person to be able to use this tutorial	21	2.71	1.24
6	Do you think blogging environment provides an opportunity to improve social skills?	21	4.14	0.71

question is "I think that I would need the support of a technical person to be able to use this tutorial".

The average score of the question was a modest 2.71. In addition, several questions had a comparatively higher number of participants giving a score of 3 or 4 compared to 5. The questions were prepared in a way so that not only perceptions about the blog, but also their previous experience with blogs, blogging behavior, opinions about blogs, learning preferences can be understood. There were also other multiple-choice and textual input questions (Table 6 and 7) that the participants had the flexibility to describe briefly. These questions are qualitatively assessed to understand the users. From Fig. 4 & Fig. 5 we can assess the usability measured as relative to users of our blogging system. The success rate was high where all the users found our blogging system was easy to use. Users satisfaction can be understood from the outcomes where users voted for the system functions being well integrated.

As stated earlier, we have divided the questionnaire into three sections so it would help us to quantitatively measure each of our research questions. The

Table 6. Qualitative analysis

Perception of collaboration	No	(%)
Gender		
Male	10	47.6
Female	10	47.6
Special	1	4.8
Age		
below 20	0	0
21–23	0	0
23–27	4	19
27–31	12	57.1
above 31	5	23.8
Preference to learn in groups		
Yes	10	47.6
No	10	47.6
Sometimes	1	4.8

Table 7. Qualitative analysis

Perception of collaboration	No	(%)
Classroom or digital learning		
Classroom learning	7	33.3
Digital learning	2	9.5
Partly both	9	42.9
Depends on subject	8	38.1
Used blogs/micro-blogs earlier?		
Yes	13	61.9
No	8	38.1
When would you comment?		
Aware of the topic and you see misunderstandings	7	66.7
Aware of the topic and like to appreciate it	6	28.6
Unaware of the topic and you ask questions on it	7	33.3
Unaware of the topic and like to appreciate it	2	9.5

section on the perception of collaboration helps us to understand, if the learners are willing to learn in groups, does this environment helps them to share their knowledge and experience with others easily, do they feel a sense of community during learning, does it help in improving social skills. For example, From Table 6, we see that there is an equal number of users who prefer to learn in groups and not. Figure 6 shows that most users feel a sense of community while

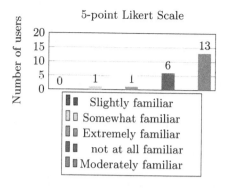

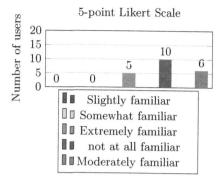

Fig. 4. I thought the blog was easy to use

Fig. 5. Various functions in this blog system were well integrated

learning with the blogging system. Also from Table 3, we can see a majority of positive feedback where they feel blog discussions help in knowledge sharing and provides opportunities to improve social skills. All these results correspond to answering our first research question on the idea of cultivating a more collaborative learning environment in the teams page of the learning management system.

The next question on how blogging helps in knowledge management, sharing, skill acquisition can be answered using the section on the sense of expressing and learning from the survey. From Table 4 we infer that majority of the users are open to having debatable learning and the systems help them to understand the topic better after reading a post. Users have also agreed that blog discussions help them to understand the discussion from others' points of view. Figure 7 shows the response among the users in feeling confident to express themselves using blogs.

Similarly using the last section on Blogging behavior will help us to answer the last research question on blog features that are useful and encouraging for the learner while using the environment. Referring to Table 5 again, we can see that most users felt the "post hit" feature useful to find more engaging and interesting posts. The share and search options were also rated necessary by most users. Interesting finds in this section from Table 7 are that most users like to spend more than 6 min in a blog post and are most likely to comment when they are "Aware of the topic and you see some misunderstandings" or Unaware of the topic and you ask questions on it. Sadly we see only 10 % of users like to appreciate others in sharing a post on a topic they weren't aware of. We could also see that the limitation to image format files in attachments was of concern to users to allow open format for attachments. Figure 8 depicts that the keywords/tags feature used was helpful and would be of great use if we could group posts based on keywords which makes it easy to look for specific posts. Similarly, Fig. 9 shows that most users felt that the commenting system is necessary to engage in discussing the topic further.

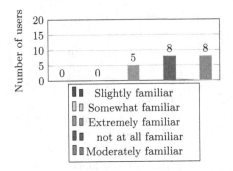

Fig. 6. Can you feel a sense of community/collaboration within the blogging system?

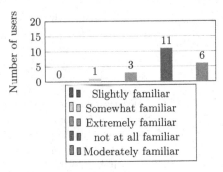

Fig. 7. Feel confident in expressing yourself using the blog?

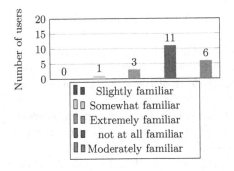

Fig. 8. Do you suggest grouping/searching posts with keywords?

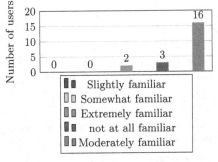

Fig. 9. The comment section is very helpful and engaging to discuss the topic further

Another topic of interest is the correlation between the responses to the survey questions. To this end, pairs of questions that should logically be correlated were statistically tested. To find the correlation between two 5-point Likert questions, linear regression can be performed on the plot of the scores of the influencing question against the influenced question. While comparing a categorical question vs a 5 point question, the average score for each category can be computed and vice versa. To capture the correlation of two categories, the average scores for each category, for each participant can be calculated, plotted on a 2D plot and the slope can be estimated by linear regression. A positive slope means the variable on the x-axis, positively influences the variable on axis y.

For example: "Do you prefer classroom learning or digital learning?" Vs "How would you rate your overall experience with the blogging system", are analyzed for the correlation between the participants' learning preferences vs their experiences of this blogging system. The choices are classroom learning, digital learning, partly both, and depending on the subject of learning with the respective average scores of 4, 4.5, 4.11, and 4.125. From a logical point of view, a person who prefers classroom learning should be expected to give a lower score than a person who prefers digital learning, with the other two choices being in between. The results also say so, but since the margins are low and sample sizes are small, we need more participants to identify such correlations accurately. The three categories of interest are Perception of Collaboration, sense of expressing, and learning Blogging Behavior. For each of the 21 participants, their average given score for each of the categories was computed. Three comparisons were performed. Perception of Collaboration vs sense of expressing and learning, Perception of Collaboration vs Blogging Behavior, sense of expressing and learning vs Blogging Behavior. So there are three 2D plots, each of which has 21 data points (N). The respective slopes for these three comparisons are as follows: 1.012, 0.889, 0.6925. All of which are positive slopes, suggesting a positive correlation between all three categories. This is expected since we could generalize that a person who had a good experience with the blog would most probably give good grades for all categories. Moreover, the statistical results we got also displayed statistically significant correlation among categories. For each respondent, one question has been selected from each category, and Pearson coefficients has been calculated along with P-Values. The strongest significant correlation has been seen between Perception of Collaboration and Sense of Expressing and Learning ($R = 0.62$, $p = 0.0029$), as well as between Blogging Behavior and Sense of Expressing and Learning ($R = 0.57$, $p = 0.006982$). A slightly moderate but still significant correlation was detected between categories Perception of Collaboration and Blogging behavior ($R = 0.52$, $P = 0.015679$).

6   Conclusion

From the responses received, it can be concluded that 85% of the users had a good overall experience with the system. The response to the question "I think that I would need the support of a technical person to be able to use this tutorial" was an interesting outlier because, despite the vastly positive feedback about the blogging system, people seem to have difficulty understanding functionalities in the system. This leaves space for improvement, to make it more user-friendly. Questions measuring the technical/collaborative aspects of the blog were mostly rated 3 and 4 on the scale, suggesting room for improvement. Proposed future improvements obtained from the survey results are grouping and searching posts based on keywords. The current search feature allows users to filter posts based on the title, content of blog posts. This feature could be enhanced further by grouping the posts based on keywords which would help users to find multiple posts that pertain to a keyword and also reduce the risk of finding irrelevant or missing relevant posts. Another possible upgrade is an open format for attachments. Currently, the blog posts only allow image files to be attached. But a blogger may need to include different file formats such as videos, which would enhance learning. Also, more users agreed to maintain an administrator to manage posts and activities around it. To conclude, our study to improve collaboration in teams page of the learning management system using blogs seems to be in the right direction as 90% of users agreed upon it. This semester, plan to further improve the system and conduct further tests before full integration to the learning management system's teams.

Acknowledgments. This work was supported by the German Federal Ministry of Education and Research [**grant number 16DHB 3008**].

References

1. Gankar, S., Wadhwani, P.: E-Learning Market Size By Technology (Online E-Learning, Learning Management System (LMS), Mobile E-Learning, Rapid E-Learning, Virtual Classroom), By rovider (Service, Content), By Application (Academic [K-12, Higher Education, Vocational Training], Corporate [SMBs, Large Enterprises], Government), COVID-19 Impact Analysis, Regional Outlook, Growth Potential, Competitive Market Share & Forecast, 2021–2027 (2021). https://www.gminsights.com/industry-analysis/elearning-market-size. Accessed 20 Mar 2021
2. Qun, Z., Xiaocheng, Z.: The design of individual knowledge sharing platform based on blog for online information literacy education. Phys. Procedia **33**, 1426–1432 (2012)
3. Obionwu, V., Broneske, D., Hawlitschek, A., Köppen, V., Saake, G.: Sqlvalidator-an online student playground to learn sql. Datenbank-Spektrum **21**(2), 73–81 (2021). https://doi.org/10.1007/s13222-021-00372-0
4. Al-Abri, A., Jamoussi, Y., Kraiem, N., Al-Khanjari, Z.: Comprehensive classification of collaboration approaches in E-learning. Telematics Inform. **34**(6), 878–893 (2017)
5. Obionwu, V., Broneske, D., Saake, G.: Topic maps as a tool for facilitating collaborative work pedagogy in knowledge management systems. Int. J. Knowl. Eng. (2022)
6. Akhrif, O., Benfares, C., El Bouzekri, Y., Idrissi, E., Hmina, N.: Collaborative approaches in smart learning environment: a case study. Procedia Comput. Sci. **175**, 710–715 (2020)
7. Beers, P.J., Boshuizen, H.P.E., Kirschner, P.A., Gijselaers, W.H.: Computer support for knowledge construction in collaborative learning environments. Comput. Hum. Behav. **21**(4), 623–643 (2005)
8. Obionwu, V., Andreas, N., Anja, H., Saake, G.: Learner centered network models: a survey. Int. J. Integrating Technol. Educ. (2022)
9. Wang, Q.: Design and evaluation of a collaborative learning environment. Comput. Educ. **53**(4), 1138–1146 (2009)
10. Obionwu, V., Broneske, D., Saake, G.: Leveraging educational blogging to assess the impact of collaboration on knowledge creation. In: International Conference on Distance Learning and Education (2022)
11. Obionwu, V., Broneske, D., Saake, G.: A collaborative learning environment using blogs in a learning management system. In: European Alliance for Innovation Conference on Computer Science and Education in Computer Science (2022)
12. Downes, S.: An introduction to connective knowledge. Stephen's Web (2005)
13. Lytras, M.D., Mathkour, H.I., Abdalla, H., Al-Halabi, W., Yanez-Marquez, C., Siqueira, S.W.M.: An emerging - social and emerging computing enabled philosophical paradigm for collaborative learning systems: toward high effective next generation learning systems for the knowledge society. Comput. Hum. Behav. **51**, 557–561 (2015)

14. Petkovic, V., Miletic, A., Djenic, S., Mitić, J., Vasiljevic, V.: Use of blogs in e-learning course (2014)
15. Robertson, J.: The educational affordances of blogs for self-directed learning. Comput. Educ. **57**(2), 1628–1644 (2011)
16. Kim, H.N.: The phenomenon of blogs and theoretical model of blog use in educational contexts. Comput. Educ. **51**(3), 1342–1352 (2008)
17. Noel, L.: Using blogs to create a constructivist learning environment. Procedia Soc. Behav. Sci. **174**, 617–621 (2015)
18. Sidek, E.A.R., Yunus, M.M.: Students' experiences on using blog as learning journals. Procedia Soc. Behav. Sci. **67**(2011), 135–143 (2012)
19. Deng, L., Yuen, A.H.: Towards a framework for educational affordances of blogs. Comput. Educ. **56**(2), 441–451 (2011)
20. Al Yateem, A.M.A., Alsayadi, S.: Designing educational blogs effect on the student's knowledge acquisition in the secondary stage: case study of KSA schools. Procedia Comput. Sci. **65**(Iccmit), 519–528 (2015)
21. Stacey, E.: Collaborative learning in an online environment. J. Distance Educ. (1999)
22. Garcia, E., Moizer, J., Wilkins, S., Haddoud, M.Y.: Student learning in higher education through blogging in the classroom. Comput. Educ. **136**, 61–74 (2019)
23. Al Yateem, A.M.A., Alsayadi, S.: Designing educational blogs effect on the student's knowledge acquisition in the secondary stage: case study of ksa schools. Procedia Comput. Sci. **65**, 519–528 (2015)
24. Halic, O., Lee, D., Paulus, T., Spence, M.: To blog or not to blog: Student perceptions of blog effectiveness for learning in a college-level course. Internet High. Educ. **13**(4), 206–213 (2010)
25. Top, E.: Blogging as a social medium in undergraduate courses: sense of community best predictor of perceived learning. Internet High. Educ. **15**(1), 24–28 (2012)
26. Strich, F., Mayer, A.S., Fiedler, M.: A social network approach to blogs: improving digital collaborative learning (2019)
27. Chu, S.K., Chan, C.K., Tiwari, A.F.: Using blogs to support learning during internship. Comput. Educ. **58**(3), 989–1000 (2012)
28. Mason, A.J., Carr, C.T.: Toward a theoretical framework of relational maintenance in computer-mediated communication. Commun. Theory **32**(2), 243–264 (2022)
29. Saba, J.: Students' perceptions and attitudes towards using blogs as a supplementary learning tool to enhance writing skills at a private university in Dubai. In: Coombe, C., Hiasat, L., Daleure, G. (eds.) English Language and General Studies Education in the United Arab Emirates. ELTTRP, pp. 161–176. Springer, Singapore (2022). https://doi.org/10.1007/978-981-16-8888-1_11
30. Kim, H.N.: The phenomenon of blogs and theoretical model of blog use in educational contexts (2007)
31. Obionwu, V., Broneske, D., Saake, G.: Microblogs-a means for simulating informal learning beyond classroom. In: International Conference on Education Technology and Comp (2022)
32. Handini, O., Hidayatullah, M.F., Akhyar, M., et al.: Analysis of collaborative learning models in online thematic learning during the pandemic covid-19. In: Universitas Lampung International Conference on Social Sciences (ULICoSS 2021), pp. 677–683. Atlantis Press (2022)
33. Schnaubert, L., Bodemer, D.: Group awareness and regulation in computer-supported collaborative learning. Int. J. Comput. Support. Collaborative Learn. 1–28, (2022). https://doi.org/10.1007/s11412-022-09361-1

34. Hmelo-Silver, C.E., Jeong, H.: Synergies among the pillars: designing for computer-supported collaborative learning. In: Handbook of Open, Distance and Digital Education, pp. 1–16. Springer (2022). https://doi.org/10.1007/978-981-19-0351-9_83-1.pdf

35. Yousef, A.M.F., Rößling, G.: How to design good educational blogs in LMS? In: CSEDU 2013 - Proceedings of the 5th International Conference on Computer Supported Education, pp. 70–75 (2013)

Integrating Agile Development Approaches and Business Analysis Foundational Knowledge into a Project Management Course

Vijay Kanabar(✉)

Boston University, Metropolitan College, Boston, MA 02215, USA
kanabar@bu.edu

Abstract. The project management profession has evolved significantly in the past few years and a new standard that reflects the full range of changes has been introduced. In this paper we address our approach to update the curriculum in project management. We made structural changes to the traditional project management Team Project to introduce business analysis core competencies to students. The group project integrates predictive plan-based and agile development approaches and introduces business analysis and requirements elicitation topics. In this paper we introduce the changes in the new standards and illustrate implementation using an exemplar project. Our conclusions of job task analysis statements reveal that students mastered traditional, hybrid, adaptive development approaches as business analysis core concepts successfully.

Keywords: Project management · Agile development · Business analysis

1 Introduction

While Agile Software Development practice is familiar to both academics and professionals for more than two decades, emerging technology and market changes has resulted in an opportunity today to integrate the same principles and practice into other domains such as hospitality or construction. In this paper we provide details of how to introduce such an approach. A search for project manager roles that employers are looking for will increasingly add competencies in agile development [1]. Additionally, there is a need for professionals who are competent in roles such as business analysis. It is within this context we seek to update the course content for a foundational course in project management to ensure that students have competencies that the workforce is seeking.

1.1 Project Management

Before we address the topic of teaching agile project management, let us first introduce the importance of teaching project management. According to PMI's 2021 Talent Gap report, 2.3 million new project management employees will be needed each year to meet

T. Zlateva and R. Goleva (Eds.): CSECS 2022, LNICST 450, pp. 233–244, 2022.
https://doi.org/10.1007/978-3-031-17292-2_19

global talent demands by 2030 [1]. There is additional evidence from other job sources for demand for students competent in the discipline of leading teams and managing projects across industry domains.

The disciplines of innovation and entrepreneurship are tightly coupled with project management. The life cycle for a project begins with aspiration. To launch any significant venture, one must embrace project management principles and practice to be successful. There is tremendous pressure on organizations to innovate, and project managers are key players in such ventures—they are responsible for managing such projects, they support innovation process by providing tools, insights, and metrics needed to successfully lead and manage innovation projects [2].

But simply possessing the innovation spirit is not sufficient to get us to the destination. Clayton Christensen suggested that 95% of product innovation projects fail and digital transformation projects fail 70% of the time [3]. Students need to be taught the art and science of taking a project idea through well-defined phases to completion. Teaching of project management is ubiquitous across domains ranging from construction to the life sciences.

It is within this context that a significant effort was initiated by Project Management Institute (PMI) to define a competency framework and curriculum model. This effort involved surveying 295 faculty members in 2014. It provided concrete evidence that a market demand exists for project management education at both the undergraduate and graduate level, and that PMI needs to support the design of a curriculum framework. The survey also revealed that there was interest in curriculum outlines with learning outcomes and case study resources such as compact teaching cases that faculty could use for teaching. Annual meetings of scholarly management associations also brought a string of inquiries to PMI's exhibit booth requesting teaching materials that could be potentially useful to faculty interested in launching a course or program in project management [3]. A comprehensive framework was eventually published and available at no cost to academics [13]. A knowledge module on the topic of agile project management and business analysis with learning outcomes was defined by faculty but not expanded upon in exemplar resources.

1.2 Agile Project Management

Any discussion of this topic always traces us back to its beginning, the Agile Manifesto "We are uncovering better ways of developing software by doing it and helping others do it. These are our values and principles –

Individuals and interactions over processes and tools

Working software over comprehensive documentation

Customer collaboration over contract negotiation

Responding to change over following a plan." [8]

The agile manifesto recently celebrated 20 years and several of the original signatories attended the virtual meeting to reflect on the achievements. There was unequivocal conclusion that the manifesto has made an impact beyond the software profession today.

Twelve agile project management principles have been defined. According to Koch and those principles may be reduce to three meta-principles. (1) Autonomy: the project team has sole discretion to make decisions and organize their work. (2) Equality: all team members work together on an equal footing. (3) Iterative delivery: without rigid objectives set out at the beginning of a project, partial objectives are regularly defined and evaluated at short project intervals (i.e., iterations) while customer feedback is integrated [4].

2 A Foundational University Course in Project Management

In this section we introduce a foundational course in project management being offered at Boston University. We will provide its context and then introduce the revised experiential project curriculum which is the focus of this paper. The new course successfully integrates agile development approaches with traditional plan-based prescriptive paradigm and introduces coverage of foundational business analysis topics.

The foundational course is housed in a business department, but the outline is relevant to any academic department and especially computer science. After all the roots of agile movement are grounded in the software industry, moreover, business analysis – especially requirements management is a core competency here.

The foundational course is a required core course for students majoring in project management at the graduate level, and it also serves as a service course for students majoring in supply chain, marketing, business analytics, enterprise risk management, and related areas.

The following overarching learning outcomes are addressed in this course to ensure alignment with the needs of the GAC accreditation [10]:

- Provide Technical Expertise associated with Management of projects to meet needs within constraints, with reference to professional standards and guides.
- Professional Behavior: Provide leadership and teamwork skills and ethical and culturally aware stakeholder engagement.
- Strategic Awareness: Contextual awareness and knowledge of strategic and operational drivers required to inform decisions and deliver sustained competitive advantage.

The key topics covered in this course are:

Module 1: Projects and Project Managers • The Project Environment

Module 2: The Fundamental Importance of Scope • The Work Breakdown Structure

Module 3: External and Internal Influences on Projects • Project Networks

Module 4: Improving Project Estimates, and Cost & Quality Management

Module 5: Earned Value, Team Leadership and Resource Management

Module 6: Risk Management • Closing and Transitioning a Project to Operations

The topic of agile project management and business analysis is now addressed in module subtopics and discussion assignments and the course now successfully addresses the following learning outcomes [13].

Agile Project Management

- Distinguish the approaches, advantages, and disadvantages of both classic and agile project methodologies, assess the deliverables and contexts best suited to each method, and apply these principles to the development of an appropriate PM strategy.
- Develop a workable PM approach that includes the typical steps, activities, and participant roles for an agile project, and evaluate how and when these agile characteristics can be integrated with steps from a traditional PM life cycle to achieve an effective hybrid approach.
- Use appropriate tools and resources for agile projects, including specific or adapted metrics that can assist the project manager in defining, executing, and controlling projects that follow an agile, or hybrid, life cycle and methodology. [13]

Business Analysis

- Construct a plan for best practices in business analysis, requirements elicitation, and requirements management that can be applied to a given project.
- Evaluate the relevance of identified tools and techniques to elicit and document requirements.
- Implement a plan to manage project changes and communicating changes to stakeholders. [13]

2.1 Alignment with New Standard

In 2021 a new global standard for project management was released in 2021 which has dramatically impacted our curriculum [5]. The motivation is described by PMI as follows, "The evolution of technology has changed the way work gets done for many professions, including project management. Practitioners are now tasked with identifying the right deliver approach (predictive, adaptive or hybrid) to get the job done and deliver value" [6]. The process groups illustrated in the modules above remain in the Models, Methods, and Artifacts section, but the substantial focus on processes is removed [6].

With the introduction of the new standard there was some urgency to update our course. Especially there was a need to make sure that we injected some of the concepts pertaining to Project Performance Domains specifically to *Development Approach and Life Cycle Project Execution Domain.*

Development Approach refers to method used to create and evolve the product, service, or result during the project life cycle, such as a predictive, adaptive, or hybrid method the development approach can demonstrate characteristics: iterative, incremental. According to the standard, "a Project Performance Domain is a group of related activities that are critical for the effective delivery of project outcomes. The Development Approach & Life Cycle performance domain addresses activities and functions associated with the development approach, cadence, and life cycle phases of the project.

The project deliverables determine the most appropriate development approach such as a predictive, adaptive, or hybrid approach. The deliverables and the development approach influence the number and cadence for project deliveries. The development approach and delivery cadence influence the project life cycle and its phases" [6]. Two additional domains introduced in the new exam content outline are shown in Table 1.

Table 1. Key domain tasks addressed in revised project [12]

Domain	Task
Adaptive and Agile Approach	Explain when it is appropriate to use an adaptive approach
	Determine how to plan project iterations
	Explain the components of an adaptive plan
	Determine how to prepare and execute task management steps
Business Analysis (BA)	Demonstrate an understanding of business analysis (BA) roles and responsibilities
	Determine how to conduct stakeholder communication
	Determine how to gather requirements
	Demonstrate an understanding of product roadmaps

Note the different expressions related to Predictive and Adaptive approaches that one can find in literature

Predictive, Waterfall, Linear, Structured, Plan-Based, Stable, Traditional
AdaptiveAgile, Iterative, Incremental, Spiral, Extreme, Evolutionary

2.2 Project Assignment

The course has been delivered historically as a group project. A quick way to assure that the new topics are being mastered was to inject the agile and business analysis topics into the group project. Students identify any project idea with the following constraints: a) It must be completed in 14 weeks b) The goal of the project must align with the Seventeen UN sustainability goals (https://sdgs.un.org/goals), c) A pilot app or prototype must be delivered.

The research posters were required to be presented on Earth Day to the entire college community to demonstrate our values to the UN sustainability goals. The project results were reviewed by faculty, students, and officers of the Project Management Club. The best student project received an award.

2.3 Key Milestones

The milestones for the projects were broken into sprints as follows with a cadence of two weeks:

Sprint 1 – Project Initiation: Charter and Scope of Project
Sprint 2 – Business Analysis & Product Road Map

Sprint 3 – Gantt Chart and Network & Release 1: Mockup of Main Menu of App
Sprint 4 – Cost and Project Budget & Release 2: Demonstrate one feature of the app
Sprint 5 – Risk Register and Mitigation & Release 3: Demonstrate one more feature
Sprint 6 – Remaining deliverables & Release 4: Final App Delivery

To assist students, we provided, where appropriate, examples and templates to aid in the creation of the project management plan elements (example: sprints, a risk register, etc.). Project management artifacts such cost and risk were being delivered alongside product artifacts such as smart phone app.

3   Methods

In this section we describe our methods and findings. Sixteen research capstone projects were presented in the Spring of 2022 to the entire college community on Earth Day. While it is not possible to describe all the projects in detail, a specific project called *Green Door App* [14] is presented so that the scope of the project can be understood.

3.1   GreenDoor App

The GreenDoor App rates sustainable organizations in the Greater Boston area in the USA. It is based on their values and impact with regards to UN Sustainable Development goals and ESG ratings. The project lasted 4 months. In the initiation, phase a charter was created and data was gathered to scope the project. A project plan was created and high-level WBS was created. A main menu was designed early on with implementation of features such as live chat. Project critical path was adhered to strictly -- initial stages of data collection of green organizations was important. This was needed to project the companies' ratings – delay here would impact the next stage and the app design and implementation would suffer. Team estimated budget to be around $50,000. Most of the budget was spent on the execution phase as expected with the implementation of the app. The project will be considered a success if users who have a choice of employers rely on GreenDoor to help them decide which organization they would prefer to work in.

The GreenDoor 1.0 app will develop and implement new features to rate organizations in the Boston area to begin with as a pilot study. See final product in Fig. 1. It illustrates the splash page and a functional page.

The Scrum Guide places importance in the definition of the product backlog as it is "...an ordered list of everything that is known to be needed in the product." Examples of user stories were articulated, and they were told to identify several. Students successfully created stories for personas such as a customer, or administrator of Green Door app. These were eventually broken down into the following items for implementation

1. Product Road Map
2. Product Design and Discovery
3. Data Collection for Ranking Green Organizations.

Fig. 1. GreenDoor App

3.2 Development Approach

There was a need to teach the traditional prescriptive approach in the course. After all, we believe more than 70% of global projects use the traditional plan-based approach to deliver projects. We determined that there were components of the group project that fits well for the predictive waterfall approach (see Table 2). However, since students were building apps, the second half of the project was delivered using Agile approach (see Table 3) (Fig. 2).

Next, we will describe how the agile development approach was introduced in the group project, i.e., via the implementation of the app. Agile terminology and concepts were used in the course – primarily Scrum because it is simple and the popular framework. Skills in Scrum based project management would be an asset to students seeking employment in the workforce.

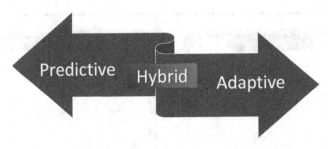

Fig. 2. Spectrum of development approach

Table 2. Predictive development approach.

Artifact	Example
Kick-off Meeting with XYZ University Project Sponsors	General requirements, needs and wants
Analysis of GreenDoor product and features	The creation of an end user survey with questions based on feature, functionality, interface, etc
End User Surveys	Gather valuable feedback from end-users to determine requirements. Customized survey question based on function and end user role
Data Collection of Boston Area Organizations	Use kick-off info, analysis, and survey data to generate final project requirements and get sign-off from project sponsors

Table 3. Adaptive development approach.

Artifact	Example
Business Analysis Sprint	Identify stakeholders, use conversational UI/UX approach to capture requirements
Design Sprint:	Technical design document is created which outlines technical architecture to be built
Features Sprint	Development and implementation of functional design of app
Testing Sprint	Verify testing results meet Project Requirements
Deployment Sprint	GreenDoor Live Version. Close the project, and evaluate lessons learned

Note: Post-Deployment activities are not conducted as the course is semester long and has time constraints

4   Findings

Research results assessed for competencies in Business Analysis and Adaptive Development are presented in this section. The Delphi approach was used to collect information from reviewers who conducted job task analysis by interviewing students presenting the posters. Summary responses were collected, and some responses from the reviewers are presented below in italics. A Delphi monitor summarized the information.

4.1 Business Analysis

The task questions are based on the new exam content outline [10].

Task 1 – Do the students adequately demonstrate an understanding of business analysis (BA) roles and responsibilities.

- Can they distinguish between stakeholder roles (e.g., process manager, product manager, product owner, etc.).

  Yes, students played roles of process manager (project manager), product owner, business analyst, sponsor, development team, UI/UX designer. Every team had one or two students who played a specialist role of business analyst.
- Can they outline the need for roles and responsibilities (Why do you need to identify stakeholders in the first place?)

By defining roles and responsibilities students removed confusion about which stakeholder played what role. They are familiar with RACI and RAM. They understand SCRUM roles. Project Leader understood the importance of empowering team members. This delegation emphasis improved team efficiency and also reduced confusion and redundancies.

Task 2 - Do the students adequately how to conduct stakeholder communication?

- Can they recommend the most appropriate communication channel/tool for business analysis? (e.g., reporting, presentation, etc.).

  The most important communication channel was the bi-weekly sprints where the UI/UX designer presented Adobe XD mockups.
- Can they demonstrate why communication is important for a business analyst between various teams (features, requirements, etc.).

Stakeholder communication brought diverse project artifacts together. The Charter, scope statement and requirements were theoretical documents until then. They understand the essential artifacts.

Task 3 - Do the students adequately know how to gather requirements?

- Do they know tools to capture requirements (e.g., user stories, use cases, etc.).

  Conversational requirements gathering approach was used at the start of the project. Students enjoyed this approach. One student played the role of a human app. Another student played the role of a customer or end user. This was recognized as a fun way to gather use cases from the customer. Surveys were created using Google Forms and these were completed by two other teams acting as customers.

- Explain a requirements traceability matrix/product backlog.

Each sprint was managed by a product backlog. And a project management tool was used to trace completion of requirements.

Task 4 - Can the students adequately demonstrate an understanding of product roadmaps?

- Explain the application of a product roadmap.
- Determine which components go to which releases.

For many project teams, requirements gathered were ambitious and excessive for the scope of the sixteen-week session. This gave students an opportunity to reduce the app features into multiple phases. They visualized a product road map for features that can be deferred into the future.

Task 5 - Do the students adequately determine how project methodologies influence business analysis processes?

- Do they know the role of a business analyst in adaptive and/or predictive, plan-based approaches?

There was an appreciation of the two different approaches for development and the importance of business analysis and the role of adaptive development vs predictive plan-based activities.

4.2   Adaptive Frameworks/Methodologies Agile Development

The task questions are based on the new exam content outline [10].

Task 1 – Can the students adequately explain when it is appropriate to use an adaptive approach?

- Compare the pros and cons of adaptive and predictive, plan-based projects. Identify the suitability of adaptive approaches for the organizational structure (e.g., virtual, colocation, matrix structure, hierarchical, etc.).
- Identify organizational process assets and environmental factors that facilitate the use of adaptive approaches.

Students were aware of the pros and cons of adaptive and predictive, plan-based development approach. They worked remotely using zoom and were collocated as well once a week. When compared with remote meetings, most appreciated colocation model. They benefitted from the professor being available to answer questions about agile methodology.

Task 2 – Can the students adequately determine how to plan project iterations?

- Distinguish the logical units of iterations. Interpret the pros and cons of the iteration.

- Translate this WBS to an adaptive iteration.
- Explain the importance of adaptive project tracking versus predictive

Iterations were planned and constrained by professor. Logical units – cadence of two weeks was required. Students translated WBS to adaptive iterations very well.

Task 3 - Do the students adequately know how to document project controls for an adaptive project.

- Can the students identify artifacts that are used in adaptive projects.

Students were confident with the topic of project controls for the predictive components such as cost variance or schedule variance as earned value is taught in depth. Some students were confused when it came to controls for the adaptive development approach.

5   Conclusion

This paper has demonstrated a successful approach to revising the project management curriculum. It describes how we can incrementally convert a traditional project management course to teach predictive, adaptive, and hybrid development approaches. The course also introduced a key topic of importance in business analysis. PMI's new exam content learning outcomes for credentialing associate project managers require students to know business analysis theory and practice. Dedicated student team members conducted business analysis tasks and translated them to requirements. We used job task analysis statements from the latest exam guidelines as a basis to inject learning goals and assess learning outcomes. In addition, we successfully presented all research projects for peer review on Earth Day as posters. Here faculty and industry experts interviewed students and provided feedback. Finally, there is an opportunity to integrate the adaptive approach more tightly in the group project. We hope to repeat this exercise in future course iterations and demonstrate outcomes utilizing numerical data.

References

1. Nick Kolakowski: How Agile, Project Management Skills Can Boost Your Job Prospects. https://insights.dice.com/2022/05/04/how-agile-project-management-skills-can-boost-your-job-prospects/. Last accessed 14 May 2022
2. Drechsler, A.: Challenges and paradoxes of teaching project management the agile way. In: Presented at the International Research Workshop on IT Project Management 2019 (2019)
3. Andriole, S.: 3 Main Reasons Why Big Technology Projects Fail – & Why Many Companies Should Just Never Do Them. https://www.forbes.com/sites/steveandriole/2021/03/25/3-main-reasons-why-big-technology-projects-fail---why-many-companies-should-just-never-do-them/. Last accessed 14 May 2022
4. PMI: Talent Gap: Ten-Year Employment Trends, June 2021 Costs, and Global Implications. (2021)
5. Kerzner, H.: Innovation project management: methods, case studies, and tools for managing innovation projects. Hoboken, New Jersey: Wiley, Hoboken, New Jersey (2019)

6. Forbes: https://www.forbes.com/sites/steveandriole/2021/03/25/3-main-reasons-why-big-technology-projects-fail---why-many-companies-should-just-never-do-them/

7. Kanabar, V.K., Messikomer, C.: New curriculum on managing projects: Responding to 21st century workforce needs. In: Proceedings of the 23rd International EDINEB Conference: Innovative Student Engagement in Business and Economics Education. EDINEB Association (2016)

8. Agile Manifesto: https://agilemanifesto.org. Last accessed 14 May 2022

9. Koch, J., Schermuly, C.C.: Managing the crisis: how COVID-19 demands interact with agile project management in predicting employee exhaustion. Br. J. Manag. **32**, 1265–1283 (2021)

10. GAC: Handbook of PMI Academic Accreditation. Fourth Edition. Project Management Institute, Newtown Sq. (2018)

11. Project Management Institute: A guide to the project management body of knowledge (PMBOK guide). Project Management Institute, Inc., Newtown Square, Pennsylvania (2021)

12. PMI: Certified Associate in Project Management Exam Content. https://www.pmi.org/certifications/certified-associate-capm (2022)

13. Task Force on PM Curricula: PM Curriculum and Resources. Newtown Square, Pa: Project Management Institute (2015)

14. Green Door: Project Green Door App In: Kanabar, V., Glusz, A., Mussabekova, S., Heeb, F., Sylla, T., Nagpal, S., (eds.) Edited Report. Boston University (2022)

ABA@BU Program Competitiveness and ABA Graduates Employability Support

Krystie Dickson, Mehnaz Khan, and Vladimir Zlatev[✉]

Boston University Metropolitan College, Boston, MA 02215, USA
{krystied,mehnazk,zlatev}@bu.edu

Abstract. We present the approach to preparing the Applied Business Analytics (ABA) graduates for successful positioning in the marketplace as a key differentiator of the ABA program competitiveness. The centerpiece of the approach is the employability support, where students learn how to (i) prepare their ePortfolio, (ii) match their skills with the current posted job offers by industry, company, and location, (iii) learn more about potential employer(s), and their expectations, (iv) adjust their initial job plans to a pragmatic job-hunting strategy, (v) prepare for job interviews with the help of technical interview simulations, and (vi) be ready to customize and repeat the previous steps in preparation for job interviews with different potential employers. The authors discuss the implementation of the employability support model and its connection to the ABA@BU Employability Database, ABA@BU Marketing & Advertising Initiatives, and the social media options for all members of the ABA Community to stay connected and actively involved in the further adaptation of our competitive approach to the challenges and opportunities ahead.

Keywords: Graduate employability support · Career-readiness experiences · Individual ePortfolio · Digication platform · Competitive landscape analysis · Professional skills · Job description analysis · Occupational analysis · Industry analysis · Applied business analytics

1 Introduction

1.1 ABA@BU Program Competitiveness

The academic programs Master of Science in Applied Business Analytics (MS-ABA) and Graduate Certificate in Applied Business Analytics (GC-ABA) have been offered by Boston University Metropolitan College, on-campus and online, since May 2017 [1]. The college is preparing to congratulate the one thousand ABA graduates in 2022. Since 2020, BU MET's online MS in ABA program has ranked #1 among the Best Online Masters in Business Analytics and Intelligence Programs by Online Masters Report; it is also recognized as the Best in Leadership Development [2].

During the 16th International Conference on Computer Science and Education in Computer Science, the authors presented the ABA approach to competitive landscape

© ICST Institute for Computer Sciences, Social Informatics and Telecommunications Engineering 2022
Published by Springer Nature Switzerland AG 2022. All Rights Reserved
T. Zlateva and R. Goleva (Eds.): CSECS 2022, LNICST 450, pp. 245–262, 2022.
https://doi.org/10.1007/978-3-031-17292-2_20

analysis on college, academic program, and student levels as one of our key differentiators and critical factors for our competitiveness [3]. It is a framework for designing, developing, and implementing a competitive landscape analysis (CLA) by comparing similar graduate programs from various universities and colleges. The CLA methodology is developed and offered for applications by program coordinators and faculty from different academic fields. They can rank and analyze competing graduate programs and make conclusions for further improvement of the educational curricula on different levels: program, course, and internal course characteristics (by lectures and course deliverables) with the help of selected key performance indicators, criteria for assessment, and uniquely developed smart analysis tables, balanced scorecards, and dashboards. The users can identify the skill set gaps between what is being taught at the university and what is demanded by the job market. As a result, this wealth of data and analysis supports the enhancement of university programs to maintain their status and exceed their competitors.

The primary purpose of this article is to present another key differentiator of our program, the approach to preparing our ABA graduates for successful positioning in the competitive marketplace.

1.2 ABA Graduates Employability Support

The ABA Graduates' Employability Support is presented as an integrated part of the ABA@BU Program Competitiveness, where students are learning how to (i) prepare their own ePorfolio, (ii) match their skills with the current posted job offers by industry, company, and location, (iii) learn more about the potential employer(s), and their expectations, (iv) adjust their initial job plans to a pragmatic job-hunting strategy, (v) prepare for job interviews with the help of technical interview simulations, and (vi) be ready to customize and repeat the previous steps in preparation for job interviews with different potential employers.

Finally, the authors discuss the implementation of the employability support model and its connection to the ABA@BU Employability Database, ABA@BU Marketing & Advertising Initiatives, and the social media options for all members of the ABA Community to stay connected and actively involved in the further adaptation of our competitive approach to the challenges and opportunities ahead.

2 The ABA@BU Graduates Employability Service Model

2.1 ABA@BU Employability Service Model

Employability of the Applied Business Analytics graduates has been a critical area of research for the ABA team to assist students in successfully positioning themselves within the job marketplace to attain their dream job. To successfully position themselves, graduates need to conduct a thorough assessment of their skills and experiences and the trends observed in the job market and proceed to bridge the gap that may exist between these two pertinent areas. Students within the field of Business Analytics (both local and international) are faced with a unique challenge of navigating through the complexities of the current job market as the field of Business Analytics is much needed across major industries, for example, Healthcare, Finance, Retail, Trade, and Manufacturing, to name a few [14]. As students embark on their job search and application process through the use of top search engines like LinkedIn [15], Indeed [16], and Glassdoor [16], they are quickly faced with the challenge of identifying their preferred job title, industry, company, and preferred location, all of which can heavily influence their pay structure and/or compensation. Some students become highly overwhelmed and paralyzed by the massive amount of information being presented to them through these sites that their decision-making strategy is reduced to two extremes, either doing nothing or sending resumes to the top one hundred jobs returned through their search efforts and hope that one of the companies selects them for an interview. Neither of these is a suitable decision-making strategy that will allow students to find their dream job or have their dream career.

The goal then quickly became to assist students in identifying successful strategies for navigating through the complexities of the job market. As a result, the Competitive Landscape Analysis framework was developed to provide insights into three critical areas for success: Program, Industry, and Student Levels [3]. The program level sought to assess the program's competitiveness compared to other universities, ensuring that our curriculum is of top quality and providing students with the skills needed to be successful in their careers. The industry level focuses on assessing the job market, including trends, identifying top required skills, etc. The student level, and the primary focus of this paper, was geared toward providing the tools to support students in their job search by providing a suitable strategy for navigating through the complexities of the job market. There was imperative to successfully execute this goal to uncover the major problems students face in the job search and application process. After conducting extensive research, which included conversations with students on the successes and failures of their job search process, the ABA research team identified the following major problem areas:

1. The Applied Business Analytics program offers students the top skills in the field. However, they were unable to articulate these skills with confidence. When asked to list their skills, students struggled to identify their top talents. They often submit applications for jobs not closely aligned to their knowledge base. This action resulted in unsatisfactory job interview performance as students were ill-equipped to demonstrate the skills needed for the role. In the event where the student was selected for the job, it resulted in poor work performance as a result of two things, the student being overqualified for the position where they were not challenged or the student being underqualified for the job, which led to a very steep and uncomfortable learning curve.

2. Students were unaware of the major industries, specifically those hiring graduates in the field of Business Analytics.

3. Outside of the significant high-tech companies like Amazon, Google, Microsoft, students were unaware of the top companies they would like to work for.

4. Students were unaware of the critical aspects of a company they should pay attention to before applying, such as company history, mission and vision statements, company growth and development, and products and services.

Based on the observed problem areas, the Student level model was designed and developed to offer three service levels, alleviating the above-outlined issues. Figure 1 below describes this model.

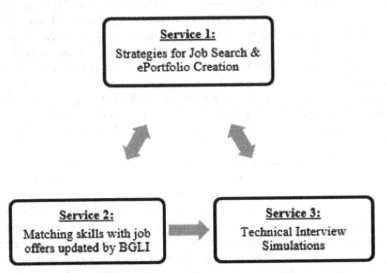

Fig. 1. Diagram displaying the student services model

The model developed focuses on three critical areas for the successful positioning of the graduates by providing an avenue to allow graduates to understand themselves better, match their skills with occupations, and prepare themselves for interviews through technical simulations. The idea here is to build our students' confidence by providing an avenue to seamlessly showcase their skills and career progression through service one. Once this is complete, students are now well-equipped with the knowledge of their skills and experiences. They are ready to match these with the jobs posted in the market to uncover the best jobs that will enhance their growth and development, offered through service two. The final task is for the student to prepare for the interview process, specifically the technical interviews, which brings us to service three.

2.2   Service 1: Strategies for Job Search and Individual ePortfolio Creation

Students' first area to be addressed when embarking on the job search process is understanding their skills and experiences. For some junior students with limited industry experience, less than two years, this task may seem daunting, deterring them from having complete confidence in themselves and their capabilities. In the job application process, employers often ask potential candidates to provide a link to their website. Employers are hoping to see the candidate's complete portfolio on this website, which includes their skills, experiences, and, vital for business analytics, a summary of significant projects completed. Employers utilize this approach to determine how the potential candidate can apply the knowledge gained to solve problems and whether the candidate can be a suitable fit for the company.

An ePortfolio or an electronic portfolio is a digital collection displaying a student's learning, growth, and development. As such, it was determined to be the most suitable solution to address the needs of our students. We conducted research and explored various platforms to host the students' ePortfolios and discovered that Boston University, in collaboration with Digication, is offering an ePortfolio tool that allows students to document their learning and share this information with various parties, including potential employers, friends, family, professors and much more [18].

The following vital issue to be addressed was determining the most suitable content to be displayed in this ePortfolio. After further research and deliberation, a model was developed to inform the design of a successful ePortfolio, as shown in Fig. 2 below. This model, named MET ABA@BU ePortfolio, comprises two key areas. The first is private, where students will store information on their personal growth and development goals, including assessing whether they are on target in achieving these goals or not. The second must be made visible to potential employers and other key persons of interest, demonstrating the student's viability for potential jobs.

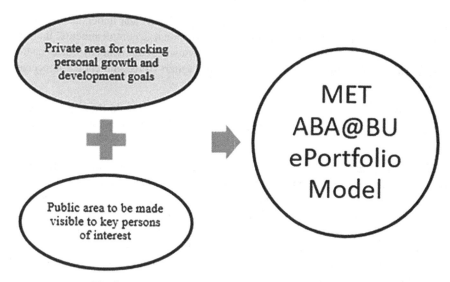

Fig. 2. Diagram of the MET ABA@BU ePortfolio model

Digging deeper into this model, it was determined that the visible public area should comprise the following seven components:

About Me. Students should be able to summarize their background and accomplishments so potential employers would better understand that student's personality.

Resume. This is an area of high importance to potential employers. Here we encourage students to upload a copy of their latest resume and preparatory badges earned throughout the Applied Business Analytics Program.

Professional Credentials. As the potential employer becomes familiar with the student's background, it's time to highlight some of their most valuable credentials. This includes listing their top technical and soft skills, certifications earned throughout their academic journey, and any professional training from a previous employer or acquired as part of a self-paced study.

Project. This section was designed especially for those students who may have limited working experience (less than two years). The aim here is to highlight some of the top projects completed by the student throughout their academic study and demonstrate a high level of proficiency in applying various Business Analytic techniques to solve real-world problems.

Courses. Often potential employers are trying to assess the depth of knowledge of an applicant to determine if they are a good fit for a particular job role. Providing a listing of the students' completed degree courses and a link to its descriptions provides the employers with sufficient information on the student's competency level gained through the successful completion of their degree program.

Recommendations. Now that the potential employer has a clear understanding of the student, their personality, and academic and professional accomplishments, the next step is to cement or solidify their impression by previewing comments by others on that student. This section allows students to upload any letters of recommendation received throughout their careers.

Contact. After reviewing all of the information presented, should the employer wish to contact the student, this is where they can find further information on how this is possible.

The private area of the ePortfolio model, identified by components eight through ten, is our competitive differentiator. Students can place their career goals (long term and short term) and keep track of their progress in achieving them. It becomes essential for Service two, level two, where students consult with various faculty members to gain advice or feedback on matching their career goals with jobs in preferred industries and companies. More to be explained on this concept in the section Service 2. The following Fig. 3 summarizes the critical components of the private area of the MET ABA@BU ePortfolio model.

Storage. Often students are required to tailor their resume based on the jobs they are applying for, paying particular attention to the Job title and industry so that students can highlight their top skills and experiences and align those to this position. The storage component allows students to save all of these versions of their resumes.

Central Resources. This component provides students with the tutorials needed to edit their ePortfolio, for example, uploading documents and images, adding badges, and publishing the ePortfolio, to name a few. It also contains links to BU Career Center resources, such as Handshake (a job posting portal) and VMOCK (an AI tool for improving resumes). [10] It also provides links to various ABA program resources, for example, LinkedIn ABA Group Page [23], ABA Programs Blackboard website [24], and BU MET Department of Administrative Sciences website, ABA page [25].

Personal Career Development Strategy. This section encourages students to think about where they see themselves in the next ten years and identify several short-term goals needed to achieve their overall vision. It also provides a simple tracker to determine their progress in achieving their vision.

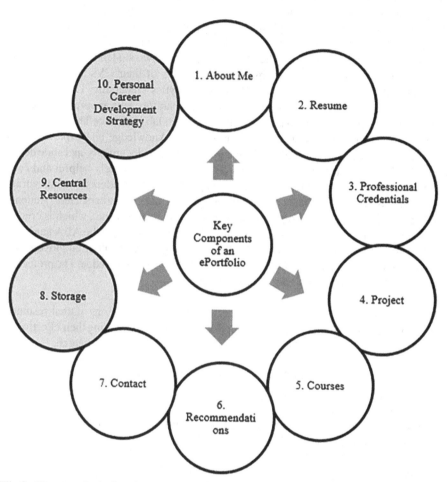

Fig. 3. Diagram displaying the critical components of the MET ABA@BU's ePortfolio model, private and public components

2.2.1   Case Study: Application of the MET ABA@BU ePortfolio Template

Benefits and Value Created by the MET ABA@BU ePortfolio Template

The ABA@BU ePortfolio model provides a strong foundation upon which students can create a successful ePortfolio, one which which capture the attention of prospective employers. To assist students in the creation of their ePortfolio, ABA faculty and graduate research assistants, in collaboration with Digication, created the **MET ABA@BU**

e-PortfolioTemplate 2022 [11, 12]. This template was specifically designed for the students in the ABA program and contains all the key components described in the ABA@BU ePortfolio Model. The role of the student is to use this template to create their own ePortfolio by adding personalized information in each of the key areas, a process which take approximately fifteen to twenty minutes.

The 'About Me' page is the first thing a person sees when visiting your ePortfolio, and this is your opportunity to make a positive, lasting first impression. Students can describe their beliefs and aspirations, highlighting their unique qualities and achievements to stand out among other students. The 'Resume' page allows students to display their academic and professional journey by including copies of their CVs and the badges to complete the recommended Applied Business Analytics Preparatory Labs badges or other non-BU professional badges. Some of these preparatory labs are prerequisites for every student. Showcasing the badges earned from each lab is an excellent opportunity for the students to showcase their hands-on analytical knowledge and experiences to employers. The tutorials provided to edit and upload images, documents, and slide decks to the 'Professional Credentials' and 'Projects' pages were extremely helpful and easy to act on. These two pages provide the perfect opportunity for students to demonstrate all of their existing achievements to potential employers and co-workers. Here, students can display their best course works, models, slides, visualizations, etc., which is crucial to stand out from others. The course page, already pre-populated for the ABA students, provides links to the descriptions of all ABA courses so that potential employers can assess the student's ability and competence level based on their knowledge. The protected areas of the ePortfolio serve a variety of purposes:

- It can be used as a storage area for students to save different versions of their resumes
- It provides links to central resources to support students in completing their ePortfolio, updating their resumes, and learning about the ABA program and research.

  - To understand the competitive landscape, students can easily access BU Career Center, Handshake, VMock, Vault [10]. Students can also get help from Burning Glass Career Insights [4].
  - The ABA program offers another based on the Burning Glass Labor Insight service and is described in Sect. 2.3.1.

- Students can use links to essential websites related to the ABA community and detailed instructions and tutorials to create their resumes or build individual e-Portfolios [11, 12].
- Personal career development strategy. This section helps the students make short-term and long-term career plans and track those plans accordingly.

ABA@BU ePortfolio template implementation (in Collaboration with Digication)
In collaboration with Digication, ABA@BU ePortfolio template was designed by a team of ambitious colleagues, including several ABA professors, ABA graduate research assistants, and volunteers. This template is regularly updated as part of our continuous research process, geared towards meeting the needs of our students and successfully demonstrating their successes, learning, and growth development to potential employers.

In communicating the value of the ePortfolio, it is also essential that students are aware of how to manage their ePortfolio as they have complete control of the privacy settings of each section of the template. Students get to choose the aspects of the ePortfolio they are ready and comfortable to publish to the world and the aspects they would like to remain hidden. Another key feature of this ePortfolio is that students will retain access to the ie ePortfolio after graduating and are on the path to a successful career. This ePortfolio can be utilized as part of their lifelong career journey as individuals can continuously update the ePortfolio as they see fit.

As with anything new, we understand that the learning curve can be frustrating. As a result, we've scheduled weekly consultation sessions so that students can receive all the support they need in completing their very own ePortfolio using the **MET ABA@BU e-PortfolioTemplate 2022** [11, 12]. There are scheduled timeslots throughout the week for this service, and no reservation is required. A tutorial containing a detailed list of instructions on how to work with the ABA@BU e-Portfolio Template and create the individual ePortfolio [12] is demonstrated with an example as follows:

Mehnaz Khan (MS in ABA, May 2022) served as a graduate research assistant during AY2021-2022, collaborated with ABA faculty on updates and revisions of the ABA@BU ePortfolio template, and tested it creating her ePortfolio. Using the ABA@BU ePortfolio template, Mehnaz presents her qualifications, experiences, and skills by providing information in each vital template area. As a final-year student, she is naturally worried about job placements and has shared her ePortfolio on several job sites and social media platforms. As a result, she has received responses from several employers. Here is a statement from her testimonial: "Boston University has provided this great platform which is helping me a lot to present myself to the employers. I have shared my badges and certificates in my ePortfolio, which I believe is helping me get the employers' attention. I have also displayed some of my course works which are helping me to make the employers understand my abilities to use analytical tools and techniques." She added, "I had the opportunity to avail the employability services provided by my department. The one-to-one ABA@BU ePortfolio consultation session has helped me set up a customized ePortfolio, connect my badges and certificates in the ePortfolio, and be creative to prepare for my competitive positioning in the marketplace. Upon creating my ePortfolio, I attended another brief consultation session on using career information provided by Burning Glass Insights. I completed a survey that portrays my skills and areas of interest and, based on that, received a customized excel report. It helped me identify my potential employers and the skills that I require to make myself more presentable and focus on the expectations of the potential employers."

2.3 Service 2: Matching Skills with Job Offerings Updated by Burning Glass Labor Insight

After the students gain a clear understanding of their skills and experiences, it is time to determine which jobs are the right fit for them by considering their unique preferences, such as preferred industry, company, and location. Based on observations and conversations with students, they were largely unaware of the industry's need for talent in Business Analytics. Students were unaware of critical statistics for hiring Business Analytics talents, such as top industries for business analytics and leading companies, based on the number of job positions posted searching for this talent and the top locations within the US where this talent is needed. The methodological framework designed to manage this problem manifests in the form of service two, which is as follows, see Fig. 4, below.

Fig. 4. Diagram displaying the methodological framework for matching individual skills with job offerings

The success of this framework relies heavily on the following key stakeholders, software platforms, and tools: ABA Consultants, ABA faculty, Burning Glass Labor Insight job platform [4], ABA Programs Blackboard website [14], and Excel.

Step 1: Submission of Request to Attend the BU MET Employability Consultation Session. The first step of this framework involves the student and their expression of interest in attending the consultation session. To submit this request, the student must complete their ePortfolio and our internally designed Employability Questionnaire. This questionnaire prompts students to answer questions on their job preferences, such as industry, location, and companies, and allows students to enter their skills. The student is submitting this request through the ABA Blackboard course site, where an administrator will review the submission and reach out to the student with a confirmation of the consultation date and time.

Step 2: Attend the Level 1 Consultation Session. During this session, our trained consultants review the information presented in the completed Employability Questionnaire and ePortfolio. This information is then entered in a standard template created by our in-house Burning Glass Labor Insight subject matter experts. In this ten-minute session, the Consultant will review the results retrieved in the form of tables and various graphical visualizations. The insights generated here provide statistics on the job market based on the students' unique preferences. An excel template with all the data is then provided to the student for further review and analysis. Level 1 of the Consultation Process is presented in Fig. 5, below.

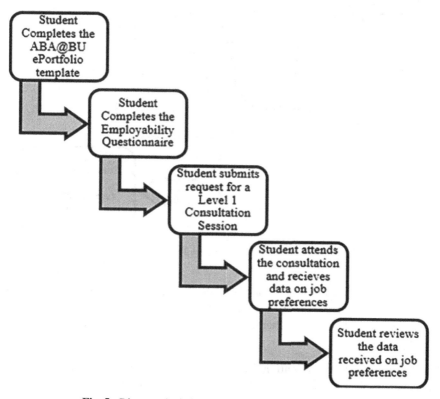

Fig. 5. Diagram depicting the level 1 consultation process

Step 3: Attend the Level 2 Consultation. The second level consultation involves a meeting between the student and a faculty member. In this session, the faculty member reviews the students' Personal Career Development Strategy presented in the private area of their ePortfolio, the students' job preferences in the completed Employability Questionnaire, and the quantitative data received from the Level 1 Consultation Session. Based on this review, the faculty member will advise selecting and applying for specific jobs and tailoring the students' resumes to demonstrate that they meet the requirements of the job. The level 2 Consultation Process is presented in Fig. 6 below.

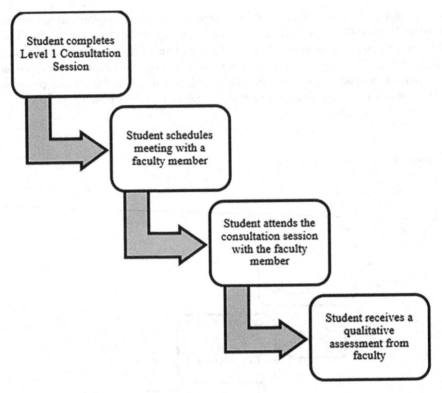

Fig. 6. Diagram depicting the Level 2 Consultation Process

Step 4: Review of Qualitative and Quantitative Data. At this stage, the student reviews the data from the Level 1 and Level 2 consultation sessions to decide the types of jobs they should apply for. That is, the positions closely aligned to their skills and expertise.

Step 5: Submit a Job Application. At this stage, the student proceeds to submit their application by sharing their resume and a link to their ePortfolio.

2.3.1 Case Study "Experience with the Employability Consultation Process"

The Level 1 Employability Consultation session, conducted by a trained ABA consultant, offers students the support needed to match their personal, professional, and educational skills with current employers' job offer. At Boston University Metropolitan College, we've utilized the tool known as Labor Insight, a software application developed by Burning Glass Technologies to make the activities surrounding the Employability Consultation session possible. The Labor Insight platform provides data on the job market, providing trends and opportunities to alter educational programs to meet the ever-changing and growing job market needs. With such a powerful tool in our arsenal, we aim to leverage its capabilities to support our employability vision.

The first step of this process requires the students to complete their ePortfolio and download the Employability Questionnaire, a specially created excel document that allows students to identify their unique preferences related to the job market. The first tab of this document provides instructions on sucessfully completing the document. The second tab of the document is divided into eight sections for student input. Sections one and two requests general information from the student, for example their Name, Boston University ID, the name of the program they are currently enrolled and their expected completion date. Sections three to seven requests that students select by clicking the various checkboxes that correspond to the data they would like to share, such as skills, preferred industry, job titles, companies, and locations. The last section, Sect. 8, provides an open text area for students to enter any additional information they would like to share with the Consultant. Once this form is completed, the student schedules a meeting to attend the level one consultation session through the ABA Blackboard course site.

The ABA consultant reviews the submitted Employability Questionnaire during this consultation session and then enters this information within the Burning Glass Technologies Labor Insight portal. Within this portal, our in-house subject matter experts designed and developed a unique template that allows the Consultants to quickly transfer student data from the Employability Questionnaire excel document to the Labor Insight platform; see Fig. 7 for more details.

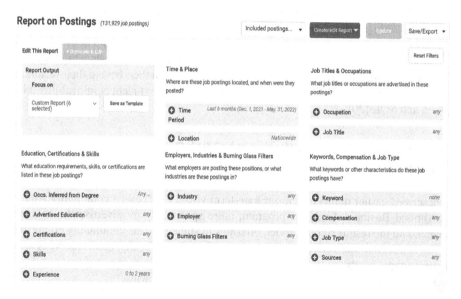

Fig. 7. Diagram depicting the labor insight template

Once this is submitted, the Labor Insight platform returns a multitude of data specifically tailored to the student's preferences. This data includes a summary of total job postings in the last twelve months, the top fifteen hiring regions, the top companies with the most job offerings displayed as a horizontal bar graph, the leading industries, skills in most significant demand, and specialized occupations. An excel template is generated with all this quantitative data and provided to the student for further review.

The next step for the ABA research team is to identify unique ways to derive insights from this data. This task must clearly understand the data collected, the methods or techniques to visualize the data, and the software applications to make this possible.

2.4   Service 3: Technical Interview Simulation

The third aspect of our student services model focuses on conducting technical interview simulations to prepare students for the technical segment of the interview process. At this stage, the student knows their skills and the jobs they should be applying for. Now comes the preparation for interviews with the company. The interview process can be highly stressful for potential candidates as they may be subject to several rounds of screening. For jobs in the Business analytics field, potential candidates may be subject to technical interviews to demonstrate their technical skills and apply them before advancing to behavioral interviews. During the technical interviews, employers are tested for competence in using the following programming languages; R, Python, and SQL [19]. They also test the applicant's ability to apply various analytic techniques to solve business problems. Some employers create test banks, including sample questions and datasets, while others rely on testing platforms like Hackerrank [21] and Coderpad [22].

We aim to replicate the technical interview process to provide our students with experience in solving problems under unique testing/interview conditions. That is, preparing students for the approach used by prospective employers to assess and select the right talent through Quantitative assessments. This experience will introduce a high level of comfort and confidence in our students so that they perform their best in their technical interviews. More of this is discussed in the article Improving student employability with Python and SQL [20].

3   Increasing ABA Visibility: ABA@BU Community Digication Portal

As described earlier in this paper, our long-term vision is to build a community around the Applied Business Analytics program, more specifically to advertise the ongoing research and the results of our service offerings to students. This community comprises employers, current students, potential students, alumni, and faculty. Each is served based on their unique needs.

For Current Students, we would like to execute the following:

1. Use this platform to educate our students on our program's latest updates, news, and industry trends.
2. Share information on Student Employability and related products and Services internally (for example, e-Portfolio creation, Burning Glass Labor Insight consultations) and externally (Center for Career development tools and services).
3. Share information on our various websites and groups (Administrative Sciences Website, Metropolitan College website, LinkedIn group, and social media groups).

Boston University Metropolitan College

Welcome to the ABA@BU Community Website

| Home | ABA Individual ePortfolios | Employers | Who are we? ˅ | Social Media | Alumni Spotlight | Services |

Forums   Professional trends and Lifelong Learning

Welcome to our Applied Business Analytics Community. Here you will find information for current students, prospective students, employers, faculty and members of staff. Please feel free to navigate throughout this site by clicking on the images below or the tabs above.
Happy browsing and we look forward to connecting with you!

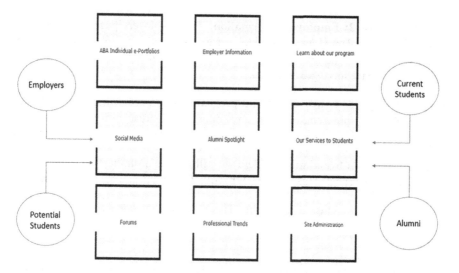

Fig. 8. Diagram depicting the critical components of the ABA@BU community website

For our Alumni, we would like to

1. Keep them connected to our community by sharing information on our latest research and other important events.
2. Collaborate in learning about their experiences in the job market

For Employers, we would like to

1. Provide an avenue to post job offerings
2. Inform them of our ongoing research, which includes studies completed by students

3. Provide a search feature that will allow employers to quickly filter through the existing ePortfolios to find the most suitable job offerings

For Potential Students, we would like to

1. Inform them of academic orientation
2. Inform them of our program offerings

The design of the website, as can be seen in Fig. 8 above, was created to meet the needs of our audience. Using the Digication platform, we were able to design this website by focusing on the following key areas:

Navigation Block 1: Individual e-Portfolios. Here the student will have the opportunity to have their e-Portfolio displayed on our community website. Employers will then have the opportunity to use our built-in search features to find talent for their specific needs.

Navigation Block 2: Employer Information. The Employers page will serve as a platform for potential employers to post job vacancies or notices of job vacancies posted on various platforms like Handshake. Also, this page will post several statistics on employers who have hired ABA alumni.

Navigation Block 3: Learn about our program. This page will display information about the ABA program, research, and community outreach efforts. Here, current students can access Blackboard, and links will be provided to the departments' websites.

Navigation Block 4: Social media. Here we will include a summary and links to our various Social media pages, for example, LinkedIn, Instagram, and our podcast episodes.

Navigation Block 5: Alumni Spotlight. This page will include advice from various alumni, where they work, the job interview process, the onboarding process, and the job experience.

Navigation Block 6: Our Services to Students. Here we will display our service model. Specially identified persons can access Burning Glass Labor insights.

Navigation Block 7: Forums. This page will be a forum for students to ask questions and communicate with the ABA team. This forum will be monitored by a member of the Applied Business Analytics administrative team.

Navigation Block 8: Professional Trends and Lifelong Learning. We will include the latest news on industry trends, emerging skills, recommended certificates, and conferences. Older news items will be archived.

Navigation Block 9: Site Administration. This page includes Tutorials, Guidelines, Content Protection & Passwords & Privacy Rules, etc.

4 Conclusion, Summary Statistics, and What Next

Our Student Services Model has been introduced to our Applied Business Analytics Community. Several of our students have engaged in creating their ePortoflios by attending consultation sessions and seeking advice from faculty members.

During the pilot phase, twenty-seven students created their ePortfolios and tested the ePortfolio template [24]. Upon completion of the final design of our ABA@BU Community Website, we will ask all current and former ABA students (over one thousand) to create and upload their ePortfolios on our community website. Our goal is to have more than one hundred listings by December 2022 and more than three hundred by May 2023.

Our students have also taken part in the Service two offerings, where they received feedback on the job market based on the students' unique preferences. Launched in Spring 2022, our interview simulations have been a resounding success, affording students the practice needed to apply the techniques learned in the ABA program to solving real-world problems.

Our next key areas of focus involve the following:

- Marketing our model to increase attractiveness among our students
- Applying our model to other program areas within the Administrative sciences department
- Developing dashboards and other visualizations displaying key insights extrapolated from the quantitative and qualitative data received in service two.
- Designing and developing a database to store all data collected in the Student Services Model.

References

1. BU MET MS-ABA: https://www.bu.edu/met/degrees-certificates/ms-applied-business-ana lytics/; BU MET GC-ABA: https://www.bu.edu/met/degrees-certificates/applied-business-analytics-graduate-certificate/
2. Best Online Masters in Business Analytics and Intelligence Programs by Online Masters Report 2020 & 2021 & 2022. https://www.bestcolleges.com/features/top-online-masters-in-business-intelligence-programs/
3. Zlatev, V., Dickson, K., Doddavaram, R.: Competitive landscape analysis on college, academic program, and student levels. In: Proceedings, 16th International Conference on Computer Science and Education in Computer Science. Boston University (September 2020)
4. Burning Glass Technology Homepage: https://www.burning-glass.com/
5. EMSI Homepage: https://www.economicmodeling.com/
6. The merger of Burning Glass Technology and EMCI: https://www.burning-glass.com/burning-glass-technologies-and-emsi-announce-merger-to-provide-deeper-labor-market-insights-and-advance-workforce-development/
7. GOUCONNECT: Homepage https://www.gouconnect.com/
8. ABA@BU Community Digication: Homepage. https://bu.digication.com/app/
9. Mehnaz Khan ePortfolio: https://bu.digication.com/mehnaz-khan/about-me
10. BU Career Center Homepage: https://www.bu.edu/careers/

11. ABA@BU e-Portfolio Template: https://bu.digication.com/app/
12. MET ABA@BU ePortfolio: Tutorial. https://www.bu.edu/adminsc/programs/applied-bus iness-analytics/ms-aba-current-students/career-advancement/
13. Preparation for ABA@BU Employability Consultation Service #2: Questionnaire. https:// www.bu.edu/adminsc/programs/applied-business-analytics/ms-aba-current-students/career-advancement/
14. Agrawal, S., at al.: Beyond hiring – how companies are reskilling to address talent gaps. McKinsey & Company (January 2020)
15. LinkedIn: Homepage. https://www.linkedin.com
16. Indeed: Homepage. https://indeed.com
17. Glassdoor: Homepage. https://www.glassdoor.com
18. Digication: BU Homepage. https://bu.digication.com/app/
19. Preparation for ABA@BU Employability Consultation Service #3: https://www.bu.edu/adm insc/programs/applied-business-analytics/ms-aba-current-students/career-advancement/
20. Yu, H.: Improving student employability with Python and SQL. In: Proceedings, 18th International Conference on Computer Science and Education in Computer Science. Sofia, Bulgaria (June 2022)
21. Hackerrank: HackerRank. (n.d.). Retrieved May 8 2022. From https://www.hackerrank.com/
22. Encrypted online notepad for secret and secure notes: encrypt and keep private notes with password: Coded pad™. Retrieved May 8 2022. From https://www.codedpad.com/
23. LinkedIn ABA Community Group Page: https://www.linkedin.com/groups/12401049/
24. ABA Programs Blackboard website: https://learn.bu.edu/ultra/courses/_52423_1/cl/outline
25. BU MET Department of Administrative Sciences website: page ABA https://www.bu.edu/ adminsc/programs/applied-business-analytics/. section Career Advancement

Plagiarism Abatement with Assignment Templates

Eric Braude$^{(\boxtimes)}$ ⓘ and Jack Polnar ⓘ

Boston University, Boston, MA 02215, USA
{ebraude, jpolnar}@bu.edu

Abstract. The ubiquity of plagiarism sites has made it imperative that faculty change assignments every time they teach a course. However, this can be very time consuming. We describe a way to make such changes that consumes a reasonable amount of time and also enhances students' learning.

Keywords: Plagiarism · IT Education · Assignments

1 The Problem

Plagiarism sites are widely used, compromising the integrity of higher education. It has become incumbent on faculty to change assignments every time they teach a course. Randomized multiple choice is one way to deal with this; however, many subjects, especially at the graduate level, require essay-type responses. To change essay assignments, however, can be very time-consuming; it requires new grading schemes and a considerable amount of review and anticipation of students' reception. We describe a way to make such changes that consumes a reasonable amount of time and improves learning at the same time.

University faculty are accustomed to creating assignments by altering existing ones. Our process systematizes and organizes this for the cyber-plagiarism age.

Much has been written about plagiarism prevention (e.g., Stabingis, Šarlauskienė, and Čepaitienė [1], and Craig and Dalton [5]); however most such writing concerns codes of ethics [4], the education of students and faculty about plagiarism (e.g., Atkinson and Yeoh [2]), the process of detecting plagiarism. Otherwise, they are at a high level (e.g., Devlin [6], East [7], Gibson, Blackwell, Greenwood, Mobley, and Blackwell [9]; Macdonald and Carroll [10]). Faculty are advised to not repeat assignments. For example, Carroll and Appleton [3] advise "rewrite/modify the assessment task each time the course is taught," but little practical guidance is provided. Sources like Joyce [8], for example, discuss prevention but not means for assignment variation. We have not found publications dealing with ways to create assignments that reduce the plagiarism problem. That is the subject of this report.

© ICST Institute for Computer Sciences, Social Informatics and Telecommunications Engineering 2022
Published by Springer Nature Switzerland AG 2022. All Rights Reserved
T. Zlateva and R. Goleva (Eds.): CSECS 2022, LNICST 450, pp. 263–273, 2022.
https://doi.org/10.1007/978-3-031-17292-2_21

2 Approach

Our approach is to write essay assignments in a generic form, creating a template from which instances can readily be created. Suppose, for example, that the class is in IT. A template would be like the following, where the system is named in place of < A > etc.

You have been tasked to install < A > with a team of < B > people in < C > months. < D > members of the development team have role < E > and reside in < F > . < G > members of the development team have role < H > and reside in < I > .

The system has the following characteristics:

< J >

...

Students are required to respond in terms of the particulars of the application—not generically.

We have found that this kind of template, together with a specific accompanying grading scheme, goes a long way to easing the assignment creation and grading burden from class to class. This is due to the faculty's familiarity with the format and evaluation, despite the factors that make the assignments quite different for students. Although the template is the same, instances can differ greatly from one another in substance, rendering solutions to other instances of little plagiarism value. It also allows students to see examples of past problems and learn from them—an asset that students appreciate. Faculty use past instances in classes as an essential means of explaining and coaching.

Section 3 Shows an example of such a framework and Sect. 4 an instance of the template. Section 5 lists the instances we have used in over more than a decade in one course.

3 Example Template

The Framework example is from MET CS682, Systems Analysis and Design. This course explores requirements analysis for information systems, software development lifecycle approaches, and design utilizing Unified Modeling Language. The course runs within a fast-paced six weeks, plus a final exam period. Students develop an 8 to 10-page requirements, project management, or design document every week which concludes as a term project and a final exam. The example below is the template for one of the weekly deliverables. The topic is software development process. Students have to consider each of the processes (Agile, Prototyping etc. or a combination of these) tailored to the given project scenario. They must provide a project roadmap and selected risk analysis and mitigation strategies.

MET CS682 ASSSIGNMENT 2
Replace this with your name

The purpose of this exercise is to (1) give you practice exploring development processes, and (2) identifying risks when embarking on a project.

Please leave the headings and the gray text unchanged except for the hints section at the end which should not be included in your solution. Observe the page limitations; however, you may include as many appendices as you wish. All appendices should be referred to in the main text. Include your last name in the file name of the assignment. (Example: Smith-Michael_CS682Assignment2.docx)

You are a project manager hired by the CEO to recommend the process and complete a risk assessment. Once the project is initiated you will be responsible for managing this project and risk mitigation strategies you have proposed. Your solution will build on the systems analysis that you developed in assignment 1. The name of the system will be the same name as the company: ...

The following project characteristics apply:
(1) ...
(2) ...
...

1. Process

Using the format below, consider each of the following development processes in terms of how suitable it would be for this project.
1. Waterfall Process
2. An iterative (Rapid Application Development) process with 3-4 iterations
3. Agile Process

1.1 Comparison of Processes

For each of the three listed development processes above, provide one strength and one and weakness relative to this particular project. Focus on what you think is the most important strength and weakness of the SDLC process specific to relevant characteristics of this specific scenario. Being selective and focused is important. Incorporate research where appropriate to add depth to your response. (up to 2 pages of 12-point text)

1.1.1 Waterfall Strength for This Project
Replace this with your response.

1.1.2 Waterfall Weakness for This Project
Replace this with your response.

1.1.3 RAD Strength for This Project
Replace this with your response.

1.1.4 RAD Weakness for This Project
   Replace this with your response.

1.1.5 Agile Strength for This Project
   Replace this with your response.

1.1.6 Agile Weakness for This Project
   Replace this with your response.

1.2 Project Roadmap

Designate one process—or a combination of processes—for this specific project, that you consider *most* appropriate (single sentence). Provide a Roadmap in the form of a Work Breakdown Structure (WBS) which clearly shows the phases of process you designated with what is being completed and by whom. In this section you do not need to explain your choices, this will be done in the next section. (up-to 1 page of 12-point text)

Replace this with your selected process.

Fill in the chart below (i.e., for this project), suitably enlarged.

Iteration	Phase	Responsibility	Expected Duration	Notes

1.3 Explanation of Process

Explain why the process (or combination of processes) and the roadmap you selected would work best supporting the characteristics of this project. Consider the strengths and weaknesses which you defined earlier. We place more weight on this section rather the roadmap itself. (up-to 3/4 page of 12-point text)

Replace this with your response.

2. Risk Analysis

2.1 Five Risks

Based on the project characteristics provided, identify five risks in this project with the highest potential to affect the SDLC process which you selected in section 1.2. In addition, give each risk a title of two to three words and create a prioritization matrix for the risks. Avoid giving a generic response: focus on this particular system under development and its particular characteristics. Note the hints below in the section "Hints on Risks." (up to 1 page of 12-point text)

Replace this with your five risk definitions – include a title for each risk. You may use the following framework:

Risk Title: (1) Underlying cause (2) Description of the risk (3) Impact should the risk materialize

Complete the chart with risk titles from above.

Risk No.	Title	Estimated Likelihood of Occurrence (L: 1-10)	Estimated Impact (I: 1-10)	Estimated cost of management (M: 1-10)	Priority ((11 – L) * (11 – I)*M)

2.2 Selected Risk

Select one of these risks and provide as below.
Replace this with your response – Risk number and title from above.

2.2.1 Likelihood
State and explain the likelihood of occurrence of this risk. Use research to support the likelihood of this risk. (up to ½ page of 12-point text)
Replace this with your response.

2.2.2 Impact
Explain the concrete impacts on the project of this risk. Use research to support the impact of this risk. (up to ½ page of 12-point text)

Replace this with your response.

2.2.3 Risk Type
State whether the risk is primarily organizational or technical and explain. (single sentence)

Replace this with either "organizational" or "technical."

2.2.4 Risk Management

Write an account of how you could mitigate the risk. Explain whether you are proposing risk "conquest" or risk "avoidance". Consider cost of management vs. impact of risk occurring as a tradeoff. Support your plan with research. (up to 1 page of 12-point text)

Replace this with your response.

3. References (based on your research)

Show that you used a wide variety of resources by listing them below and clearly indicating in the body above where you used. Make sure to use proper referencing in your paper. We suggest using APA format, but other formats are fine as long as it clearly distinguishes your work from work of others in your response—be mindful of plagiarism rules.

[1] your first reference replaces this
[2] ...

Evaluation

	D	C-	C+	B-	B+	A	Letter Grade	%
Clarity	Disorganized or hard-to-understand		Satisfactory but some parts of the submission are disorganized or hard to understand	Generally organized and clear	Very clear, organized and persuasive presentation of ideas and designs	Exceptionally clear, organized and persuasive presentation of ideas and designs		0.0
Technical Soundness	Little understanding of, or insight into material technically		Some understanding of material technically	Overall understanding of much material technically	Very good overall understanding of technical material, with some real depth	Excellent, deep understanding of technical material and its inter-relationships		0.0
Thoroughness & Coverage	Hardly covers any of the major relevant issues		Covers some of the major relevant issues	Reasonable coverage of the major relevant areas	Thorough coverage of almost all of the major relevant issues and researched where appropriate	Exceptionally thorough coverage of all major relevant issues and researched where appropriate		0.0
Relevance	Mostly unfocused	Focus is off topic or on insubstantial or secondary issues	Only some of the content is meaningful and on topic	Most or all of the content is reasonably meaningful and on-topic	All of content is reasonably meaningful, and on-topic	All of the content is entirely relevant, and meaningful		0.0
						Assignment Grade:		0.0

The resulting grade is the average of these, using A+=97, A=95, A-=90, B+=87, B=85, B-=80 etc.
To obtain an A grade for the course, your weighted average should be >93. A->=90. B+ >=87. B >83. B->=80 etc.

Please do not include Hints section from your solution.

Hints on the *Process* Sections

Clarity:
- When you choose an Interpretation, an approach, or a technique, an explanation will contribute well here towards clarity, thoroughness
- There is no such thing as a 100% "right" answer to this question. For that reason, it is important that you explain how you made your selection.
- Check for consistency.

Technical Soundness
- Understand and outline the key differences between Waterfall, RAD, and Agile processes and explain these thoroughly and clearly within the context of the scenario. The Waterfall, Rapid Application Development (RAD), and Agile processes are referenced in module 2 Part 1.
- Note that RAD and Agile are both iterative in nature.
- Pages 5 through 17 in the textbook will help. The notes and the textbook are not identical: there are many variants on system analysis concepts, and we encourage broad reading and experimentation, this is where research comes in.

Thoroughness and Coverage
- Review your solution after completing both part 1 (Development Process) and part 2 (Risk Analysis)—you may uncover additional considerations—as well as check for consistency.
- Research similar business and different SDLC process characteristics to have a better understanding on how they compare and contrast.

Relevance
- Reference the specific characteristics of the project in your justification. Don't be generic. Explain any trade-offs you made developing your recommendation(s).

Hints on the *Risks* sections

Clarity:
- Risk should be defined precise and to the point stating the issue, what may happen and impact.

Technical Soundness
- Show understanding between conquest and avoidance

Thoroughness and Coverage
- Use references to support risk identification, likelihood, cost of impact and cost of management.
- Make sure that you explain how you would mitigate the risk, be explicit about whether your strategy is conquest or avoidance—or perhaps a combination.
- Review your entire solution after completing it—you will uncover additional considerations. Check for consistency.

Relevance
- A strong solution has to concentrate on real risks rather than on very unlikely situations.

4   Example Instance of the Template

Using the template in Sect. 3, we fill in a new scenario on the first page every semester. Starting with the Process section, everything is the same, semester to semester. The framework itself is fine-tuned as we find improvements.

MET CS682 ASSSIGNMENT 2
Replace this with your name

The purpose of this exercise is to (1) give you practice exploring development processes, and (2) identifying risks when embarking on a project.

Please leave the headings and the gray text unchanged except for the hints section at the end which should not be included in your solution. Observe the page limitations; however, you may include as many appendices as you wish. All appendices should be referred to in the main text. Include your last name in the file name of the assignment. (Example: SmithMichael_CS682Assignment2.docx)

You are a project manager hired by the CEO to recommend the process and complete a risk assessment. Once the project is initiated you will be responsible for managing this project and risk mitigation strategies you have proposed. Your solution will build on the systems analysis that you developed in assignment 1. The name of the system will be the same name as the company: *RemoteAssist that assists employees in their remote work*

The following project characteristics apply:
- The CEO is interested in features for *RemoteAssist* which conflict with what investors think is both important and can be delivered in the initial release. For example: The CEO believes that *RemoteAssist* must have exceptional user experience and integrate with social media, however investors disagree considering health and safety features are critical—at least for the initial development.
- Along with the CEO and yourself, your initial team has 1 systems analyst who is also a subject area expert and 1 developer experienced with programming of this type of system: 5 additional developers and 3 QA personal are needed for this type of project to be delivered in the timeframe of the initial release based on your previous experience of working on similar projects.
- The system analyst/subject area expert and the experienced developer reside in time zones with substantial difference. The experienced developer is very talented; however, family priorities will limit their availability on this project, potentially in most critical moments.
- Believing that it keeps costs low, the CEO would like to hire as many offshore developers and QA staff as possible, even though they would probably be in very different time zones, potentially with deep cultural differences. You may account for the effects of pandemic, war, sanctions, and unrest impacting the offshore development team.
- You are to assume the timeframe of the initial release and or iterations depending on your process selection

1. Process
...

5   Instance History

Outlined below are some of the scenarios which we have utilized using the framework in Sect. 3. We usually use current industry trends so that students think through applications that they may well encounter as they enter the IT field.

- BestPurchase- an app focusing on retail with automation and or recommendation capabilities.
- StayHealthy- an app which helps users manage a healthy lifestyle in the age of COVID.
- FinanceAdvisor provides personal finance advice to clients, mainly via proprietary applications.
- The COVID pandemic has required much more flexibility from event management systems, such as capacity, social distancing and vaccination considerations. You are to specify a system called FlexEvent that facilitates flexible management for events and or venues.
- The GardenByDesign company specializes in landscaping, garden design, lawn care, and specialty items such as koi pools and bonsai.
- VolunteerFit specializes in matching volunteers and donations to organizations that have needs.
- SmartBots, maker of autonomous home vacuums, wants to branch out into the travel business by introducing a personal travel companion robot.
- Suppose that your organization specializes in city tours and would like to introduce a new app called AugmentedCityTour. AugmentedCityTour provides tourists options for tour booking and in-tour navigation and narration via Augmented Reality (AR) overlay for landmark information, and in-your social interaction capability.

6   Assessment

The classes we reference in this paper are assessed by means of student evaluations. Since the assignments are a central part of the course, student evaluations of the course are therefore a reasonable indicator. We began refining the template approach in approximately 2016. The results are shown in Fig. 1.

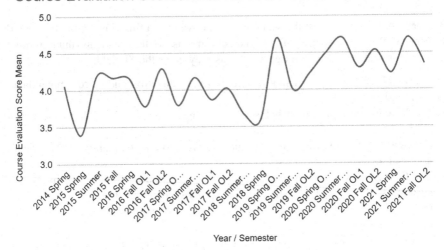

Fig. 1 Course scores in CS 682 since 2014

7 Conclusions

The template approach to creating repeated unique assignments is a reasonable response to the plagiarism epidemic. Evaluations show good results in terms of student reception. Pre-existing assignment / solutions, rather than being part of the problem, become legitimate learning aids for students.

References

1. Stabingis, L., Šarlauskienė, L., Čepaitienė, N.: Measures for Plagiarism Prevention in Students' Written Works: Case Study of ASU Experience. Procedia - Social and Behavioral Sciences **110**, 689–699. https://doi.org/10.1016/j.sbspro.2013.12.913
2. Atkinson, D., Yeoh, S.: Student and staff perceptions of the effectiveness of plagiarism detection software. Austr. J. Edu. Technol. **24**(2), 222–240 (2008)
3. Carroll, J., Appleton, J.: Plagiarism: a good practice guide (2001). Accessed from https://i.unisa.edu.au/siteassets/staff/tiu/documents/plagiarism—a-good-practice-guide-by-oxford-brookes-university.pdf
4. Code of Academic Ethics of ASU (2012). Accessed from https://www.asu.edu/aad/manuals/acd/acd204-01.html
5. Craig, R., Dalton, D.: Understanding first year undergraduate student perception on copyright and plagiarism: development of platform for a culture of honest inquiry and the academic construction of knowledge. In: June 2013 International Conference on Plagiarism across Europe and Beyond (2013)
6. Devlin, M.: Policy, preparation, and prevention: proactive minimization of student plagiarism. J. Higher Edu. Policy and Manage. **28**(1), 45–58 (2006). https://doi.org/10.1080/13600800500283791

7. East, J.: Aligning policy and practice: an approach to integrating academic integrity. J. Acade. Lang. Lear. **3**(1), 38–51 (2009)
8. Gibson, J., Blackwell, C., Greenwood, R., Mobley, I., Blackwell, R.: Preventing and detecting plagiarism in the written work of college students. J. Diversity Manage. **1**(2), 35–42 (2006)
9. Joyce, D.: Academic integrity and plagiarism: australasian perspectives. Comp. Sci. Edu. **17**(3), 187–200 (2008). https://doi.org/10.1080/08993400701538062
10. Macdonald, R., Carroll, J.: Plagiarism – a complex issue requiring a holistic institutional approach. Asse. Evalu. Higher Edu. **31**(2), 233–245 (2006). https://doi.org/10.1080/02602930500262536

Reflections on the Applied Business Analytics Student Writing Project

Greg Page[1,2]([⊠]) and Huey Fern Tay[1,2]

[1] Princeton University, Princeton, NJ 08544, USA
[2] Boston University, Boston, USA
{gpage,hftay}@bu.edu

Abstract. In this paper, the authors describe a student article writing project run by a Professor in Applied Business Analytics at Boston University's Metropolitan College. Through this project, students write and self-publish articles on various topics related to data science. The project enables students to build and refine their data modeling skills, and to build a portfolio of content related to the data science field. The authors trace the history of the project, point out some of its notable successes and setbacks, and identify some thoughts about how the project should continue to evolve.

Keywords: Data science · Data mining · Data science education

1 Introduction

Beginning in the Fall of 2020, Greg Page, a Senior Lecturer in Applied Business Analytics (ABA) at Boston University's Metropolitan College, queried several students in a Marketing Analytics class to ask whether any were interested in collaborating on articles related to data science. Three students from the section stepped forward, and expressed a desire to involve themselves in such a project.

Those three students – Jiawen Huang, Qiuyue Wang, and Abhishek Kumar – worked with Professor Page to release the first "wave" of articles. The students published each of these articles to Medium, a web-based, self-publishing platform. For the most part, these articles consisted of more in-depth analysis and refinement of topics introduced in ABA specialization courses.

Page's idea to collaborate with ABA students on data science articles stemmed from an experience during the previous summer. In June and July of 2020, Page worked with Yiting Wang, a recent ABA graduate, on two data science articles that were posted to Medium. The first of these, written by Wang, explained the point scoring system in a video game called Animal Crossing [1]. The second of these, written by Page, was titled, "What's the story with those dynamite sticks on my bar plot?" [2].

Seeing the positive experiences across the summer and fall of 2020, and the potential for future benefits as well, Page institutionalized this group in Spring 2021. He opened it to all members of the ABA community, dubbing it the ABA Writers' Group. Since that

T. Zlateva and R. Goleva (Eds.): CSECS 2022, LNICST 450, pp. 274–281, 2022.
https://doi.org/10.1007/978-3-031-17292-2_22

time, the group has met continuously, on a weekly basis, via Zoom. During the twice-annual ABA webinars, Page and the current group of student participants deliver a slide presentation to current and incoming ABA students. This webinar serves to update the ABA community about the group's efforts and progress, and to advertise the group to students who may be interested in participating.

The topics covered by this paper include:

- The student article writers' process, from idea generation to publishing;
- The structure and pacing of the weekly Zoom meetings;
- Examples of successful student outcomes;
- Challenges and setbacks associated with the project; and
- Conclusions and final thoughts from the authors

2 The Operational Concept, from Brainstorming to Publishing

During the weekly Zoom sessions, Professor Page cycles through the student participants, in order of their arrival time to the meeting. The "check-in" period offers the student a chance to offer updates about recent progress and/or to identify any recent roadblocks or sticking points. Once a student's check-in time is completed, the student is free to either stay in the meeting, to observe the other topics and ideas, or to depart. Throughout the meetings, Professor Page maintains the meeting notes via a Google Doc that is shared with all student participants.

Students are encouraged to generate their own article ideas – when students have done this, they are more likely to take ownership of their projects, and less likely to perceive it as something akin to a class assignment. When students attend for the first time, and are searching for a topic, Page first encourages them to think about their interests. For instance, a student passionate about movies could analyze a cinema revenue dataset, or a student with a keen interest in finance could analyze stock market returns. Kegui "Gary" Zhuo is one student who combined his strong passion for NBA basketball with some data manipulation skills by using the popular R package dplyr [3] for his analysis.

A second option for any student is to choose a single function or concept, and to demonstrate it using either Python or R. Shang Ding's "Cross-Validation Techniques: k-fold cross-validation vs Leave-One-Out Cross-Validation [4]" encapsulates this approach. This student had first gained exposure to the cross-validation concept while taking AD654: Marketing Analytics, an ABA specialization course. Prior to writing the article, however, she had not yet acquired firsthand experience with the technique known as leave one out cross-validation.

If a student wishes to participate but is completely at a loss for a domain area or a data science angle, Page suggests starting points for the student to explore.

Students have the option to write an article entirely independently, or with some level of direct involvement from Professor Page. A student choosing the former option could of course pick any topic to explore. In such a case, Professor Page's role would be purely 'behind-the-scenes', and the article's by-line would belong entirely to the student. For a student choosing the latter option, the byline would be split (by the student, with Professor Page).

It is essential that Professor Page clearly outlines the roles and expectations from the outset. For this project to work, it is essential that students "buy in" and take ownership of the exploration and article drafting. This is essential for two reasons: first, because to use an alternative, in which the professor was truly the one performing the coding, drafting, and conclusions, would not lay a genuine foundation for a student-led writing project; second, this would not be sustainable. A truly student-led writing project can scale up or down easily as the number of participants changes.

These stories are published primarily through Medium (a self-publishing platform), or through specialized sub-channels of Medium, such as Towards Data Science, Codex, and Nerd For Tech. Others are posted to R-Bloggers, a site that aggregates content related to the R programming language and statistical environment.

Students can write a single article on a single topic as a "one-off" sort of project, or could use a series of articles to explore a topic in more depth.

Huey Fern Tay, an online ABA student with a background in journalism and marketing communications, did both.

Tay wrote a series of articles on variable imputation after joining the project upon completion of ADR100 in Summer 2021. She started with an explanation of the Last Observation Carried Forward, setting the story within a fictional scenario involving the local weather in Melbourne during the Australian Open. She then wrote about imputation with a categorical average, followed by linear regression model imputation using the simputation [5] library in R, emphasizing the *impute_lm()* function which is used to replace missing values in a dataset with the results of a linear model, built with the values of known, related variables as inputs [6].

Those articles have reverberated around the data science community, helping to build a digital footprint around Tay as an authority on data science. Tay's articles have been shared on Twitter by several data scientists, and by the Towards Data Science platform itself.

The final installment of the imputation series revolved around the perils of zero imputation as well as the occasions when the method is appropriate. This piece was subsequently cited in a Masters thesis by a graduate student from Utah State University.

3 Establishing a Regular, Predictable Rhythm – with "All Volunteers, No Hostages"

Although the meeting time block may change from semester to semester, once it is set, it remains firmly in place throughout the term. The maintenance of a regular, steady meeting time reduces the friction that would otherwise arise if meetings with individual student authors had to be scheduled separately. New student writers are often reminded that they can choose to attend these sessions as their schedules permit, rather than view the meeting time block as a fixed, firm obligation.

To reinforce this, Page even asks the students not to RSVP when they are unable to attend. Discouraging student RSVP emails is a way of reminding students that the sessions are meant to be loose, free-wheeling, and completely optional.

An important tenet of the ABA Writers' Group is that all the members are there voluntarily. Students are regularly reminded that the writing project is not a class, or even an extracurricular obligation. Professor Page often reminds the students that if the writing group begins to feel like a burden, or obligation, they should simply take time away from it, and return when their schedule is freer.

Attrition is fairly common – approximately 1 in 3 students who visit do not return for a second meeting. While this attrition rate may sound high at first, there are some positive ways to view it. Chief among these is that it shows that students understand the messaging around the project – those who lose interest in article writing do not stay affiliated out of a sense of obligation.

Meeting attendance fluctuates considerably, sometimes based on the natural rhythm of the academic semester. Meetings have included as many 12 separate ABA students and recent graduates, and have also been as small as just a single student meeting directly with Professor Page.

4 Student Success Vignettes

Students can benefit from participation in the writing project in several ways.

First, students will gain more expertise on the topic that they select for their article. Generating the code required to demonstrate a concept, and then articulating the steps and results in words, forces a student to carefully assess the concepts involved..This benefit can apply to both the domain knowledge involved, and to the data science concepts illustrated in the article.

In addition, student writers can expand on the coding and modeling skills that they learn in their ABA courses. Given the rapid pace of all ABA courses – whether on-campus or online – there is often not enough time in the semester to cover every single topic in considerable depth. A student who encounters a theme or concept of interest in class can supplement that knowledge with extra material through the writing project, such as Tay, whose piece about detecting multicollinearity was inspired by the final project in her AD699 Data Mining course.

As students explore the datasets, they train themselves to troubleshoot data quirks that need to be addressed before the start of an analysis (e.g. missing values, illogical values, the data format of multi-response surveys). The process of problem solving helps students build confidence around those decisions. Furthermore, students can begin to establish an article portfolio that may be of interest to future employers. The 'Animal Crossing' analysis written by Yiting Wang is a case in point. Her analysis involved relatively straightforward techniques such as 'groupby', 'mean', and 'sort' but her subject matter left an indelible impression on readers, including a member on the interview panel at Wayfair, a Boston-based home furnishings company. Yiting got the job.

Recent graduates of the program can use the article writing as a way to continue to bolster their data science skills while they are otherwise immersed in the job hunt. During the long, stressful, and often discouraging process that students encounter with the job search, students often experience intensifying feelings of frustration. Involvement with a project such as this one may not only alleviate some of those feelings, but could also offer them a topical, relevant answer to the question, "What have you been doing lately to sharpen your analytics skill set?".

Student participants may also gain some networking benefit by participating in the weekly check-ins. Naturally, some conversational topics arise during these sessions, beyond the immediate focus on the articles. These side topics sometimes include job interview experiences, including takeaways about employers' expectations, and the skills valued by potential employers. Students armed with this 'market intelligence' gain an edge in a competitive market by being better prepared for the job interview process. One of the student authors found that during interviews with Meta, and with a food delivery app service, several of the fundamental data handling questions that arose overlapped with other students' article topics.

Finally, the practice with writing and editing may be helpful for English language learners, especially as they prepare for job interviews and corporate recruiting, as the descriptive experiences assist them in structuring their thought process and explanatory skills.

5   Limiting the Scope

To help students narrow their scope, Page reminds students to consider publicly available datasets that can be found on data science websites such as Kaggle where datasets can be filtered according to analytics techniques or genre. He also reminds them to consider the abundance of data from the realms of sports, government, and finance – such information is often easily obtainable.

Sometimes, students begin with extremely ambitious ideas – they want to write something far-reaching that explains a topic in great depth. However, an effective article often succeeds due to its focus, rather than its breadth. Most data science blog posts are concise, and they serve a single, important purpose. They enable a student in a university course, or a working professional, to answer a question about how to accomplish some particular purpose. Students who wish to tackle a topic in considerable depth are encouraged to break their content up into multiple parts.

6   Challenges and Frustrations

Students new to analytics generally do not appreciate the benefit and value that can come with descriptive techniques. Often, when a student arrives at the Writers' Group meetings for the first time, and is in search of an idea, Professor Page will suggest an article that demonstrates a single concept, function, or type of data visualization.

An example of such an article is Xiangyu Wang's "Exploring the World of Hexagonal Bin Plots [7]." In this article, the author describes the problem that arises when scatterplots are built with enormous datasets – there is so much overplotting that the points become impossible to distinguish from one another. Hexagonal bin plots address this problem by dividing the graph into distinct regions, and then filling those regions based on the count of observations that fall within that area. Xiangyu goes through several modification options in the article, including adjustments to the hexagon sizes, color scheme alterations, and even the decision of whether denser areas should be filled with lighter or darker shades [8].

An article like the one described above is ideal for someone who initially attempts a scatter plot and wonders how to address severe overplotting that cannot be solved by transparency or jitter adjustments. It also might be a great find for a student in a

University course tasked with making a hexagonal bin plot, but not sure where to start, or which 'levers' to pull to achieve the desired outcome.

Even after seeing an article such as the one described here, students often resist the idea of writing about a specific type of visualization. Most likely, this is because such articles lack the "punch" of something like an advanced tree algorithm, neural network, or matrix decomposition.

Some students may approach the writing project with a degree of wariness; after all, if they are new to analytics, what can they contribute to the field? How would it provide unique insight or value? To address these questions, Page often reminds students to reframe the issue – rather than expect to write something groundbreaking and Nobel Prize-worthy from the outset, they can simply pick a single idea, and tackle it. At a bare minimum, the resulting article will help the student to better understand the chosen topic, and could be a "nice to have" item on a resume.

The language barrier may also present a challenge. Students may begin with a strong sense of motivation, but then run out of steam when the time comes to draft the article. To the best degree possible, Page can become involved when he senses that this is creating a barrier – he can ask the student to generate a first draft, and then to "pass the torch" to him for a review and a round of edits.

Ideally, the process flow would look something like this:

1. Professor Page works with the student to help shape the article concept and scope;
2. The student explores the topic and/or any related datasets independently;
3. The student checks in during the weekly sessions for guidance and/or the chance to "sanity check" any ideas or concepts being explored in the draft;
4. If the student reaches a complete impasse, Page can take the student's existing code and narrative under review, for a round of edits;
5. The student makes a final round of reviews and edits, before sending the article back to Page for review;
6. After Page gives the code and written content a final "okay", the student posts the article directly to a destination site.

7 Publicizing the Work

There is not a single "go-to" location for publishing the students' work. When the project started, all of the articles were simply posted to Medium. Xiaotong "Claire" Ding was the first student to publish to r-bloggers, with a detailed description of nearZeroVar(), a function from R's caret package [9]. Ginna Gomez was the first student to post to Towards Data Science, back in May of 2021. A specialized channel within Medium, Towards Data Science is focused specifically on its eponymous field. Articles submitted to Towards Data Science are screened by a team of editors prior to approval; the site, therefore, carries more prestige than Medium.

After an article is published, there is not a single standard used for publicizing the students' work. When the project started, Professor Page shared all of the student articles in the ABA LinkedIn group page. This is an internal page, accessible only to members of the ABA community. Page has also shared some articles on his own LinkedIn page, helping gain more exposure for the group.

Professor Page has registered the domain GoodWaveData.com. This summer, he plans to link all of the existing published body of student work to this site. He intends to develop this site into a hub for topics related to learning, and teaching, data science.

In one case, a student author created a website to showcase her work.

Going forward, student authors can be encouraged to share their content through the ePortfolio platform offered by Digication. This platform offers students a standard, visually appealing way to tell their story and to share their work.

8 Conclusions

From its beginnings in Fall 2020, the writing project's meetings have been entirely virtual. With COVID-19 now in its endemic phase, and in-person meeting restrictions lifted, it may be worth experimenting with face-to-face sessions in addition to Zoom. No matter what, the Zoom format should be maintained – that is what enables remote learners to participate in the process.

Among the cases in which the articles had a significant, positive impact on a student's job search, the common theme among them is the popularity of the subject matter, rather than any specific analytics insights featured in the article. One of the best such examples is Lujia Wang's 2021 piece, "Data Insights from Reddit WallStreetBets" posts [10]. Wang released this post on March 12, 2021, when the hoopla surrounding the Reddit WallStreetBets forum was still fresh in the minds of many investors and stock market analysts. The article received considerable social media "buzz" in the form of shares, comments, and likes. Wang spoke to a class at the University of Washington about her findings, after the course professor saw her article on LinkedIn. She was asked about the article during her hiring process with Applied Materials, a semiconductor company based in San Jose, California, where she now works.

While the benefits that can accrue to participating students have been noted above, it should also be noted that Professor Page benefits from the experience, too. The topic development and data exploration bolster his subject matter knowledge and help him to develop and refine his instructional style. This semester, he embedded two of Tay's articles into assignment prompts for AD699. The writing project also enables Page to spot truly remarkable talent among members of the ABA community, which can help the department to identify future facilitators, adjunct instructors, and project partners. Recognizing the need for a marketing analytics textbook that balances substantive Python instruction, statistical rigor, and contemporary marketing concepts, Page reached out to Tay this spring to suggest a collaboration on this project. They are now co-writing a marketing analytics textbook, set for release in digital and print editions by Labor Day of this year.

References

1. Wang, Y.: Animal Crossing: Secret of Miles Rewards with Python Visualization. (24 Jun 2020). https://medium.com/self-training-data-science-enthusiast/animal-crossing-secret-of-miles-rewards-with-python-visualization-a441aa6238f5

2. Page, G.: What's the Story with those 'Dynamite Sticks' ono my Barplot?. Medium (30 Jun 2020). https://medium.com/@greg.page_41455/whats-the-story-with-those-dynamite-sticks-on-my-bar-plot-c9820e4788e9
3. Wickham, H., François, R., Henry, L., Müller, K.: dplyr: A Grammar of Data Manipulation (2021). R package version 1.0.7. https://CRAN.R-project.org/package=dplyr
4. Ding, S.: Cross-Validation Techniques: k-fold cross-validation vs Leave-One-Out Cross-Validation. Medium (21 May 2021). https://shangding.medium.com/cross-validation-techniques-k-fold-cross-validation-vs-leave-one-out-cross-validation-2dcfb7d5deb3
5. van der Loo, M. Simputation: Simple Imputation (2021). R package version 0.2.7. https://CRAN.R-project.org/package=simputation
6. Tay, H.F.: Using R's simputation to handle missing values. Towards Data Science (25 Jul 2021). https://towardsdatascience.com/how-much-money-did-we-make-again-using-simputation-to-balance-the-books-f8e5c7b74f51
7. Wang, X.: Exploring the World of Hexagonal Bin Plots. Medium (15 Jan 2021). https://xiangyuw.medium.com/exploring-the-world-of-hexagonal-bin-plots-1562c65f3f94
8. Wickham, H.: ggplot2: Elegant Graphics for Data Analysis. Springer-Verlag, New York (2016)
9. Ding, X.C.: Function with Special Talent from the caret package in R: NearZeroVar (04 Sep 2021). https://www.r-bloggers.com/2021/09/function-with-special-talent-from-caret-package-in-r-nearzerovar/
10. Wang, L.: Data Insights from Reddit's Wall Street Bets Posts. Medium (12 Mar 2021). https://lujiaw.medium.com/data-insights-from-reddit-wallstreetbets-posts-8f95dbd59a6c

Digital Learning Technologies – Supporting Innovation and Scalability

Leo Burstein(✉) ⓘ, Andrew Abrahamson ⓘ, and Courtney Pike ⓘ

Boston University, Boston, MA 02215, USA
{bur,andrewa,cjpike}@bu.edu

Abstract. Present-day student success is often defined as achieving career goals within a rapidly changing modern workplace, in an educational environment that embraces different lifestyles and learning preferences, makes learning available at any time and place, individually or in teams, and encourages continuous communications with faculty and fellow students. How can technology help to achieve these objectives while assisting faculty in their pursuit of teaching excellence and research quality? How do technology innovations interplay with support scalability, and how to inspire motivation and achieve competitive advantage in the age of cloud computing and SaaS platforms? We provide examples of enhancing the learning ecosystem and streamlining support efforts by leveraging our infrastructure that integrates educational technologies and provides a stage for innovation.

Keywords: Digital learning · Learning technology · Student success · Support scalability · Innovation platform

1 Superior Learning Environment and Scalable Support

Boston University Metropolitan College (MET) has a long and successful history of offering online and hybrid graduate academic programs. Using the fundamental educational principles of achieving an optimal balance of structure and dialog, and leveraging the latest technological capabilities, our programs help students achieve a broad spectrum of educational goals. From building a solid academic foundation to developing their independent learning skills, students consequently learn business competencies, build long-lasting professional relationships, and position themselves for success in their professional careers. We constantly track the latest trends in higher education, trying to combine the proven benefits of online technologies with the effectiveness of face-to-face communications. We believe that our main challenge is positioning these emerging technologies not as obstacles, but instead as tools that help to achieve two objectives. First, they facilitate the creation of a superior learning environment that enables effective communications between faculty and students and makes the learning content interactive and always available – both to learn and to create, at any time and from any place. Second, they enable effective and scalable support for both students and faculty.

T. Zlateva and R. Goleva (Eds.): CSECS 2022, LNICST 450, pp. 282–288, 2022.
https://doi.org/10.1007/978-3-031-17292-2_23

Two classes of digital learning technologies, including Learning Management Systems (LMS) and video conferencing, emerged as the key requirements to ensure structure and dialog [1] in any online or blended academic program. However, digital learning technologies and instructional practices are not limited to online education. In fact, they can significantly enhance traditional on-campus learning [2]. In this paper, we will talk about technology innovation and scalability as it applies to all learning modalities: online, on-campus and hybrid.

2 Innovation Platform

In our modern economy, it is difficult to imagine a business process that is not based on some type of information system. However, recent IT trends have created certain challenges to grass-roots innovation. As on-premises computing infrastructure is being replaced with managed hosting, and ultimately with "...as-a-Service" (SaaS, PaaS, IaaS, etc.) platforms, the ability for customers to experiment and innovate within these platforms often depends on platform vendors, who use the same systems to support all their clients. Functional application changes are possible only within the vendor-envisioned configuration parameters, and any changes beyond this space require platform updates and modifications. Achieving an innovation-driven competitive advantage in this situation is somewhat difficult, as all changes are subject to the vendor's priorities and, when implemented, become instantly available to all platform customers, including the competition.

Fortunately, there is an approach to bypass the *aaS platform limitations. The widely used Application Programming Interface (API) framework allows for a standardized flow of data and commands between heterogeneous systems. Companies can create their own "innovation platforms" while still maintaining focus on their core competencies. Allowing for integrations with "generic" 3rd party systems, these platforms deliver a competitive advantage by combining the best of both worlds: the efficiency of *aaS platforms and the effectiveness of custom core competency applications.

MET applied this "innovation platform" concept [3] to integrate our main digital education platforms: Blackboard LMS, Zoom video conferencing, and other data from the university systems. We leveraged the new platform to deliver the additional functionality that was critical to support our innovative learning initiatives, which are promoting student success and increasing faculty satisfaction. Our innovation platform is integrated with the main transaction platforms in two directions using APIs: we not only automatically get the real-time information we need, but we can also automatically manipulate these platforms based on our business rules and needs. Having these capabilities is critical for our ability to innovate, and the level of automation is critical to achieving scalability (Fig. 1).

In the next sections, we will provide some examples of how we use the MET innovation platform to achieve new learning capabilities and improve student and faculty support.

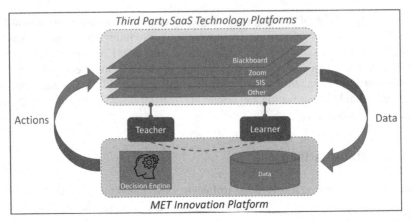

Fig. 1. Maintaining a competitive edge with SaaS clouds: two-way integration between 3rd party technology platform and MET Innovation Platform enables streamlined communications and brings new functionality to create a superior learning environment.

3   Course-Centric Integration

The extended use of online conferencing technologies, even before COVID-19, created a need for the seamless integration of these technologies into the teaching and learning process. When defining this integration philosophy, MET drew a parallel from the online classroom to a physical space where instructors and students meet. Like a physical classroom or a course conferencing website, our online classroom is always linked to a specific course. This "course-centric" integration is different from a traditional web-approach, where online meetings are scheduled by individual users and are linked (and licensed) to their personal accounts.

Our course-centric integration solution leveraged the MET Innovation Platform to interconnect Blackboard Learn SaaS with Zoom's cloud platform, through API. By having all the necessary data, we facilitated the ability to automatically create, start and join Zoom meetings, and provided this as an add-on to the Blackboard system. In this process, we successfully created and deployed a "Launch Meeting" button to solve two business objectives (Fig. 2):

Fig. 2. Automatically created menu and one-click button for faculty and students to enter a course-specific online meeting.

Connection Transparency. Because online classrooms are "hardwired" to courses, anybody in a course is guaranteed to meet in the same online space, which is accessed through the Blackboard course site. It is simply not possible for instructors and students to end up in the "wrong" meeting, as joining a course meeting is as simple as clicking a button. Even when instructors teach multiple courses, each course has a specific "button" with information dynamically generated for the course in which it is deployed. There is no need for any coding or manipulation of the standard element for faculty or students.

Time Savings. The button eliminates the need for instructors to partake in many standard Zoom processes, including obtaining licenses, using their "personal" account/meeting room, setting up meetings, distributing links to students, ensuring meeting security, downloading and distributing recordings, or tracking attendance. All these tasks are completely automatic. The course-centric Launch button is ideal when a course has co-instructors, substitute instructors and/or teaching assistants. Everyone uses the same button, and instructors and teaching assistants always join the correct meeting with their students, eliminating the need to exchange links in advance.

4 Managing Student Progress

Providing faculty with the tools to achieve teaching excellence, and students with the motivation to absorb the learning material are our key exploration areas for technological innovations. Combining data from multiple systems, we develop new tools to help monitor, visualize, and track student progress in courses. At the same time, we use the functional capabilities of our innovation platform to make the digital learning content more interactive, support different learning preferences, and enable instant feedback.

Managing Prerequisites. To prepare our students for successful careers in the modern workplace, our academic programs make practical knowledge and hands-on skills a priority for learning. This often assumes that students have a solid background in quantitative disciplines, basic programming skills, etc. Because our students have different backgrounds and varying levels of experience, we provide non-credit modules that help students better prepare and succeed in specific graduate courses. Managing this network of pre-requisite relationships between learning modules is challenging. Based on all information available in our innovation platform, we developed an algorithm to automatically enroll students into the relevant modules, so that by the time their courses start, they can catch up on the skills they need to master their course materials. This proactive enrollment gives students more time to prepare, saves faculty and administrators time, and reduces potential errors (Fig. 3).

Providing Additional Motivation. To provide additional motivation for students and to keep track of their progress, we developed a system of "mini-badges" that are tied to workplace-relevant skills acquired during their studies. These badges are automatically awarded upon completion of specific learning modules. Badges are augmented by the automatic distribution of digitally signed electronic certificates that students can use to demonstrate their newly mastered career skills to their colleagues or potential employers. To offer a view of this progress in the course context, we implemented the Badge Dashboard, a tool provided by the innovation platform to show students their course-relevant badge status and to show instructors all their student badge statuses in a particular course.

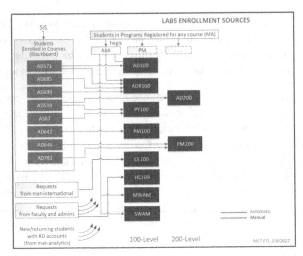

Fig. 3. Complex relationship matrix between academic programs, graduate coursework, and preparatory modules.

Managing Skills and Tracking Progress. Many of the preparatory pre-requisite modules are offered in a self-paced, rolling enrollment format often without the active presence of an instructor. To help make up for this, we leveraged the data we collect from the innovation platform to develop a set of reports that show weekly student progress since their enrollment. They show both the individual student progress and weekly statistics of completing the different units of the learning module, including awarded badges. These statistics help to identify situations where individual students might need help or encouragement, as well as specific parts of the learning content that are more difficult to learn and might require updates. They also help to identify situations when adding an active instructor for a few weeks would be beneficial, to provide additional guidance to the struggling students. The conceptual reporting structure is described in Sect. 5 below.

5   Scalability of Support

With a focus on streamlining consistent delivery of a quality course experience across hundreds of annual course offerings, spanning multiple content delivery formats, we leveraged the capabilities of the innovation platform to construct a set of scalable course support tools targeted at specific business needs. These tools aid in the direction of support actions and provide insight in a form that dramatically increases the efficiency of our internal support activity and maximizes the support leveraged from our support partners. Both proactive and responsive support activities benefit from this implementation. The tools draw on data aggregated from heterogeneous sources, provide new aggregated information, manage access based on our organizational roles, and enable automation across platforms in response to defined business rules.

We will present here two examples of these scalable support resources. The first is an educational technology dashboard that draws on aggregated data resources. The second is a functional reporting model that brings process and data visibility to relevant actors with specific business needs and process requirements. Together, these provide transparent and efficient data access in service of both college-level and individual/group level oversight and support activities.

Course Site Dashboard. The course site dashboard draws on data aggregated from the university systems and 3rd party platforms to provide a technology deployment overview for the entire college across a given semester. In addition to centralized access, the course site dashboard provides direct links to specific external resources. This saves time by reducing the need to rely on often disconnected and incompatible user interfaces, and workflows across multiple systems, to execute routine academic support tasks.

The dashboard serves a set of processes performed proactively by support staff to prepare and maintain the learning infrastructure. These processes principally concern the timely availability of course content, collaboration technologies, schedules, etc. This availability is viewed from the faculty, student, and cross-functional support perspective. The range of support staff capable of performing tasks has broadened as a result, reducing the load on faculty and staff with administrator roles on 3rd party technology platforms. This is possible because the dashboard's access is managed by our innovation platform, and not through the restrictive roles that are defined in the 3rd party platforms. The implementation of the dashboard vastly reduced both the time elapsed to resolve support requests and the time spent by faculty and staff working around suboptimal access control mechanisms.

Functional Reports. Functional reports are built on the same set of aggregated data that feeds the course site dashboard but are targeted at more individualized business requirements. The innovation platform design (see Fig. 4) allows data queries to be developed quickly, independent from the presentation views, which are shared across all reports and controlled by function-specific access rules. Three examples of such functional reports are provided below.

- Report for support staff without high-level administrative LMS access to obtain visibility into enrollment information across all supported courses.
- Report for faculty and teaching assistants to facilitate assignment of students to teams working on course assignments.
- Exceptions report to ensure all registered students have access to the corresponding course sites, the sites had been properly prepared and open for students, and access is promptly removed when students drop or change courses.

These reports bridge the gap between the flexibility of the application programming interfaces and the ease of use provided by a dashboard optimized to match the internal support processes. Time is saved by providing access to views not available on the 3rd party platforms due to the lack of implementation or user-level access controls. The result has greatly increased our support process effectiveness and efficiency.

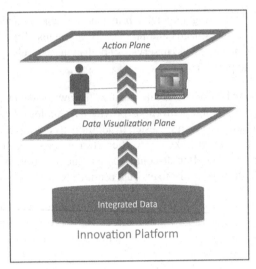

Fig. 4. Integrated data is visualized for subsequent decision-making performed by a human actor or a computerized algorithm.

6 Future Work

Data providing visibility into the learning process helps faculty analyze and manage student progress. Additionally, it provides an opportunity to automate some routine functions related to sending timely reminders, tracking due dates, etc. We believe that adding a rule-based algorithm to automate such routine tasks will provide value for faculty and students. The innovation platform allows us to experiment in this area and explore the opportunities of applying emerging artificial intelligence technologies to education.

References

1. Moore, M.G.: The theory of transactional distance. In: The Handbook of Distance Education, 2nd edn., pp. 89–108. N. J. Lawrence Erlbaum Associates, Mahwah (2007)
2. Burstein, L., Chitkushev, L., Kanabar, V., Zlateva, T.: Innovative instructional practices in design, implementation and execution of blended programs. In: Proceedings of the Boston University Instructional Innovation Conference, Boston, MA (2011)
3. Cusumano, M., Yoffie, D., Gawer, A.: The future of platforms. MIT Sloan Manag. Rev. 26–34 (2020)

Improving Student Employability with Python and SQL

Hanbo Yu[✉]

Department of Administrative Sciences, Boston University Metropolitan
College, Boston, MA 02215, USA
`yuhanbo@bu.edu`

Abstract. This paper introduces the author's educational approaches and achievements related to analytical and technical skills required by companies during the hiring processes of graduates in MS in business analytics. The author mainly focuses on Python and SQL, the core competencies that many employers currently value significantly. In this paper, the author shares his experiences on curricula development and execution of an elective course, AD 599 Introduction to Python and SQL for Business Analytics at Boston University, such as introducing data structures and algorithms to students and designing standard operating procedures for data projects, improving the employability for students by preparing students for technical job interviews such as job description cracking analysis and real-life data challenge bank building, lessons learned, and prospects of future.

Keywords: Python · SQL · Algorithms · Data structure · Standard Operating Procedure · Employability improvement

1 Introduction to Course AD599

1.1 Introduction to Boston University MS-ABA Program

The Master of Science in Applied Business Analytics (from now on MS-ABA) at Boston University's Metropolitan College (MET) is designed for business analysts, data scientists, data analysts, or others looking for transitions into data-driven roles such as management consultants. It can help people harness the concepts, techniques, and tools to transform available data into business insights or strategies [1]. The MS-ABA ranked No. 1 in Best Business Analytics & Intelligence Programs of 2021, No. 5 in Best Online Master's Business Analytics of 2022, and No. 10 in Best Online Master's in Business Programs (Excluding MBA program) [2]. In recent years, graduates from the MS-ABA program joined famous companies such as Google, Boston Consulting Group, Amazon, Wayfair, Tencent, L'Oréal, P&G, etc., and have made significant achievements and accomplishments in their professional areas.

The MS-ABA program has trained and prepared its students well in their data analytics skills and job searches. The author believes that MS-ABA will perform better in the future as new developments of new courses are coming in.

T. Zlateva and R. Goleva (Eds.): CSECS 2022, LNICST 450, pp. 289–301, 2022.
https://doi.org/10.1007/978-3-031-17292-2_24

1.2   Introduction to AD599 Introduction to Python and SQL for Business Analytics

The course AD599 Introduction to Python and SQL for Business Analytics (referred to as AD599) primarily serves students in the MS-ABA program. Many employers require specific Python and SQL experiences and skill levels in their data analyst/data scientist/business analyst positions. However, not all students in the MS-ABA program have former experiences in Python or SQL. This course, AD599, can give students a preliminary idea about Python and SQL, which can be a good foundation for students to dig deeper in these areas.

The pilot offering of AD599 was in the Summer 2 semester of 2021. Based on students' feedback and recommendations by the initial teaching team, the author reviewed and revised the content. The administrative sciences department approved the content revisions and asked the author to teach the course in the Spring semester of 2022, face-to-face and online.

So far, 70 students have completed this course AD599. Overall, the students' feedback is positive, stating they have learned valuable knowledge, techniques, and skills in Python and SQL needed for managerial decision-making and business analysis applications.

2   Course Content Upgrade and Development

2.1   The First Version of the Course Content Upgrade in November 2021 and Preparation for Online and On-Campus Teaching of AD599 Spring 2022

The author started his job search endeavors before his graduation from the MS-ABA program in January 2021. During his job search journey, the author noticed that Python and SQL working experiences are valued a lot by most employers who were hiring in the labor market. The author did some statistics, randomly picked 500 data analyst/data scientist job descriptions from LinkedIn [3], and found that 77.6% of these jobs required Python knowledge, 85.8% of these jobs required SQL knowledge, and 54.4% jobs required both.

The author then realized that Python and SQL are a crucial part of the core competency of being a data analyst/data scientist and business analyst. As he entered more and more rounds of interviews with various companies, he noticed another requirement for the Python application part. Most data scientist/data analyst jobs do not involve algorithms and data structures in the professional field or in daily life. However, companies still test them, mainly in online assessment, on platforms such as Hackerrank[4] and Coderpad[5]. These companies also leave "data challenges" or "take-home data projects" to candidates, which are common issues that data analysts/data scientists need to solve in daily life.

For the SQL part, the author also noticed that the basic SQL techniques he learned from school were not enough to solve some interview questions. During the author's learning process at Boston University, he did not use one convenient technique in SQL, Common Table Expression (referred to as CTE), and window functions. However, in the interviews with different companies, he noticed that these were necessary to stand out from all candidates. Therefore, after extensive self-training, he successfully gained these skills and knowledge and finally obtained two job offers, one from a local company in Boston and another from a consulting firm on Wall Street.

The original version of the course contents included twelve lectures in six modules, four individual assignments, four quizzes, five discussion topics, and one final project.

During the initial review of the original course contents of AD599, the author discovered the need to introduce algorithms and data structures, data projects, or CTE and window functions. To improve the employability of students who will take this course, the author included the new content in the revised course materials for the Spring 2022 offerings of AD599.

The author added the following contents to the Python part of lectures in AD599 during the first version of the update and development of course contents: data structures such as Stack, Queue, Linked List, Hash Table, and Trees; Basic Algorithms and related concepts, such as Time Complexity, Linear Search, Binary Search, Bubble Sort, and realization of data structures[6].

The author also added a new part of the data modeling section to the Python-related lectures in AD599. This data modeling section included Introductions to regressions, basic rules and coefficients of regressions, realizations of regression models in Python, and regression model selection by cross-validation score.

The author added CTE and window functions to the SQL part of the lectures. This part included the syntax and use case of CTE and window functions such as Partition By, Over, Order By, Rows Between, Row Number, Rank, Dense Rank, Lead, Lag, N Tile, Count Percentile, etc.

With such significant changes in the content of the lectures, the author also adjusted the assignments, discussion topics, quizzes, and the final project to guarantee that all deliverables from students comply with the lecture notes. In addition to a content redesign of the third individual assignment, a brand new two parts final data project is offered. It is similar to the take-home challenge in real-life technical skills interviews. CTE and window functions are part of the final project. The test banks of all quizzes and questions related to characteristics of data structures and algorithms were included as well. The content of the discussion topics is harmonized with the in-class learning of the students. The new version of the study guide can be found in the Appendix section at the end of the article.

The student feedback at the end of the online delivery of AD599 Spring 2022 is positive - students appreciate the changes and the possibilities that the changes bring.

2.2   The Second Version of the Course Content Upgrade in April 2022 and Preparation for Online and On-Campus Teaching of AD599 Summer 2022

During his teaching process, as the spring semester of 2022 comes to an end and related information and feedback from students are already available, the author noticed that another revision of the course content is possible and submitted for an internal review by the ABA faculty a proposal to upgrade the course contents of AD599 before Summer 2022.

In this version of the course content upgrade, the author added more content related to Algorithms into the Python part of the lectures, such as the QuickSort algorithm, which has a lower time complexity than common sorting algorithms; he also added practical SQL techniques such as Limit, Offset, Between, Like, Union All, Case When clauses, etc., to the SQL part of the lectures, which he believes could be helpful for students to solve SQL interview questions.

To match the lecture notes better, the author also redesigned individual assignments one, two, and four in this upgrade version. He also expanded the four quiz banks even more so more questions are included in the quizzes.

After the approval of this upgrade proposal, compared to the original version of course contents, 50% of lecture contents are upgraded, 100% of individual assignments are redesigned, 100% of quizzes are expanded, 100% of the final project is improved, and 40% of discussion topics are revised.

3   Course Content Execution

3.1   Interactive Teaching Approach

The author taught the course AD599 both on-campus and online. The contents of the on-campus class and online class are identical. The only difference is the teaching speed since the length of the on-campus class is fourteen weeks and of the online course seven weeks. This significant difference requires different teaching approaches.

The author delivered the lecture contents swiftly yet effectively in class for the online session. He also provided extra consultation sessions for students if they had any questions or problems. Though without in-class practices, the students still comprehended the lecture contents well since most of them could deliver satisfactory results in the assignments, quizzes, and the final project.

The author implemented an interactive teaching approach for the on-campus delivery mode. He walks among students and asks and answers their questions in the classroom. Before introducing any lecture topic, he would use a real-life example to intrigue the students. When the students started to get interested and pay attention, he could deliver the core spirits of the topics more efficiently and effectively.

For instance, when discussing a critical application of data analytics, Forecast, the author pivoted an angle with stock price forecast to emphasize the importance of accurate predictions. The author briefly introduced the origin of stocks, which can trace back to the age of sails[7]. Back in history, since people did not have the methods to make accurate forecasts, their stock exchange activities were complete guesses. In contrast, we have multiple approaches to making more accurate forecasts nowadays, and the stock exchange activities are much more reasonable and rational. The students happily embraced this brief introduction of relevant knowledge, it drew their attention, and the whole lecture went well.

The author also used detailed explanations when introducing new concepts. When he introduced the most significant difference between Stack and Queue, he used this skill to make things clear. The queue is known to follow the First-In-First-Out rule (referred to as the FIFO rule). Stack is known to follow the Last-In-First-Out rule (referred to as the LIFO rule). To compare the FIFO and LIFO rules, the author made a series of calculations for the profit that an imaginary company could get within a fiscal year with different rules. The calculation results were precise, with different rules, and the company's profit within a fiscal year is also not the same. By showing this to students, they immediately realized the difference between rules and better understood the difference between Stack and Queue.

3.2 Teamwork Spirit Building

The author's top priority was always helping students master the necessary skills in Python and SQL, and when that purpose was fulfilled, he sought to help the students a bit more.

The author understands well that teamwork spirit is vital in professional fields. Therefore, the author asked the students to group up as four-person or five-person teams in class and work together. The author also understood that some people might not be able to work well together. In every class session, he gave students chances to swap their groups until they found people with whom they could work. The grouping process entirely depended on the students themselves; the author would not intervene unless some people were left out without any group.

Python and SQL require a lot of practice. Therefore, after all, groups were settled, the author would assign in-class exercises related to topics learned for students to work on as a group. The author would walk around the classroom, approach each group, and check on their progress multiple times for each practice question.

This approach built their teamwork spirit successfully since the final project of AD599 was also group work. Seven out of ten teams delivered results more than satisfactory. The author believes that this teamwork experience can help students in their future working environment and professional fields.

3.3 Standard Operating Procedure of Data Analytics

The author understands the importance of a Standard Operating Procedure (SOP). SOPs can specify working steps to standardize products and quality [8]. In Data Analytics, the products are the results of data analysis, such as insights and forecasts. With the assistance of an SOP, the quality of data analytics projects can be standardized and guaranteed.

In class, the author showed students the SOP of a full data analysis project of Bavarian Motor Works Vehicle Price Forecast. The whole project started with data retrieves and data import through data type determination and conversion, null value detection and replacement, data cleansing, variable selection, train-set, and test-set split, model fitness test with cross-validation scores, model selection, and model building, to the final step which was price forecast of an imaginary vehicle. The students worked in groups and tried to find out the meanings of each step and realized the significance of SOP, which resulted well in their individual assignment three outcomes.

3.4   Retrospective Analytics

It is widely known that most people can make mistakes; it is also not unusual that people make mistakes at the early stages of data analysis projects/consultation projects/data science research when they do not have enough information. The author knows and understands this fact; therefore, he took a proactive approach in teaching this course AD599.

The final project of AD599 is comprised of three parts, phase one, phase two, and the final report. The author emphasized multiple times in class that if students made mistakes in phase one, it was normal and acceptable since they had not learned all skills and techniques in the class; however, as they obtained more knowledge and information, they should look back from the start and check if they had used the wrong methods or made any mistakes. The author called this "retrospective analytics," which resulted well since seven teams out of ten delivered optimal results in Phase two and the final report.

The author believes that making mistakes is normal and not the end of the world. However, realizing one's mistakes and correcting them is the vital part. He shared this idea with students, and from the positive results, most students accepted and understood it.

4   Extra Curricula Activities for Improving Student Employability

4.1   Employability Consultation Service

Other than the attempt to improve students' employability by revising the course contents of AD599 and its proactive execution, the author volunteered and contributed as a consultant in Employability Consultation services organized by the MS-ABA program. The author interviewed multiple companies during his job search process and collected technical interview questions such as online assessments and take-home data challenges from big companies such as Tesla, LinkedIn, Lyft, Airbnb, BNY bank, etc. Instead of wasting these good resources, the author built a technical interview test bank based on his collected material and then shared it freely with students who needed employability consultation services.

The author hosted a consultation session in March 2022. Although not many students attended, the attendees all showed gratitude and appreciation afterward. As more and more students graduate and start their job search, it is imaginable that these students will share their interview questions with the author, and hence, the test bank will grow bigger and stronger and be able to help more students.

4.2   Personal Consultation Sessions for Students

Outside the employability consultation services, the author also provided personal consultation sessions for students from course AD599 on the evening of each Friday. During the sessions, the author offered his advice on how to modify resumes, how to prepare for behavioral interviews, and how to succeed in technical screenings. He shared his own interview experiences with students and his takeaways and lessons learned. From the feedback of students, these sessions were more than helpful in their job search process.

4.3   Job Description Cracking Analysis

The author helped many students with their job search, among which there is an appropriate example for this article. The author has a teaching assistant who also possesses a master's degree in Data Analytics from another university and is currently seeking a job. This teaching assistant is a competitive individual, and he is interviewing with the located in Boston company New Balance for a Data Analyst, product costing position[9]. Since he did not have too many interview experiences, he asked the author for help.

The author analyzed thoroughly and carefully the job description[9] and found an appropriate angle to "crack" it. He told his teaching assistant that, since this was a product costing data analyst position, showing one's knowledge and understanding of the importance of cost control could make one easily stand out from candidates. There are many links between raw materials and final products on shelves in the modern manufacturing industry, and each link contains a cost. If such costs can be reduced and controlled, the manufacturer can have an advantage in the final sale price. They can either use this advantage to obtain more market share or publish it in their quarterly financial statements to boost stock prices. The teaching assistant took the author's advice and expressed his knowledge and comprehension in this matter. Soon, good news came that the teaching assistant is now in the third round of interviews and very close to an offer. The author feels happy and achieved in this event and will continue providing similar services to students.

5   Lessons Learned and Next Steps

So far, the author's attempts to improve student employability have returned positive results. Most students in the author's class expressed gratitude for this endeavor, which helped them with their academic studies and significantly improved their employability in interviews.

Moreover, the labor market is constantly evolving, and the author will continue improving and refining the course contents, including lectures, quizzes, assignments, etc., and building the technical interview test banks.

The author's effort to improve students' employability will not stop here. As more and more students graduate and get job offers, the precious data on employability will be available. The members of the Administrative Sciences Department of Boston University Metropolitan College, including the author, can gather the data and build a SQL-based database for further analysis. They can use methodologies of statistics, data mining, machine learning, natural language processing, etc., to analyze which key features play the most crucial part in whether a student is hired or not. This project possesses excellent potential and is worth a considerable amount of effort.

Appendix Study guide of AD599

Module 1 Study Guide and Deliverables	
Topics:	<ul><li>Introduction to the Python language, installation, first programs, workspace options, and current applications.</li><li>Script programming, data types, variables, mathematics, list operations, and data structures (stack, queue, linked list, hash table, tree).</li></ul>
Readings:	Module 1 online content
Discussions:	Discussion 0: Introduce yourself
Class Time:	Monday, Jan 24 from 6:00 - 8:45 PM ET Monday, Jan 31 from 6:00 - 8:45 PM ET

Module 2 Study Guide and Deliverables	
Topics:	<ul><li>Modules, flow control, conditional logic, Text and strings, formatting and printing, loops</li><li>Functions, tuples, lists, and dictionaries</li></ul>
Readings:	Module 2 online content
Discussions:	Discussion 1: <ul><li>Initial post due by Thursday, Feb 17 at 11:59 PM ET.</li><li>Respond to at least two of your classmates' posts by Sun-</li></ul>

	day, Feb 20 at 11:59 PM ET.
Assignments:	Assignment 1, due by Sunday, Feb 20 at 11:59 PM ET
Assessments:	Quiz 1, available between Saturday, Feb 19 at 9:00 AM ET and Sunday, Feb 20 at 11:59 PM ET
Class Time:	Monday, Feb 7 from 6:00 - 8:45 PM ET Monday, Feb 14 from 6:00 - 8:45 PM ET

Module 3 Study Guide and Deliverables	
Topics:	• Advanced topics for functions, Introduction to Algorithms, Common Algorithms, Realization of Data Structures • Numpy/Scipy (functions and capabilities), Pandas.
Readings:	Module 3 online content
Discussions:	Discussion 2: • Initial post due by Thursday, Mar 3 at 11:59 PM ET. • Respond to at least two of your classmates' posts by Sunday, Mar 6 at 11:59 PM ET.
Assignments:	Assignment 2, due Sunday, Mar 6 at 11:59 PM ET.
Assessments:	Quiz 2, available between Saturday, Mar 5 at 9:00 AM ET and

	Sunday, Mar 6 at 11:59 PM ET
Class Time:	Tuesday, Feb 22 from 6:00 - 8:45 PM ET (President's day Holiday, no class on Monday) Monday, Feb 28 from 6:00 - 8:45 PM ET

Module 4 Study Guide and Deliverables

Topics:	• Statsmodel and Sklearn • Regressions, Cross-Validation, and Model Selection
Readings:	Module 4 online content
Discussions:	Discussion 3: • Initial post due by Thursday, Mar 24 at 11:59 PM ET. • Respond to at least two of your classmates' posts by Sunday, Mar 27 at 11:59 PM ET.
Assignments:	Assignment 3, due by Sunday, Mar 27 at 11:59 PM ET.
Assessments:	Quiz 3, available between Saturday, Mar 26 at 9:00 AM ET and Sunday, Mar 27 at 11:59 PM ET
Class Time:	Monday, Mar 14 from 6:00 - 8:45 PM ET Monday, Mar 21 from 6:00 - 8:45 PM ET

Module 5 Study Guide and Deliverables

Topics:	• Database and SQL Introduction, basic syntax and environment, Creating and Populating Databases, basic queries and filtering • Intermediate queries and subqueries, sets and joins, Grouping and Aggregation, Views
Readings:	Module 5 online content
Discussions:	Discussion 4: • Initial post due by Thursday, Apr 7 at 11:59 PM ET. • Respond to at least two of your classmates' posts by Sunday, Apr 10 at 11:59 PM ET.
Assignments:	Assignment 4, due by Sunday, Apr 10 at 11:59 PM ET. Final Project, Phase 1, by Sunday, Apr 10 at 11:59 PM ET.
Class Time:	Monday, Mar 28 from 6:00 - 8:45 PM ET Monday, Apr 4 from 6:00 - 8:45 PM ET

Module 6 Study Guide and Deliverables

Topics:	• CTE and Window functions • Integration of Python and SQL

Readings:	Module 6 online content
Discussions:	Discussion 5: • Initial post due by Thursday, Apr 21 at 11:59 PM ET. • Respond to at least two of your classmates' posts by Sunday, Apr 24 at 11:59 PM ET.
Assignments:	Final Project, Phase 2, by Sunday, Apr 24 at 11:59 PM ET.
Class Time:	Monday, Apr 11 from 6:00 - 8:45 PM ET Monday, Apr 18 from 6:00 - 8:45 PM ET

Final Presentation

Topics:	• What is next, and overall wrap-up • Q & A
Assign-ments:	Final report, due Monday, May 2, at 11:59 PM ET Presentation, due Monday, May 2, at 11:59 PM ET
Class Time:	Monday, Apr 25 from 7:00 - 8:30 PM ET

References

1. MS in Applied Business Analytics. Master of Science in Applied Business Analytics|BU MET. https://www.bu.edu/met/degrees-certificates/ms-applied-business-analytics/. Accessed 8 May 2022
2. Best Online Masters in Business Analytics and Intelligence Programs by Online Masters Report 2020 & 2021 & 2022. https://www.bestcolleges.com/features/top-online-masters-in-business-intelligence-programs/
3. Data Analyst jobs in the United States - linkedin.com. https://www.linkedin.com/jobs/search/?currentJobId=3064176256&keywords=data%20analyst&refresh=true. Accessed 8 May 2022
4. Hackerrank. HackerRank. https://www.hackerrank.com/. Accessed 8 May 2022
5. Encrypted online notepad for secret and secure notes. encrypt and keep private notes with password.: Coded pad™. https://www.codedpad.com/. Accessed 8 May 2022
6. Cormen, T.H., et al.: Introduction to Algorithms, 3rd edn. MIT Press, Cambridge (2009)
7. Woodward, D.B.: A new guide to the public funds, or, every man his own stock-broker containing the origin of the funding system, causes of the fluctuation of the prices of stocks, manner of transferring stock
8. Pearce, O.: What are sops? and why does my organization need them? #StayConnected. https://blog.montrium.com/experts/what-are-sops-and-why-does-my-organization-need-them#:~:text=SOPs%20specify%20job%20steps%20that,failure%20or%20other%20facility%20damage. Accessed 8 May 2022
9. Data Analyst product costing in Lawrence, Massachusetts, United States of America: Administration at New Balance. New Balance. https://jobs.newbalance.com/global/en/job/R25113/Data-Analyst-Product-Costing. Accessed 8 May 2022

Author Index

Printed in the United States
by Baker & Taylor Publisher Services